WARPED MOURNING

Cultural Memory
in
the
Present

Mieke Bal and Hent de Vries, Editors

WARPED MOURNING
Stories of the Undead in the Land of the Unburied

Alexander Etkind

STANFORD UNIVERSITY PRESS

STANFORD, CALIFORNIA

Stanford University Press
Stanford, California

© 2013 by the Board of Trustees of the Leland Stanford Junior University. All rights reserved.

No part of this book may be reproduced or transmitted in any form or by any means, electronic or mechanical, including photocopying and recording, or in any information storage or retrieval system without the prior written permission of Stanford University Press.

Printed in the United States of America on acid-free, archival-quality paper

Library of Congress Cataloging-in-Publication Data

Etkind, Aleksandr, 1955– author.
 Warped mourning : stories of the undead in the land of the unburied / Alexander Etkind.
    pages cm. — (Cultural memory in the present)
 Includes bibliographical references and index.
 ISBN 978-0-8047-7392-8 (cloth : alk. paper)
 ISBN 978-0-8047-7393-5 (pbk. : alk. paper)
   1. Russian literature—20th century—History and criticism. 2. Grief in literature. 3. Socialism and literature—Soviet Union. 4. Collective memory and literature—Soviet Union. 5. Collective memory and literature—Russia (Federation) 6. Victims of statesponsored terrorism—Soviet Union. I. Title. II. Series: Cultural memory in the present.
 PG3020.5.G75E75   2013
 891.709'35847084—dc23
                                           2012028868

ISBN 978-08047-8553-2 (electronic)

Contents

List of Illustrations — ix
Transliteration Note — xi
Acknowledgments — xiii

Introduction — 1
1. Mimetic and Subversive — 5
2. Mourning and Warning — 25
3. The Parable of Misrecognition — 44
4. Writing History after Jail — 60
5. On Tortured Life and World Culture — 83
6. The Debt to the Dead — 110
7. The Cosmopolitan Way — 134
8. The Tale of Two Turns — 159
9. The Hard and the Soft — 172
10. Post-Soviet Hauntology — 196
11. Magical Historicism — 220
    Conclusion — 243

Notes — 249
Index — 295

Illustrations

1. A 500-ruble banknote in circulation in the Russian Federation from 1995 to the present. 6
2. Boris Sveshnikov, Untitled (n.d.). Ink on paper. 90
3. Boris Sveshnikov, Untitled (1949–1950). Ink on paper. 91
4. Boris Sveshnikov, *Encounter* (n.d.). Oil on linen on panel. 92
5. Boris Sveshnikov, *The Coffin Maker's Workshop* (1961). Oil on linen. 95
6. Boris Sveshnikov, *Last Alms* (1992). Ink on paper. 103
7. Boris Sveshnikov, *Spring Grove* (1957). Oil on linen. 104
8. Boris Sveshnikov, *Untranslated* (1998). Ink and gouache on paper. 108
9. The ghost of the father in *Hamlet* (1964), a film by Grigory Kozintsev. 143
10. Hamlet and Laertes in *Hamlet* (1964), a film by Grigory Kozintsev. 152
11. Hamlet and Laertes in *Beware of the Car* (1966), a film by Eldar Riazanov. 153
12. The final scene of *Beware of the Car* (1966). 154
13. *Moloch of Totalitarianism* (1996), a memorial at the Levashovo Cemetery near St. Petersburg. 187

Transliteration Note

In the main body of the text, the transliteration of Russian names has been simplified with a view to making them easier on the Anglophone reader's eyes (hence, for example, Yury Brodsky rather than Iurii Brodskii). Likewise, where established conventional English spellings of particular names and place names exist, these have been given preference (hence, for example, Mandelstam, not Mandel'shtam). In the footnotes and bibliography, Russian names and sources have been transliterated according to the Library of Congress system. The acronym for Gosudarstvennoe upravlenie lagerei (State Administration of Camps) should be rendered as "GULag," but I have opted to spell this word "gulag" and understand it in a broader meaning. All translations are mine unless stated otherwise.

Acknowledgments

This book is rooted in the history of my family, the Etkinds, and in my background, as part of the ex-Soviet intelligentsia. Decades ago, my father, the art historian Mark Etkind, told me that he wanted to write a book about the artists who perished during Stalin's terror. He died soon afterward and did not have the chance to write it, but he could have written some of the pages that appear in my book. My uncle, Yefim Etkind, inspired many of my speculations, and I refer to his brilliant writings—his memoirs as well as his scholarship—often, though not often enough. This book is my work of mourning for both of them, and also for my stepfather, Moisei Kagan, a prominent philosopher who fought in World War II, survived ideological purges, wrote excellent books, and lived long enough to lose faith in the Soviet regime, though not in Marxism. Apart from my family, I knew only a few of the figures about whom I have written in the following chapters. Once, however, in 1986, Dmitry Likhachev helped me win what seemed a hopeless conflict; more recently, his writings—memoirs and scholarship—have helped me to make sense of my own conflicting ideas. I also know Lev Klein, another camp survivor and brilliant scholar; it so happened that many years ago he published my first article. I have no reason to think that these persons would agree with me if they read these pages: the work of mourning is as rebellious as it is mimetic. But I cherish my belief that they would, and actually did, support the effort.

A long time ago my conversations with the leaders of the Memorial Society in St. Petersburg, Veniamin Iofe and Irina Flige, helped me to elaborate the general framework of this book. Later, this project benefited from several awards that were equally important. In 1999, I was a fellow at Wissenschaftskolleg in Berlin, where I chatted over lunches with Aleida Assmann, the leading expert in German memory, and Stephen Greenblatt, the leading Shakespeare scholar. Their impact on my thinking is much appreciated. In 2001, I received a grant from the Open Archives of the Central European University. I am grateful to Istvan Rev, the director of the archives, not least because I also used this grant to take my wife, Elizabeth Roosevelt Moore, on a honeymoon doing research at several sites of the former gulag in the Russian North. We later continued with a tour through the former plantations of the American South. Many of my current ideas were conceived in my conversations with Elizabeth, as we both tried to explain and understand our legacies. In 2006, I received a fellowship from the Davis Center for Historical Studies at Princeton University, and I want to send my thanks to Gyan Prakash, Michael F. Laffan, Anson Rabinbach, and Stephen Kotkin for the many fruitful exchanges and events that followed. Readers of my book will note the influence of my cofellow at the Davis Center, Ronald Schechter.

In 2010, I received a large grant from HERA (Humanities in the European Research Area) for the collective study *Memory at War: Cultural Dynamics in Poland, Russia, and Ukraine*. With the support of the Department of Slavonic Studies at the University of Cambridge, we have created a unique research environment for studies of memory and mourning across eastern Europe. My colleagues at Cambridge, Simon Franklin, Emma Widdis, and Rory Finnin, helped me to shape the *Memory at War* project, and this is another opportunity to thank them. The participants of *Memory at War* have given me invaluable inspiration and feedback, and I want to thank, among others, Julie Fedor, Uilleam Blacker, Ellen Rutten, Sander Brouwer, Galina Nikiporets-Takigawa, and Jill Gather. Among the many interactions in the larger European framework connected to this project, those with Jay Winter, Andrzej Nowak, and Andriy Portnov were particularly helpful.

I received valuable feedback after my talks at the Research Seminar of the Slavic Department of Princeton University (2008); the conference "Finding a Place in the Soviet Empire" at the University of Illinois at Urbana-Champaign (2011); the conference "Memory and Theory in Eastern Europe" at King's College, Cambridge (2011); and the joint seminar "Memory and Literature after Auschwitz and the Gulag," which Dominick LaCapra and I gave at the University of Colorado at Boulder in 2011. A series of Interdisciplinary Mellon Seminars in East European Memory Studies, which Harald Wydra and I gave to a fantastic group of graduate students and colleagues at CRASSH (the Cambridge Center for Research in Arts, Social Sciences, and Humanities) in the spring of 2010, helped me to articulate some long-standing ideas.

This book has benefited greatly from discussion of its emerging parts with many friends and colleagues around the globe. Comments by Jana Howlett were important for chapter 3. Comments by Maya Turovskaya were crucial for chapter 7, which also benefited from the advice of Dmitry Bykov, Lilya Kaganovsky, Emma Widdis, Susan Larsen, and Simon Lewis. I conceived chapter 5 during my visit to the Zimmerli Art Museum, New Brunswick, where Jane Sharp, Allison Leigh-Perlman, and Jochen Hellbeck provided much-needed guidance through its collections; Allison Leigh-Perlman kindly read this chapter and helped me to improve it. Comments by Eric Naiman, Caryl Emerson, and Tim Portice were important for chapter 11. At the later stages of this project, Dmitry Bykov provided much-needed inspiration. Nancy Condee and Julia Vaingurt generously commented on the manuscript and helped to correct some of my mistakes.

Scholarship often entails disagreeing with friends, but it is equally important that friendship survives the arguments. Sometimes openly and sometimes implicitly, I argue in this book with Alexei Yurchak, Svetlana Boym, Yuri Slezkine, Mark Lipovetsky, Leonid Gozman, Eli Zarecky, Mischa Gabowitch, Natan Sznaider, Oleg Kharkhordin, Ilia Kalinin, Kevin Platt, Caroline Humphrey, Dirk Uffelmann, and Ilia Kukulin. Thanks to them all, and I hope that our arguments will continue.

I am extremely grateful to Julie Fedor, who read and edited my manuscript, corrected many of my mistakes in style and substance, and challenged me to rework some parts of the book. Julie's contribution to this work is very much appreciated, and I can only wish to be able to reciprocate her help in the future.

Finally, my warmest thanks go again to Elizabeth. Her eye, taste, and care helped me to write this book from the start to the end.

* * *

Some chapters of this book have been published, in different versions, as journal articles. A part of chapter 3 was published as "A Parable of Misrecognition: Anagnorisis and the Return of the Repressed from the Gulag," *Russian Review* 68 (October 2009): 623–640. A version of chapter

6 was published as "Sedlo Siniavskogo: Lagernaia kritika v kul'turnoi istorii sovetskogo perioda," *Novoe literaturnoe obozrenie* 101 (2010): 280–303. A version of chapter 8 was published as "The Tale of Two Turns: *Khrustalev, My Car!* and the Cinematic Memory of the Soviet Past," *Studies in Russian and Soviet Cinema* 4, no. 1 (2010): 45–63. Early versions of chapter 9 appeared as "Vremia sravnivat' kamni: Kul'tura politicheskoi skorbi v sovremennoi Rossii," *Ab Imperio* 2 (2004): 33–76, and "Hard and Soft in Cultural Memory: Political Mourning in Russia and Germany," *Grey Room* 16 (Summer 2004): 36–59. A part of chapter 10 was published as "Post-Soviet Hauntology: Cultural Memory of the Soviet Terror," *Constellations* 16, no. 1 (2009): 182–200. Parts of chapter 11 were published as "Stories of the Undead in the Land of the Unburied: Magical Historicism in Contemporary Russian Fiction," *Slavic Review* 68, no. 3 (Fall 2009): 631–658, and "Magical Historicism: From Fiction to Non-Fiction," *East European Memory Studies* 4 (March 2011): 2–5. This book benefited from the editorial work and feedback that were provided by these journals' editors: Irina Prokhorova, Mark Steinberg, Michael Gorham, Marina Mogilner, Birgit Beumers, Alexander Skidan, Felicity D. Scott, and Ian Zuckerman.

WARPED MOURNING

Introduction

After the French Revolution, relatives of the guillotined victims used to gather regularly for Bals des victimes, or Victims' Balls. Women wore a red ribbon marking the point where the guillotine cut. They cut their hair to bare their necks, imitating the haircut given the victim by the executioner. Inviting the women to dance, men would jerk their head sharply downward in imitation of decapitation. Dancing and flirting, they manifested their mourning for their fathers and mothers in macabre details.

It is possible that the whole story of these Victims' Balls is a subsequent, nineteenth-century romantic legend.[1] Many authors have repeated it, however, as I am doing now. Whether the French decadents of the postrevolutionary generation really gathered at Victims' Balls or not, they fantasized about doing so, passing these fantasies on through generations, all the way to us. These legendary balls provide a prototypical case of what I call mimetic mourning—a recurrent response to loss that entails a symbolic reenactment of that loss.[2] This re-presentation of the past—making the past present, if only in symbolic, detoxicated form—addresses the questions that constitute the core of mourning: How did it happen? Where and when? Why did it happen this way? Could it have happened differently? Could I have done something to prevent it? The mourner addresses these questions to herself and others, who might be either witnesses to the loss or its fictional narrators. Whether the mourner has evidence that testifies to the circumstances of the loss, or whether the reminiscence and the witness are pure fantasy, these re-presentations—bringing the dead back to life in imagination, text, social interaction, or performance—are at the core of mourning.

It may be that, in general, the story of terror consists of two parts: the ascending part of history and loss, and the descending part of memory and mourning. While the ascending slope is all about mass murder and lonely deaths, the descending one is about symbolizing, sharing, and bonding. In Victims' Balls and mourning plays, poetry, humor, and pleasure play strangely prominent roles. For the descendants of the French revolutionary Terror, there was some pleasure in dancing at the Victims' Balls, composing stories about them, and sharing them with their peers and juniors. In contrast to some later concepts, such as Freud's repetition compulsion and the connected ideas of trauma and the posttraumatic, the stories of Victims' Balls presume that their participants operate in full consciousness of their individual losses and their collective mourning. Sharing experience is a source of pleasure, and this is why we retell such stories also with some residual pleasure.

In the stories of Victims' Balls, participants come together physically in a ritual of collective mourning, a behavior that we often observe among survivors of a catastrophe and the first generation of their descendants. Later generations continue to mourn and share, but they do not feel the need to bond and dance with their peers. As time passes and generations replace one another, their mournful, mimetic performances migrate to the increasingly virtual spaces of theater, art, and literature, and then to film, television shows, and social media. Academic historiography also plays its role in this broad process.

This book is part and parcel of this long-term development. I submit that, haunted by its unburied past, late-Soviet and post-Soviet culture has produced memorial practices that are worthy of detailed study. While the American historian Stephen Kotkin perceives a "Shakespearean quality" in the post-Soviet transformation, it is no surprise that the participants of this process employ equally dramatic metaphors, partially invented and partially imported, in their attempts to understand what has happened to their civilization.[3] In fact, the leading cultural genres in Russia often seem to be building on Gogol rather than on Shakespeare, and they manifest unusual, maybe even perverted, forms of mourning the past and comprehending the present.

Working independently on different continents, two leading cultural critics have formulated a "Fifty-Year Effect": this is how long it takes for literature to estrange the tragic past, process its experience, and elaborate a convincing narrative capable of gaining wide if not universal acclaim. Stephen Greenblatt proposed this Fifty-Year Effect in his study of Shakespeare's, and specifically *Hamlet*'s, relation to the Reformation.[4] Dmitry Bykov applied the same idea to Russia's historical prose, from Lev Tolstoy to Aleksandr Solzhenitsyn.[5] Fifty years, or two cultural generations, is how much is needed to make the work of mourning culturally productive. I would speculate that the historical processes of catastrophic scale traumatize the first generation of descendants, and it is their daughters and sons—the grandchildren of the victims, perpetrators, and onlookers—who produce the work of mourning for their grandparents: mass graves for the generation of terror, trauma for the first postcatastrophic generation, and mourning for the second.

Written in the 2000s, the current book is largely focused on the 1950s and 1960s, the productive time of post-Stalinism that would define many features, good and bad, of the forthcoming postsocialism. But in culture, any regularity is an invitation to violation, and the scope of this book extends far beyond the events that happened fifty years ago. Its early chapters examine the experience of those authors who were incarcerated in the 1930s and wrote their texts of scholarship and trauma in the 1950s. Then, the central chapters discuss the mourning processes of those whose parents were murdered or jailed in the 1930s, though some of the mourners were themselves also jailed in the 1960s. Finally, this book's concluding chapters lead the reader to the cultural products that have been composed by the current generation of writers and filmmakers, who have been looking at the terrible past of their ancestors and teachers from the distance of fifty years and beyond, with a focus that shifts in time with every passing year.

Warped Mourning discusses many cultural genres, from films to memorials, but its focus is on literature. The book begins with a discussion of the relations between mourning and other cultural and psychological processes, such as trauma, repetition, revenge, and humor. In chapter 2, I argue that mourning for the past is often connected to warning about the future, a correlation that is particularly clear in the aftermath—and anticipation—of man-made catastrophes. Chronologically, the action of this book starts in the dark decades, from the 1930s to the 1950s, when the Soviet state arrested its citizens, tortured them in specialized camps, and let some of them return home, where these survivors met again with their families and colleagues. As I demonstrate in chapter 3, the cultural consequences of these encounters were both important and unusual. Under a regime that refused to acknowledge its own violence, mourning its victims was a political act, an important and sometimes even dominating mechanism of resistance to this regime. The book continues into 1956, when Nikita Khrushchev blamed the now-deceased Stalin for the "unjustified repressions," and then into the Thaw of the early 1960s, which I interpret as the era of Soviet Victims' Balls. In contrast to those balls that allegedly occurred in the period of the Restoration in France, the revolutionary regime was still in power when the mourning games started in Russia. In chapter 4, I read and contextualize some of the deepest, though disguised, stories of trauma and mourning that the surviving victims of terror, many of them professional historians, published after their release from the camps or exile. Chapter 5 shifts to other cultural genres of mourning, such as visual art and poetry. In chapter 6, the book takes its step into the mid-1960s, when intellectuals played melancholic games with the Soviet courts. The weird combination of mimetic mourning and political resistance led the most consistent mourners precisely and inexorably back to the sites of memory of Soviet terror, into the camps. In chapters 7 and 8, I discuss how late-Soviet and post-Soviet Russian films unfold their mourning for the victims of the past in narratives, high and low. Chapter 9 surveys monuments to the Soviet victims and speculates about their relations to texts of poetry and prose, fiction and nonfiction. In chapters 10 and 11, the reader will learn about the current state of the post-Soviet mourning. It is as warped as ever, though in a new Russian way, of course.

1

Mimetic and Subversive

Both Russian citizens and foreign visitors know this image well: the 500-ruble banknote, which has been in use for the past two decades. It shows the Solovetsky monastery, a magnificent edifice on an arctic island, one of the most cherished sanctuaries of the Orthodox Church. But look closer and you will spot an odd detail: instead of onion-shaped cupolas, the cathedral is topped with wooden pyramids.

There was a period in the long history of this monastery when awkward planks roofed the cathedral towers. In the 1920s and 1930s, the cathedral was used as a gigantic barracks for a prison camp that was deployed on this island.[1] Its convicts destroyed the leaking cupolas and built the pyramidal roofs, which survived until the 1980s, when the reconstruction started. The Solovetsky camp was the earliest and "exemplary" camp in the gulag system that defined twentieth-century Russia. In cultural memory, this camp functions as a metonym for all Soviet camps—a part that stands for the whole and embraces all the horror and suffering of the Soviet victims. The title of Aleksandr Solzhenitsyn's great book *The Gulag Archipelago* alludes among other things to the Solovetsky Archipelago. The memorial stones that mourn the victims of Stalinism on the central squares of Moscow and St. Petersburg were both brought from these islands.

In the twenty-first century, the monastery has fully restored its onion-shaped cupolas and other features of its ancient past. The monastery houses a historical museum that tells the story, albeit incompletely, of

6   *Mimetic and Subversive*

FIGURE 1. A 500-ruble banknote, which shows the Solovetsky Monastery as it looked in the late 1920s, when it housed the exemplary camp of the gulag. The banknote has been in circulation in the Russian Federation since 1995.

the murderous camp that once functioned within its walls. However, after many years of struggle between the monastery and the museum, in 2011 the Russian government decided that the museum should move from the island to the mainland. The Solovetsky story was to be streamlined. One part of its past would become the whole; another part would be excised and sent elsewhere. Simultaneously, Russia's Central Bank decided to revise the image on its note; on September 6, 2011, the bank announced the issuing of a new version of the note, which now features the onion-shaped domes of the Solovetsky monastery. Though the bank did not comment on these changes, their meaning is clear: there is no place for the memory of state terror on the state currency.

The post-Soviet series of banknotes showcase noncontroversial sites of national glory, from the Monument to the Millennium of Russia to the Bolshoi Theater. It is all but impossible to imagine that a concentration camp would be deliberately included among these images. But as I write, the 500-ruble banknote with pyramidal towers is still in circulation. This version of the note—a memorial to the Solovetsky camp, not the Solovetsky monastery—was continuously printed and reprinted from 1995 to 2011. The image survived several modifications of the note, including its redenomination in 1997, when the banknote of 500,000 rubles was exchanged for 500 rubles, with the same image of the concentration camp.[2]

Whether millions of Russians are aware of this or not, it is the mournful images of the Soviet gulag that they carry in their wallets, touch, handle, glance at, and exchange daily. But this site of memory is as warped as it is common. Perhaps the 500-ruble banknote carries a double message, representing the Solovetsky monastery for pedestrians and the Solovetsky camp for connoisseurs. With its layers and contradictions, this double image exemplifies the typical complexity of mourning for the Soviet victims. Sometimes the proverbial Russian censorship plays a role in these mourning games, but sometimes we know that censorship is not an issue. It would be brash to suspect the officials of the Central Bank of a subversive conspiracy, nor would I dare to speculate about their unconscious motivations. Probably the most realistic, down-to-earth way to understand this amazing banknote is to see it as a ghostly apparition. Whatever the actual design- and decision-making process that shaped the note may have been, the note's cultural role is very close to that of a ghost. It is unknown who brought the banknote image into being, and how; the same is true for ghosts. The picture on the banknote reminds those who are in the know about a hidden secret of the past—a specialty of ghosts. This is probably how ghosts come to us these days, to haunt the public sphere and marketplace rather than aristocratic manors and deserted graveyards.

Though I do not know who created the 500-ruble banknote, I know who uncovered its meaning. A local scholar of the Solovetsky Archipelago, Yury Brodsky, noticed the unusual towers on the bill, identified the image as belonging to the gulag period, and published his revisionist story.[3] As a result of this interpretative act, the meaning of a routine artifact changed from one of self-celebration to mourning.

Too Much Memory?

In contrast to the Nazi terror that featured a crystal-clear boundary between the victims and perpetrators, the Soviet terror targeted many ethnic, professional, and territorial groups. Though in some waves of terror the Poles, the Ukrainians, the Chechens, or the Jews suffered more than others, there were other waves when the terror chose Russians. Some of these operations focused on the peasants, and others targeted the intelligentsia, but some periods extracted a particularly heavy toll from the state and party apparatus. It was a rule rather than an exception that the perpetrators of one wave of terror became victims of the next. Though in every singular act of torture or murder the victim and the executioner were separated by an enormous distance, the fact was that a little later, in several months or years, the executioner would likely become a victim of the same treatment. This rotation makes it very difficult to reach any historical, philosophical, or theological—in fact, any rational—understanding of these events. Nikolai Shivarov, an investigator who forced Osip Mandelstam and several other poets and writers to acknowledge their "criminal" enmity toward the Soviet system, committed suicide as a convict of the gulag in 1940.[4] After hundreds of thousands perished on the construction site of the Belomor Canal, the head of this construction project, Semen Firin, was sentenced and shot in 1937. After millions died in the gulag, its organizer and chief administrator, Matvei Berman, was sentenced and shot in 1939. Thousands of perpetrators were purged, arrested, tortured, and executed in the waves of repressions that decimated the bureaucratic bodies responsible for repressions, the People's Commissariat of Internal Affairs (NKVD) and related bodies of the Communist Party, in Moscow and the provinces. Victims and perpetrators were mixed together in the same families, ethnic groups, and lines of descent. Sometimes they also found themselves mixed together in the same cells and barracks. Unlike their peers in the colonial domains of the socialist empire such as Ukraine or the Baltic states, who felt oppressed by a foreign power and were eager to resist it, and unlike even the peasants in Russian villages who perceived collectivization as the ruthless imposition of an urban and therefore foreign order, the victims from the Russian intelligentsia perceived the terror as senseless and monstrous precisely because it was self-inflicted. Indeed, at the Moscow trial of 1992 that failed to ban the Communist Party as a criminal organization, its attorneys produced a bizarre argument: since Communists suffered from "repressions" more than others, their organization could not be blamed for these crimes, even though it had organized them. Since their peers have already punished some perpetrators, this argument goes, there is no need to punish these people again.

If the Nazi Holocaust exterminated the Other, the Soviet terror was suicidal. The self-inflicted nature of the Soviet terror has complicated the circulation of three energies that structure the postcatastrophic world: a cognitive striving to learn about the catastrophe; an emotional desire to mourn for its victims; and an active drive to find justice and take revenge on the perpetrators. As in Shakespeare's *Hamlet*, these three impulses—to learn, to mourn, and to avenge—compete for the limited resources of the melancholic mind. The suicidal nature of the Soviet atrocities made revenge all but impossible, and even learning very difficult. To learn about oneself is the toughest among the challenges of learning. Mourning, however, has had no limits.

There is no umbrella concept to embrace all the branches and institutions of the Soviet terror. In cultural memory, the Solovetsky camp represents the system of the gulag, and the gulag represents the Soviet terror. However, victims of the Soviet regime also suffered in many other institutions of the criminal state: during the arrest when the state came into their homes, searched their belongings, and separated them from their families; in investigative prisons, where the state applied the most inhuman (and illegal, under that state's own laws) methods of torture; in various forms of "administrative exile" and "special resettlement" that broke up families and dictated where people must live, often forcing them to move to isolated and remote locations where conditions were so harsh as to be life-threatening; in grand-scale social experiments such as collectivization and forced industrialization, with famine and urban poverty as their results; and also in other institutions of disciplinary power such as psychiatric hospitals, orphanages, and, last but not least, the Soviet army, with its universal draft and endemic brutality.[5]

The popular word that renders the horror of the Soviet penitentiary system is "*zona*," the fenced zone of a prison or a camp. "The zone" means everything that is the opposite of "freedom" (*svoboda*), which, in this usage, embraces all that is the life beyond the fence. "The zone" is, essentially, the gulag from the prisoner's point of view. The institutional framework of the gulag is much broader, and I follow the tradition of using this concept, "gulag," as an imprecise but convenient term for the whole variety of Soviet-era penitentiary institutions.[6] Historically, the word "gulag" is the bureaucratic acronym of the Stalin-era's State Administration of Camps, which was closed down in 1960. But the potential for meaningful generalization of this concept is huge. Veniamin Iofe, probably the most impressive intellectual of the Memorial Society, has defined the gulag as a kind of shorthand for Soviet oppression in all its forms. "Our compatriots still have the gulag within," wrote Iofe in 2001.[7] With this range of definitions, it is not surprising that the number of gulag victims is uncertain; the available estimates range between 5 and 30 million. Even the number of their official "rehabilitations" is unknown; it ranges, by different accounts, from 1.2 to 4.5 million. Indeed, the only certainty about the Soviet catastrophe, apart from its massive scale, is its very uncertainty. We do not have anything like a full list of victims; we do not have anything like a full list of executioners; and we do not have adequate memorials, museums, and monuments, which could stabilize the understanding of these events for generations to come.

Unlike the treatment of former Nazi officials in Germany, no professional ban was ever instated for former leaders of the Communist Party of the Soviet Union, let alone its rank-and-file members. Only negligible compensation has been provided to those victims who have been officially "rehabilitated." Many more of those who were robbed by the Soviet Communists, such as the millions of collective farmers, for example, will never see any form of compensation whatsoever. This unfinished business is one of the reasons for the obsessive return of history in contemporary Russian culture and politics.

There was no external authority, such as occupying forces or an international court, to dispense justice; and there has been no serious philosophical debate in Russia, secular or religious, over problems of collective guilt, memory, and identity. Despite an attempt made in the early 1990s to initiate such a debate by the historian and gulag survivor Dmitry Likhachev (see chapter 4), Russian intellectuals have not produced anything comparable to the great book by Karl Jaspers, *The Problem of Guilt*.[8] In Germany or France, denial of the Holocaust is a crime, but in Russia a politician or professor can disseminate propaganda for the Soviet past and ignore or deny its crimes without subjecting himself or herself to the slightest risk. While Europeans are talking about the "mnemonic age," a "memory fest," and a growing obsession with the past "around the globe," some Russian authors complain about the "historical amnesia" in their country.

In fact, "nostalgia," rather than "amnesia," has become a fashionable word and an important element of post-Soviet culture.[9] Allusions to the past make up an important part of the political present. Political opponents in Russia differ most dramatically not in their understanding of economic reforms or international relations, but in their interpretations of history. Discussions of current policy issues rarely go without reference to historical experience. Concepts and labels like "Stalinism," "the cult of personality," and "political repressions" are rhetorically employed as often as modern legal or economic terms. The events of the mid-twentieth century still make up a living, contentious experience that threatens to return again and therefore feels frightening and uncanny (see chapters 10 and 11).

In 2011, one of the most popular Russian journalists, Oleg Kashin, who had just recovered from injuries inflicted in a beating reminiscent of the manner in which the Soviet state treated its dissidents, said that Stalin was "the third person sleeping in every one of our beds. . . . Napoleon has long become a brand of cognac, and Stalin should have become the name of a kebab or a sort of tobacco, but we constantly drag him out of the grave."[10] Post-Soviet memory operates as a living combination of various symbols, periods, and judgments, which are experienced simultaneously. The present is oversaturated with the past, and this solution refuses to produce any sediment. As Tony Judt put it, in western Europe, the problem is a shortage of memory, but in eastern Europe and Russia, "there is too much memory, too many pasts on which people can draw."[11]

Too much or too little, one thing is clear: the very nature of the Soviet terror makes it difficult to comprehend, remember, and memorialize. To the scholars of Stalinism, there is nothing more foreign than the German-Jewish idea of the uniqueness of the Holocaust, and the reason for this is not only the desire to receive the proper recognition for the victims of Stalinism on a par with the victims of Nazism but also the intuitive understanding of the multitude of "repressions"—genocides and democides—that constitute Stalinism.[12] There were many waves of "repressions," and most of them were repetitive, chaotic, confusing, and overwhelming. Even though their total numbers can be set forth in the homogenous language of demographic losses, in other respects they defy standardization, spread out as they were over a good part of the twentieth century and across the gigantic space of Eurasia. The descendants of these repressions' survivors do not share the concepts that were crucial for the perpetrators and fatal for the victims. The "kulaks," the "saboteurs," the "bourgeoisie," the "social parasites," the "anti-Soviet elements," and other "class enemies" were exterminated for belonging to these categories, which have no meaning for us.

Remembering the Soviet terror often entails disbelief that such things could have happened. This is a productive feeling, but the least appropriate response to it would be a redemptive narrative that demonstrates the functionality of terror.[13] The victims' suffering and the perpetrators' intentions are both unbelievable in man-made catastrophes, and "suspension of disbelief," a popular literary convention, cannot help us to learn their lessons. The Holocaust historian Saul Friedlander writes about disbelief as a deep and common response to the Nazi terror. He states that though a common goal of historical writing is "to domesticate disbelief, to explain it away," the research on the Holocaust should resist this temptation.[14] Scholars of the Soviet period should aspire to do the same. Writing history does not imply resolving its warped contradictions in a smooth, functional narrative. Making sense of the memory of the past does not require sharing its weird presumptions. We do not need to comprehend the murderer's motives in order to mourn his victim, though many mourners do know the desire to understand what happened, and why, and what it meant.

At the end of the twentieth century, many influential thinkers, particularly in the field of economics, connected socialist ideas with Stalinism and claimed that striving for full equality and universal justice logically leads to state-sponsored terror. Yet we also know ample historical instances of terror committed for the sake of private property, both in colonial and domestic contexts. Whether socialism inescapably led to Stalinism or whether the latter was a result of unique and unfortunate choices and circumstances, there is no doubt that the Soviet regime compromised the ideas of socialism gravely, and maybe even irreversibly. As a result, mourning for the human victims of the Soviet experiment coexists with mourning for the ideas and ideals that were also buried by this experiment. This is double mourning, for the people who were murdered for the sake of ideas and for these ideas, which were also killed by this violence—a warped concept in itself.

The Work of Mourning

For many years, Nadezhda Mandelstam had a painful, persistent nightmare: she is standing in line to buy food and her husband, Osip, is standing behind her; but when she looks back, he is not there. Not recognizing her or not willing to talk to her, he walks away. She runs after him to ask, "What are they doing to you 'there'?" But Osip never responds.[15] Importantly, Mandelstam put the word "there" in quotation marks, as if she saw these quotation marks in her dream; though she had no way of conceptualizing "those" who had taken away her husband, she needed a grammatical fiction or placeholder, which remained unspecified but which, with an element of self-irony, she put into quotation marks.

It is not the pain of knowing, but rather the desire to know—"What are they doing to you 'there'?"—that lies at the heart of mourning. This desire to know the unbearable is also a desire to share its burden, to express it in clear words or images, to tell the story—what "they" have done to him "there"—to the close community of equals, and then to others as well. At this stage, Victims' Balls become textual; in other words, communicative memory about the terrible past flows into cultural memory, where it stays indefinitely.[16] With a somewhat similar meaning, Walter Benjamin said that "memory is not an instrument for exploring the past but its theatre. He who seeks to approach his own buried past must conduct himself like a man digging."[17] Two barely compatible metaphors—theater and digging—reveal the problem of mourning. A man who digs into his own past is also a performer who plays his role in public. Whether he performs digging in the soil, in the archive, or in popular culture, this is a practical activity, the work of mourning. But this work does not end once the past has simply been dug up and revealed. Only when they become public, as in a theater, do these excavations of the past, buried and unburied, complete the work of mourning.

From Pushkin's major works *Boris Godunov* (1825) and *Eugene Onegin* (1833), both of which analyze remorse for an unjustifiable murder, to Dostoevsky's *Crime and Punishment* (1866), and then to Aleksandr Blok's *Retribution* (1919), the classics of Russian literature provide spectacular templates for mourning, shame, and repentance. Rediscovering these classical examples after a long period of revolutionary enthusiasm, the late-Soviet culture produced its own ways of coming to terms with the horrible past. Three cultural genres led the Soviet mourning: literature, music, and film. In literature, mimetic mourning and political protest melded in such works as Boris Pasternak's *Doctor Zhivago* (published in the West in 1957 and in Russia in 1988), Anna Akhmatova's *Requiem* (1963, 1987), the memoirs of Nadezhda Mandelstam (1970–1972, 1999), Aleksandr Solzhenitsyn's *The Gulag Archipelago* (1973, 1989), Varlam Shalamov's *Kolyma Tales* (1978, 1987), and Vasily Grossman's *Life and Fate* (1980, 1988). Another leading genre was music, a traditional medium of mourning that had the additional advantage of being impenetrable for the censors. Dmitry Shostakovich composed a series of major works that mourned the victims of the Soviet period, from his "Leningrad" *Symphony No. 7* (1942) to his late works (1962–1972) that combined music with political poetry. I argue in this book that a number of major Soviet films belong to the same pantheon of mourning.

I rely on the concept of mourning more than on other concepts that have been tested in this field, most notably trauma.[18] As Sigmund Freud classically defined it, mourning is an active, realistic, and healthy process. It has its limits, both in time and in intensity. It has its interminable counterpart, melancholia, though of course there is much uncertainty about the boundary between them. Freud was a great mourner in his late years, and the concept of mourning was at the center of his thinking, close to but different from the concept of trauma. Trauma is a response to a condition that had been experienced by the self; mourning is a response to a condition of the other. An individual subject who has suffered a trauma, such as shell shock, cannot represent the traumatic situation; this representational inability is precisely what constitutes trauma.[19] In contrast, mourning is all about representation. Nadezhda Mandelstam knew exactly whom she lost, when she saw him for the last time, and what the circumstances of his arrest were. There is no such knowledge in trauma.

Remembering its losses, a postcatastrophic culture lives on through the subsequent generations, as the survivors who struggle with their traumas give way to the descendants who mourn the victims of the catastrophe. We mourn for our grandparents whether we remember them or not, and we mourn for the victims of the Jewish Holocaust or the French Revolution whom we do not remember. It is easier to understand Marianne Hirsch's concept of "postmemory" as a domain of mourning rather than a domain of trauma or the posttraumatic.[20] The alternative idea, that trauma with its subtle psychological dynamic can be passed down through generations, is conceptually more complex and empirically less verifiable.

Different in their relations to representation, the two conditions, mourning and trauma, are similar in relation to repetition. In mourning as well as in trauma, the subject obsessively returns to certain experiences of the past, and these returns obstruct this subject's ability to live in the present. Sometimes—in those cases when, as Freud put it, the subject loses her ability "to love and work"—this obsession with the past is clearly pathological, but sometimes it is temporary and reversible. After World War I and the revolutions that ended it, Freud formulated his newest discovery, the "compulsion to repeat." Easily explained by the pleasure principle when the repetition involved pleasurable gratification, it became a puzzle when, as Freud observed, the material and the process of repetition were both excruciating. It is not only that wounding experiences of the past turned into painful memories in the present. Freud discovered more than this: the past's uncanny ability to contaminate the present. To account for this anachronistic phenomenon, Freud revised his whole system, looking far (though not far enough, in my opinion) beyond the pleasure principle. The new dichotomy that he devised juxtaposed remembering, which relates to the past as past, and repeating, which reenacts the past in the present.

Repetition and remembering make present selected features of the past. Refined by Shakespeare, Coleridge, and other connoisseurs of mourning, the English language renders the relevance of these time-bridging processes better than German or Russian, which do not have any precise equivalent for the English prefix "re-," with its universal but deep meaning. Indeed, the word "representation" captures with elegance the mechanism of making the nonpresent relevant for the present, while "remembering" connotes, in a crisper way than is available to theory, reconnecting the lost member with its peers, the reciprocal relations between the reconstitution of the community and the return of its repressed, prodigal elements.

As Freud notes, his patients tended "to *repeat* the repressed material as a contemporary experience instead of, as the physician would prefer to see, *remembering* it as something belonging to the past." The physician would prefer to see remembering, but like his distant colleagues, historians, he often sees repetitions. In remembrance, the past and the present are distinct; in repetition, they are fused, so that the past prevents the subject from seeing the present. The therapist's duty is to short-circuit these cyclical reverberations of the past by helping the patient "to re-experience some portion of her forgotten life" so that it might be remembered rather than reenacted. "The ratio between what is remembered and what is reproduced varies from case to case," but the patient needs "to recognize that what happens to be reality is in fact only a reflection of the forgotten past." Commenting on this idea, the anthropologist Michael Taussig postulates a "double action": the subject both reexperiences her past and distances herself from it; the subject is both in and out of this past, and it is at that point that she realizes that what she is confronting "is not the past but a memory."[21]

In his introduction to the German translation of Dostoevsky's *The Brothers Karamazov*, Freud gives a challenging example of the mimetic nature of mourning. Interpreting Dostoevsky's epileptic seizures, Freud declares: "We know the meaning and intention of such death-like attacks. They signify an identification with the dead person, either with someone who is really dead or with someone who is still alive and whom the subject wishes dead."[22] Though mourning usually strives to revivify the past, it can also be anticipatory: the subject imagines or rehearses a future horror, something that he fears could happen, or something that he fears he will bring to pass through his own guilty desires. In this remarkable construction, Freud allows for the possibility of redirecting the energy of mourning toward other purposes, such as revenge, rebellion, or forewarning.

The dichotomy between repeating and remembering is central for Freud's "technique," but culture blurs these processes. Only an "impulsion to remember," writes Freud, can overcome the "compulsion to repeat," but the forces of resistance work against this process: "The greater the resistance, the more extensively will acting out (repetition) replace remembering."[23] On the stage of postcatastrophic memory, the dialectics of repetition and remembering produce warped imagery, which combines the analytic, self-conscious exploration of the past with its reverberations and transfigurations. Spirits, ghosts, demons, and other creatures conflate reenactments with remembrances in creative forms that can be naive or sophisticated, regressive or productive, influential or isolated. What we usually fear is the uncertainty of the future, but we often imagine this future as a repetition of the past.

Though Freud did not elucidate the overarching logic of his post–World War I works on repetition, mourning, and the uncanny, it can be formulated in a few simple words. If the suffering is not remembered, it will be repeated. If the loss is not recognized, it threatens to return in strange though not entirely new forms, as the uncanny. When the dead are not properly mourned, they turn into the undead and cause trouble for the living. Freud begins his famous essay "The Uncanny" (1919) by arguing that the uncanny is "secretly familiar," something that "has undergone repression and then returned from it." "Estranged . . . through being repressed," an image feels uncanny and, moreover, frightening when it returns to the subject, writes Freud. In his literary analyses, Freud emphasizes a particular way of rendering the uncanny experience that later scholars would call "metonymic." He notes that stories by E. T. A. Hoffman and other mystical romantics often feature "severed limbs, a severed head, a hand detached from the arm," and other corporeal metonymies.[24] The experience of the uncanny depends upon the lost and found members of human bodies, which are sometimes autonomous and sometimes incorporated into other, now monstrous bodies. Presenting living and dead human and animal parts in creative combinations is how people represent death and the world after it; Bakhtin described this method as "gothic realism" (see chapter 4). When a living or revenant part represents the perished whole, this part feels uncanny. The past is large, integrated, and self-sufficient; what returns from it is dispersed, fragmented, and scary. Freud's formulas defined the uncanny as a particular form of memory, one that is intimately connected to fear. The combination of memory and fear is, precisely, the uncanny. The higher the energy of forgetting, the greater the horror of remembering. When ghosts talk to us, as the ghost of Hamlet's father talked to Hamlet, they substitute someone whom we know: they speak in these persons' voices, tell their secrets, and complete the business that they have left unfinished. But as Hamlet felt acutely, the act of recognition does not deprive a ghost of its strangeness and otherness. The uncanny is the strange turned familiar; the ghostly is the familiar turned foreign.

In matters of mourning, Freud based his distinction between the healthy and the sick on the subject's ability to acknowledge the reality of the loss. But this distinction did not work well in the terrorized Soviet Union. Millions of victims were convicted for long terms of imprisonment "with no right of correspondence," and long silences followed their arrests. Many were shot before they ever reached a camp; others returned months, years, or decades later. For millions of relatives and friends, the uncertainty was external and realistic rather than internal and pathological. Many prisoners were released earlier or later than the terms laid down in their sentences. Many died in the camps and prisons, but the news of their deaths might take years or decades to reach their families and friends. The sentence had little or no predictive value. The gulag did not provide reality checks for either hope or mourning. In an indefinitely large part of the Soviet experience, death could not be recognized as death, and survival could not be relied upon as life. The state, the source of the repressions, was also the only source of information.[25] This is a condition of uncertain loss, in which the beloved person disappears for reasons that nobody understands; in which she may be alive and might possibly return; in which no information about the loss is available or trustworthy. However, what happens to mourning or melancholia in conditions of uncertain loss and untestable reality has not been theorized. What we know is that this condition is destructive both for the survivors and for the memory of the dead. As Jacques Derrida put it, "Nothing could be worse for the work of mourning than confusion or doubt; one has to know what is buried and where. . . . Let him stay there and move no more!"[26]

Psychoanalytic studies of posttraumatic syndromes in Germany suggest that traumatic experience is transmitted transgenerationally. The second, and even third, generations following a social catastrophe manifest "subnormal" psychological health and social performance, and this is claimed to be true both for the descendants of the victims and the descendants of the perpetrators.[27] Following the classic study of "phantoms," which was based on deciphering a secret language of Freud's Russian patient Sergei Pankeev, some scholars believe that similarly subtle, mysterious mechanisms govern the transmission of transgenerational memory.[28] I believe that before formulating such complex hypotheses, we need to look at what culture, high and low, presents in the plain view. In the modern world, novels, films, school textbooks, museums, monuments, guided tours, and, finally, historical studies present rich narratives about the past and transmit these narratives from generation to generation.[29] Though this book employs some elementary ideas from psychoanalysis and deconstruction, it is predominantly an exercise in cultural studies, which I tend to reformulate as a historical discipline.

In Russia, a land where millions remain unburied, the repressed return as the undead. They do so in novels, films, and other forms of culture that reflect, shape, and possess people's memory. The ghostly visions of Russian writers and filmmakers extend the work of mourning into those spaces that defeat more rational ways of understanding the past. Embracing the confusion of present and past, the obsessive reenactment of the loss, and the disturbed and disjointed nature of the relationship to the present, the melancholic dialectic of reenactment and defamiliarization produces a rich but puzzling imagery.

Clorinda

Analyzing the allegorical world of the baroque mourning play, Walter Benjamin believed that "pensiveness" is the most characteristic feature of the mournful. Other emotions alternate between attraction and repulsion; mourning is unique because it intensifies without ambivalence.[30] Mourning has an unusual ability to deepen the contact with reality, but only with the reality that has vanished. Creative but isolating, this mournful world needs to be understood by others before its subject can attain relief from it. Like Freud's study of the work of mourning (*Trauerarbeit*), Benjamin's study of the *Trauerspiel* combined factual observations, personal projects of mourning, and recipes for relief. Freud wrote, "The inhibition of the melancholic seems puzzling to us because we cannot see what it is that is absorbing him so entirely."[31] Benjamin probably had this seminal text by Freud in mind when he stated, "the theory of mourning . . . can only be developed in the description of that world which is revealed under the gaze of the melancholy man." Supplementing Freud, Benjamin proposed the rhetorical concept of allegory as the clue to the melancholic world. He saw "the will to allegory" as a kind of primary desire, which he confined to the internal structure of melancholy: "The only pleasure the melancholic permits himself, and it is a powerful one, is allegory," said Benjamin.[32]

Exhuming the past buried in the present, the scholar watches memory turning into imagination. In the postcatastrophic condition, many authors and readers share a desire for a poetic reenactment of the catastrophic past, which they perform in their fictions. Referring to the mythical protagonists of the sixteenth-century Italian poet Torquato Tasso, Freud gives a striking example of this process. In a poem about the First Crusade, the knight Tancred kills his beloved Clorinda while she is disguised in the armor of the enemy. After her burial he finds himself in an enchanted forest that strikes the crusader with terror. At the height of his grief, he slashes with his sword at a tree; blood streams from the cut, and Clorinda's voice tells Tancred that he has wounded his beloved once again.[33]

> "I was Clorinda, not the only soul,
> lodged here in rough, hard plants . . .
>
> These branches and these truncks can feel. If you
> hew down their wood, you murder what you hew."[34]

Freud sees in Tancred's action a compulsion to repeat: driven by this compulsion, he repeated his murder, and the process would replay itself without end. This element of Freud's analysis of Tancred's story has become a staple of trauma theory.[35] However, Freud and his followers in the field of trauma studies do not do justice to other wonderful details of the story. As Tancred repeated his action, its object was transformed, magically but inescapably, from a living woman to her remote symbol, a tree. Tancred is the same, but Clorinda is different; she "was Clorinda," she says. What Tancred meets in the magic forest is, the narrator tells us, "a simulacrum horrible and dire." A noble savage, a female victim, and now a monstrous simulacrum, Clorinda is far more interesting than Tancred.[36] However, we see and hear Clorinda's posthumous experience through Tancred, who is alive and horrified but does not seem to be traumatized: he has not forgotten Clorinda's words, but renders them as he heard them, in quotation marks. Tancred's mourning takes the poetic shape of his lover hybridized with a tree and speaking, like a ghost imprisoned in a weird body, in a recognizable and familiar voice. Tancred, the mournful perpetrator, does feel a compulsive drive, but this is not a compulsion to repeat the murder. Rather, it is a compulsion to remember and reenact the lost love— a feat that can only be achieved using magical means. In this important example, Freud's idea of compulsive repetition works only if we assume a "double action" in which Tancred physically reenacts the past and magically distances himself from it, acknowledges his loss and reincarnates the lost object, and turns the sensual reality of the beloved Clorinda into the fearsome imagery of the monster. For Tancred's mournful mind, Clorinda transgresses many dichotomies that defined their earthly lives— between friend and enemy, man and woman, the living and the dead.

His mourning for the lost, human Clorinda shapes the monstrous image of Clorinda-the-tree, which is now a figment of Tancred's imagination. He incorporates in his mourning the major preoccupations of his peers, the crusaders—guilt, fear, gender ambivalence, exotic longings. Reflecting and revealing the major issues of their cultures, mourners follow Tancred in this mechanism that makes mourning a culturally productive—enriching and not only impoverishing—experience.

Another way of naming this relation between mourning and difference is to use a foundational concept of the Russian formalist school: estrangement, or defamiliarization. Estrangement, a creative variation in the repetition of the past, fights and often overcomes the Freudian death drive, that mechanism of eternal repetition of the traumatic memory. As Joseph Brodsky put it, what distinguishes art and literature from life "is precisely that they abhor repetition."[37] Even though Tancred reimagines his magic forest again and again, he also sees it as strange and different. Estrangement can be lifesaving for a mourner, and sometimes literally so; when mimetic performances come too close to the original loss, they can lead to suicide or homicide. Remembrance detoxifies repetition; healthy remembrance is about playing it safe. Mimetic mourning emulates but does not reproduce the loss, and the differences between the lost past and its mimetic model are no less important than their similarities. With the help of magic, humor, or analysis, the mourner develops *markers of difference* that enable her to vary the serial re-presentations of the past.

I believe that post-Soviet memory can be productively situated at the crossroads of three epistemologies, one of which is rooted in the Freudian psychoanalysis of mourning; another in Walter Benjamin's idea of the second life of religious symbols in mass cultural products; and the third in Russian formalism, with its idea of estrangement. Magic is one toolbox from which mourners draw their markers of difference; artistic culture with its mechanisms of estrangement is another; and humor is a third. They are strange bedfellows, but their close relations to mourning are recognized every time mourners share ghost stories, gather for a meal, or write obituaries. Coleridge believed that "the terrible, by the law of the human kind, always touches on the verge of the ludicrous."[38] Benjamin remarked that "the pure joke is the essential inner side of mourning which from time to time, like the lining of a dress at the hem or lapel, makes its presence felt."[39] If humor is the inner side of mourning, the external side takes the form of the monument. If jokes often protect the mourner from mimetic excesses that could destroy his authorship, monuments mark the difference in a serious, ceremonial way.

There are museums on the sites of the Nazi concentration camps, and now on some sites of the gulag as well. The designers and staff of these museums strive to reconstruct the life and world of the camp in minute detail and with the greatest possible historical accuracy. Historians, curators, and architects take great care in their efforts to reproduce the material trappings of the original camp: the fence, the barracks, the watchtower. But at the center of this grim and gloomy zone these same historians, curators, and architects almost always erect a monument: an obelisk or a figure that is visible and recognizable, ideally, from every corner of the memorial zone. This double structure is visible in various memorials, created by different cultures: on the sites of Nazi camps in Germany and Poland; on the battlefields of the Civil War and on the sites of black slave rebellions in America; on the Russian battlefields of 1812 and 1941–1945. While the historical parts of these museums and memorials are all different, the monumental parts are more uniform, indeed all but universal, and this is striking. The obelisks were not there when the camps functioned as camps, but they seem to be essential when these camps function as museums. It is as if our historicizing drive to reproduce the horror of the past finds its limit precisely at the center of the site of memory, and this limit is marked out in such a way as to leave no part of the site untouched by its presence. Reproducing the past for the sake of mourning, we need a marker of difference to remind us and reassure us—powerfully, centrally, and unmistakably—that this is only mimesis and not an original. This obelisk is a functional analogue for quotation marks, as dominating in the field of vision as they are in the field of text. Quotations are all different, but the signs marking their boundaries are the same.[40] As mourners, we need to see all the original camp details, but we do not want to return to the camp, because to do so would be all but suicidal. Like quotation marks, the obelisk highlights the difference between the present and the past, the copy and the original, the reenactment and the act. The obelisk provides us with the certainty that enables us, "in spite of everything, to recognize that what happens to be reality is in fact only a reflection of a forgotten past."[41] Take note of Freud's "in spite of everything": a mourner's drive to repeat, reenact, reimagine—her death wish—is enormous. In many cases, only humor—a construction that is lower than obelisks but sometimes more powerful—protects the subject by estranging the past.

Quotation marks, monuments, humor, and interpretation—these are all indispensable elements of cultural memory that were simply not there in the past, when the events happened for the first time. In respect to the past, truth claims are fluid, as are their relations to the ethical or political concerns of the present. As Russian examples generously teach us, yesterday's truth may differ from that of today. Cultural memory is a living realm that changes with history. Works of fiction that do not claim truth (for example, historical novels) or genres with unverifiable validity (for example, memoirs) are crucial genres of memory. In a democratic society, various institutions compete in their striving to patrol the borders between truth and myth in the representation of the past. With the passage of generations, the borders between myths and truths shift and curve. These movements of truth in the space of memory comprise, in their turn, an important part of cultural history.

The contemporary descendants of the victims of the Nazi terror now live in conditions that are vastly different from the conditions in which their forebears lived and died. Today, however, many of those who are shaping cultural representations of both the Nazi Holocaust and the Stalinist terror belong to the third postcatastrophic generation. They rarely own oral histories or family photographs, but they all operate within the public sphere, with its variety of multigeneric cultural products.[42] In post-Holocaust Europe the process of mourning embraces the descendants of the victims as well as the descendants of the perpetrators: with the passing of generations, their mutual hatred is transformed into a coparticipation in mourning. For the third generation after a catastrophe, joint mourning has a reconciliatory, cosmopolitan potential. If memories of the Holocaust helped shape the new, potentially pan-European culture of human rights, memories of the gulag, famines, and other socialist atrocities have also contributed to the formation of Western ideas of rights and recognition.[43] However, these ideas become less certain when one crosses the well-guarded borders that segregate Europe into its western and eastern parts. There in the East, memories of the socialist terror are salient and militant, as are memories of World War II. The Soviet regime disappeared forty-five years later than the Nazi regime, and its collapse was entirely different (see chapter 10). In this part of the world, tragic stories of the socialist past are still more divisive than economic or political issues of the present. The living generation remembers the serial catastrophes of "real socialism" and lives through its never-ending "transition" to another condition, which is still as distant as the horizon. Rather than sharing the multidirectional experiences of suffering and emancipation, various groups—ethnicities, generations, and even professions—cultivate their different versions of the past, versions that shape their identities, define their friends and foes, and endow their changed and changing worlds with meaning. In this lively situation, memory wars are inescapable. They are fought between those who claim to feel compassion for the victims and those who insist on their continuity with the perpetrators. They are fought between national states, political parties, and cultural figures. And they are also fought over interpretations of cultural artifacts, such as the Solovetsky banknote, and the films, novels, pictures, and sculptures that I discuss in this book.

2

Mourning and Warning

Poet and person of remarkable courage, Osip Mandelstam was arrested in 1934 after he wrote a satirical poem about Stalin, an act that he understood as suicidal. After investigation, he was sentenced to a mild exile, and, exceptionally, his wife, Nadezhda, was allowed to accompany him. Several years later, he wrote an ode to Stalin, a complex piece of poetry that essentially glorified Stalin.[1] It seems that Stalin read the brutal caricature of 1934 and, paradoxically, liked it.[2] Stalin probably read Mandelstam's reverent ode of 1937 as well, though we do not know how he understood it. We know only that Mandelstam was arrested again and subjected to the standard treatment: separation from family, transportation to eastern Siberia, barracking with criminals, hard labor, hunger, and lack of medical care. Nothing more was heard of Mandelstam until the collapse of the gulag system in the mid-1950s, when random survivors returned from the camps to tell partially true, partially fantastic stories about their victims. Yulian Oksman, a sober literary scholar who survived ten years in a camp also in eastern Siberia though thousands of miles away from Mandelstam, wrote to an émigré colleague in 1962:

Already during the transportation Mandelstam began to demonstrate signs of insanity. Suspecting that the camp officials . . . had received an order from Moscow to poison him, he refused food. . . . Neighbors caught him stealing their bread rations and beat him brutally, until they realized that he was mad. . . . He was thrown out of the barracks, lived near trash pits, and ate garbage. Dirty, covered with grey hair, long-bearded, in rags, crazy—he had been turned into the camp's scarecrow.[3]

In Auschwitz, these people were called *Muselmänner*, or Muslims.[4] In the Soviet camps, they were called *dokhodiagi* ("goners" or "the soon-to-be-dead").[5] By all accounts, these goners constituted a large proportion of the camp population. Since the Soviet camps did not practice the Nazi procedures of "selection," which were aimed at eliminating the sick and weak, many of those who perished in the gulag spent their last weeks and months as goners.[6] Wasting precious resources, the goners were a nuisance; but there was no official guidance on what to do with this never-decreasing group of people. Some of these individuals might be cured or killed, but any consistent program of elimination—or, by the same token, of support—would be punishable. Only the camp medics had concepts and contexts within which they could handle these people, but even if they wanted to do so, their resources were inadequate. Sometimes the goners were even released "for medical reasons," a strategic response that improved the camp mortality statistics. More often, they were left to die in the camp.[7] Produced by the gulag in huge numbers, the goners personified the abject world of the camps, its ideal type (to borrow a concept from the social sciences). Julia Kristeva defined the abject as "a massive and sudden emergence of uncanniness . . . a weight of meaninglessness on the edge of non-existence and hallucination."[8] These words might serve as a portrait of Osip Mandelstam, who prophetically wrote in 1931, "Only my equal can kill me,"[9] and a collective picture of the millions of his equals in the gulag.

Having survived the camp, Solzhenitsyn understood its functioning by analogy with the body, which cannot exist without getting rid of its waste products; thus the gulag developed a means of ejecting "its principal form of waste," the goners. Like Primo Levi, Solzhenitsyn stated that no witness could relate the experience of the goners, the central phenomenon of the camps:

Philosophers, psychologists, medical men, and writers could have observed in our camps, as nowhere else . . . the reduction of the human being to an animal and the process of dying alive. But the psychologists who got into our camps were, for the most part, not up to observing; they themselves had fallen into that very same stream that was dissolving the personality into feces and ash.[10]

Transformative Torture

Analyzing the early reports of the survivors of the Nazi and, in a few cases, Soviet camps, Hannah Arendt identified in these writings a common tone, which she described as a "curious air of unreality." She focused on the incomprehensibility of the camps, which their inmates frequently described as a nightmare. From the commonsense point of view, "neither the institution itself . . . nor its political role makes any sense whatsoever." Nothing offends common sense more, Arendt said, than "the complete senselessness" of the camps where the innocent suffer more than the criminal, labor bears no fruit, and crimes do not benefit their authors. This reign of pure violence needs an explanation, but the task of providing one presents an "extraordinary difficulty." Responding to this puzzle, Arendt presented the camps as "laboratories in the experiment of total domination," a goal that can be achieved only in a "human-made hell."[11]

It was not the logic of production that organized the life and work in the gulag, but the logic of torture. Investigative torture has become one of the most memorable features of the Stalinist terror. However, investigative torture was applied mostly in prisons rather than in camps, where millions were kept under a different kind of torture. In the camps, the effects of hunger, hard labor, untreated illnesses, freezing temperatures, separation from families, isolation from the world, and vulnerability to violent attacks by fellow inmates combined in an overwhelming pain that, being purposefully inflicted by the regime, should also be considered as torture. As Elaine Scarry reveals in her classical analysis, "torture consists of acts that magnify the way in which pain destroys a person's world." Pain, Scarry argues, has a unique ability to destroy language by degrading speech to the sounds anterior to language. If pain destroys the sufferer's world, torture has an additional element: it expands the torturer's self and its self-perceived power. The pain of torture results in the dissolution of the boundary between inside and outside, conflation of private and public, and substitution of the victim's agency by that of the torturers. "The torturer's growing sense of self is carried outward on the prisoner's swelling pain."[12]

Soviet concentration camps were torture camps, not extermination camps, and if people died in high numbers it was the result of negligence rather than purposeful intent. In the language of Arendt and Scarry, the gulag's primary function was to destroy the convicts' language and their world. If the need for information, as Scarry shows, is a false justification for investigative torture, the economic needs of the Soviet state were a similarly false justification for the torture endemic to the camps. Economic productivity in the labor camps was about 50 percent of the average level achieved by free labor in the same industries; moreover, this estimate does not take into account those prisons and camps where millions of convicts did not perform any labor. Many of the gulag's projects had no rational justification, and many have never been completed. Those that were finished, such as the Belomor Canal, proved to be economically useless. The gulag managers' permanent problem was not a deficit but a surplus of labor. They did not arrest people in order to realize their projects; they invented projects in order to occupy the prisoners.[13] The regime partially recognized the nonutilitarian nature of the camps when it talked about their ideological, educational, and psychological—in a word, transformative—functions.[14] Osip Mandelstam's swift degeneration in the camp demonstrates the brutal efficiency of this low-tech treatment. Used universally in the prisons and camps of the gulag era, transformative torture—"remolding and reforging human nature," to use the language of Stalinism—efficiently turned those who were generously endowed with language, creativity, and what Arendt called "the world" into goners who were indifferent to everything but their next morsel of bread or their hated neighbor.

Seeking a philosophical means of representing the horror of the Nazi camps, the Italian philosopher Giorgio Agamben develops the concept of bare life, or *homo sacer*, defined as "life that may be killed but not sacrificed."[15] Indeed, only life that has value may be sacrificed. By contrast, the bare life of the camp victims fills an irrelevant space or time between social and biological deaths. Not defined by law, custom, or faith, bare life enters into a direct relation with the sovereign: he who can declare a state of emergency can also define which of his subjects might be wasted at will. Agamben argues that camps are permanent zones of exception from the law, and therefore life in these zones cannot be described in terms that are meaningful outside of these zones. There are archives for all kinds of life but bare life. Scarcely self-conscious due to humiliation, hunger, and disease, bare life of the camps has been largely forgotten.

However, in the Stalinist context, Agamben's analysis looks incomplete. The idea of sacrifice relies on the religious concepts of the ancient

Greeks and Romans; for moderns, this is a very ambiguous concept.[16] In secular terms, one could define sacrifice—for example, a loss of soldiers at war or fire fighters on duty—as based on the voluntary participation of the potential victims and the retroactive acknowledgment from the public sphere. In other words, sacrifice is voluntary, public, and meaningful to the public. In contrast, a mass murder in a gas chamber, in a state-organized famine, or in a Soviet camp does not conform to this definition because it is neither voluntary nor public.

Agamben's sacrificial definition of bare life and his archaic concept of *homo sacer* need serious adjustment before they can be applied to the gulag. Revising Agamben, Eric Santner proposes the concept of "creaturely life," which reflects the "ontological vulnerability" of humans. According to Santner, those cultural institutions and human communities that attempt to shelter their members from various threats often intensify their vulnerability by exploitation and tyranny.[17] Following both these authors and also Elaine Scarry, I propose a more specific construction, "tortured life." This is life that has been stripped of meaning, speech, and memory by torture. Like creaturely life, tortured life is created by destitution, but this is a kind of destitution that is generated by the purposeful efforts of the state and its institutions. Like bare life, tortured life is situated in direct relation to the sovereign, because it is the sovereign who tortures. Tortured life is a temporary condition, though if the torture is skillfully performed, it can be drawn out over a prolonged period of time. This life can survive and recover, but the posttraumatic consequences are unavoidable.

Soviet people were not just objects of ideological manipulations and violent coercion on the part of the institutions of the state. These institutions were also created and run by people who shared the same nature—class, ethnic, and human—as those who were tortured or murdered in the gulag. The historiography of Stalinism has featured a long-lived and enduring debate between the so-called totalitarian school and the revisionists. The revisionists carried the day in Western universities in the 1990s, though much to their chagrin the totalitarian model would largely be embraced in post-Soviet Russia. While the totalitarianists revealed the top-down control and coercion in Soviet society, the revisionists emphasized the intrinsic agency of the common people and of the low-level structures of the state. After the demise of the Soviet Union, a new generation of historians has shifted the focus of these debates toward the self-disciplining practices employed in the hearts and minds of Soviet citizens, practices that are viewed as the construction of a particular kind of subjectivity.[18] One consequence of this body of new research has been to displace to the margins the massive violence that was the definitive feature of Stalinism. While Hannah Arendt and, more recently, Tzvetan Todorov see terror as the essence of totalitarian government,[19] the new wave of historiography has focused on Soviet diaries, autobiographies, and dreams, all of which are manifestations of subjectivity that preserve some features of freedom even under terror.

These approaches, one that focuses on violence and another that focuses on discourse, should be creatively combined. The state-sponsored violence of the high Soviet period (1928–1953), always massive and ever increasing, imposed self-disciplinary practices on the Soviet subjects. These practices would not have developed without the omnipresent backdrop of the gulag, where discipline was external, diaries forbidden, and human life returned to its animal origins. During this period, any member of the Communist elite could be sacked, arrested, tortured, and killed at any moment and for many reasons, one of which could be insufficient loyalty. An understanding of the environment of coercion, violence, and angst is crucial for the analysis of the ideology, culture, and discursive practices of the Soviet period. The resulting complex of feelings—fear, bewilderment, resentment, compassion, and mournfulness—was a permanent feature of the Soviet life. Theoretical reasons for ignoring the Soviet violence are as thin as historical ones. The most important inspiration for the studies of Soviet subjectivity, Michel Foucault, did not ignore violence as a historical phenomenon, but rather emphasized it.[20]

Nevertheless, overlooking violence has become an important trend that pervades even the best studies of Soviet life. One example is the acclaimed book by anthropologist Alexei Yurchak, which focuses on "the last Soviet generation" but necessarily starts the analysis by digging into the earlier periods. Having developed an original methodology for studying ideological performances as speech acts, Yurchak describes Stalinism in purely discursive terms, as the reign of an "authoritative speech." In Yurchak's formulation, Stalin was "the Master of discourse" and its "editor" who "legitimized the ideological discourse from a position external to it."[21] Yet Yurchak does not explain how this paradoxical mechanism—the control of ideological debates by nonideological means—worked in practice.

I submit that only violence—threats, purges, arrests, torture, show trials, executions, and the gulag—could force an ideological debate into the margins dictated by an external power. Stalin could control—"edit," as Yurchak puts it—other people's utterances only because he had sheer physical, and not merely discursive, means of power at his disposal. In one of his examples, Yurchak refers to an interesting Soviet publication, *The History of the Civil War in the USSR*.[22] The very title of this work is stunningly disingenuous. In fact, the volume tells the history of the civil war in Russia and adjacent territories in 1918–1922, that is, before the creation of the USSR in 1922. Furthermore, this history makes no reference to the subsequent Soviet terror that was, strictly speaking, the civil war in the USSR. According to Yurchak, "Stalin carefully reviewed the text," and the editors accepted 700 corrections that he suggested. The first volume of the planned multivolume edition was printed and circulated in half a million copies in 1936. But Yurchak does not say what happened next. During the following year, two out of eight members of the editorial board and eight out of eighteen contributing authors were "repressed": eight were sentenced and executed, one committed suicide in fear of arrest, and one fled abroad. Probably because of these events, the subsequent volumes were never published. Typical for the period, this story lays bare the mechanisms of Stalin's "metadiscourse": physical violence turned the editors and authors, many of them heroic soldiers and radical politicians in the past, into a flock of sheep who slavishly accepted hundreds of "corrections" to their own memories and histories. The results were also typical: lives were lost, volumes were left unwritten or unpublished, and the civil war in the USSR continued. As Arendt declared, violence cannot create power but actually destroys it.[23] Symbolized and largely realized by the gulag, violence was both catalyzer and corroder of the Soviet discourse.

Boomerangs of Violence

"Everything flows," wrote Vasily Grossman, but in Soviet Russia, this flow was swirling and warped, as in a whirlwind. Based on routine, massive, and ever-increasing violence, political models fanned out from the metropolitan centers to the cultural and geographic periphery and then returned with fresh force, legitimized and magnified, to the centers.

Comparing Nazism with Stalinism and both with colonialism worldwide, Hannah Arendt formulated the idea of the "boomerang effect," whereby the practices of colonial governance were transferred back to the metropolitan country.[24] With its aboriginal roots, the boomerang metaphor encapsulated the old, Kantian nightmare that the European peoples would be ruled as if they were savages who could not rule themselves. After Arendt, anthropologists have repeatedly stressed the role of colonies as "the laboratories of modernity," where the newest technologies of power were tested before they were brought to Europe.[25] In contrast, the Soviet terror's waves and cycles were mostly centrifugal. Sent from Moscow to all corners of the enormous country, executives of terror developed their local methods of torture and murder, but the "quotas" of terror were tightly controlled from Moscow (though regional leaders often requested permission to increase them). I will show, however, that Grossman proposed a more complex understanding of terror, which he developed in parallel to Arendt's.

In Grossman's *Everything Flows*, a novel written between 1955 and 1963, the protagonist, Ivan Grigorievich, is returning from the northern camps of the gulag, where he has spent twenty-nine years of his life. He visits Moscow and Leningrad, the cities of his youth, and then settles in a provincial town of southern Russia. While reading this novel, we never move beyond the borders of the Soviet Union, but the narrative is surprisingly cosmopolitan. Scenes in the camps emphasize the multiple ethnicities of the prisoners, from the Russians to the Jews to the Poles and Crimean Tatars. The most passionate and detailed parts of the novel tell us not about the camp experience of the protagonist but about events that happened thousands of miles away from his camp. These are the chapters that describe the famine in Ukraine, and this is the best depiction of the Ukrainian famine that has been written in Russian. But with his work of mourning, Ivan Grigorievich takes us farther than Ukraine. Born in the Caucasus, on land where the memories of colonization by the Russian Empire were still recent and living, he frequently revisits his childhood in dreams that are narrated in the novel. The place where his father built his house had formerly been populated by the Circassians, a rebellious tribe that led the militant resistance of the Caucasian peoples against Russian domination. Thousands of Circassians were killed during the Russian colonization of the Caucasus; in the mid-nineteenth century, many were expelled to Turkey. Growing up among the ruins of this civilization, the young Ivan would come across the remains of abandoned Circassian gardens and cemeteries among Russian fields and roads. Once, after coming home from such a walk, he broke down and wept: "It was as if, there in the half-dark of the forest, someone were lamenting, searching for people who had vanished, looking behind trees, listening for the voices of Circassian shepherds or the crying of babies." Ivan asked his father for an explanation, and the father answered with a popular Russian saying that was often used for explaining the Stalinist terror, but is here applied to the colonization of the Caucasus: "When you chop down the forest, splinters fly": the victimization of the Circassians was a fair price for Russian, and later Soviet, imperial glory.[26]

Thinking about his childhood in the colony, Ivan Grigorievich describes both his shame for the past and premonitions of future disasters. This combination of political guilt, sentimental nostalgia, and apocalyptic mindset is typical of the childhood reminiscences of postcolonial thinkers who grew up in settlers' colonies. Grossman himself was in fact born and raised in Berdichev, one of the centers of the Jewish Pale of Settlement, a colonial institution of the Russian Empire that practiced apartheid for two centuries. Grossman's life experience was thus essentially the opposite of that of Ivan Grigorievich: the former was a native victim of apartheid, the latter an imperial settler. By giving his ethnically Russian protagonist, Ivan Grigorievich, who stands here as a quintessential victim of Stalinism, childhood roots in a settlers' colony in the Caucasus, Grossman presents us with the living trajectory of Arendt's boomerang: a sweeping loop that turned Ivan Grigorievich, a descendant of imperial perpetrators in the colony, into a victim of internal violence at home. Emphasizing this construction, the novel reaches its finale with Ivan Grigorievich's pilgrimage to his home in the Caucasus (see chapter 3 for more details of his trip). The family house is no longer there, but the novel ends at this site of memory, having described a full circle like a boomerang.

Long musings about Russia's unfreedom precede this finale. According to Grossman, Russian progress and Russian slavery were shackled together by a thousand-year-long chain. Essentially, Grossman understands the Soviet horrors of collectivization, mass famines, and concentration camps as the resurgence of serfdom, which the Empire abolished in 1861.[27] In the twentieth century, speculates Grossman, the Soviet state extended serfdom to social and ethnic groups that historically had never experienced it, such as miners in Ukraine or the Tatars in the Crimea. Grossman explains both the old czarist and new Soviet serfdom as the result of Russia's geographic space—the "tragic vastness," as he put it. Like Arendt, Grossman perceives an affinity between the Nazi and the Soviet totalitarianisms, or, as Grossman formulated it: "the unity of the barbed wire stretched around Auschwitz and the labor camps of Siberia." This intuition is also central for Grossman's great novel, *Life and Fate*.

In Grossman's philosophical vision, serfdom was thus the primary manifestation of Russia's internal unfreedom that continued through the millennia. However, in Grossman's poetic vision, Ivan Grigorievich's imperial childhood foreshadowed his experience in the gulag. One boomerang flies back to the gulag from the site of the external colonization, in this case, the Caucasus. Another boomerang returns from Russia's internal colony, which was serfdom. In this stereoscopic picture, we find two centripetal movements that both returned from Russia's geographical and social periphery to its core, which was the gulag.

The First Collapse

We can only speculate about what would have happened if Nazi Germany won World War II: would Hitler's successor have denounced the Holocaust? In the Soviet Union, the very same institutions and personalities that had organized the mass crimes later revealed them voluntarily. Ironically, Stalin's major achievement, the military strength of the Soviet Union, created a unique situation in which his regime had to analyze, exculpate, and dismantle itself. There was nobody else to do it. But under this kind of control, the process of working through could not achieve closure.

In 1956, the head of the Soviet state, Nikita Khrushchev, started the de-Stalinization process. There is no doubt whatsoever that he was personally implicated in the "repressions" that he oversaw through the decades of his service as the party leader of Ukraine and Moscow, some of the bloodiest of the bloodlands.[28] There was nothing coercing Khrushchev to confess other than his own guilty memory of the terror and his fear of the terror's reenactment.[29] This autonomous, self-imposed character of Khrushchev's revelations makes them unique, even unprecedented in the history of the twentieth-century violence.

In 1953, there were 166 labor camps in the Soviet Union, plus a large number of other penitentiary institutions, from prisons to special settlements. Many millions served time in these institutions. Almost all of them were released between 1954 and 1956.[30] The enormous system of the gulag melted away with amazing ease, foreshadowing the collapse of the Soviet Union a few decades later. At the moment of his celebrated confession at the Twentieth Congress of the Communist Party in 1956, Khrushchev was at the height of his power. But according to his son, Khrushchev was "ceaselessly returning to Stalin, poisoned by Stalin, trying to expunge Stalin out of himself and failing to do so."[31] Whether his incomplete revelations were driven by individual atonement or political calculation, he explained them using the vaguely Hegelian and, to some extent, Freudian idea that a crime should be acknowledged in order to prevent its repetition. "Never again" resounded as a leitmotif both in his report to the Twentieth Congress and later in his memoirs. Mourning and warning were tightly linked in his rhetoric, with the latter providing political arguments for the former. You may feel no remorse, he kept warning his peers, and you are not required to confess your own crimes; but if you do not mourn your victims, your fate will be the same as theirs. Khrushchev succeeded in transforming his milieu to such an extent that he escaped the worst: deposed in 1964, he was left in peace to live for many more years, dictated his memoirs, and was buried by his family. As the Soviet phrase went, he enjoyed the supreme luxury of dying in his own bed—a luxury that, in his case, was well earned.

Desperately in need of a conceptual apparatus that neither Marxist tradition nor the Stalinist legacy could provide, Khrushchev coined two operational concepts: "unjustified repressions," to embrace mass arrests, tortures, and deportations, and the "cult of personality," to describe the accompanying ideological practices. Both concepts served to scapegoat Stalin. "Unjustified repressions" blamed the preceding ruler for the meaningless, unmotivated man-made catastrophe. The quasi-religious concept of the "cult of personality" accused Stalinism of violating two fundamental tenets of Marxism—rationality and egalitarianism. These conceptual contributions were substantial if euphemistic, and Khrushchev's language is still with us.

If the Nazi Holocaust was ended and exposed by others, the Soviet terror was ended and exposed by its former perpetrators, who were also its potential victims. For the speaker and the researcher, self-applied concepts present notorious epistemological problems. I suspect that many of Khrushchev's political difficulties were connected to this paradoxical logic of self-reference, which was first exemplified by the Cretan sage of 600 B.C., Epimenides, who said, "All Cretans are liars." If all Cretans are liars, of course, then this statement is a lie, too. If every Communist believed in the lie, could they reveal the truth? Khrushchev relied on dialectics rather than logic, and this Hegelian method provided some relief. However, self-applicability does make it difficult to comprehend, represent, and remember the Soviet terror. In retrospect, its agents and targets seem blurred, agency dispersed, purpose uncertain, causality cyclical, and renunciation incomplete.

Two readings of the term "repression(s)," the Freudian and the Khrushchevian, are intimately correlated. After Stalin died, the long-mourned, secretly familiar, inadvertently forgotten returnees were received with mixed feelings that ranged from horror to compassion to indifference and hostility. They returned with an experience of violence, humiliation, and suffering that was out-of-scale for their family, friends, and neighbors. Familiar and alien, they were uncanny. In Freud's famous definition, the uncanny "is something which is secretly familiar, which has undergone repression and then returned from it": the return of the repressed.[32] After the collapse of the gulag, the victims of repressions were coming back from their camps as uncanny returnees. While perpetrators saw the dead returning to take a terrible revenge, others imagined the fate of the repressed with horrifying details that mixed oral histories, personal fears, and literary paradigms (see chapter 3). The whole country turned into a "contact zone" between the innocent victims of the gulag and the guilty survivors who managed to escape it.[33] In 1956, Anna Akhmatova said: "Now two Russias are eyeball to eyeball. Those who were in prison and those who put them there."[34] But these two Russias were also aware of the third, which died in the process. Shaping a zone of indistinction between bare life and state law, between repression and rehabilitation, and finally, between mourning and oblivion, this triangular relation determined the cultural dynamics of the late-Soviet period.

Mourning and haunting have etched their imprints on many products of late-Soviet and post-Soviet culture. Striving to understand and appreciate this culture, scholars need a particular sensitivity to the warped, the uncanny, and the ghostly. According to a credible witness—the trained historian, Soviet dissident, and later leading post-Soviet human rights activist Liudmila Alexeyeva—in 1953 the Moscow public was accustomed to stories like this:

> One night the general was found in a cold sweat, screaming, "Forgive me, Dmitry Ivanovich!" His wife asked him who he was talking to; he did not respond. After a few weeks, the general started talking to the invisible Dmitry Ivanovich while awake. After they took him to the insane asylum, his wife learned that Dmitry Ivanovich was a man the general shot with his own revolver in 1937.[35]

A similar effect—mournful and somewhat mystical experience of the belated justice—was felt everywhere among the Communist sympathizers, some of them defectors at this stage. Resigning from the French Communist Party in October 1956, the Martiniquan author and politician Aimé Césaire wrote:

> Khrushchev's revelations concerning Stalin are enough to have plunged all those who have participated in communist activity, to whatever degree, into an abyss of shock, pain, and shame. . . . The dead, the tortured, the executed—no, . . . these are not the kind of ghosts that one can ward off with a mechanical phrase. From now on, they will show up as watermarks, . . . obsession, . . . malaise, . . . wound at the core of our consciences.[36]

Despite the enormous difference between the criminal Soviet general and the sophisticated postcolonial intellectual, we see similar metaphors for the new situation that remained beyond comprehension: they both perceived the ghosts of the dead returning to torment the living. But within his party, Khrushchev failed to rally support for his courageous repentance. His sympathizers were mainly intellectuals in the Russian capitals and provinces who were numerous and important in the technocratic and still-ambitious Soviet Union, but he failed to address them directly. This intelligentsia included scores of gulag survivors and their relatives. Ilia Ehrenburg, a popular writer who outlived Stalinism, named this period "the Thaw." Defrosting three decades of Stalinism (1924–1953), this remarkable decade ended in 1964, when a vigorous protest from the Communist Party against Khrushchev's capricious reforms led to his dismissal.[37] During the long, dreadful Stagnation that followed (1964–1985), the authorities resumed their attempts to escape from the memory of Stalinism. Playing with the two meanings of "repression," I call this dark period of memory "the repression of repressions." However, those inconsistent moves revealed as much as they obscured. Banished from politics and transferred to culture, the work of mourning became the most sensitive ideological issue in the late-Soviet period.

Tragically incomplete, the Thaw was the most successful of Russia's de-Stalinization projects. Led by poets and writers, Russia's mourners had their moment of recognition that eventuated in their unprecedented popularity during the Thaw and in the later period. Less than ten years after Stalin's death, Khrushchev staged a performative act of major importance: the removal of Stalin's corpse from the mausoleum on Red Square (1961). Announced on televisions that the Soviet people had only recently obtained, the news about this removal was watched with wonder and relief. I was a child in Leningrad, and I remember watching this news together with my father, who was inexplicably moved by it. Watching my father who was watching Stalin's removal happened to be the first political experience of my life, though of course I did not know what would follow.

Cosmopolitan Memory?

The periods that within the Soviet Union were called the Thaw and Stagnation coincided with what has gone down in global memory as the central phase of the Cold War between the Soviet Union and the Western world. Throughout this period, the memory of the gulag was preserved internationally, by American and European historians, activists, writers, and politicians, and by Soviet dissidents and memoirists. As the legacies of Hannah Arendt, Isaiah Berlin, and many others can testify, the Cold War struggle against the Soviet expansion was also a struggle for human rights within the Soviet Union and for the historical memory of its victims. The Cold Warriors smuggled, translated, and published manuscripts by Solzhenitsyn, Grossman, Osip Mandelstam and Nadezhda Mandelstam, and many others; they produced magisterial pieces of scholarship such as Arendt's *Origins of Totalitarianism* (1951) or Robert Conquest's *Great Terror* (1968); and they gathered an amazing array of Soviet artworks, such as Norton Dodge's collection that preserved precious pieces of art from the gulag and other places (see chapter 5 for some examples).

In the aftermath of genocides and other catastrophes, global memory has played various roles. Sometimes it has been a supplement to national memories, sometimes a catalyst, and sometimes a substitute. The prominent Holocaust historian Dan Diner recently reexamined this problem. Starting with Maurice Halbwachs's classical argument that collective memory requires a remembering collective, Diner comes to the conclusion that nations can preserve memory while some other social groups, such as classes, cannot. Diner states that the Nazi crimes "entered the ethnicized memory" of Germans because the regime eliminated those whom Germans considered to be "part of a culturally and historically different collective." In contrast, the Soviet regime defined both victims and perpetrators "as part of the same historical mnemonic collective."[38] Therefore, Diner concludes, German guilt and Jewish mourning have been passed down through generations, while the Soviet crimes vanished from memory.

Naturalizing ethnic differences, Diner denies the ability of nonethnic groups to structure "mnemonic collectives" and remember their dead in a collective way. Even in the German-Jewish case, I find this argument questionable. Germans were not "fundamentally different" from Jews; it was the Nazis who invested enormous efforts into construing this religious group as the national Other. Unavoidably, the "thesis of a fundamental difference" between ethnic and other groups underestimates those types of solidarity that transcend and transgress national borders. According to Diner's argument, the repressions of "kulaks" or "*nepmen*" could not and do not remain in the collective memory, either because these groups were ideological fictions created by the Bolsheviks with their theories of class warfare or because these groups were successfully exterminated and did not leave descendants to mourn them. Diner characterizes such crimes as historically describable but mnemonically nontransmissible. With some hesitation, Diner makes an exception to this rule for those Soviet groups who suffered from repressions that were defined by ethnicity. Diner mentions Ukrainians here, but he could give many more examples—for instance, Chechens, Crimean Tatars, or, indeed, Jews after World War II. However, my central question addresses not these ethnically defined cases but a more general picture that Diner draws here: is Diner's nationalization of memory (that is, the identification of the remembering collective with the nation) historically true and morally defensible? I do not believe so. Diner's concept of collective memory seems to be custom-made for the Nazi Holocaust. Designed to clarify comparisons between the Holocaust and other cases of mass murder, it precludes many of these comparisons. Diner seems to operate within a simplified distinction between two types of human collectives, nations and classes. Marxist efforts to furnish classes with self-conscious identities do not seem convincing to Diner, but the idea that nations have identities, and therefore subjectivities, is something he appears to take as a given.

It is individuals who feel guilt or sorrow. However, these individuals have the ability to pass on, preserve, and exchange their feelings; culture provides them with the instruments for these purposes. Culture allows people to share their experiences without requiring physical encounter. Various media and genres of culture transmit and distort memory, which moves between individuals, communities, and generations. Using cultural means, some individuals and groups are able to shape the feelings of other individuals and groups. With the help of texts, images, and other cultural instruments, some individuals even create new groups and collectives. Besides nations and classes, there is a third type of collective: associations, as Alexis de Tocqueville first described them.[39] The post-Soviet transformation has not happened within an undivided—classless, nationless, subjectless—unity. It has been a struggle between myriads of collective subjects, who construct themselves according to a variety of principles, from the ethnic to the political to the generational to the memorial, and shape their identities in this struggle.

The concept of cultural memory is close to the concept of collective memory but is significantly broader.[40] Cultural memory presumes a remembering collective only in the broadest and loosest sense. In the modern world, the cultural communities of those who subscribe to a certain journal or take part in online chat play the role of "mnemonic collectives." The turn from "collective memory" to "cultural memory" de-emphasizes the remembering collective and focuses on the materials of which memory is made. It is a turn from the sociology of memory in the tradition of Maurice Halbwachs to cultural studies of memory in the tradition of Walter Benjamin. "Multimedia collages" of cultural memory integrate multiple types of signifiers: from memoirs to memorials; from historical studies to historical novels; from family albums to museums and archives; from folk songs to films to the Internet.[41] The leading role of the Memorial Society, a typically Tocquevillian association, in preserving memory of the Soviet victims, monitoring human rights, and struggling for Russia's democratization, exemplifies the post-Soviet type of the remembering collective and testifies to the powerful role of memory in structuring the social space.

In the mid-1980s, Mikhail Gorbachev launched glasnost, a sweeping project of public truth-seeking that revealed more about the Soviet past than about Russia's present. Newly published memoirs, archival findings, and popular histories documented the processes, institutions, and personalities of the Soviet terror in unprecedented detail.[42] The great texts of the Thaw that remained unpublished at the time—Solzhenitsyn, Shalamov, Grossman—were all published in large print-runs. Hundreds of memoirs and autobiographies published in the 1980s dealt with the sufferings of their authors or their parents under the Soviet regime. In 1993, the literary historian Marietta Chudakova, then an adviser to President Yeltsin, wrote that such writing would fulfill the function of a "Russian Nuremberg," staged not in the courtroom as in Germany but on the pages of memoirs.[43]

This hope failed to materialize. In fact, historians and journalists often lament the cynicism of the post-Soviet public, which instead of learning about pluralism has learned a sad lesson about the dependency of historical truth on the changing interests of those in power. Though the memories of social catastrophes have a long life, the feelings of survivors differ from those of their children, and the feelings of the second and third postcatastrophic generations are different again. The so-called second de-Stalinization, which began in Russia in 1985, was smothered during the second Stagnation period, which stabilized and coagulated in 2000.

Dispersed and marginalized, the intelligentsia of early twenty-first-century Russia have been deprived of their economic or political relevance. Nostalgia for the Soviet past has been purposefully spread by the state-controlled television, and its manifestations have become increasingly frequent on the printed page and the computer screen. Among the historical novels, biographies, films, and documentaries that have been disseminated in abundance during this period, a growing share belongs to conspiracy theories and propaganda that effectively deny the crimes of the Soviet period. Often, this "restorative nostalgia" has more to do with the drive to criticize the current Russian government than it does with any genuine sympathy for the world of communal apartments, collective farms, and the gulag.[44] But the booming social media in Russia and their decisive role in political processes in the 2010s testify to the truth of Tocqueville's words that he wrote, by quill, in the 1830s:

> Among the laws that rule human societies there is one which seems to be more precise and clear than all others. If men are to remain civilized or to become so, the art of associating together must grow and improve in the same ratio in which the equality of conditions is increased.[45]

There is no doubt that the increasingly consumerist and also sociable Russian society has become less interested in the Soviet guilt than it was fifty, or even twenty, years ago. However, references to this legacy are surprisingly robust in political debates and cultural products of the post-Soviet era. During this decade, the challenging task of making sense of the Soviet past has also produced original and important novels and films (see chapter 11). About 2010, some intellectuals started talking about a third de-Stalinization. Equivocally supported by President Medvedev, this initiative entailed a series of meetings and declarations, with the most important result being the projected plans for two national museums of the "totalitarian terror," one in Moscow and one in St. Petersburg. It will be the next decade, and maybe the fourth de-Stalinization, that will hopefully see these museums open.[46]

For the Soviet regime, an insistence on its own definition of truth was crucial; as soon as it faltered in this, it collapsed. In the twenty-first century, Russia's authoritarian "transition" demonstrates the tortured complexity of its postcatastrophic situation, in which the past haunts the citizenry, divides the society, and limits political choice. If the second and third generations live on the same territory where the catastrophe happened; if the political regime on this territory, despite having gone through multiple transformations since the catastrophe, remains ambiguous in its treatment of the catastrophic past; if the perpetrators are not condemned, the victims are not compensated, the criminal institutions are not banned, the monuments are not built—the postmemory of the catastrophe acquires intense and peculiar forms. The very concept of postmemory is not easily applicable to this situation because, strictly speaking, this is not yet a *post*memory. Transforming time in a way that is typical for the posttraumatic condition, the mourned and dreadful loss, the subject of remembrance, continues into the present and shapes the future. The memory of the past becomes indistinguishable from the obsessive fear of its repetition, and the dread of the future takes the shape of compulsory repetitions or creative remembrances of the past. Mourning merges with warning, shaping a temporal zone of indistinction, which combines the past and the future in a joint effort to obscure the present.

3

The Parable of Misrecognition

In 1930, Grigory Etkind was arrested at his apartment in Leningrad. Five months later, his son came home from school one day and asked a gray-bearded man, who was sitting on the staircase, "May I pass, please?" "Fima," said the man, using his son's nickname. Later that night, Grigory explained to the twelve-year-old Yefim what had happened. Along with hundreds of other "*nepmen*" who had launched small businesses a few years earlier, Etkind was arrested for not being able to pay the exorbitant taxes with money he did not have.[1] Etkind and his fellow prisoners were kept in overcrowded cells where they had to stand on their feet for weeks, tortured with unbearable heat, blinding light, sleep deprivation, and continuous interrogation.[2] After months of this treatment, an official gathered a large crowd of prisoners and announced that four of them, including Etkind, were to be executed. These four were removed and shoved into a paddy wagon. After a short trip, Etkind was thrown out of the speeding car onto the pavement in front of his home. He waited for his family, not knowing if they themselves had been arrested, until he saw Yefim and realized that his son did not recognize him. The next morning, Grigory went to the barber and asked for the "full renovation" (*polnyi remont*). But the psychological damage was irreversible; Yefim wrote that his father never returned to his former self.[3]

A sophisticated scholar and effective memoirist, Yefim Etkind knew how to begin his story so that a feeling of horror would haunt his readers. He began with the scene on the staircase: one day he came home from school and did not recognize his own father. He also used two literary comparisons to relate this event to his readers. Comparing his father's experience to the mock execution of Dostoevsky in 1849, Etkind wrote that when he worked on Dostoevsky in the 1990s, he was still thinking about his father's mock execution and anticipation of death. In another attempt to capture this horror, Etkind compared his father's story with *A Terrible Revenge,* the novel by Nikolai Gogol. "What I heard from my father seemed to me even scarier than Gogol's *Terrible Revenge.* How one can possibly live with this? I do not remember how I managed to handle my disgust with the world."[4]

Looking more closely at this novel, we might get a better idea of the twelve-year-old Yefim's response. *A Terrible Revenge* (1832) tells a story of magic, incest, and murder. A sorcerer seduces his daughter; the dead rise from their graves; the earth shudders as if alive. In the end, yet another apparition of magical forces punishes evil and restores peace. What happens at the start of the story, however, resonates with the terrible but unavenged experience of Grigory and Yefim. Gogol's story begins at a wedding party where the father-sorcerer arrives in disguise; even his daughter does not recognize him. People are scared by his foreign appearance, but they also feel as though they have seen him before; maybe he has come from hell? He is the familiar become unfamiliar and frightening. He is the uncanny.

Grigory Etkind was not a sorcerer. He was a small entrepreneur who recycled old books and magazines into folding paper. It was the treatment that he received in prison that made him unrecognizable. The horror of power attached to its innocent victim and accompanied him even after this power released him. With surprise, I found similar situations in other stories that describe the return from the gulag. Some of these stories read as true; others are definitely fictions; probably, most of them present a mixture of memory and imagination.

Why Misrecognition?

Starting from 1953 and until the end of the decade, millions of returnees were coming home, though many of them no longer had any home to come back to.[5] The millions of people who had never seen the gulag welcomed its living remains, the returnees, with mixed feelings. This chapter analyzes several stories in which those who returned from the gulag were misrecognized by their loved ones. I do not claim that cases of misrecognition were statistically frequent in real life. However, the prominence of these narratives in the memoirs, imaginative literature, and films about the gulag deserves study.[6]

Recognition is a concept from classical poetics that made its way into philosophy and political theory. Developed by Hegel and advanced by the French-Russian philosopher Alexandre Kojève (Kozhevnikov), the problem of individual and group recognition has been revisited by James Taylor, Pierre Bourdieu, and other Western philosophers.[7] Nancy Fraser and Axel Honneth juxtapose the struggle for recognition, which aims at achieving respect for cultural differences, with the struggle for redistribution, which aims at reaching economic and legal equality.[8] The possibilities for applying these ideas to socialist societies have not been adequately debated.

In his *Poetics*, Aristotle defined recognition as "a change from ignorance to knowledge, and thus to either love or hate, on the part of personages marked for good or evil fortune."[9] Depending on this fortune, "anagnorisis," or misrecognition, played different roles in tragedy and comedy. In comedies, acts of misrecognition created distances, swapped statuses, and deconstructed the social order.[10] In tragedies, misrecognition does not drive the plotline as in comedy but provides a summary reflection and sometimes a culmination to it. When the act of misrecognition occurs inside the family or among friends, it demonstrates the power of fate, which tragically overwhelms individual love. Fate transforms a hero beyond recognition: even those who love him do not recognize him. Odysseus's wife and son did not recognize him after his decades of wandering (his dog and wet nurse did). Oedipus failed to recognize the father he did not know; Hamlet hesitated before he recognized the ghost of his father. A corollary of misrecognition is imposture, when an individual denies her identity and continuity by pretending to be a different person. In a touching moment in Pushkin's *Boris Godunov*, when the impostor deceives everyone into accepting his false identity, he discloses his real self to the only person whom he loves. Ironically, only when everyone misrecognizes him in the way he desires does he realize his deepest desire to be recognized as his real self. Characteristic for feudal Russia, impostors also played an unusually big role in Soviet history.[11] Among the many reasons for this is their ability to generate allegories for crucial ideas about identity, power, and recognition.

In 1919, the young Osip Mandelstam told his girlfriend and later wife, Nadezhda, that the two themes most important to him were death and recognition. "He was thinking not only about the process of recognition of what we had already seen and known," according to Nadezhda, "but about the spark which accompanies the recognition of something hidden and still unknown, but appearing in the proper moment, such as fate." Osip's strong definition of recognition as the grasping of fate was connected to his understanding of death. "I had the feeling that death for him was not the end but the justification of life," wrote Nadezhda Mandelstam decades later.[12] But Osip's lonely death in a distant camp, the typical death of a goner, was far from being "the justification of life." These goners were semicorpses whose suffering deprived them of any decency, hope, and memory (see chapter 2). In a sense, everyone in the country was a "goner," said Nadezhda; "on both sides of the barbed wire, all of us have lost memory."[13] However, this transformation happened in different ways on each side of the barbed wire, with the result being a deep lack of communication, a kind of mutual nonrecognition.

A monument to the recognition of the Other, Nadezhda Mandelstam's memoirs read as a remarkable document of mourning, arguably the most important Soviet-era text of atonement. The attitude that the author and the readers have toward Osip Mandelstam, a great poet and unique personality, contrasts with the impersonal, nonsacrificial character of his mortification in the camp. Osip simply died in a camp, eliminated like millions of others. Boldly, Nadezhda made no attempt to ascribe a redemptive meaning to Osip's death. Describing the challenge he threw down to the authorities before his arrest, she did not attempt to construe his death as an act of self-sacrifice. After all the detective work that she had done in order to delineate the circumstances of her husband's murder, she saw it with clear eyes, as a senseless act that had no reason, purpose, or justification. The rhetorical effect is created by the tremendous disparity between the attitude of this author and her readers toward Osip Mandelstam and the senseless, nonsacrificial character of his annihilation. In the course of the memoir, this effect interacts with another feature of the Soviet mourning—the uncertainty surrounding the deaths of the victims. The time, place, and circumstances of deaths in the camp remained unknown, as if such deaths were simultaneously both a state secret and a matter of mere detail, not even worth mentioning. The uncertainty of the loss meant that incompleteness would be a central feature of the work of mourning.

I take the story of misrecognition as a trope, which means more than it says, and my interests here are both rhetorical and historical. Historians know that those victims of the camps who survived and returned to their families experienced multiple social and personal problems.[14] The surviving goners struggled with massive psychological transformation. Famously, Primo Levi committed suicide after many years of writing about the Nazi camps. The agony of his Soviet counterpart Varlam Shalamov is less well known (see chapter 5). Scholars of Holocaust literature state that "only few of the few who survived the camp believed they had remained 'themselves' throughout their ordeal."[15] Multiple memoirs of the gulag survivors and their relatives say, as a cliché, that those who returned from the camps *returned as different people.* With the return of the survivors, the identity loss of these people—still alive but no longer themselves—became visible and horrifying. If the internal perspective on this transformation was uncertain and inexpressible, the act of misrecognition of a survivor by her family illustrated the nightmare of the identity loss in a short, clear plot. In a bitter irony, this plot manifested the victorious power of the state, which had achieved its transformative goal by changing its targets beyond recognition. By the same token, this plot expressed the despair of survivors and their families, who felt their estrangement precisely in the moment of the long-awaited reunion. Emphasizing the external, physical change of face, body, posture, dress, and hair, the story of misrecognition worked as a parable for the deeper feelings of internal, psychological change. In cultural memory, the parable of misrecognition became a potent device for expressing the horror of the camps, the guilt of those who escaped them, and the lack of communication between those two parts of Soviet society.

Misrecognition of the Returned

A short story by the highly successful author and singer-songwriter Bulat Okudzhava, "Woman of My Dreams" (1985), describes Okudzhava's memory of his mother's return from the gulag in 1947.[16] The protagonist is a twenty-two-year-old student whose mother is serving ten years in the gulag. He studies Pushkin at the University of Tbilisi and lives in a communal apartment with an elderly neighbor. The student is poor and lonely. He feels "no despair" but admits to yearning for his mother. He has a few photographs of his mother, and he cherishes her "dear and ghostly" image.[17] His neighbor, a heavy, aged man "with widely spread ears with grey wool sticking out of them," plays some role in the story. He never talks to the student and avoids meeting his eye. Gradually, the student realizes that his neighbor has recently returned from the camps. Now he seems ghostly: "nobody saw him entering the doors," and the student imagines him flying "in and out of the window." Suddenly, the student's mother sends a telegram announcing her release. She is coming to live with her son and will soon arrive by train from Kazakhstan. The student is petrified by the fear that he will not recognize his mother upon her arrival. He fantasizes that she is an old, hunched, gray woman. With horror, he imagines that she will see that he does not recognize her and that his misrecognition will aggravate her suffering. But he imagines how happy they will be together and how they will talk endlessly about their lives in separation. When he finally meets her, he does recognize her. To his relief, she has barely changed physically; she is still strong and young. They hug each other and go to his home. He wants to ask her about her life in the camp, but "her face was hard, stony." Her eyes were "dry and empty; she looked at me but did not see me." She would not answer the questions addressed to her personally, such as "Do you want some cherries?" In response, she would say, "Who, me?" When the neighbor comes to say hello, the mother starts talking with him, but the son does not understand them. Communicating with strange words and gestures, they go through the ex-convict ritual of reeling off and comparing lists of the gulag sites where they were held, exchanging geographical place-names that mean nothing to the son. They seem to speak a secret language that the son does not share.

In an effort to revive his mother's old self, the son takes her to the cinema to see a famous movie that was brought back from Germany by the Red Army as a trophy, *The Woman of My Dream*.[18] This film is important for the son. Watching a beautiful actress living her happy, peaceful life on the Danube is "the most precious" experience that this student has. The son hopes that this film will have a similar effect on his mother, helping to restore her, as if the film were "a prescribed medicine or even better, a miracle." In fact, for the mother this movie is intolerable; she leaves the cinema in the middle of the film.

The "feel-good" foreign film reveals to the mother and the son the tragic foreignness that separates them. Watching this movie with her, he thinks the "implausible thought" that "the shiny Austrian carnival on the banks of the glorious Danube was impossible to combine with those circumstances" in which his mother lived in the camp. In the analysis that Okudzhava eloquently presents here, the twenty-two-year-old protagonist could not establish any contact with women of his own age and culture, because his development was delayed by the "black mystery" of his mother's arrest. With her release, his feelings of confusion and guilt only deepened. Love for another woman would feel like a betrayal of his mother, and this betrayal seemed a heinous crime not so much because she was his mother but because she was a gulag returnee. In this story, the cinematic "woman of my dream" works as a transitory object of desire, which the protagonist can enjoy without betraying his mother. The Nazi film star who played this role, Marika Rökk, probably seemed more attractive because she was a foreigner and, even better, a screen image. The student feels that his admiration of Marika must surely be shared by "everyone in Tbilisi"; now that his mother is with him, he wants to share with her his fascination. But his mother has no patience for Rökk. The student is left alone with his desire for the foreign woman of his dreams and compassion for his long-suffering mother. This unsteady mix would unfold further in the inconsistent cultural developments of the Thaw, of which Okudzhava became a leader. Later, another famous poet and bard, Vladimir Vysotsky, married a star whom he first saw in a French film. Their romance would constantly have to do battle with Soviet visa restrictions, meaning long separations that he described in his songs.

The inability of mother and son to reconnect amounts to tragedy. The internal transformation that this woman underwent during her ten years in the gulag is so deep that "she is entirely different," the student tells his neighbor with horror. This neighbor seems to understand what has happened; the author and the reader who, unlike the mother and the neighbor, have not experienced the camps do not understand it. Set inside the most intimate relationship between mother and son and rendered even more painful by the unusually good physical condition of the mother, this gap is deeply unsettling. Since she cannot talk about her experience to her son, there is no way for them to bridge their mutual estrangement. Punished by her withdrawal, he does not ask questions either: "I wanted to ask how she lived there but I was scared and did not ask." Two lives, one in the camp and another "in freedom," are incommensurable.[19]

Yevgenia Ginzburg's *Journey into the Whirlwind,* a classical camp memoir, documents a symmetrical moment of misrecognition from the opposite perspective of the exiled mother who misidentified her son. In 1948, Ginzburg, then in exile in Kolyma, managed to arrange for her son, Vasily Aksenov, the future writer, to join her there. At sixteen years of age, Vasily had not seen his mother for eleven years. They met at the house of the local big shot, who was hosting a party. The hostess, who had overcome many obstacles in order to carry out her good deed of delivering Vasily to his mother, now entertained her guests by suggesting that Vasily guess which one of two women was his mother. The mother and son recognized one another. However, Ginzburg recognized Vasily because he looked like her elder son, Alyosha, who had died years earlier; she only remembered Vasily as a four-year-old. Even though she knew that this was Vasily and otherwise controlled her emotions very well, she inadvertently blurted out the name "Alyoshenka!" at the moment of her reunion with Vasily. At this moment, her mourning for the dead son outweighed her joy at finding the living one.[20]

This part of Ginzburg's life-story is set in the same historical moment as Okudzhava's "Woman of My Dreams." Both narratives include reunion scenes involving two future leaders of the Thaw and their repressed mothers. Both involve moments of misrecognition. Okudzhava's story is written from the perspective of a son who imagines misrecognizing (even if only for a moment) his mother after separation, while Ginzburg's story is written from the perspective of the mother who really does (even if only for a moment) misrecognize her son after separation. In addition, Ginzburg's story presents a social game in which the long-suffering victims have to recognize one another for the amusement of their benevolent masters. Okudzhava's story is written as a fiction with an explicit autobiographical element; Ginzburg's story is written as a memoir—that is, a true story of the past with some measure of selection or exaggeration. But the most important difference lies in the follow-up to the moment of misrecognition. Okudzhava's character remains distanced from his mother; in this case, the fear of misrecognition prefigured the actual alienation. On the contrary, Ginzburg and her son immediately developed a deep relationship. During their first night together, she told him the detailed story of her arrest and life in the camps; this was, she writes in her memoirs, the first oral performance of the future book of these memoirs. In both narratives, the moment of misrecognition illustrates the tremendous change in the personalities involved, but it does not predetermine the subsequent development of their relationships.

Misrecognition by the Returned

In Vasily Grossman's novel *Everything Flows* (1955–1963), Ivan Grigorievich returns from the camps. Ivan had been arrested as a student and imprisoned in the camps for twenty-nine years; his fiancée, friends, and relatives thought about him for a long time, but not that long. Grossman analyzes the process of forgetting the camp prisoners by using the Soviet concept of "*propiska*," local right of residence, which he combines with Freudian metaphors: "First, the man lost his right of residence in life and travelled into people's memory. Then, he lost his right of residence in memory and moved into the subconscious. From there, he showed up sporadically, like a jack-in-the-box, and frightened people with these unexpected, instantaneous appearances."[21] Survivor's guilt manifests itself in fear or even hostility toward the victim's memory.

Ivan Grigorievich is constantly preoccupied with the issue of recognition. Once, after his release from the gulag in 1955, he saw his late mother in a dream. She was walking along a road full of trucks and tractors, a road that he had seen in the camp; he cried, "Mama, mama," but she could not hear him in the noise. "He had no doubt that if she looked back, she would recognize her son in the grey prisoner; if only she heard, if only she looked back." This fear of having changed so much that he would not be recognized, as a physical individual, even by his mother, is soon realized by the actual situation of not being recognized, as a moral individual, by his cousin. Arriving back in Moscow, Ivan Grigorievich visits his cousin, Nikolai Andreevich, a prosperous scientist. Decades earlier, the cousins loved one another, but both feel discomfort when they meet again. Nikolai Andreevich wants to ask Ivan Grigorievich about his experience in the camps. He also wants to tell Ivan Grigorievich about his guilt for some of the compromises that he had made in his life as a typical Soviet *intelligent*. But he cannot bring himself to start asking and confessing. Both have survived and both feel survivor's guilt, but their feelings are as different as their modes of survival; neither of the cousins is ready to discuss them. To describe the gap between them, Grossman uses stunning metaphors of "foreignness." Ivan Grigorievich's face seems "foreign, unkind, and hostile" to Nikolai Andreevich. "It was the same feeling that Nikolai Andreevich felt during his trips abroad. There he felt it impossible, unthinkable to talk to foreigners about his doubts, to share with them the bitterness of his experience." Now he feels the same way toward his cousin. By the same token, the old prisoner, Ivan Grigorievich, does not want to share his pain and mourning with his cousin either. "Ivan Grigorievich imagined how he . . . would talk about those who had gone into the darkness. Their fates were so intolerably sad that even the most tender, quiet, and kind word about them would feel like the touch of a dumb, abrasive hand to a bloody heart that had been torn open." Avoiding this theme of mimetic mourning, the only one of interest to him, he chooses an exoticizing metaphor for his camp experience: talking about it would be like telling fairytales of a thousand and one polar nights. Ivan Grigorievich and Nikolai Andreevich recognize one another as physical persons; they do not deny that they are the same relatives who have maintained their physical continuity from those times when they knew and loved one another. However, they deny one another their mutual acknowledgment as moral individuals. Both of them experience the changes that the other has gone through, not just as an aging and development of the same person but as a radical transformation of identity, as though the remembered person had been replaced by a stranger or even an impostor. "Who is the actual Kolia?" Ivan Grigorievich asks himself: is it the Kolia he remembers, or the Kolia standing in front of him now? At several points, Grossman underlines emphatically the fact that what both cousins actually end up saying to each other is "entirely opposed" to what they wanted and intended to say.

From his formerly beloved cousin, the calamity of misrecognition is transferred to Ivan's formerly beloved city. Traveling to Leningrad where he had lived before his arrest, Ivan Grigorievich simultaneously "recognized the city and did not recognize it."[22] He sees his dead camp-mates there, greeting him from behind corners, and smells "the spirit of the barracks," which he fears has now spread inexorably across the whole country; from now on, he will always be fighting against the compulsive desire to return to the camps or their ruins. As the story develops, Ivan Grigorievich finds a job, a room, and a woman. She dies soon afterward, but he keeps talking to her about love, camps, and history. As we saw in chapter 2, the story ends with Ivan Grigorievich's trip to his parental house in the Caucasus. Of course he does not find the house; but on its site, he is rewarded by a vision of his late mother's tenderness to him. Like the mysterious pilgrims described in one of the young Joseph Brodsky's first poems (see chapter 5), at the end of his pilgrimage Ivan Grigorievich finds consolation in the intransigence of his life-world. Despite all the transformative efforts of the state that moved people, things, and the country beyond all recognition, "The world has not altered. No. It has not altered. It is what it has been," wrote Brodsky in 1958.[23] "The same, unchangeable" are the final words of the story about Ivan Grigorievich. Everything flows, but he is still recognizable, and this is his victory.

Varieties of Misrecognition

Identity has many levels, and so does identification. Andrei Bitov's *Pushkin House* (finished in 1971, published in 1978), a novel that gained cult status among the late-Soviet intelligentsia, presents a literary scholar who was celebrated in the 1920s, imprisoned in the gulag in 1929, and released in the 1950s. Though the protagonist had survived his twenty-seven years in the camps, he abandoned his scholarship. Having returned to Leningrad, he spent his time drinking with his former camp warden.[24] All that he wanted was to get back to the camp, or at least to the ground on which the camp had once stood. His grandson, the young literary scholar Leva, longs to meet his famous grandfather. He had seen many photographs of his grandfather, all of them taken before his arrest. Leva read and admired his grandfather's works; he wanted to be the heir and follower of his grandfather's ideas. "With pride, Leva felt in his own face, the face of his grandfather."[25] But upon finally visiting his grandfather's apartment, Leva is greeted by a person whom Leva immediately rejects; there is no way that this person could be his grandfather. The person has a weather-beaten and tanned face, a red neck, and a dumb expression on his face. Even his drinking companion, the former chief of his camp, looks more intelligent. "I have become a different man," the person who opened the door, Leva's grandfather, tells him. The trauma of the camp turned an erudite, innovative scholar into a husk of a man, compulsively seeking out reenactments of his trauma, and bent on self-destruction. As Bitov said later, he based this character on real-life scholars who had spent many years in camps or exile, such as Mikhail Bakhtin (see chapter 4).[26] When the old man eventually disappeared, his family assumed that he had gone back there, to the site of his former camp, to die. Once he was safely out of the way, the Leningrad Institute of Russian Literature established a cult around the late scholar, in which Leva also took part. Bitov's feat of imagination is astonishing. Writing fiction with no autobiographical underpinnings, he exploits his license with an intensity that the actual memoir cannot afford. The misrecognition of the grandfather by his admiring grandson and the grandfather's disgust in response to this admiration both demonstrate the scale of transformation that the gulag imprinted on its prisoners.

In 1952, another future leader of the Thaw, Andrei Siniavsky, met his father, Donat, upon the latter's release after a nine-month prison term. Right from the gates of a provincial prison, Donat took his son deep into the forest to talk. He told Andrei that he had become the subject of a "scientific experiment" in prison: he was now connected to a frightening electric apparatus, and "they" were controlling his thoughts and words by a kind of radio communication. "They" were listening to this conversation as well, the father believed, and so he cut off the conversation. The son was in despair. Writing about this situation decades later in his autobiographical book *Goodnight!*, Siniavsky was self-consciously ambiguous about his father's condition: maybe this was a hallucination caused by psychological trauma, or maybe his father really was under surveillance using some secret technological device invented by "them." What is clear from Siniavsky's account is that the father's revelation caused a painful alienation between the father and the son. Tortured by this irresolvable gap between his adored father and himself, Siniavsky ends this episode with a confession of filial guilt:

The joy of seeing my father was mixing with an inexhaustible longing; it was as if by finding him I lost something forever. . . . We intensely enjoyed the sight and smell of one another. But still, we were distant, as never before. . . . I had to rush back to Moscow, having left my father alone with his haunting voices, with no help, in this uncanny desolation. He could not help me in my solitude, either. He would never learn what I was thinking and where I was going. I could not burden him. But my guilt before him is not decreased by that.[27]

Siniavsky presents this conversation with his father as his initiation into the particular kind of literature that he would practice as a writer. Calling it "grotesque" or "fantastic," Siniavsky believed that he received from his broken father a mysterious ability to communicate with improbable worlds. Overcoming the gap that separated him from his father, he developed a new identification with him. Thus the future Abram Tertz developed his strange literary style. "Spirits were at work. I could not disentangle myself from them, being elevated by a sense of something like a poetic horror . . . on the edge of the sublime. . . . My father passed his condition to me." The shock of seeing his father transformed by his unimaginable experience to the point of nonrecognition shaped Siniavsky's literary career (see chapter 6).

Yearning for their imprisoned parents, the Soviet orphans imagined them as exotic heroes or romantic martyrs. It was not easy to recognize them in the aged and exhausted victims of senseless terror who actually returned from the camps. Trying to imagine the incomprehensible, their friends and relatives construed the prisoners' bodies and experiences as strange, foreign, and uncanny. Again, Nadezhda Mandelstam documents the quasi-melancholic process of this incomplete work of mourning in the situation of the uncertainty of loss. "There is nothing more frightening than a slow death," wrote Mandelstam, meaning not a slow dying but the slow acceptance of death. Her nightmare, in which she asked Osip, "What are they doing to you?," haunted her until she received an official paper that informed her about Osip's death, though it did not specify when he had died. This paper dispelled the dream, but not the hope. Nadezhda finished her first book of memoirs with doubt (maybe he is still alive?), and she ended the second with a letter addressed to him, in case she should die first.

Like Freud's melancholia, Nadezhda's mourning did not recognize the loss. In contrast to Freud's melancholia, her psychological process was realistic; it did not deny the reality of the loss through wishful fantasies on the edge of delusion, but responded to the actual uncertainty of the information about the loss. In her efforts to learn the fate of her husband, Mandelstam actively sought evidence, developed conjectures, and subjected the available information to reality checks. She found and interviewed several ex-prisoners who said that they had met Osip in the camps, but their stories were not credible. One of them was the poet Yury Kazarnovsky (1904–1956?), a goner who survived and bore witness.[28] Nadezhda Mandelstam's critical words about Kazarnovsky's stories of Osip's death are exemplary: "his memory had turned into a huge soured pancake, where the facts and realities of living in the camp were baked along with fantasies, legends, and mere fiction." She wanted facts, actually one single fact: "What are they doing to you 'there'?" But Kazarnovsky told her about his own miraculous survivals. Mandelstam believed that this pancakelike memory was characteristic for many survivors whom she happened to know, particularly those who were released early in the 1950s (later, ex-prisoners often recycled other people's stories). For life that had been reduced to its bare essence, only death was meaningful enough to enter the narrative. Survivors, wrote Mandelstam,

did not draw a firm line between facts, which they witnessed, and the legends of the camps. . . . In the consciousness of these stricken people, places, names, and events mixed together into a roll that I had never been able to untangle. Most of these camp stories, as I learned them, were confused lists of those bright moments when the narrator was on the brink of death but miraculously survived.[29]

While Mandelstam tested the reality of her loss, Kazarnovsky tested the reality of his survival. Focused on their fictional realities, they could not find common ground. In the gulag and around it, the tortured uncertainty about one's life or death reflected the melancholic uncertainty about the death of the other.

Personal Recognition and Social Distribution

Depicting the situation that was difficult for both those who returned from the camps and for those who remained "free," various authors converged on a rare and striking event. They document the actual moment of misrecognition or the anticipation, fantasy, or nightmare of such misrecognition. The momentary failure to recognize one's returning father or one's arriving son; the fantasy of misrecognizing one's mother or being unrecognized by her; the nightmare of not being recognized by a husband—all this opens a gap in the most intimate texture of the self. The gap has to be filled by a narrative construction that can take a lifetime to produce. Whether such misrecognition actually happened or was imagined, its meaning is still the same: it stands as a parable of terror, an all-embracing allegory for the subjective experience of "repressions."

Unlike the recognition-acknowledgment of political and cultural groups, which is normally a subject of struggle, recognition-identification inside the family is usually taken for granted. Family life relies on the recognition of personal identities, which are construed as continuing throughout a lifetime. Precisely because of this, misrecognition among people who are connected by family relations and common experience has an enormous impact on those involved. When misrecognition occurs between those who love each other, it is charged with guilt and fear. These uncanny moments testify to the loss of compassion, trust, and solidarity. Short moments of misrecognition are attributed to larger factors, such as historical shifts, unlawful incarcerations, or the flow of hostile, irreversible time. These holes in the ego need to be filled by communication, imagination, and writing. In the personal narrative of a survivor, misrecognition of a significant other works as a powerful device, a trope of the utmost intensity. It demonstrates the scale and degree of the transformation that people underwent at the hands of the state. It admits the unforeseen alienation between those who were "free" and those who were "repressed." It reveals the pain of the victim and the guilt of the survivor. This story, of a person whom the state had changed to the point where even her closest others failed to recognize her, works as a condemnation of the transformative power of the state. This is my explanatory hypothesis for the stories about misrecognition and the return from the gulag.

On the next level of interpretation, the plotline of misrecognition stands as a parable for the story of Soviet socialism, its idealistic aspiration and tragic failure. According to its ideological purposes and legal foundations, the Soviet system sacrificed the recognition of individual and group differences for the sake of redistribution of material goods, such as food, housing, basic services, and, ideally, all forms of capital. Despite its massive violations on all counts, this normative principle of socialism was not questioned throughout the Soviet period.[30] In order to eliminate what the system called "classes," it split itself into two vastly different regimes, making their difference larger than people could have imagined before, after, or outside of this process: "free citizens," on the one hand, and the prisoners of the gulag, on the other. In lieu of all human differences, one bipolar dimension of disparity was constructed. All differences were compressed into this binary opposition. The state invested all its power in enlarging this difference. The project was largely successful. When the inhabitants of these two worlds met, they could not communicate, talk about their different experiences, or cohabitate in common spaces. They did not recognize one another.

Though no single narrative can embrace the Soviet terror, the story of misrecognition serves as its allegory. In an uncanny way, scenes of misrecognition of a father by his son, of a son by his mother, of brother by brother, illuminate the extent of the Soviet state's radical intervention into the most private aspects of family and kinship. The closest of relatives did not recognize each other because the state effectively transformed one or both of them. With the collapse of the gulag and, later, the USSR, the story of the misrecognition of the returned became a trope for the tragedy of "repressions" and the futility of "rehabilitation." Strikingly, the interminable mourning for those who did not return but were not known to be dead transformed the longing of love into its opposite, the horror of the uncanny.

4

Writing History after Jail

History was a high-risk profession in the Soviet Union, and many Soviet historians spent months, years, or decades in various branches of its penitentiary system. Some of them died there; others survived and went on to resume their professional activities. Their writings after the gulag have left us with a rare experiment on the nature of the historical profession, a unique source that we should read respectfully and in detail.

Most of these historians were trained within the mainstream traditions of archive-focused historiography or classical philology. Some of them added to this training their philosophical interests, which ranged from neo-Kantianism to Marxism. Some were haunted by their gulag experience and felt a compulsive drive to represent it, which meant producing historical parallels and analogies to this experience; others were less affected. The postmodern idea that historical writing is a genre of storytelling that reflects the life experience of its authors (and readers) would sound foreign to most of these scholars. But they would willingly agree that their understanding of their contemporary environment was infused by their professional knowledge. The opposite was true as well: their historical ideas developed under the influence of their Soviet experience and, specifically, their experience as survivors of and witnesses to the gulag.

Many memoirs testify to the fact that history was a frequent subject of conversation in the camps, among nonhistorians and historians alike. When two former officers of the victorious Red Army, Lev Kopelev and Aleksandr Solzhenitsyn, met in a camp barrack soon after the end of

World War II, they immediately started debating Russian and European history. Solzhenitsyn was a mathematician and poet, but his experience in the camps turned him into a popular historian. History was the process that had brought the camp into being and delivered suffering to its prisoners. In and after the camp, the process of working through this experience often took the form of individual speculations and public debates on history. The gulag was a pathological symptom on a huge scale, and like an individual patient who excavates his past in order to recover from his symptoms, the gulag prisoners dug into the past in order to diagnose the troubled state of their nation, empire, and world. After the collapse of the gulag in 1953–1956, the broader society became as interested in historical therapy as the convicts had been earlier. Writing history became central for the post-Stalinist public sphere, and remarkably often, ex-convicts would become its most popular historians.

The Historians' Affair

In 1929, the Soviet political police arrested the most prominent historians of Leningrad. They were accused of plotting a coup and shaping an alternative Russian government. More than 150 people were arrested, almost all of them academic historians or archivists. This massive trial, one of the first of its kind, has been remembered as the "Historians' Affair." The leaders of the historical discipline were arrested along with their wives, daughters, and graduate students. Most of them received relatively short terms, three to five years, and spent them working on the construction of the notorious Belomor Canal. Their fates and subsequent academic careers varied dramatically.

Matvei Liubavsky, a senior historian who before 1917 had been the rector, or head, of Moscow State University, was exiled to Bashkiria. There, in one of Russia's internal colonies, he wrote a major treatise on Russia's colonization and then died in 1936. His book was not published until about six decades later. One of Liubavsky's students, Yevgeny Tarle, who was also arrested in connection with the Historians' Affair, was more fortunate. Tarle spent one year in prison and two in exile in Kazakhstan. He survived this experience and had a glittering academic career, becoming a full academician and Stalin Prize laureate. Stalin personally liked

Tarle's biography of Napoleon (1936), which does read as if it was modeled after Stalin. Tarle's magisterial work was a global history of colonialism (1965). It is important that both these historians, Tarle and Liubavsky, wrote their major treatises on colonization, a direct, unlimited manifestation of power. However, their two books, the definitive Soviet work on the subject, on the one hand, and a subversive, unpublishable manuscript, on the other, could not be more different. Tarle wrote a standard Marxist narrative of colonialism as a stage in the development of capitalism, with British, French, and other empires competing and dividing the world. Liubavsky wrote a history of colonization as an internal Russian affair, in which Moscow invaded Novgorod, Siberia, and many other lands, including Bashkiria, where he wrote this book.[1]

A younger survivor of the Historians' Affair was Nikolai Druzhinin, a social historian who had already taken part in revolutionary activism, World War I, and the Russian civil war. In 1930, he spent ten weeks in a cell with fifty prisoners; there was not enough room for them to lie down on the floor simultaneously, so they organized a roster system to make sure that everyone had a chance to rest.[2] In the daytime, they organized lectures on technology, history, and Pushkin. During interrogation, Druzhinin confirmed that the arrested historians, some of them his teachers, were hostile to the Soviet state, but denied his own involvement in their conspiracy. Atypically, his female investigator released him. Druzhinin would go on to a long and successful career, becoming the foremost Soviet historian of Russian agriculture. Decades after his imprisonment, Druzhinin learned that his investigator had herself been arrested in 1938, spent eight years in the gulag, and died shortly after release. Druzhinin died almost a centenarian in 1986. Shortly before his death he wrote a memoir of how he had informed on his teachers, and how his persecutor had saved him before herself becoming a victim. It was a dry report. Druzhinin offered no explanation or apology, but it was evidently important to him that the story be recorded for posterity.[3]

After his release in 1930, Druzhinin started work on a monumental two-volume study of a peculiar Russian institution, state serfdom, and a nineteenth-century bureaucrat, Count Pavel Kiselev, whose reforms aimed at improving the management of the so-called state peasants, serfs who belonged to the state rather than to private owners. This book could be read as an optimistic model helping to boost the legitimacy of the ongoing collectivization; published in 1946, it received the Stalin Prize. Even the most vigorous Stalinist critics did not detect any sign of dissidence in this book, but I do. Druzhinin was writing about the imperial "attempts to achieve total control over the life of the state peasants" and about the "personal freedom that was the foundation for peasants' economic initiative."[4] There were obvious parallels here to the Soviet state's treatment of the peasantry. Soviet collectivization was an unprecedented event that subjected millions of peasants, from the Arctic to Central Asia and from the Carpathian Mountains to the Pacific coast, to a unified regime of work and life that was shaped to suit the state's convenience.[5] Russian intellectuals, and historians first and foremost, could not help but reflect on the relation of this collectivist regime to the specifically Russian traditions, those that previous generations of intellectuals had almost unanimously deemed to be oppressive, such as serfdom, and those that they believed to be progressive or even prophetic, such as the peasant commune. Collectivization renewed interest in the Russian peasantry and in the history of those movements that were ideologically focused on the peasantry, such as populism and Tolstoyanism. As Druzhinin was accumulating the academic regalia of status and power in the 1950s and 1960s, he managed to consolidate a coherent, relatively productive branch of Soviet historical studies that was focused on the history of the peasantry. Interestingly, this direction of historical studies outpaced its more famous counterpart in Russian literature, the so-called village prose movement, by roughly one decade.[6]

The Cosmic Academy of Sciences

With the start of the double Soviet movement of collectivizing the peasantry and repressing the townfolk, the gulag in its various manifestations, from the prison to the camp to exile, became a zone of contact between the intelligentsia and "the people," which meant everyone else from the hugely diverse Soviet Union. Nobody documented this situation better than the historian Dmitry Likhachev, who became the leading intellectual of the perestroika era in the 1980s.[7] Arrested in 1928 together with other members of his student circle, the "Cosmic Academy," Likhachev was condemned to five years of hard labor, which he served in the

Solovetsky Special Purpose Camp and on the Belomor Canal, until he was released in 1932. The Solovetsky camp was the starting point of the growing gulag system and its experimental base. Entrusted with the ideological and even artistic reeducation of the masses of prisoners, convicts with connections to the unusually large camp administration led relatively safe lives. For those masses, however, at times the Solovetsky camp was not much different from an extermination camp. Characteristically, there was a high turnover of camp authorities, with the managers of the camp often becoming its victims. This constant change and uncertainty added chaos to the rigid system of status hierarchy, so that nobody's survival was secured in this "exemplary camp."[8] Though Likhachev survived this camp because he was employed by an internal agency that specialized in the reeducation of the adolescent inmates, he attributed this miracle to his friendships with one or two authoritative criminals who exercised informal power over the camp.[9] He also derived scholarly benefit from his friendships with the criminals. Starting with an article in the Solovetsky camp newspaper, which he then developed into a series of extended research essays, Likhachev focused his first publications on the criminal language and other aspects of the cultural world of the "thieves" who were held in the camp.[10]

Studying criminals as "the people," Likhachev continued an age-old tradition of the Russian intelligentsia. In the gulag, the distinction traditionally drawn in Russian ethnography between "the people" and the intelligentsia was reconstituted in the contrast between criminal prisoners, on the one hand, and the political prisoners, who came from the intelligentsia, on the other. Focusing on the "criminals," Likhachev's essays were well informed both in terms of his empirical evidence and his theoretical background. Before Likhachev, the conventional wisdom held that the criminal argot should be viewed as one of the "secret languages," which certain ethnic, religious, or professional groups developed in order to protect their communication from more powerful groups. Launched in the mid-nineteenth century by Vladimir Dal and his circle, who founded Russian ethnography as an instrument of imperial administration, this understanding of argot as a "secret language" feels curiously similar to modern postcolonial models, such as James Scott's anthropology of "hidden transcripts."[11] Likhachev vigorously rejected this understanding. In his view, the criminals were, on the contrary, marking themselves through their argot; far from making themselves inconspicuous, they made themselves noticeable by using it. Speaking both the colloquial Russian and their argot, they were bilingual, and they shifted from one language to another at will. The key to this argot was emotional and not functional, claimed Likhachev. By using his argot, a criminal wielded a magical power over his world. As a magical tool, the words of argot conflated the signifier with the signified. The fine rational distinctions that modern languages develop to communicate human experience—between words and facts, or between subjects and predicates—collapsed in the criminal argot, which Likhachev deemed a regression or even degeneration from the modern to the primordial, primitive state of language. Apart from scores of examples drawn from the living speech of the convicts, Likhachev referred to a surprisingly broad assortment of philosophers and anthropologists, from Lucien Lévy-Bruhl to Bronislaw Malinowski. Comparing thieves to shamans, he claimed that the argot of the "criminals" in the Solovetsky camp was a kind of missing link, a clue shedding light on the historical evolution of language.

An inadvertent anthropologist, Likhachev construed his mission as bearing witness to his unlikely bedfellows in the camp. His story was unusually articulate and sympathetic to people who were so radically different from himself. His "thieves" were as exotic, inaccessible, and dangerous as the most remote of the tribes, and his careful anthropology of this largely unknown world should be recognized as a major achievement. In his study of the "emotional expressivity" of the thieves' argot, Likhachev highlighted the fact that this language, which sounded so grim and threatening to outsiders, was in fact notable for its wit and creativity. The key to this divergence is humor or, as Likhachev put it, that which is funny. Many elements of argot vocabulary, speculated Likhachev, were originally born out of jokes. When used in the context of the argot, these words might still hint at jokes of the past and express their "inerasable wittiness." Argot thus manifests and reproduces funniness in its "diluted form." Connected to a particular worldview that focuses on and venerates chance, fate, and risk, argot is a defensive mechanism because it downplays danger, mocks it, and neutralizes it by holding it up to mockery. Argot circulates within isolated communities and does not feel "funny" outside of these communities. Merging the magical with the comical and looking for the linguistic manifestation of this combination in one of the most dangerous, violent social environments, Likhachev's theory of argot was a remarkable construction.

66   *Writing History after Jail*

Likhachev's empirical study of the criminal argot was contemporaneous with a literary discovery of the Renaissance carnival that another convict, Mikhail Bakhtin, made in the same years in remote exile in Kazakhstan. Bakhtin was arrested a few months after Likhachev and a few months before the eruption of the Historians' Affair. Like Likhachev's thieves' argot but on a broader scale of generalization, Bakhtin's carnival merged poetry with magic and irony with obscenity. Both authors imagined a life that was radically different from the everyday routine, and both projected it into cultural performances rather than in racial or tribal identities. There is much in common between these observations, though their textual references were very different. Why did these two authors, Bakhtin and Likhachev, draw such similar conclusions from studies that were so remote and disconnected, both empirically and methodologically? And why was it the case that decades later, precisely these two authors became the best-known cultural historians of Russia?

Mores Ancient and Modern

Another historian and convict, Boris Romanov, triangulates this relation and helps to understand it. Romanov was arrested in 1930 as part of the Historians' Affair. After thirteen months of investigation, a period that he later described as the worst time of his life, he was convicted to five years of hard labor; he served three and a half years working on the Belomor Canal. Later, when he applied for rehabilitation in 1956, he pleaded "a deep psychological trauma" that was "an obstacle to scholarly work" and had "various medical consequences." He received psychiatric treatment for this condition. In the private letters that were recently published by one of his former students, Romanov wrote about his enduring fear of being rearrested, "a horrible burden" that was still with him even in 1953, more than twenty years after his incarceration.[12]

In 1947 and after many delays, Romanov published a book, *The People and Mores of Ancient Russia*, a pioneering work of historical ethnography based on a close reading of medieval Russian sources. Critics accused Romanov of pessimism and pornography in depicting "the people"; "misanthropy" was a word that Romanov's critics used extensively. They were quite right. In his book, Romanov described medieval Russia as a world of "lawlessness and violence." Analyzing the etymology of the Russian word for "work" (*rabota, strada*), he demonstrated its ancient connection to the word "slave" (*rab*), its correlation with "suffering" (*stradanie*), and its contrast with the idea of freedom. Focusing mainly on one social group, the slaves (*kholopy*), Romanov cited their laments and argued that the legal position of slaves was indistinct from that of cattle. Forced to work with no contract or any legal protection whatsoever, a slave could be killed by his master with impunity. The state imposed no penalty for such crimes, and the church was indifferent. Romanov also gave a deeply sympathetic account of medieval opposition to the centralizing efforts of the state. One twelfth-century author, Daniil Zatochnik, provided the inspiration for many of these conclusions. Romanov presented Daniil in a way that embraced his own experience: "This free man dived deeply into the boiler of people's life. . . . He sent consolation to some and warning to others, . . . saw multiple falls into the depth of slavery, and experienced it, to some extent, on himself." Daniil's nickname, Zatochnik, means "convict." Indeed, the Moscow prince exiled him to a distant land near Kargopol, quite close to the place where his future historian, Romanov, would serve on the Belomor Canal.[13]

After an ideological debate on this book, Leningrad State University sacked Romanov. Dmitry Likhachev was one of those few who tried to defend him. Much later, in his book *The Laughing World of Ancient Russia* (1976), Likhachev combined the experience of his youth in the Solovetsky camp with Bakhtin's carnivalesque intuition and Romanov's bitter readings of Russian sources. Likhachev's accomplishment in this book was a coherent, widely accepted picture of medieval Russian life as the world of a fundamental dualism. Prosperity and order dominated in one part of this world; poverty, hunger, and confusion governed the other. Absurd, mocking, and laughing, this second world was populated by "troubled" people "on the run"; it was also a "counter-culture" and an "anti-world." This world was "unrepresentable," wrote Likhachev, and the men of this world were "naked" and "bare." In their bareness, men were equal. They possessed nothing that was dear to them, and nothing revealed the former origin, status, or class that they had left behind in the first world. This bareness made them bitter, honest, and daring.

A common reading of this book claims that the laughing world is organized as a carnival. But while it is true that Likhachev does sound like

Bakhtin, it is equally true that sometimes he sounds more like Agamben. Likhachev construes his antiworld not as a cyclical event in this world but as its permanent part, a cursed place, a hell on earth. In this laughing world, "debauchery replaces the church and the prison courtyard replaces the monastery." Therefore the laughing world is simultaneously the world of darkness—a difficult combination for the unprepared reader. To depict this world, Likhachev uses an interesting word, "*kromeshnyi*," best translated as "ghastly," and normally used in Russian in conjunction with "darkness."

Two decades after *The Laughing World* was published, Likhachev revealed its secret source. In his memoirs, Likhachev wrote clearly that the ghastliness of his medieval laughter was drawn from the camp. In the Solovetsky camp where he spent three years of his youth, he observed the convicts striving to "remedy the criminal, shameful world of the camp as the laughing world." Boldly applying to the camp the eponymous concept (*smekhovoi mir*) from his best-known work of scholarship, Likhachev clearly stated the epistemological (rather than historical) connection between the modern world of the camp and the medieval world of the carnival. In his memoirs, he described the camp as a ghastly world of hard labor, routine violence, enforced sociality, hysterical discharges, and creative obscenity. The tortured convicts had nothing that was dear to them, and in moments of leisure they mocked everything and everyone. According to Likhachev, the folkish humor of prisoners was a defensive mechanism: "humor, irony told us: all this was not real." Combining the magical and the comical, the laughing world of these people was a fantasy rather than reality, perhaps an imaginary compensation for their life in a shameful world. Literally, in the Solovetsky camp "debauchery replace[d] the church and the prison courtyard replace[d] the monastery."[14]

In his works on Russian laughter, Likhachev referred to Bakhtin respectfully, but in his memoirs he presented a more complex picture of the relationship between the intellectual journeys of these two major thinkers. He described the atmosphere in his student group, the Cosmic Academy, as self-consciously carnivalesque. They performed an extended parody of their university; for example, Likhachev held the title of "Professor of Melancholic Philosophy." In fact, Likhachev hints that Bakhtin derived his idea of the carnival from the rumors he had heard about Likhachev's Cosmic Academy.[15] These words suggest an anxiety of influence, and also a prisoners' rivalry. Likhachev did not want to be dependent on Bakhtin; in his memoirs, he reversed this relation. Having survived one of the harshest of the Soviet camps and having discovered there firsthand its extreme traditions of obscene argot and folkish laughter, Likhachev did not want to cede his primacy to a fellow convict who sat out the years of terror in mild and boring exile.

The three Soviet historians of the laughing world, Likhachev, Romanov, and Bakhtin, were all survivors of terror. They had much to share, and reading their books one is struck by a strong sense of an external agenda in their speculations about the distant past. Eloquent and penetrating, their ideas do not grow from the textual material itself; rather, an external agenda has organized their material in a way that its authors found intuitively plausible. As readers, however, we do not necessarily share this intuition, since we do not share the basics of their life experience. Still, we respond to their works, finding in them not only richness of detail but also creativity and compassion. Because of the Soviet censorship and for other reasons, these three authors did not acknowledge the formative influence of prison, gulag, and famine on their works. Only Likhachev's memoir interprets his earlier studies as echoes of his extraordinary personal experience. Applying templates forged through recent and common ordeals to distant and variegated pasts, these works of history repeat rather than remember, act out rather than work through. But they have all proved highly successful with later generations of readers. Circulating among survivors, the creative energy of mimetic mourning produced an unusual but coherent worldview that many admirers have cherished, appreciated, and, to some extent, understood.

Gothic Realism

Arrested in 1938, Olga Berggolts, poet, philologist, and graduate of the Institute of History of the Arts, was severely tortured and gave birth to a still-born child. After seven months she was released. Like many intellectuals of the time, she kept a diary, which was confiscated, read and marked, and then returned. She commented on this fact bitterly: "Now my tortured, defiled diaries are in my desk. No matter what I write, I keep feeling all the time that my words will be highlighted by the red pencil. . . . Oh, shame! shame! shame! Never ever was there such unfreedom!" After her release, her diary entries returned again and again to her prison experience. "Why did they subject me to that torment? . . . And what was the point of that unlimited, boundless, savage human suffering, into which my own suffering dipped deeply, but also broadened to the point of madness?" She perceived the long hours of interrogation as unforgivable violations of her subjectivity: "They removed my soul, dug around inside it with their stinking fingers, spat into it, shat on it, then stuffed it back in and said, 'Carry on with your life.'" She believed that those months in jail had destroyed her not only as a person but also as a Soviet writer: "How will I write the novel about our generation . . . the novel about the agency [*sub'ekt*] of the epoch, the agency of consciousness, when my consciousness has been subjected to such pogroms, when it has lost its pre-prison balance?"[16] But in prison, she also read the other prisoners her verses about Stalin. These verses had already gained her some popularity before her arrest, and the prisoners "loved" them. She stayed in Leningrad throughout the siege of 1941–1944 and would later be celebrated as the major poet of this tragic and heroic time.

Mikhail Bakhtin wrote his treatise on the Renaissance carnival, the most influential book ever written by a Russian cultural historian, in a situation not much different from Berggolts's. Arrested in 1928, after interrogations Bakhtin was sentenced to five years in the Solovetsky camp, but because of his poor health, the sentence was commuted to a Kazakhstan exile. It may have been the case that there, too, he received special treatment on health grounds. He was unusually lucky, described the treatment in the investigation prison as "humane," and never complained about the conditions in exile. Despite his poor health, he outlived his investigator, who was shot in 1936, by many decades. Compared to Likhachev and Romanov, Bakhtin was an armchair observer of the underbelly of the Soviet camp system. At the time of his arrest, Bakhtin had already completed his book on Dostoevsky; exceptionally, it was published while he was in jail. From his exile in the steppes of northern Kazakhstan, he watched the collectivization and the resulting famine, which was devastating in that part of the country. His term of exile was completed in 1936, but he did not return to the metropolis. He survived the subsequent years by voluntarily staying in the same remote location, then moving to another odd and remote place, Mordovia, in European Russia, occasionally changing his addresses and effectively "becoming illegal," as he put it decades later.[17] It seems that he complemented his luck with an unusually smart understanding of his time, combined with the competent management of his own life and work.

Several of Bakhtin's friends were shot while he was in exile. One of them, Pavel Medvedev, was a professor at Leningrad State University and the first editor of the personal documents belonging to the greatest poet of the prerevolutionary era, Aleksandr Blok (according to Bakhtin, Medvedev received the documents from Blok's widow after becoming her lover). Shortly before Medvedev was arrested and shot in 1938, he helped Bakhtin to obtain a teaching position.[18] Another close friend, poet and mystic Boris Zubakin, was accused of organizing an anti-Soviet Masonic lodge, which in this case was a true charge. He was shot in 1937. Yet another friend, the engineer Vladimir Rugovich, shared the same fate. Other members of what we know now as "Bakhtin's circle," philosophers Matvei Kagan, Lev Pumpiansky, and Valentin Voloshinov, all died young men in the late 1930s.

According to his biographers, Bakhtin was also close to a major political figure, Nikolai Sukhanov. An active member of the populist party the Socialist Revolutionaries, Sukhanov converted to Marxism and in 1917 joined the Mensheviks, the dissenting part of the Social-Democratic Party. More important, Sukhanov was the author of one of the most detailed memoirs of the revolution of 1917; Lenin read and reviewed Sukhanov's memoir shortly before his death, and was furious. Sukhanov was also a journalist and editor who published many luminaries of the Russian prerevolutionary Left in his journal, *New Life*. In the mid-1920s in Moscow, Sukhanov was trying to relaunch the old debates about the Russian peasant commune, an explosive theme on the eve of collectivization. The intense political divisions of early Soviet life ran through his family. Sukhanov's wife, Galina Flakserman, was a Bolshevik who worked for Lenin and other top leaders of the revolution; in fact, the vote on the decision to launch the Bolshevik coup of 1917 took place during a conspiratorial meeting held in the couple's apartment. Reportedly, Flakserman typed some of Bakhtin's manuscripts for him.[19] If Bakhtin needed fresh material on the paradoxes of politics and culture, he could not have found a better source than this family.

Bakhtin was a survivor. His strategy enabled him to outlive Stalinism, physically as well as intellectually. Never talking explicitly about his fear, mourning, or guilt, would appear to have been a part of this strategy. But until the end of his life, Bakhtin was deeply interested in the history and meaning of Russian revolutions and eagerly discussed these topics. Only in 1973 did he feel safe enough to express his regret that in 1917, Prime Minister Aleksandr Kerensky had not suppressed the resurgent Bolsheviks by force.[20]

Bakhtin was always engaged in Russian literature, from Gogol to the early twentieth-century symbolists, as well as particular manifestations of the Russian folk religion.[21] Yet his arrest did seem to bring about a shift. Before his arrest, Bakhtin had been writing a book on a classic of Russian literature, Dostoevsky; in exile, he changed his subject to a classic of European literature, Rabelais. In this effort, Bakhtin was exploring mournful spaces of "world culture," where the poet Mandelstam, the composer Shostakovich, and the artist Sveshnikov also felt at home (see chapter 5). Before his arrest in 1934, Mandelstam famously said that he belonged to a poetic movement that was defined by a "longing for world culture."[22] Cut off from their roots and living, as Mandelstam wrote in his epigram that mocked Stalin, "without feeling a country under our feet" (see chapter 2), these people were longing for world culture, but in the most unusual ways. In his paradoxical treatise written in 1933 in anticipation of arrest, *Conversation about Dante*, Mandelstam challenged the received wisdom by describing Dante as "a tortured and hunted man," full of "internal worries and heavy, vague uneasiness," who "during all the course of *Divina Commedia* does not know how to behave, how to step, what to say, how to bow." If Dante the narrator had descended to hell without Virgil, speculates Mandelstam, we would have had "no saga of ordeals and attractions, but the most grotesque buffoonery."[23] This was a longing for the other combined with a projection of the self, a feeding ground for creative and deconstructive exercises. Like Mandelstam, Bakhtin expressed his fear and mourning in terms of "world culture," which for him meant Rabelais and other great figures of the European Renaissance, from Cervantes to Shakespeare. Like Mandelstam, Bakhtin perceived this culture in highly original ways.

Bakhtin's carnival is an event in which social roles are swapped and established truths mocked. The powerless become strong, subalterns are eloquent, authorities agree to be ridiculed, and the whole social machinery reveals its contingent and laughable nature. Bakhtin speculates that in medieval Europe, historical carnivals were regular feasts of "popular culture," which in the later cultural epochs migrated into the literary works of authors such as Rabelais, Goethe, and Dostoevsky. However, he is also inclined to understand whole epochs as carnivalesque. In periods of social turmoil, "when truths change," all life becomes a carnival: this is the closest Bakhtin comes to dealing with Russia's revolution in this work. Another crucial concept in his dissertation is "gothic realism." Later, Bakhtin would drop this warped concept from his vocabulary, but in the dissertation that he wrote in Kazakhstan and Mordovia, he argues that "gothic realism" infused a large part of medieval culture, including chimeras and monsters on cathedral walls; stories of the descent into the kingdom of the dead; fables about animals and spirits; and obscenity in popular language, which regularly refers to the "gothic" enigma of fertile death. Other examples of "gothic realism" provided by Bakhtin include the art of Bruegel the Elder and Hieronymus Bosch, two masters of the monstrous, and also images of "pregnant, laughing death," which, Bakhtin says, is the very essence of the grotesque (see chapter 8). These images represent "two bodies in one," the dying body and the new body about to be born. Despite his lifelong infatuation with Freud, Bakhtin is rarely interested in sexuality as such: when he mentions genitals, they are symbols of procreation, which in this gothic world happens on the edge of death. Representing the collective and immortal body of the people rather than any egotistic and perishable personality, Bakhtin's gothic realism is positive and cheerful: "The very flow of time, the very change of epochs became the subject of ambivalent laughter." In modern times, laments Bakhtin, this complex imagery has degenerated into "moralizing consolations or theoretical utopianism," which loosens its connection to both mourning and laughter. All of this is crucial for the Bakhtinian history of literature: "fragments of gothic realism fill the literary space of the last three centuries."[24] Because these double-bodied symbols resurge during the gothic carnival, "there is nothing that is entirely dead: every meaning will celebrate its revival." Having been to hell and back, Bakhtin plays Virgil rather than Dante: he leads the reader to the "most grotesque buffoonery" but softens its horror with rational explanations and spiritual consolations.

Completed as a dissertation in 1945, Bakhtin's work on carnival became famous twenty years later when the new, post-Stalinist generation of intellectuals helped to publish and publicize it. This powerful and ambiguous text sends many messages at once, but one thing is undeniable: a feeling of historical and personal loss infused Bakhtin's study. His emerging book was searching for a meaningful way of dealing with these losses, a way that would promise their compensation or even redemption without "dialectically" erasing the reality of the loss.

In this bitter, self-conscious position, Bakhtin was close to his German contemporary and fellow victim of terror Walter Benjamin. Arguably the most profound analogy to Bakhtin's dissertation on Rabelais is Benjamin's dissertation on the seventeenth-century German *Trauerspiel*, tragic drama of the German Counter-Reformation. One written in 1925 on the Italian island of Capri and the other written throughout the 1930s in the Kazakh town of Kustanai, these dissertations overlap in their politicized readings of the Renaissance and the early baroque period, in their common emphasis on popular culture, and in their themes of mourning and humor. As Bakhtin did with his carnival, Benjamin deliberately extended the meaning of *Trauerspiel* far beyond its historical period: "For these are not so much plays which cause mourning, as plays through which mournfulness finds satisfaction: plays for the mournful." Also in a Bakhtinian way, Benjamin wrote about "the characteristic feeling of dizziness" that "the spiritual contradictions" of the baroque epoch induce in the modern reader. Both thinkers sought justification for nascent cultural forms in the distant past, though Benjamin was clearer when he highlighted the "remarkable analogies" between the baroque plays of mourning and expressionism; he even wrote that the authors of *Trauerspiel* were more successful in their work of mourning for the victims of the Thirty Years War than his contemporary artists who had seen World War I and the failed revolution in Germany. Both Benjamin and Bakhtin struggled to distance their respective subjects, the *Trauerspiel* and carnival, from the idea of tragedy. Having received the aesthetical tradition that spread from Aristotle to Nietzsche, they both thought it to be inadequate for the new, twentieth-century experience. If in tragedy death is the "ever immanent reality," said Benjamin, in mourning plays death "frequently takes the form of communal fate." These mourning plays were so "offensive or even barbaric to refined taste" that they were said to be "written by brutes for brutes." Like Weimar and early Soviet cultures, mourning plays were "haunted by the idea of the catastrophe" but fought against the "historical ideal of the restoration."[25] Though they never met or read one another, Bakhtin and Benjamin would happily have agreed about many of their historical observations. Even more important for this hypothetical consensus is their similar political experience on the margins of emerging dictatorships, and similar intellectual sources: classical philology, Marxism, Freudianism, and messianic mysticism.

Benjamin and Bakhtin transformed their personal feelings toward their sorrowful times into powerful idioms that became sharable by their followers, both in their countries and abroad, though with very significant delays. Benjamin would work on many different subjects after Capri, but Bakhtin kept rewriting his Kustanai study for decades. Much of the powerful mythology of the first version remained in his book as it was published in 1965 and translated into English in 1993. However, in the new atmosphere of the Thaw, Bakhtin substantially revised the text. He probably thought that the earlier version was too personal a document and hoped that his revisions would make it more objective, less like a dream or myth and more like a conventional piece of scholarship. In the final version, the carnival became more optimistic than it was in the first, less like a mourning ritual and more like a rite of spring, though Bakhtin's thesis in both versions was that these two events were one. Many additional details and some terminological novelties, such as the replacement of the "gothic" with the "grotesque" and the erasure of the concept that was crucial for the first version, "gothic realism," worked in this sanguine direction.[26] As we know, Benjamin failed his dissertation, but Bakhtin defended his successfully.

White Negroes

Leonid Pinsky, a historian of European literatures, was in jail from 1950 to 1956, and after release, submitted an essay, "The Tragic in Shakespeare," to a literary journal. His friend, the Shakespearean scholar Aleksandr Anikst, was surprised to see that Pinsky had not revised this essay at all since his arrest. Anikst asked Pinsky: "Is it possible that a hard life experience did not compel you to deepen your understanding of the tragic?"

Pinsky responded, "My mind does not change just because they beat my ass." Anikst, both of whose parents spent many years in the camps, commented that this response was typical for Pinsky: in his longing for world culture, he refused to see a relation between real-life experiences and the work of a cultural historian.[27] The responses of other ex-convicts could not have been more different. In 1936, a prominent historian of Russian literature, Yulian Oksman, was arrested in Leningrad. After a year in prison and nine years in some of the harshest camps of the gulag where he worked as a lumberjack, shoemaker, and bathhouse attendant, Oksman developed a set of entirely new ideas, which experts have called his "post-camp worldview." He told a friend that two terms in the gulag were needed for his epiphany, which he also called his "healing": for a transformation of this depth, he said, "one term would be insufficient, I did need precisely these ten years."[28] Before his arrest, Oksman was a major expert on Pushkin and the senior editor of the collected works of Pushkin in seventeen volumes, a major accomplishment of the Soviet "science of literature." It was launched, in a macabre way, in 1937 to commemorate the centennial anniversary of Pushkin's murder. By then Oksman was already in northern Siberia, in the notorious Kolyma camps.

In many ways an opposite to Bakhtin, Oksman was an archival scholar, a successful bureaucrat, and an active, sometimes aggressive public intellectual. His lifelong passion was the historical and political context of Russian literature, a subject that fit easily with the dominant Marxist worldview that Oksman shared with the 1930s Soviet elite, of which he was a member. He left his legacy in textual work with manuscripts and commentaries, and shunned interpretative speculations. Scholarly contributions of this kind tend to be lacking in glamour, and no biography of Oksman has been written. However, several major publications document his rich correspondence, which presents not only the stoicism of a survivor but also a persistent search for historical metaphors capable of explicating, or even explaining, what it was that had happened to him. Always interested in the rebellious moments of Russian history and literature, after serving his decade-long sentence Oksman focused on the defiant nineteenth-century critic Vissarion Belinsky. Oksman devoted years of work to an encyclopedic volume on Belinsky, but his true labor of love seems to have been the annotated publication of a single, rather obscure document: the letter that Belinsky wrote to Gogol in 1847. Oksman emphasized the fact that he had begun his study of Belinsky's letter straight after his release from the Kolyma camp, and characterized this work as his "testament." After a great deal of trouble with the censors, Oksman finally republished this letter, accompanying it with many pages of commentary. Reading the document in question helps us to understand how this textological work was connected to survival in a torture camp.

In the letter, Belinsky commented on Gogol's last book, which called upon the reader to support the monarchy and proposed a pious compliance with Orthodox teachings as the way to both civil peace and salvation. In strong and creative language, Belinsky accused Gogol of misguiding the reader. "One cannot keep silent when lies and immorality are preached as truth and virtue under the guise of religion and the protection of the knout," wrote Belinsky. "You failed to realize that [what] Russia . . . needs is not sermons . . . but the awakening in the people of a sense of their human dignity lost for so many centuries amid dirt and refuse; she needs rights and laws." Instead, wrote Belinsky, Russia "presents the dire spectacle of a country where men traffic in men." Belinsky means serfdom, and he uses the striking phrase "white Negroes" to describe the Russian peasantry.[29] Refuting doubts raised by some previous scholars, Oksman proved the authenticity of this astonishing letter, which is indeed one of the strongest appeals for freedom that has been written in Russian.[30] He also demonstrated the importance of this letter as a source for the later Russian practitioners of revolution, such as Mikhail Bakunin. It was Oksman's agenda to show that Russian literature and criticism led Russian politics and revolution.

A textual example gives a glimpse at what Oksman was trying to achieve through his unusual methods of scholarship. In a fragment of Belinsky's letter, he spotted an infelicitous wording, "dignity lost . . . amid *dirt and refuse*" (*v griazi i navoze*). He wrote to a friend that he had doubts about the accuracy of this standard reading of Belinsky's manuscript. Having reviewed three available drafts of this letter, he reached an alternative reading that satisfied him more: "dignity lost . . . amid dirt and unfreedom" (*v griazi i nevole*) was his preferred reading.

It took three years for Oksman to obtain official permission to publish his study. Twenty-five separate internal reviews of the publication were commissioned, and the publication was discussed at ten meetings of the editorial board, but still was not approved for release. In 1952, Oksman presented an ultimatum to the provincial university in Saratov where he taught: either his study of that letter would be published, or he would leave the university. This time, he won, but his version of this subversive text did not make its way into many of the subsequent collections of Belinsky's and Gogol's works. When American or Russian university students read Belinsky's famous letter to Gogol today, it is unlikely that they are reading Oksman's version.

Oksman's correspondent, Kornei Chukovsky, a charismatic critic and children's poet, wrote to him in 1961 that Belinsky's anniversary in Moscow "went as they [the authorities] wanted it to be. At least it was clear that the great freedom-lover was foreign to them—foreign and hostile."[31] When Khrushchev's campaign of de-Stalinization reached its peak in 1962, Oksman decided that the time for more direct action had arrived. Among all the intellectual survivors of the gulag, he seems to be the only one who understood his mission as one of not only mourning for the victims but also taking revenge on the perpetrators. In 1963, he passed to an émigré Russian press an article in which he named the colleagues who had denounced him, and many others, in the 1930s-1950s; these people still held power in Moscow and Leningrad. This publication was unprecedented; moreover, Oksman did not deny his authorship.[32] The same year Oksman also passed Akhmatova's *Requiem* and some of Mandelstam's verses for publication in the West.[33] In response, KGB agents would search Oksman's apartment once again, this time on the basis of the mistaken hypothesis that it was Oksman who was publishing stories in the West under the pseudonym Abram Tertz (Siniavsky would be revealed as the real author behind Tertz about a year later).[34] But strangely, Oksman was not rearrested. Toward the end of his life, he had plans for an epic, large-scale memoir that would survey the whole path of the intelligentsia through the Soviet era. He died before he managed to realize this bitter project.[35]

Intellectual prisoners often returned from the camp with a particular interest in the deep, primordial mechanisms that drive humanity in the conditions when the commitments of culture and civility have been forgotten by some and never learned by others. The military translator and future ethnographer Eleazar Meletinsky was arrested in 1942, released in the chaos of war in 1943, arrested again in 1949, and served time in the gulag until 1954. His experience ranged from five months of solitary confinement to the overcrowded barracks to the camp hospital, where he was saved from hunger and death. Later a charismatic scholar of myth and folklore with a cosmopolitan breadth, he once interrupted his long, detailed memoir of his camp experience with an interesting aside. Why was it, he asked himself, that he found himself mentioning the ethnicity of every friend or enemy whom he met in the camps? In the overfilled cells and barracks, he explained, when everyone had an equal—and equally uncertain—fate, ethnicity was the anchor that helped to sort out human relationships. It is clear that Meletinsky's subsequent interest in deep, archetypical mechanisms of myth, folklore, and primordial culture was sparked and developed during his time in the prisons and camps. Another survivor of the gulag with somewhat similar interests who also shaped the Soviet and post-Soviet humanities, Lev Gumilev was the son of Anna Akhmatova and her first husband, the poet Nikolai Gumilev, who was shot by the Bolsheviks in 1921. Lev Gumilev served in the northern camps from 1938 to 1944 and then again, in Kazakhstan and Siberia, from 1949 to 1956. There he developed his idiosyncratic but highly influential theories about mechanisms of "ethnogenesis" and the role of "passionarity" in nation building. There was not much that was similar in the conclusions of these two scholars, one Jewish, cosmopolitan, and thoroughly structuralist, the other nationalist, anti-Semitic, and desperately judgmental.[36] However, their starting point was the same: the cramped, all-male, deliberately primitive cells and barracks, and this experience defined their lifetime interests. In the Europe and America of the 1960s, the overwhelming preoccupation with the primitive had postcolonial roots; in the Soviet Union, former inmates of the gulag promoted and propelled parallel developments.

The World Upside Down

Unsurprisingly, a historian and survivor wrote the best analysis of the Soviet labor camps after Solzhenitsyn. In 1981, an archaeologist and professor at Leningrad State University, Lev Klein, was arrested for his alleged homosexuality. He was convicted and sentenced to three years in prison; a retrial shortened his term, and he served about eighteen months in a prison and labor camp. A prolific scholar whose books range from a reading of Homer to the origins of the Russian state, Klein summarized his camp experience in a short book, *The World Upside Down*.[37] In a narrative that combines a personal story with ethnographic analysis, Klein reveals the hierarchical structure of the community of inmates; the unconditional power of charismatic "thieves" and the pathetic life of the rogues; and the unlimited violence that was applied routinely all across this community. Klein believes that "the subculture of Soviet labor camps," with its strict hierarchy and unlimited violence, is unique in modern times, though he sees many analogies for this structure among the primordial tribes, as anthropologists know them. The subculture of the camps shares with these tribes such rituals and institutions as initiations, castes, tattoos, self-mutilation, and others. Klein also documents the sexual dynamics of this all-male community, with its sharp distinction between active and passive homosexuals and the subordinate, stigmatized position of the latter. Initiation rituals, beatings, and rapes underline the informal hierarchy of the camp and structure many aspects of its life. Klein also tells the story of his own survival in this harsh environment. He makes it clear that the late-Soviet camp, which he observed in the 1980s, in many ways represents an even more brutal and debased version of the old Stalinist gulag system. Detailed and analytical, Klein's book called for a radical transformation of the Russian penitentiary system, one of the most vicious and also most enduring of the Soviet legacies.

Interestingly, Klein is the only historian who analyzes the structure of power in camp and prison with such clarity. It is not only the absence of censorship that makes this new analysis feasible but also a late-Soviet and post-Soviet disenchantment with old romantic sentiments. There is no trace of populism in Klein's relentless narrative, no belief in the self-generating morality of the common folk. Klein's only hope is the disciplining force of "culture," which he understands in moralistic, elitist terms that seem obsolete in the Western context. For Klein, "culture" means the enlightening, civilizing, and standardizing "culture" as Matthew Arnold understood it, not the playful and relativist culture of postmodern thought. But this top-down attitude does not prevent Klein's narrative from expressing a very human compassion for the victims of the state that had created the camps and of the gangs that ruled them.

Many of the details that Klein relates in this book are so cruel and transgressive that reading it is almost unbearable. However, in 1990, after a heated debate in their professional journal, Russian ethnographers largely endorsed Klein's conclusions. A professional ethnographer who served in a labor camp between 1949 and 1954, Vladimir Kabo supported Klein. In his own memoir, Kabo remembers how he first developed his interest in the history of magic and religion in the gulag; decades later, he became an expert on the aboriginal cultures of Australia and emigrated to that country in 1990. In his response to Klein's essay, Kabo notes differences between his experience and Klein's.[38] Kabo confirms that in his experience, the camp of the early 1950s had not featured the sadistic, systemic violence to the extent that Klein describes in his essay on the late-Soviet camps. During the thirty years that separated their terms, Soviet camps have only become crueler, says Kabo.

Looking at the historical interests of the camp survivors, I discern several major preoccupations. In and after jail, one group of historians focused on the macrohistory of power. Theirs was a history from above, focused on external and internal colonization, and I discern in their works grand-scale parables of collectivization and the gulag. Another group of historians worked on the microhistories of violence, misery, and humor that they discovered in the camps. Theirs was a history from below, and they developed a sharp, human, and consistent view on this history. In the primitive and the primordial, these historians found allegories for their camp experience. They strove to synthesize this experience with their historical material, but the very nature of this experience meant that their lives and sensibilities were radically different from their readers'. This is why some of these historians puzzle, surprise, even shock us, and polarize our responses. The most extreme and for us almost inconceivable experience of violence and survival in prison and the camps left its traces on these historical works.

First, this was a bitter experience of social injustice, evil, and contingency. The intellectual prisoners thought and talked through such problems ceaselessly. Is it mere chance that I am in prison? If my suffering has been caused by the Soviet regime, should this regime be viewed as a random and arbitrary freak of nature, or a matter of law-based historical necessity? As a prisoner, Dmitry Likhachev gave an improvised talk to his peers on the problem of chance. He essentially denied its existence. Every person defines his fate, consciously or not, and there is no such thing as contingency, said Likhachev. For example, romantic poets lived short lives while realist writers lived long ones, and in both cases this was a matter of choice. In the same way, each and every prisoner, he said, determined the circumstances of his own arrest. This was what Likhachev believed in 1928; when he composed his memoirs fifty years later he mocked these juvenile ideas as the kind of nonsense that was typical among the prisoners.

Second, being in the camp broadened the survivors' social horizon to an extent that was unimaginable elsewhere. An intellectual like Likhachev met many kinds of people in the Solovetsky camp that he would have been unlikely to meet otherwise: Orthodox monks, serial murderers, old Bolsheviks, professional thieves, religious sectarians, navy officers, Uzbek nationalists, and many others. Almost inescapably, the surviving intellectuals in the camp became lay ethnographers. On a more general level, for these and other intellectuals the wild, suffering population of camps and prisons became the Soviet Other, a distant analogue of the noble savage of the Enlightenment.

A third feature of the gulag's intellectual life was its radicalism. In the life of the camp that Likhachev found "fantastic," "monstrous," and "nightmarish," the routine mechanisms of reality testing did not work. Rationality and common sense are calibrated for civilized life, not for the "theater of the absurd" that was the camp. Therefore, wrote Likhachev, the ideas that he and his peers discussed in the camp were typically "extravagant" and "contrarian." They espoused "impossible theories" and set out to demolish "the common views," that is, the views that were common outside of the camps and that had now been so radically destabilized by their camp experiences. When the old, blind, and very established Likhachev dictated these lines, his attitude toward his own past was highly ironical. But he could still remember the appeal and the power of these radical ideas. He could still make out the unmistakable music of the gulag in the background of both Bakhtin's book on the carnival and the literary scholarship that Siniavsky produced in the camp, forty years after Likhachev had served his term.[39] The intellectuals from the camps still recognized one another from afar.

5

On Tortured Life and World Culture

In 1944, the secret police arrested the young philologist Tatiana Gnedich. She would spend twelve years in the gulag, mainly because of her acquaintance with Leonard Wincott, a British Communist who worked in Leningrad and later also spent years in the camps. In prison, Gnedich produced what became the definitive Russian translation of Byron's *Don Juan*. She memorized both the original and her translation, and the investigator was so impressed that he supplied her, against the rules, with paper and pen. Released in 1956, she found temporary board with my uncle, the translator and scholar Yefim Etkind. She had two cherished possessions: her translation manuscript and the quilted jacket that had kept her warm through the years. The jacket stank, and Yefim threw it away despite Tatiana's protests; it could not stay in his communal apartment. Later, Yefim introduced Tatiana to a famous theater director who staged her translation of Byron with huge success. This launched her career, though Yefim wrote that in her later translations, she would never approach the level of her prison work.[1]

In his memoir, Yefim could not reconcile his two feelings: his disgust at the filthy jacket that was Tatiana's personal site of memory, and his veneration for her talent, which enabled her to produce, huddled under this jacket, an astonishing cultural achievement. These feelings had to be kept separate; though they focused on one and the same person, they had nothing in common. Two sentiments that the compassionate public felt toward the survivors of the camps—fear and shame, on the one hand, caring concern and admiration, on the other—knew no compromise. But still, one had to live with both feelings. There was no place for a gulag survivor's quilted jacket in a friend's home; but throwing it away was not a guarantee that it would not return in disguise. Indeed, Yefim notes in the same sparkling memoir that Gnedich's precious manuscript, the cherished translation of *Don Juan* that she brought from the camp, stank as much as her jacket.[2] But there was no way to dispose of these papers.

The Unbearable Quilt

Though many details of the Gnedich story are extraordinary, the presence of a wandering, southerly Don Juan in the cold, solitary confinement of a Leningrad prison was not.[3] In 1933, Osip Mandelstam spoke about "the longing for world culture" as a definitive characteristic of his poetry and a broader literary movement (see chapter 4).[4] This longing was much more than a desire to worship the classics and expound on great texts. It was also a mode of self-expression, the only one available to these authors who were working in an environment of increasingly tight censorship and surveillance. As the émigré musicologist Henry Orlov wrote in 1976 about Dmitry Shostakovich, "quotations, . . . ellipses and hints, had developed over the decades into a special method of self-expression. . . . Shostakovich excelled in making gestures of reassurance to the prison guards while surreptitiously releasing his true thoughts to the world outside."[5] Many others, Mandelstam included, were less effective at this double-pronged writing, and, in any case, literature could hide less than music.

Hannah Arendt's idea of worldliness makes the meaning of Mandelstam's terminal "longing for world culture" more explicit. Writing about "humanity in dark times," Arendt revealed how people respond to the collapse of the public sphere by pressing up against each another, eliminating distances and defenses, and mistaking "warmth" for the "light" that only the public sphere can provide. This is how they develop the "unworldliness" that is characteristic of pariahs. "The world lies between people," Arendt wrote, but oppression or persecution destroys this "in-between." Those who have been formed by "dark times," she wrote from experience of her generation, "have been inclined to despise the world and the public realm, to ignore them . . . in order to arrive at mutual understandings with their fellow men without regard for the world that lies between them." Arendt contemplated a peculiar theory of emotions, which she defined by their relations to the world: fear shrinks back from the world and hope overleaps it, while laughter and anger reveal and expose the world. "Under the pressure of persecution the persecuted have moved so closely together that the interspace which we have called world . . . has simply disappeared. This produces a warmth of human relationships which may strike [us] as an almost physical phenomenon." Human warmth could help people to survive but did not compensate for the loss of the world: "for what was wrong, and what no dialogue . . . could right, was the world." Such worldless networks Arendt saw as characteristic for pariahs and, even worse, barbarians: "worldlessness, alas, is always a form of barbarism."[6]

Arendt's analysis helps to reveal the mechanism of those remarkably tight groups of mutual support that many memoirists depict in the Soviet communal apartments, in intellectual salons, and sometimes even in prison cells: "a nexus of intimacy and terror," as Irina Paperno calls it.[7] Longing for world culture was a defense or maybe a compensatory mechanism for those who felt smothered by these tight, warm groups. As a classical analysis of Mandelstam's poetry showed, the poet identified these close-knit communities with the rhetorical tautologies that they produced, and he hated both.[8] It is no surprise that Mandelstam did not survive the worldlessness of the camp life. In the same essay on "dark times," Arendt emphasized freedom of movement as a primary condition for connecting with the world, something that she found even more important than freedom of thought. Indeed, there is no better way to deprive people of the world than to restrict their movement; this was the rationale of the gulag. And of course nobody was less worldly than the pariahs of the camps like Mandelstam, the goners who were desperate and exhausted to the point that they did not express their pain, did not communicate with their peers, and did not tell their stories.

Agamben notes that only victims could possibly tell the truth about the camps.[9] Survivors wrote memoirs, not victims; the latter often lost their ability to tell their stories well before their physical death. Survivors did not share the most extreme experiences of the life in the camp, such as scapegoating or terminal illness, because these experiences made survival impossible. In the Soviet camps, however, all the boundaries—between victim and perpetrator, between victim and survivor, between bare life and *vita activa*—were more fluid than in the Nazi camps. As we have seen, some of the perpetrators ended up in the gulag just a few months or years after their victims. Many survivors were psychologically mutilated to such an extent that they also qualify as victims. Some survivors retained their true belief not only in the Communist idea but even in the progressive nature of the gulag.[10]

Addressing the Soviet camps in her memoirs, Nadezhda Mandelstam resolved the paradox of witnessing in the same way that Agamben did decades later: "Only those who were about to perish in the camps, but accidentally survived, can testify about them."[11] She had already learned that she had lost her husband to the gulag, and she had read both Shalamov and Solzhenitsyn. These authors introduced the world of the gulag from two opposing perspectives, the former from the perspective of a goner and the latter from the perspective of a survivor.[12] In his pathbreaking portrait of a convict, Solzhenitsyn presented Ivan Denisovich, a shrewd jack-of-all-trades whose folksy vitality would endure the gulag. One of those soon-to-be-dead who, by an arbitrary quirk of fate, was saved by a camp doctor, Shalamov described his characters as semicorpses whose suffering from hunger, labor, and humiliation deprived them of any decency or hope. While Solzhenitsyn presented his experience of survival as a moral lesson for humankind, Shalamov steadfastly denied any value in the gulag experience. Individual survival could be accidental, or it could be earned by skills and tricks like those that Ivan Denisovich demonstrated; for Shalamov, the vanity of survival was as absurd as the whole gulag system. In one story, Shalamov presents deliberately variegated people (generals, kolkhoz members, religious sectarians, and so forth) who are all hungry and exhausted. They are alive mainly because they do not have the energy to die; when, after a change in the camp leadership, they are suddenly given a proper meal, the strongest of them, a sectarian, responds by attempting to escape, and is shot dead by the guards.[13] The minimalist form of Shalamov's literary work—his hatred of what he called "belletrization," the seeming lack of organization in his *Kolyma Tales*, and the multiple repetitions that are conspicuous in his writings—exemplify his refusal to inscribe meaning into suffering.[14] Shalamov's characters are not heroes or martyrs. They are victims who are sometimes endowed with a rare understanding of their fate. This ability distinguishes them from bare life, and it is fairer to understand them as "radical stoics," as Walter Benjamin described some characters of the German "mourning plays." In Benjamin's analysis, these characters respond to the external state of emergency with "the stoic technique," which builds up a "fortification against the state of emergency in the soul."[15] In both Benjamin and Shalamov, these radical stoics are "anti-historical creation[s]" in the sense that, as Benjamin commented wryly, they do not seem historically real.

There are several ways to invest redemptive meaning in the gulag experience.[16] The functional argument speculates that terror was instrumental for the state, and therefore those who understood its function and collaborated with the state were heroes. The survival argument proposes that survival in the gulag required rare human qualities, and therefore those who survived the gulag were heroes. The witness argument posits that the survivors' mission was to tell the truth about the gulag, and therefore those who survived in order to bear witness were heroes. Shalamov is the best singular source for disproving these arguments individually and all at once. In one of Shalamov's stories, the narrator speculates that a horse would not survive what he had survived. This narrator saw no more meaning in his labor than a horse would; strikingly, Shalamov did not try to find consolation in his authorship either. Primo Levi wrote that he wanted to survive Auschwitz so that he could bear witness; Shalamov never said this. Having survived three terms in the gulag and, between and after these terms, many years of Soviet life, Shalamov died in a retirement home in Moscow in 1982. To one visitor, this facility looked like a gulag: "the smell of urine, dirt, and rot . . . a huge broad corridor and on its vinyl floor, entirely helpless people were crawling." Deaf, convulsing, and delusional, Shalamov was one of those people; still, he was composing poems.[17] The monument on Shalamov's grave was vandalized in 2002; robbers removed its bronze head from the granite pedestal. Meanwhile, the house in Vologda where he was born is now a museum. Against his own wishes, it is as a witness to the gulag that Shalamov is remembered today.

Dominick LaCapra distinguished between two typical responses to a trauma, the constructive "working through" and the obsessive "acting out" of the disturbing event.[18] I would add a third mode, "making sense" of trauma or catastrophe. Affirming himself by creating zones of exception, the sovereign denies responsibility for the abuses committed in these zones. But with the passing of time and with the scale of abuses revealed, the sovereign changes his strategy. His last resort is a redemptive narrative, which in the Soviet context presents victimhood as sacrifice and suicidal perpetrators as cruel but sensible strategists. Psychologically, this sacrificial interpretation responds to the desperate need of descendants to find meaning in their losses. Morally, it amounts to normalization of the terror that killed millions. Historically, it requires the service of hired professionals who are paid to produce a smooth narrative of a false and tragic variety. Politically, it enables the continuity of the state with its obsolete self-definitions of sovereignty. An alternative solution to the conundrum of post-Soviet memory is the recognition of the "unjustified" (Khrushchev) and "senseless" (Shalamov) nature of the terror. Terror has no positive meaning or function; the assertion of any such function borders on justifying the enormous suffering of its victims. Self-conscious negativity, on the other hand, is a difficult strategy; not for nothing was Shalamov accused of nihilism.[19] I would see his position rather as existentialist.

Taken together, the textual portraits of Shalamov's goner and Agamben's *homo sacer* bear an unmistakable resemblance to yet another figure that embodies the tragic flow of history, Walter Benjamin's "Angelus Novus." Contemplating a drawing by Paul Klee, Benjamin describes the angel of history. "Where we perceive a chain of events, he sees one catastrophe." This warped creature would like to stop the flow of history and awaken its dead victims, but he is not free to do so; the "storm irresistibly propels him into the future to which his back is turned. . . . This storm is what we call progress."[20] In Benjamin's time, this angel's final destination was the camp. Benjamin's soon-to-be-fallen angel gazes compassionately, though helplessly, at a soon-to-be-dead convict.

Soviet Surrealism

Unlike Catholicism, Eastern Orthodox Christianity did not develop any equivalent of the doctrine of purgatory, which played such a prominent role in shaping the ways in which pre-Reformation Europeans imagined life after death and the possibilities for talking with ghosts. Also relevant for the roots of Soviet culture, the Jewish tradition did not have this doctrine either. This lack may be one reason why the Soviet and post-Soviet cultures in their longing for world culture have tended to be indiscriminate in their appropriation of the Western imagery of the undead. In the early phases of this process, in the 1950s and 1960s, it was specifically Catholic (and often Counter-Reformation) imagery, from Dante to Bosch to Goya, that the Soviet authors chose as particularly close to their needs.[21]

These references were central for the most important Russian artist among the gulag survivors, Boris Sveshnikov (1927–1998). During his eight-year-long term in a labor camp in northern Siberia from 1946 to the end of 1953, and then during his long life after his release from the camp, Sveshnikov created amazing works of art that throw a new light both on the gulag and, more generally, on the Soviet experience. Entering the camp when he was nineteen, he developed a surprisingly mature understanding of what had happened to him and to his country. One of his camp drawings interprets power as a monstrous blade that shaves the town, an operation that is consistent with the sovereign's narcissistic gazing at his own reflection, and with the treatment that the naked citizens—bare, tortured life—receive under his command. Well composed as a whole, this picture also works like a comic book, or a Russian icon, with the successive stages of the story unfolding simultaneously on a single page. While the sovereign's hand shaves the city in one part of the picture, the citizens are undressed and prepared for the worst in another; to the left, a terminal broom is already sweeping away their remains. A deeper look reveals in this fascinating drawing a satire on the Hobbesian sovereign who treats his victimized citizens as though they were whiskers of his beard, human trash that he shaves off the state body at will.

Some of Sveshnikov's camp pictures emanate a pure horror. In one drawing, ratmen perform mysterious experiments on human females in a prison or a laboratory, a place that looks and works like the gulag. An analogy to Sveshnikov's drawing is the famous series by the American artist Art Spiegelman, who rendered the horror of the Holocaust by showing its victims as mice and perpetrators as cats.[22] But in Spiegelman's work, the victims are mice; in Sveshnikov's pictures, the perpetrators are rats.

Sveshnikov was sent to jail when he was nineteen, after a fellow student bragged that he was planning to kill Stalin. Sveshnikov spent eight years in a remote camp in the Northern Urals for his acquaintance with this would-be assassin. By his own account, he was already a goner when a chance visit saved his life. The visitor was Arkady Steinberg, a doctor

FIGURE 2. Boris Sveshnikov (Russian, 1927–1998), Untitled, n.d. Ink on paper 27.9 x 39.3 cm (11 x 15 1/2 in.). Collection Zimmerli Art Museum at Rutgers University, Norton and Nancy Dodge Collection of Nonconformist Art from the Soviet Union 2003.0872 / 21097. Photo by Jack Abraham.

at a larger camp, himself a prisoner who was serving his second term. A charismatic personality, Steinberg was an officer who was decorated for his heroism in World War II, a trained artist, poet, and translator. In the gulag where he spent eleven years, he went through medical training and became a camp doctor. His colleagues, members of a powerful but risky profession who sometimes felt sympathy for intellectuals, also saved other celebrated survivors, such as Varlam Shalamov and Aleksandr Solzhenitsyn.[23] On the walls of Steinberg's hospital, Sveshnikov found reproductions of his beloved Dutch and Italian artists. After his recovery in this hospital, Sveshnikov worked as a night watchman in a workshop, a privileged position that Steinberg helped him to obtain. This meant that Sveshnikov was able not only to survive, but to spend time working on his paintings, for which he reportedly used the hospital linens, the ink that his parents brought him on their annual visits, and oils that the camp was

FIGURE 3. Boris Sveshnikov (Russian, 1927–1998), Untitled, 1949-1950. Ink on paper 28.3 x 37.8 cm (11 1/8 x 14 7/8 in.). Collection Zimmerli Art Museum at Rutgers University, Norton and Nancy Dodge Collection of Nonconformist Art from the Soviet Union D22301. Photo by Jack Abraham.

allocated for propaganda purposes.[24] Rescued by a Latvian ex-prisoner and then by an American collector in a feat of cosmopolitan memory, many of Sveshnikov's works are now kept in the Zimmerli Art Museum in New Brunswick.

Let's look at one of his paintings, which presents the camp experience in a strikingly unusual way. We see a dramatic confrontation between two men, one leading the other to an unknown destination, a service, perhaps, or an experiment. With a cross on his robe, the leader looks like a priest or monk. The contorted movement of his hands, which we see but the other man does not, betrays the leader's tension and doubts. He appears to be wringing his hands, in despair or in supplication. With his twisted and restrained movement, the second man looks like a sacrifice in a ritual that the first man is performing, albeit reluctantly. The leader seems to look upon the victim with sorrow; the victim's face is calm, as if he has

FIGURE 4. Boris Sveshnikov (Russian, 1927–1998), *Encounter*, n.d. Oil on linen on panel 80.1 x 70 cm (31 9/16 x 27 9/16 in.). Collection Zimmerli Art Museum at Rutgers University, Norton and Nancy Dodge Collection of Nonconformist Art from the Soviet Union. 2003.0750 / 21676. Photo by Jack Abraham

accepted his destiny. He is dressed in a robe that leaves his back naked and defenseless; one might see some eroticism in this image. If we assume that the first man's robe is of the same fashion, then the second man is looking at the naked bottom of the first man. They are looking at one another and we are looking at them; we are trying to grasp what the hell is, literally, going on here. The figures are set against the background of a northern landscape that looks like Sveshnikov's camp, which he depicted in many drawings: the camp is cold, inhuman, and strangely elegant in these pictures.

While some aspects of this image, such as the architecture of the camp, are historically correct, other aspects are fantastic. There is no doubt that crosses were not allowed in the gulag, and that the inmates' winter uniforms were anything but sexy. Uncanny images of memory combine faithful representations of the past with deep, frightening transformations of that past. It is precisely in these transformations that the agent of memory invests his feelings about the past. The proponents of nonrealistic styles in art, such as expressionism or surrealism, made this discovery long ago: the subjectivity of the artist expresses itself in the distortions of the visual image. In fact, I think that human memory generally works in this way. We would understand it better by analogy not with realist art but with expressionism or surrealism, with their distortions for the sake of expression.

Walter Benjamin's essay on surrealism (1929) helps to appreciate Sveshnikov's art in the camp. Benjamin wrote this analysis of the French artistic scene after his visit to Moscow, and used a recognizably Russian term in its subtitle: "Surrealism: The Last Snapshot of the European Intelligentsia." In this essay, Benjamin proclaimed the idea of the collective body as the key to the new poetics and politics. "The collective is a body, too," claimed Benjamin, and cited Trotsky in confirmation of this idea. According to Benjamin, building a collective body needs ecstasy that may come from two sources, intoxication and revolution. Surrealists were too engaged in the former and too little in the latter, lamented Benjamin. But intoxication does not necessarily come from drugs, Benjamin said: the "most terrible drug—ourselves . . . we take in solitude."[25] Despite this melancholic clause, Benjamin's essay is infused with sublime revolutionary hope. If Benjamin and some of his surrealist heroes called for revolution, Sveshnikov—also a visionary—found himself on the opposite slope of the historical pass from revolution to disenchantment. Many of his drawings are sharp criticisms of that very concept of the collective body that both Benjamin and Bakhtin ventured to glorify and mourn. Having drunk his fill of the "most terrible drug" of solitude, Sveshnikov developed an anti-utopian imagery that could be compared only with the great twentieth-century novels of this genre.

In a series of camp drawings and paintings, Sveshnikov presents scenes from a fabulous collective feast, with abundant food, drinks, sunshine, and flesh, a very Bakhtinian imagery in which the top and the bottom gleefully swap places. This carnival is set in an unidentifiable historical time, as if Sveshnikov did not hope to find it among his contemporaries and did not want to leave a clue any more specific than "world culture"; the gulag is surely one of the last places we would expect to find this sumptuous feast. Exaggerated, naked female bottoms are a permanent presence in these images. One can understand these almost all-female, sunny, hedonistic, and gregarious images in a structuralist way, as a binary opposition to the all-male, frozen and hungry world of the camp: a dreamlike compensation for the actual horror of life on the edge of death. But the light is too intense and the voluptuous bottoms too heavy, and we feel a healthy dose of self-irony in this man's fiction. Sveshnikov's fantasies of unavailable sex could be quite vicious, as in a drawing in which a naked woman is making love to a gigantic, bipedal fish, or one in which rats pump air into the naked bodies of pretty women. Sveshnikov's friend remembers him as a person who was "invariably sad,"[26] and his transgressive, carnivalesque feasts are disturbing rather than cheerful.

Sveshnikov's camp pictures offer an endless variety of images of horror. In one frightening painting, we see two skaters, one of them with a grinning skull, the other still living. Compared to the previous couple, the monk and his companion, these two skaters have successfully adjusted to their environment. Accompanied by a devilish orchestra, they skate vigorously and in step, a gesticulating corpse and a man with steady eyes that look straight at us. The image is discomforting, as if he were begging us to hold his gaze, pleading to be remembered before he is taken away forever. Sveshnikov's art set the uncanny images of the camp against a universal, pan-European background, which the artist borrowed mainly from Dutch and Flemish predecessors, gloomy witnesses of the Counter-Reformation and the Thirty Years War.

FIGURE 5. Boris Sveshnikov (Russian, 1927-1998), *The Coffin Maker's Workshop*, 1961. Oil on linen 79.5 x 74.7 cm (31 5/16 x 29 7/16 in.). Collection Zimmerli Art Museum at Rutgers University, Norton and Nancy Dodge Collection of Nonconformist Art from the Soviet Union. 2000.1462 / 16784. Photo by Jack Abraham.

Sveshnikov told the story of the gulag from the perspective of its victim, of a goner. Later, in 1961, Sveshnikov portrayed this figure as a man already in the coffin; praying to the heavens, at the same moment he enjoys his still-erect penis, the only drop of color on his bloodless body. This is probably the best image of a goner, to which only some of Shalamov's stories can add a thing or two. But with his baroque propensity for historical image-making, Sveshnikov presented the camp and the world in a way that was profoundly different from Shalamov's minimalist stories. Unexpectedly, Sveshnikov feels closer to Bakhtin's Europeanist imagery.[27] Theirs was tortured life perceived through "longing for world culture." Both Bakhtin and Sveshnikov were wise enough to see themselves alienated from their carnival scenes in the position of the outsider that, for better or worse, is intrinsic to both the historian and the artist.[28]

When the young historian of art Igor Golomstock saw Sveshnikov's art for the first time in the late 1950s, he identified him as "our home-grown surrealist." But he also thought that the sense of solitude that emanated from Sveshnikov's pictures was different from European surrealism as he knew it. After meeting Sveshnikov, Golomstock learned that Sveshnikov had not even heard the word "surrealism" when he was arrested in 1946, and had elaborated his ideas and images independently, in the isolation of the gulag.[29] At the time, Sveshnikov gave the impression of a person who "had not entirely melted after the camp." Golomstock introduced him to Andrei Siniavsky, and Sveshnikov's art became for this generation of mourners one of the very first sources of their imagery of the terror. Indeed, these uncanny fantasies became available to Golomstock, Siniavsky, and their friends before they read those texts, from Bakhtin to Shalamov, that help us today to understand both Sveshnikov and the gulag. It is no wonder, then, that Siniavsky should have gone on to author his own appreciative essay on Sveshnikov, though he did so only after he had served his own term in the camp. Siniavsky particularly admired the double meaning of Sveshnikov's drawings, which both are and are not about the camp: "Anyone who didn't know this was a camp would never guess it."[30] Siniavsky's essay on Sveshnikov was clearly autobiographical: he eagerly identified his own camp memory with Sveshnikov's much earlier one. No less informed about the camps (see chapter 6), Golomstock saw in Sveshnikov's drawings and canvases "something akin to the post-apocalyptic: it was as if time curdled and the artist contemplated the still new, inexplicable offspring of human life."[31]

Mourning Plays

In a recent essay, the anthropologist Alexei Yurchak describes a group of Leningrad artists who became active in the late 1970s and called themselves Necrorealists. They were focused on death, the dying body, and what they called "non-corpses." They pored over medical atlases and luxuriated in the gory details of death by hanging and other, preferably slow, ways of dying. They owned a lifelike, uncanny-looking human mannequin, which they would beat in public spaces, shocking passers-by. In 1984, this group staged a brawl in central Leningrad on the fifth floor of a building, from which they were visible to the pedestrians below. Screaming, they continued their wrestling until their leather mannequin fell down to the street. Its head tore off, the crowd was furious, and the police arrived. Though the police saw this action as a "provocation," they struggled to come up with an offense with which to charge the group. According to Yurchak, at first the Necrorealists produced these mimetic scenes as a kind of street theater or living installation. From early on, however, their performances developed into individual practice rather than public art. One of the group spent nights all alone in the forest, "as if becoming for a night neither a man nor an animal but both, like a folkloric werewolf."[32] Later, in the 1980s, the group wrote stories and produced films that developed its favorite theme of the dying, wandering non-corpses. Yurchak draws a parallel between this repetitive imagery and David Cronenberg's movie *Crash* (1996), whose protagonists obsessively reenact car crashes; Cronenberg explained his film as "a metaphor for those people who undergo life-shattering experiences . . . and [are] finding strange ways to relive that experience and so come to understand it."[33]

The leader of the group, Yevgeny Yufit, directed several "necro-films" that feature werewolves, man-tree hybrids, and other mute, violent mutants that are by-products of some Soviet scientific experiment. As Yurchak writes, "The more the Necrorealists turned to artistic projects the more their texts, installations, and films became populated by human, semihuman, and hybrid life-forms."[34] Having discovered this fascinating group of lay artists and introduced them to the global audience, Yurchak interprets their actions in Agamben's terms. The Necrorealists, he says, pursued a "politics of indistinction," which aimed at suspending known political identities and exploring bare life. According to Yurchak, these artists purposefully created a space that made them indifferent to the Soviet system within which they had to live and experiment. In a larger study, Yurchak has elevated this zone of indistinction between the political and nonpolitical to being the leverage of the Soviet collapse.

At this point, it is worthwhile to recall Agamben's original way of using these concepts, bare life and zone of indistinction: "Testimony [about the camps] . . . takes place where the silent and the speaking, the inhuman and the human enter in a zone of indistinction in which it is impossible to establish the position of the subject."[35] Like Eric Santner with his concept of creaturely life, Yurchak presumes the ability of bare life not only to express itself artistically but also to understand itself in creative, "bioaesthetic" ways that are incomprehensible to the sovereign state. This would be unimaginable for Agamben's *Muselmann* or Shalamov's goner. Yurchak is clearly talking about memories of bare life and mournful reenactments of suffering, which are cultural processes that involve contemplation and aestheticization, rather than about the actual experience of dying, which is largely incommunicable and foreign to anything aesthetic. Reading the explications that Necrorealists have given for their own actions, Yurchak follows them too closely. Like his subjects, he shuns a connection between their performances and a very specific situation of post-Stalinist Russia. He believes that the rich imagery of the Necrorealists is "interested not in death but in alternative forms of vitality,"[36] a concern that he connects to biopolitical problems of clinical death, euthanasia, and other modern difficulties with distinguishing between life and death. It remains unclear why these Soviet artists of the late 1970s and early 1980s were "intuitively concerned," as Yurchak puts it, with these issues years earlier than European intellectuals discerned their importance, and decades earlier than Russian intellectuals noticed them. Rather than connecting the cultural production of the Necrorealists to the global and distant future, I would rather link them to the immediate Soviet past.

Offspring of the uncompleted Thaw, Yufit and his followers performed the work of mourning for the victims of Soviet terror in a fresh, innovative idiom. Along with many late-Soviet artists, musicians, writers, and filmmakers, they played out their Victims' Balls. Their mimetic reenactments of violence, victimization, and slow death followed the experience of the Soviet goners in literal and detailed ways. Like Bakhtin who refigured and sublimated his fear and mourning into a panhistorical concept of gothic realism, the Necrorealists also strove to explain their actions and concerns in ways that they found both challenging and appropriate. There are close parallels between the performances of the Necrorealists and the earlier work by Daniel, *This Is Moscow Speaking* (see chapter 6), the contemporaneous art of the Mitki, a group of artists from Leningrad, or the later prose and screenplays by Vladimir Sorokin (see chapter 11).

Revealing similar themes by purely textual means, Joseph Brodsky's reminiscences provide an instructive commentary to the performances of the Necrorealists. When he was sixteen, Brodsky worked with corpses. The future Nobel laureate dropped out of high school and never studied at a university, but in 1956 he got a job as a dissector's assistant in a Leningrad morgue. As he related about thirty years later, he "dissected corpses, removed their guts, and then sewed them back." With obvious pleasure, Brodsky went into macabre detail: "an old lady's corpse . . . yellow skin, very flabby, it bursts open, and your finger slips into a layer of fat. To say nothing of the smell." Brodsky quit the job after a bizarre episode: "A gypsy came to see us in the morgue. I gave him his two children—twins, if I am not mistaken. When he saw them all cut up . . . he decided to pin me right where I was. . . . Jean Cocteau was a piker compared to the surrealism that went on there!"[37] Whether this scene was taken from Brodsky's fantasy or memory, his presentation competed with the "world culture" of French surrealism. But it was the local roots that provided this scene with its political and biographical meanings. "The morgue shared a wall with the Crosses," Brodsky notes. The Crosses (Kresty) is a Leningrad prison that served as a filtration center of the Great Terror, a gateway to the gulag. It was an important site of memory both for Akhmatova, whose son was held in the Crosses in 1938–1939, and for Brodsky, who was imprisoned there in 1964. Brodsky admired Akhmatova's *Requiem*, a poem that is set near the walls of the Crosses, where the mothers and wives of prisoners would stand and wait. It was there that Akhmatova spent many days in 1949 trying to pass food to her son and to obtain information about him, and where she wanted to be commemorated by a monument.

In the early 1950s, Brodsky's parents were scared by the ongoing anti-Semitic campaign and were preparing themselves for "the long trip" to the camps in Siberia. Remembering 1956, the year when he worked in the morgue, contemplated the Crosses, and heard about Khrushchev's revelations, Brodsky emphasized the communication that was established with the victims at that time: "Prisoners [of the Crosses] would toss notes out to us."[38] Indeed, fears of the Soviet Jewish Holocaust dissipated after Stalin's death, but in 1956 Brodsky did end up making a "long trip" to the land of gulag. Right after his experience in the morgue next door to the Crosses, he volunteered to take part in geological parties to northern and eastern Siberia.[39] Brodsky left no doubt that many of his peers in geological parties were ex-prisoners, that they often visited former camps during their trips, and that the mores in the expeditions were not much different from those of the gulag; he even used the term "picaresque" to describe his one-night stands with the former inmates of female lumberjack camps. As often happened to Brodsky, he moved against the current: this was the time of the mass release of prisoners from the gulag, and they were drifting in the opposite direction, from Siberia to European Russia. Five years of these Siberian expeditions—Brodsky's chosen way to spend the time of the Thaw—provided him with the material for some of his earliest poems, including the famous "Pilgrims":

> past the world, and past sorrow,
> past Rome, and past Mecca . . .
> the pilgrims are trekking.
> They are hunchbacked, they hobble.
> They are hungry, half-naked . . .
> birds screech to them hoarsely:
> The world has not altered.
> No. It has not altered.
> It is what it has been.[40]

In my reading, this enigmatic poem is a synopsis of the poet's pilgrimage to the sites of the gulag, and also of the gulag prisoners returning, "past arenas and temples," to their homes, which, in some sense that they wanted to believe in, had not altered (see chapter 3).

Starting with the morgue, looking at the prison, and then surveying the geographical span of the gulag, this Brodsky monologue works as an elaborate, meaningful text of mourning. Driven by the spatial contiguity between the morgue and the Crosses and the essential proximity between terror and death, Brodsky's monologue segues smoothly from his work with corpses through his Siberian pilgrimage to his own incarceration in

1964: "The funniest part is that later, when I landed in the Crosses myself, I observed all this from the other side."[41]

The German-American philosopher Theodor Adorno famously said that writing poetry after Auschwitz was a barbarity. Brodsky altered Adorno's statement into "How can one write poetry after the gulag?" and added: "and how one can eat lunch?" Brodsky believed in his capacity to write poetry after both the Nazi Holocaust and the Soviet terror. Empowered by his poetic license, Brodsky testified to the fact that representing the unimaginable is an ordinary, indeed indispensable, human activity. He described his generation as "born precisely at the time when the Auschwitz crematoria were working full blast, when Stalin was at the zenith," and he saw this generation's mission in continuing "what, theoretically, was supposed to be interrupted" by the Nazi and Soviet camps. In his Nobel lecture, Brodsky mourned "the tens of millions of human lives destroyed by other millions," with the Soviet camps' death toll "far surpassing" that of the Nazi camps. "In the real tragedy, it is not the hero who perishes, it is the chorus," said Brodsky: in contrast to the classical tragedies in which the surviving chorus mourns the perished hero, the mass tragedies of the twentieth century disposed of their choruses. It is the mission of the lonely survivors to mourn the perished masses.[42]

An indisputable part of world culture, Brodsky's vision was both poetical and political. Stating with pride that along with his Russian contemporaries, he had produced a literature that was "neither a flight from history nor a muffling of memory," he emphasized the formative role of his own, and other writers', prison experience. "Prison is essentially a shortage of space made up for by a surplus of time." This ratio, he said, echoes man's situation in the universe. This is why incarceration is a metaphor of metaphysics and, "practically," the midwife of literature. Poetry, he said, is the genre of choice in solitary confinement, while imaginative prose blooms in shared cells (he did not consider nonfiction, unfortunately). In the popular mind, he said, prison compares to death, and solitary confinement to a coffin. Relying on his experience, however, Brodsky advised the reader to follow these metaphors in the opposite direction: "prison writing shows you that hell is both man-made and manned by man."[43]

Barracks Poetry

In 1954, Sveshnikov was released from the camp but, like many returnees, was still forbidden from settling in Moscow or other major cities. He joined his camp savior, Arkady Steinberg, in the town of Tarusa, not too far from Moscow. Overcrowded with returnees, this picturesque town became the intellectual and poetic center of the Thaw. Nadezhda Mandelstam wrote her memoirs there and interviewed the returnees about Osip. It was in Tarusa that Steinberg, after his eleven years in the camps, translated John Milton's *Paradise Lost* and many other works by English, French, and Chinese poets.

A member of Steinberg's circle, Sveshnikov also frequented another village near Moscow that became famous in the history of Soviet art and poetry, Lianozovo. After a camp on the local railway was dissolved, its barracks remained in place, and provided a shelter and living space for some returnees, vagrants, and intellectuals. A tower and parts of the fence of this former camp were still intact—an accidental monument to the bygone era of the gulag. The Kropivnitsky family led the local group of counterculture intellectuals. Lev Kropivnitsky, Sveshnikov's classmate, was also arrested for the same conspiracy to assassinate Stalin. He served eight years of his term in the same camp as Sveshnikov and the remainder in Kazakhstan. Released in 1956, he joined his father, Yevgeny Kropivnitsky, an influential artist and musician, who lived near Lianozovo. When another young artist, Oskar Rabin, married Yevgeny Kropivnitsky's daughter, the couple moved into a barrack of the former camp. This barrack—a living site of memory—became an intellectual salon and informal exhibition center that housed what became the most consequential among many "companies" of the Thaw.[44]

Like many ex-convicts, Sveshnikov drew a sharp dividing line through his life-story. Emphasizing the role that the camp played in his life and work, Sveshnikov divided his oeuvres into two periods, "in the camp" and "after the camp," and marked many of his best pictures just by the name of the camp and a date. Unlike Mandelstam, who did not survive the camps, Sveshnikov lived long enough to find his communion with world culture. For many years, he worked as a book illustrator for a Moscow publishing house. He illustrated his favorite German tales by Hoffman, Goethe, and the Brothers Grimm, as well as many other books

FIGURE 6. Boris Sveshnikov (Russian, 1927–1998), *Last Alms*, 1992. Ink on paper 30.5 x 42.8 cm (12 x 16 7/8 in.). Collection Zimmerli Art Museum at Rutgers University, Norton and Nancy Dodge Collection of Nonconformist Art from the Soviet Union. D22567. Photo by Jack Abraham.

of fantasy and miracles. In his illustrations, frozen woods and Gothic castles look like improved versions of his aestheticized camp. He still saw himself as an ugly, estranged observer or dreamer who had no access to the life of the permanently feasting community. In a 1992 drawing, he portrayed a male figure against the background of the camp barbed wire, a person with no legs but with a gaze focused straight ahead and trained on the spectators. As in some of his camp paintings, this gaze makes us uncomfortable, as if by looking at us the protagonist demands more than we are willing to give. In another picture, the feast of world culture takes place on the upper floor while the only nonparticipant, a pathetic creature with whom the artist seemingly identifies, watches or dreams about it from the cellar. In this position toward the carnival that Bakhtin called "out-findedness," the artist felt safe.

In Lianozovo, Igor Kholin, a former World War II officer who was imprisoned for a couple of years in the local camp and served in its internal

FIGURE 7. Boris Sveshnikov (Russian, 1927–1998), *Spring Grove*, 1957. Oil on linen 70 x 50 cm (27 9/16 x 9 11/16 in.). Collection Zimmerli Art Museum at Rutgers University, Norton and Nancy Dodge Collection of Nonconformist Art from the Soviet Union. 2003.0762 / 21677. Photo by Jack Abraham.

security, wrote a new kind of poetry, which he called "barracks poetry." He started to write these verses "standing on the camp tower," as a friend of his would put it decades later. Then the camp vanished, but Kholin stayed on in the village, worked as a waiter, and wrote:

> Isn't it amazing,
> This human ability
> To cry
> And appeal for pity
> In such a strange way?
>
> Why animals
> Don't cry,
> And houses
> And cars?
> . . . . .
> I want to tell you
> About world-wide weeping
> When the universe
> Shudders
> And everything merges into
> A single scream,
> A deep-drawn sigh.[45]

The human ability to weep and mourn is strange indeed. The magic of mourning turned the stinky attributes of the gulag life, things like a quilted jacket or a camp barrack, into subjects for poetic imagination or sacred worship. Among the unusual personalities who frequented this Lianozovo community was Eduard Limonov, who would become an émigré writer in the 1970s, a scandalous returnee in the 1990s, a prisoner in the 2000s, and a political figure in the 2010s. The writer Andrei Bitov remembers his own visit to Lianozovo as a trip to the end of the world; with awe, he describes a long path to the barracks that stretched along the barbed wire in the snow. The local memory of the camp was a leitmotif in many of the texts that were written by members of the Lianozovo group.[46]

The works of Leonid Chertkov, the leader of a poetic circle in Moscow that was cotemporaneous with the Lianozovo group, started in 1953 with a fascinating cycle, "The Salt of the Earth." In these three poems, which one of Chertkov's friends characterized as "cool like cannibals," the narrator is part of a firing squad in an unidentified army. At times, this could be a modern Western colonial army or a Russian medieval one; at other times, we seem to be dealing with Soviet troops. "They always recognize us at a distance," the narrator recounts; his squad suppresses a rebellion, captures a deserter, sets fire to a field, and rapes the town-folk. In some lines, the narrator and his comrades are imprisoned; a few lines later, they are burning, raping, and shooting again. These activities are described in regular, romantic verses, which bear the recognizable stamp of Kipling and early Soviet poetry. I read in these verses a rare attempt to imagine the world of the perpetrator and to mock it by parodying the language that this perpetrator would eagerly recognize as his own. Twenty years old when he wrote these extraordinary verses, Chertkov was an assiduous student of Russian literature and a translator of English poetry. As it happened, Chertkov's work of mourning led him to mimetic self-sacrifice, and in 1957 he was arrested for anti-Soviet propaganda and went on to serve five years in the latter-day gulag. After release, he emigrated to France, where he continued to pursue his literary and historical studies. In an obituary, a perceptive observer grasped the meaning of Chertkov's historical obsession: "His literary scholarship was of a romantic kind. He felt a lack of an actual literature for his studies. . . . He suspected that an unheard-of literature still existed somewhere and he searched for it in the archives."[47]

In 1963, the KGB investigated the artistic community at Lianozovo and incriminated its patriarch, Yevgeny Kropivnitsky, who was duly expelled from the Union of Artists.[48] It was probably at this point that the KGB experts coined the phrase the "Lianozovo school." Two interrelated forces, cultural mourning and political protest, drove the consolidation of companies of local poets, artists, and returnees in places like Lianozovo, Tarusa, or Moscow. One such poet, Genrikh Sapgir, said: "We knew that prison was a threat to us, but we never talked about it. . . . There were many prisoners then, and many were released. . . . What we saw around us was life on the edge of death. And we needed to express this."[49] He sounds like a Necrorealist, though his poetics is very different. In 1964, Vsevolod Nekrasov, a member of still another group whose poetry would become known as "conceptualist," wrote his best-known poem:

Freedom is
Freedom is

> Freedom is
> Freedom is
> Freedom is
> Freedom is
> Freedom is freedom.

It is difficult to disagree with Nekrasov's statement when it finally emerges, but in fact we do not know which freedom the author had in mind—freedom as a philosophical category, or freedom from jail, or (most probably) both. With time, this tautological minimalism would become a characteristic feature of the Lianozovo school. Retreating from the heights of world culture, the survivors and mourners of the Soviet terror focused their intuition on the intrinsic dignity of bare life. In a situation when the official culture denied the victims of the gulag their grievability, the cult of bare life emerged as an important, even crucial expression of mourning and protest.[50] This cult did not need world culture; its point was to affirm the value of bare life as it is, in its inarticulate, primitive shape that is barely able to express itself. After all these megatons of torture, "The world has not altered," as Brodsky's pilgrims said to themselves. Referring to the German literary tradition, Eric Santner reveals the construal of creaturely—and also creative—life in the sublime poetry of Rilke and the prose of Sebald. In Russia, a similar discovery or invention came later and in a different way, among the generation who overcame both their trauma of the gulag and the longing for world culture. This break with the longstanding tradition of the intelligentsia brought an incredible popularity to the Mitki, an informal group of Leningrad artists and poets who, from the late 1970s to the 1990s, built a new version of a group subculture that practiced and worshipped a self-conscious primitivism, genial brutality, and humorous innocence. In various ways the Mitki presented their new civic ideal of a friendly alcoholic who enunciated aphorisms of pleasure and unworldliness. But they also produced some horror doggerel (*uzhastiki*) that in the late-Soviet period became a part of the popular, anonymous folklore.

> A boy in the village found a machine-gun.
> Now in the village there lives no one.[51]

Combining the childish innocence of the poetic form with the brutal or even sadistic cruelty of the story, these ironic, catchy replicas of the

FIGURE 8. Boris Sveshnikov (Russian, 1927–1998), *Untranslated*, 1998. Ink and gouache on paper 28.4 x 38 cm (11 3/16 x 14 15/16 in.). Collection Zimmerli Art Museum at Rutgers University, Norton and Nancy Dodge Collection of Nonconformist Art from the Soviet Union. D22571. Photo by Jack Abraham.

Soviet past should be understood as another genre of mimetic mourning. The pleasures of the creaturely, senseless, homeless life on the edge of death have never been celebrated with such directness. Consciously apolitical, the Mitki presented a startling contrast to the deep involvement of the intelligentsia in the perestroika processes that dominated this period. In contrast to the previous tradition, the Mitki did not produce a meaningful response even to the arrest and imprisonment of one of their leaders, the poet Oleg Grigoriev. In the 1970s, he spent about two years in prison, reportedly because a chief of the Soviet literature objected to his children's rhymes.

The aging Boris Sveshnikov responded to these new tendencies in his own way. In one of his last pieces he showed an anarchic carnival composed of culture and nature together, in a kind of spiral whirling, which advanced dangerously close to the lonely hero. But he is still able to conjure it away by one of the strange, unearthly movements of hand that Sveshnikov presents so well. In these last pieces, when he became almost blind and his technique deteriorated, his horror returned to him, and he reverted to the imagery of the camp. It was as if he understood his new physical limits of his age and the approaching death in the terms and metaphors of his old—indeed, at this point fifty-year-old—memory of his life in the gulag.

"He who seeks to approach his own buried past must conduct himself like a man digging," wrote Benjamin.[52] This digger recovers facts like an archaeologist but also creates artifacts like an artist. It is all digging for him, and he does not separate the two roles—of the historian and the artist—that he plays in the process. In a postcatastrophic situation, the digger of the past—the historian-cum-artist—needs mechanisms of estrangement, with humor being the most important and frequent of these mechanisms. Materializing memory in the public sphere often entails fiction rather than truth, allegories rather than facts, and irony rather than tragedy. These allegoric images both retain their dependency on the past and affirm the present's striking difference from it. Mimicking the past, they also assert that the past has passed. As long as the survivor survives, his obsessive remembrances of the catastrophe do not equal its actual return there, but rather constitute its disempowered, detoxified representations. Sometimes recognizable as traces of memory and sometimes so heavily distorted that the historical past is transformed beyond all recognition, these allegoric images work as mnemonic tools that revive the past and, simultaneously, as artistic devices that celebrate its death.

6

The Debt to the Dead

When the writer and scholar Andrei Siniavsky came home from the strict regime camp where he had served six years (1965–1971), he felt as though he had been split into pieces:

And I began to weep . . . not for my lost youth but because of the *ridge*, as I called it, that had suddenly been erected in my mind, splitting me into two halves, into a *before* and an *after* my exit from behind the barbed wire, as though foreseeing how difficult it would be to return from there to people and what a chasm now lay between us and them.[1]

Siniavsky's major philological works were all written or conceived in the camp, and these works both reflected his camp experience and mourned other victims of the Soviet terror. Following Soviet culture through to its final stages and beyond, Siniavsky's scholarly writings deserve consideration on a par with his literary fiction, which has received more attention.[2] In both its quality and quantity, Siniavsky's camp output is remarkable, but not entirely unique. There are deep analogies to Siniavsky's camp oeuvre in the works of other authors who also spent years in camp or exile. They feature the unrestrained, radical "theses that sharply contradicted the conventional wisdom," which one of these ex-convicts, Dmitry Likhachev, believed to be characteristic of the writings that were produced in the gulag.[3] Focused on Siniavsky, this chapter also illuminates a fascinating but largely forgotten group of cultural activists of the Thaw who were members of Siniavsky's circle before his arrest. It has become traditional to distinguish several strands in the Soviet scholarship and criticism: official, émigré, and dissident. I believe that camp criticism represented an additional, separate, and original strand of twentieth-century Russian scholarship.

Siniavsky and His Company

The son of an active member of the revolutionary movement who was imprisoned, with tragic results, in 1952 (see chapter 3), Andrei Siniavsky was a doctoral student at the elite Institute of World Literature in Moscow. One of his fellow doctoral students was Stalin's daughter, Svetlana Allilueva, also an expert on Soviet literature.[4] According to another classmate, Siniavsky "amazed his peers with his knowledge of the literature that we did not know—the symbolists, the Silver Age."[5] For his dissertation, Siniavsky chose Maxim Gorky's mammoth novel *The Life of Klim Samgin*, the story of an intellectual protagonist who falls in love with a female leader of the Khlysty sectarian community. This erotic and heretical plotline follows a long-standing Russian literary tradition, but Gorky's longest novel continues to baffle critics. The Russian peasantry and its unorthodox religiosity had enchanted many Russian and early Soviet authors, just as they had impressed Siniavsky's father in his populist youth, and this seems to have been one of Siniavsky's lifelong interests.[6]

The Thaw was a time when a routine human experience of getting together with a group of friends felt like a new and radical phenomenon. According to a well-informed participant, Liudmila Alexeyeva, friends' companies "emerged in a flash in the mid-1950s, stayed vibrant for a decade, then faded away. . . . They performed the functions of publishing house, salons, billboards, confessional booths, concert halls," and much else: an improvised, highly personal version of the Habermasian public sphere in a society where this sphere had been suppressed for half a century.[7] A graduate student of history in the late 1950s, Alexeyeva describes her own "company," in which recent returnees from the camps debated the events of the Thaw together with future writers, bards, and human rights activists. In the next decade, some of these people went on to become cultural stars and some, political prisoners. Two young and ambitious authors, Yuly Daniel and Siniavsky, both of whom, as it would later be discovered, were smuggling their works abroad at the time, were at the center of this network. Siniavsky's student, and later a superstar of Soviet popular culture, Vladimir Vysotsky, entertained their mutual friends by singing camp songs, some of them authentic: "Vysotsky did not compose his own songs at that time. He sang old camp songs . . . but he sang them in such a way, slow and passionate, that they felt new and tragic, like those songs that he would compose in the future."[8] From 1961, the earliest songs that Vysotsky wrote himself were all stylizations of camp songs, *blatnye pesni*.[9] Using first-person narration and singing in the low, hypermasculine voice of a convict and drunkard, Vysotsky inserted into his songs references to the geography of the gulag, concepts that were specific to camp life, and a recognizable aesthetics of this folkish genre. It was due to Vysotsky that the companies of the 1960s sang "camp lyrics" in their living rooms or around the campfire, and he owed his popularity to the fact that broad circles of the intelligentsia at the time were longing for an art that would express their preoccupation with the victims of the Soviet system. In a 1964 song, "Not Everyone Was Admitted to Our Circle," Vysotsky told the story of a victim whose friend had turned out to be an informer; the narrator, now in a prison or camp, is contemplating revenge. Siniavsky remembered how Vysotsky sang this song on Yuly Daniel's birthday shortly before the real-life arrest of Siniavsky and Daniel, which would enact the song's plot (one of their friends turned out to be an informer).[10] Vysotsky's lifelong efforts brought this folkish art into the mainstream of literature and theater. Siniavsky took his literary pseudonym, Abram Tertz, from one such camp song about a legendary Jewish thief. He encouraged Vysotsky to write and play these songs, and was disappointed to find out later, after his release from the camp, that Vysotsky had not committed himself exclusively to this genre. Like his teacher, Vysotsky was often on the edge of imprisonment because of his dissident poetry and deviant lifestyle. He was lucky enough to avoid arrest, but the way he performed his camp songs convinced at least one ex-prisoner, Vadim Tumanov, who had spent six years in the Kolyma camps, that the singer must certainly be a fellow ex-prisoner.

A remarkable personality, Tumanov was a commercial sailor and champion boxer before he was imprisoned in 1948. In the 1960s, after a long odyssey involving fights, flights, retrials, and narrow escapes, this charismatic survivor launched a gold-mining "cooperative" in Kolyma that made him into one of the first Soviet millionaires. In 1977, when Siniavsky was already teaching at the Sorbonne, Tumanov took a group that included Vysotsky, the star poet Yevgeny Yevtushenko, and several scientists on a guided tour through the ruins of the Kolyma camps. Described in Tumanov's memoir in exhaustive detail, this tour was a veritable pilgrimage. They visited a makeshift camp cemetery, where wooden boards bearing the personal identification numbers of the dead convicts written in indelible copying pencil marked the graves spreading over the permafrost to the horizon. Yevtushenko took one of these boards as a souvenir, and kept it on his desk in his house near Moscow, wrote Tumanov.[11] Vysotsky composed several songs about Kolyma. His plans to make a film about the camps never came to fruition, but he did coauthor a novel about them, *The Black Candle*.[12] One of his most popular songs takes as its setting the Vacha River, where Tumanov's ex-convicts panned for gold in the tundra: "I go to the Vacha weeping, I return from the Vacha grinning."

Another friend and a member of Siniavsky's "company" was the art historian Igor Golomstock. He was five years old when his father was arrested in 1934. Several years later, his mother would voluntarily move to the gulag zone of Kolyma together with her son and second husband; she worked there in a camp as a doctor. Golomstock spent four adolescent years, 1939–1943, among the camp guards, the prisoners, and their children. He makes it clear in his memoirs that these years were formative for his "character, preoccupations, and worldview," and particularly for his future interest in cultural history. In the paranoiac atmosphere of the 1950s, when some of their friends were reporting on them, Golomstock and Siniavsky could trust one another as fellow sons of political prisoners. Golomstock was one of the first experts to appreciate the work of Boris Sveshnikov, another ex-prisoner (see chapter 5); he also introduced Sveshnikov to Siniavsky. Golomstock and Siniavsky shared an interest in the folklore and writings of the noncanonical religious movement, the so-called Old Belief. From the summer of 1958, they sailed the north Russian rivers in pursuit of rare Old Belief manuscripts. On the way to these hidden treasures, they visited the old sites of the gulag, which reminded Golomstock of his Kolyma childhood. Siniavsky and Golomstock coauthored the first Soviet book on Pablo Picasso, presenting him mainly as the author of *Guernica* and other tragic images of the war. A few years later, Golomstock took part in the Daniel and Siniavsky trial and was convicted for refusing to cooperate with the court. After his emigration to England, he turned to the history of unofficial Soviet art and published a pioneering comparison of the arts under totalitarian regimes, from Nazi Germany to the Soviet Union and China.[13]

When his Moscow friend, psychiatrist Miron Etlis, also a former prisoner, felt the need to escape from his jealous wife, Golomstock recommended that he go to Kolyma, as his mother had done decades earlier. Etlis followed this advice, and in fact ended up settling there permanently. Decades later, Etlis became the leader of the local Magadan branch of the Memorial Society, a major organization that deals with the memory of the victims of the Soviet and post-Soviet states. In 1989, he negotiated with the émigré sculptor Ernst Neizvestny the erection in Kolyma of a fascinating monument to the victims of the Soviet terror, *The Mask of Sorrow* (see chapter 9).[14] This company of friends was consequential.

Liubimov and Moscow

Siniavsky's novella *Liubimov* (1963) presents the well-known events of Russian revolutionary history as a series of miracles, ghostly apparitions, and collective hallucinations. Lenia, a little man in a provincial town, has the power to hypnotize the local population. He confiscates all property in Liubimov, institutes round-the-clock surveillance over citizens, and organizes their collective labor. Supported by the hypnotically induced enthusiasm of the masses, his regime lasts until everyone, the leader and the masses, has exhausted their transformative energies. Curiously, Lenia received his hypnotic skills in the local library, where he borrowed an old mystical book; its author, a mid-nineteenth-century Freemason, visits the library as a ghost. The librarian, a hybrid character who is sometimes under Lenia's hypnoses and sometimes possessed by the nobleman's ghost, narrates the whole story. The Soviet government attacks the rebellious Liubimov, but Lenia is able to hypnotize its spies and soldiers. Lenia's rival and prototype, Lenin, is presented as a werewolf. The Liubimov citizens take the waters of the local river for champagne and Lenya for a dictator, but they feel happy only for so long as the hypnosis lasts. In the meantime, Lenia marries the local beauty. It then becomes clear that he is more interested in men than women, and so he turns a Soviet agent into his closest friend. The story ends when an Orthodox priest prays the Masonic ghost back into his grave, Lenia loses his power, and Soviet tanks raze Liubimov to the ground. An attempt to deconstruct the improbable course of Russian history by magical means, the novella anticipates many subsequent efforts of the writers who would become known in the 1980s or later.

Siniavsky's international renown as a writer, a dissident, and, after his emigration, a professor at the Sorbonne has overshadowed extraordinary works that his friend Yuly Daniel wrote before their arrests. Siniavsky's fellow defendant in the trial of 1966, Daniel spent five years in the camps. Among the stories that brought him to the Soviet court was his novella *This Is Moscow Speaking*, which he composed sometime between 1960, when its action takes place, and 1962, when he published it in Washington, D.C. under the pseudonym Nikolai Arzhak. Born in 1925 and trained in philology, Daniel fought and was seriously wounded in World War II. He donated elements of his own biography—combat, wounding, womanizing, and freethinking—to Tolia, the narrator of *This Is Moscow Speaking*. A fictional memoir of fantastic events, the novella starts with a company of friends holidaying at the dacha, drinking, flirting, and discussing politics. Suddenly, the radio announces: "This is Moscow speaking. . . . By decree of the Supreme Soviet, Sunday 16 August, 1960 is declared Open Murder Day." This decree endows every citizen of the USSR with the right to kill any other citizen, "with the exception of persons who are listed in the attachment to this decree." Initially the protagonist, Tolia cannot believe his ears. His friends' responses are varied. One friend, a member of the Communist Party, dismisses the broadcast as an American provocation. Another friend, a Jew, worries that the decree is the opening shot in a new anti-Semitic campaign. A fellow resident of Tolia's communal apartment, a survivor of the gulag, approves of the decree because he believes that "it is the right and duty of the state to pass its power into the hands of the people." Tolia has no patience for any of these ideas. "Didn't you learn anything in your camp?" he feels like asking his neighbor. Tolia's lover suggests that she and Tolia use Open Murder Day as an opportunity to kill her husband so as to get him out of the way. Tolia is appalled, and shows her the door; she is contemptuous, and calls him a "sissy." Having lost his girlfriend to Open Murder Day before it has even started, Tolia is astonished: "We cheated on him . . . we spent his money on drink, we ridiculed him . . . but to kill him?"

Whatever the ideological framework, which nobody understands in any case, people use Open Murder Day for sorting out their mundane troubles and settling personal scores. Tolia, who killed Germans during the war, reflects on the nature of hatred. Is there anybody whom he hates as much as his former girlfriend hates her husband? He becomes aware of his hatred toward the authority figures of his time, the fat, inarticulate members of the Soviet elite. "What about them? Can we forgive them? What about 1937? . . . They think that since they've shat on the grave of the Mustached One, that makes [Stalin] all right?" A recent soldier, Tolia contemplates taking revenge on the Soviet authorities. In anticipation of Open Murder Day, his fantasy reverts to his wartime experiences, the naked physical aggression of a foot soldier with a grenade and a machine gun.

Collective remembrances of the terror of the 1930s, the sacrifice of the 1940s, and the madness of the 1950s punctuate the narrative. More interestingly, Tolia sees the Moscow of the early 1960s as poised on the verge of a new cycle of terror. He takes his metaphors from architecture. The neoclassical edifices of Stalinist architecture still dominate Moscow, but the newest constructions that, as they crumbled into disrepair in subsequent decades, would go down in history under the name of the Khrushchev slums (*khrushchoby*) embody the hope of emancipation from the Soviet terror. Daniel lists the modest symbols of this hope: imported Finnish furniture, translations of Hemingway, and the sleek trousers that were in fashion at the time. But this world of new prosperity is threatened by the menacing, monumental gray structures that were built in the 1930s. With a "dark sense of their superiority," these buildings are waiting only for their architect, Stalin, to rise up from the grave and to level the tender green shoots of new life. The fashionable, modern housing of the Thaw would be helpless against the impending attack of the grand multicolumn skyscrapers of the Stalin era. This feeling of the imminent return of the terror and the fragility of the post-Stalinist order would become a permanent feature of late twentieth-century Russia.

Daniel speculates about the nature of violence throughout the story. In a dialogue with a friend, Tolia formulates a hypothesis about Open Murder Day as a technique whose objective is to accustom the population to violence, to make violence routine. The difference between Stalinism and Open Murder Day, he says, is the cynical absence of an ideological justification of violence in the case of the latter. There was "a sauce" in 1937, an ideological dressing that endowed the events with meaning, at least for true believers. But in the case of the coming Open Murder Day, no explanation was given. "Now we are on full self-service," thinks Tolia.

A week or two later, Tolia notices a strange agitation in the streets. Restless groups of people sing songs, declaim verses, share jokes, and brew their anxiety in a carnivalesque way that was typical for the Thaw. In a warped way, the anticipated horror is transformed into a cheerful solidarity shared by "companies" of friends, these new communities of fear, mourning, and resistance. Daniel's novella includes damning portraits of Thaw-era bohemians, of their empty talk, and the unlimited compromises they are prepared to make in order to accommodate the regime. Tolia uses or even invents a symbol capturing this combination of imaginary freedom and actual conformism characteristic of the Thaw-era intelligentsia: *"figa v karmane,"* an obscene finger gesture performed inside the pocket, a stronger Russian version of "tongue in cheek." The solidarity of the post-Stalin generation does not facilitate but rather obstructs collective action. Gradually, Tolia realizes that the Open Murder Day has failed to bring the "full freedom of homicide." Fending off an attack by a stranger on Red Square, next to Lenin's mausoleum, Tolia realizes that this man is an assassin sent by the party authorities to kill him, Tolia.

After a prolonged period of stunned silence and shock in which nobody mentions the events of Open Murder Day, Tolia's friends gather for another drinking party, and someone breaks the taboo on mentioning Open Murder Day. This prompts an outpouring of rumors and speculations about the events of that day. There is talk of secret lists of victims; mass murders of Armenians in Nagorno-Karabakh and Russians in Central Asia; a boycott of Open Murder Day in the Baltic republics; and plans to make Open Murder Day an annual event. A survivor, Tolia celebrates his victory with a new girlfriend. But his would-be assassin also survives; Tolia did not kill him, even though he had the opportunity to do so.

Daniel and Siniavsky wrote their stories as anti-utopias, and they complement one another. *Liubimov* is about symbolic and *Moscow* about physical violence. *Liubimov* is about the provinces and *Moscow* about the capital. *Liubimov* is about the past and *Moscow* about the future. *Moscow* is narrated by a survivor of catastrophe and *Liubimov* by its historian. The key literary references in both novellas belong to the vast genre of satirical anti-utopia; both mention *Don Quixote* by Cervantes. In Liubimov's library, people talk ceaselessly about Ernest Hemingway (his novel *Fiesta* is specifically mentioned) and Lion Feuchtwanger. Preparing for Open Murder Day in Moscow, people read *Revolt of the Angels* by Anatole France and an unnamed novel by Aldous Huxley, most probably a reference to *Brave New World*.

Tolia's fictional father is a Bolshevik commissar who perished in the gulag in 1936. Yuly Daniel's actual father was a Yiddish writer who died of consumption in 1940 in Kiev and therefore escaped both the Nazi Holocaust and the Soviet terror. Yuly Daniel's son has become a leader of the Memorial Society. Passed through generations of this family, the memory of terror generates fictional narratives and social activism, but does not seem to weaken or fade. A unique feature of Daniel's and Siniavsky's narratives, however, is that we have authentic and detailed documents of authorial intentions and readers' responses: the records of the famous trial of 1965–1966.

In his testimony, Daniel repeatedly insisted that he wanted to warn the public that the Stalinist "cult of personality" could return then, in 1960, in new and even more vicious forms. However, Daniel's personal theory of Stalinism was quite different from Khrushchev's. Instead of blaming the cult of personality, Daniel imagined decentered, allegedly spontaneous but in fact subtly manipulated massacres, which are probably close to historical Stalinism. A KGB expert informed the court that Daniel presented "our country as a huge concentration camp"; that the Soviet people in this novel were "oppressed, frightened, and enraged"; and that the authorities there "introduce the wildest measures that throw our country back to an almost primordial condition." This is a correct reading of the novel, which the critic continued by using one of the favorite concepts of both Daniel and Siniavsky: this fiction, he wrote, was "monstrous."[15] At the trial, the prosecutor said that the novel incited violence against the Soviet leaders, and characterized Daniel's novel as "wild fantasy," "furious slander," and "jeering at the Soviet people." The court agreed.

A few years after the Siniavsky and Daniel trial, Hannah Arendt commented in connection to the student unrest of 1968 that violence and power were opposites: "when the one rules absolutely, the other is absent." Reflecting on the Soviet occupation of Czechoslovakia and the first translated novel by Aleksandr Solzhenitsyn, *The First Circle,* Arendt stated that "rule by sheer violence comes into play where power is being lost.... Violence itself results in impotence."[16] This formula is quite close to the fantasies of Daniel and Siniavsky. Both nightmares, of total massacre in *Moscow* and total hypnosis in *Liubimov,* fail to create anything close to stability and legitimacy of power. While Siniavsky's story mocked the idea of "totalitarian" rule based on ideological transformation from above, Daniel's parable was similar to a subtler version of the so-called revisionist school of Soviet history, which emphasized the spontaneous, unplanned development of terror from below. However, it is also different from this position. Indeed, in Daniel's story, it was the central administration that decreed the regime of free, unpunished murder. In this imagined situation, the administration did not withdraw its control but implemented it through secret agents, lists, bribes, and amnesties.

Predating *One Hundred Years of Solitude* by Gabriel García Márquez (1967), Siniavsky's *Liubimov* and Daniel's *Moscow* share with this masterpiece of magical realism its complex narrative structure and freewheeling experimentation with history. Siniavsky and Daniel are the two most important predecessors of leading post-Soviet authors such as Vladimir Sharov, Vladimir Sorokin, and Dmitry Bykov, who would continue their experiments with violence, libraries, and time (see chapter 11). Most important, one could read both of these unusual texts, *Liubimov* and *Moscow,* as Victims' Balls (see Introduction), imaginary rituals of mimetic mourning that would have run amok had they been realized. But can we be so sure that they were never realized?

There are details in the life stories and court trials of Daniel, Siniavsky, Brodsky, and even Vysotsky that make me think that, with all the ambivalence that one can imagine, these figures provoked their persecutions and imprisonment through their actions, which we might read as a form of mimetic mourning. After the collapse of its major structures between 1953 and 1956, the gulag became a sacred place, but reaching this destination required a very serious effort. The undertaking of the pilgrimage to the gulag was a task for the writer, the priest of the emerging culture of mourning. Some made the pilgrimage as tourists, and brought back souvenirs from the mass graves for their writing desks. Some made the pilgrimage by turning themselves into prisoners—the way of mimetic self-sacrifice. Some imagined these visits for their readers.

A Voice from the Chorus

If in Moscow Siniavsky spoke as a soloist, in the camp he was part of the chorus. The camp was the place for the chorus of the Soviet tragedy, and Siniavsky liked being there. He saw "an impassable boundary" between the camp and the home. Crossing this border in both directions is traumatic, but he tended to downplay the trauma of imprisonment and emphasize the trauma of liberation.[17] Paradoxically, Siniavsky depicted his arrest and long term in the camp as predictable events, a sort of destiny, while his release from the camp features as an unexpected and troubling event, a point of rupture. His novel *Goodnight!* describes his return from the camp to Moscow as an expulsion from home and a loss of vision. He compared himself to a boy who had completed his prison term and was now supposed to go home, but could not bear to leave, so he wept and begged to be let back into the camp; the guard drove him away, but he kept coming back again and again, unable to bring himself to set off for home. There is a meaningful resemblance between Siniavsky's self-documented desire to return to the camp and the story that Bitov tells in his *Pushkin House* of the ex-convict who does return to the site of the camp, to die there (see chapter 3).

After his release, Siniavsky found that he needed to wear eyeglasses. He understood this loss of vision as a symbol of a deeper regress that he experienced when he returned home. He wrote that through his glasses, one of his eyes contemplated the alien Moscow life, while the other eye looked back to the camp. Life in the camp was "more complete and more inspiring" than life in Moscow. Even the prison, the worst place of all, had a "style and rhythm" he never saw again, either in Russia or abroad— "frightening, attractive, and joyful."[18]

Both of the memoirists who were closest to Siniavsky—his wife, Maria Rozanova, and his friend Igor Golomstock—emphasize the long-expected nature of Siniavsky's arrest, which all three viewed as practically inevitable. "We are waiting for the arrest," wrote Rozanova, and when her husband was arrested, she noted in bold: "**Finally.**"[19] In his *Goodnight!*

Siniavsky mentioned that even when she agreed to marry him, his wife had known that he would eventually go to jail. She never liked to hear him state this as a fact, but he would do so "more and more often" as the arrest drew closer.[20] Much in the history of the famous Siniavsky and Daniel trial becomes more comprehensible if one accepts the paradoxical idea of the internal temptation that prison represented for those who belonged to the mournful leaders of the Thaw.

For Siniavsky, the difference between camp and home also meant a difference of genre. He wrote fiction in civilian life and nonfiction in the camp. There he wrote his most successful book, *Strolls with Pushkin*, and sent it to his wife in dozens of letters by the camp mail, evading the half-literate censorship by inserting fragments of this scholarly and playful text in the middle of routine letters. There in the camp, he also wrote *A Voice from the Chorus*, a remarkable collection of notes and aphorisms, and the first and major part of another scholarly book, *In the Shadow of Gogol*. He also drafted in the camp parts of those books on Russian folk life and on the Soviet civilization that he would complete and publish much later, in Paris. By any standard, his output was amazing. Neither in Moscow, where Siniavsky was employed by the leading academic institution, nor even in Paris, where he worked at the Sorbonne, did he ever write scholarly works that surpassed his camp production. In *Strolls*, Siniavsky said that Pushkin was full of his highest poetic potencies when perched on the very edge of a plague pit.[21] In a similar way, Siniavsky was at his fullest when writing his mournful texts from the vantage point of the Soviet camp.

There were several factors that explained the climax of creative energy that Siniavsky experienced in his camp in Mordovia. This post-Stalinist camp for political prisoners, an "exemplary" institution that survived and succeeded the gulag, was a literal realization of the Soviet utopia—a classless, all-male, purposefully unproductive society that built discipline and order on an irrational, unjustifiable foundation. There was nothing better to confirm Siniavsky's double feelings of historical mourning and political protest than the reality of the camp. It was also a social milieu that was entirely different from the rarefied, select circles of the Soviet intellectual elite. Many members of the intelligentsia experienced a surge of energy when they were emancipated from its institutions, whether through emigration to the West, "internal emigration" into hermetic circles of connoisseurs, or even incarceration. In the camp, Siniavsky met unusual people whom he would otherwise have never encountered, such as Russian sectarians, Ukrainian nationalists, shadow entrepreneurs, and many others who had been criminalized by Soviet law. These people were radically different from "the people" whom his father, a socialist revolutionary, worshipped together with several generations of the populist intelligentsia. Siniavsky followed Shalamov in the conclusion that the experience of the camp undermined the most basic beliefs that had found their expression in the masterpieces of Russian literature, from Gogol to Tolstoy.

Scholarship requires libraries; there was a library in the camp where Siniavsky served the major part of his term, but its holdings were very limited. Using this library, Siniavsky also asked his wife to send books or bring them during her annual visits. Their correspondence is full of such requests, which give an idea of his reading in the camp: it was Russian symbolist poetry and the European high-brow and mystical literature of E. T. A. Hoffmann, Maeterlinck, Kafka, and even Hermann Hesse, translations of which had become fashionable among the intelligentsia. He also read books and essays on Russian folklore, which had been likewise coming into vogue. More surprisingly, he read rare sources on Russian sects, which the sectarians in the camp lent him. Later, when he could use the libraries of Moscow and Paris, his pet subject became Vasily Rozanov, a sophisticated fin-de-siècle thinker who combined eroticism and mysticism. Having produced a profound reassessment of Russian and Soviet values, Siniavsky had to invent a new language of critique and resistance. The originality and richness of his camp-time scholarship were linked to this task. But everything that Siniavsky learned and felt in the camp, he expressed in his speculations about Pushkin and Gogol. Not surprisingly, these speculations were unusual.

After decades of state terror, the camps of the 1960s were full of ghosts. With a deliberate ambiguity, Siniavsky wrote to his wife: "Everything here is a bit fantastic, even flowers and encounters.... The sun is lower on the horizon, and therefore the shadows are longer.... My neighbor is spectral, we slept and ate together, and suddenly it turned out that he is a specter" (2:62). Those who were released from the camp also felt illusory or hallucinatory, but for a different reason: "they have immediately become spectral and unearthly, as if they were dead" (2:169). Everything was ghostly because of the camp's boredom and loneliness; everything was haunted because of its history and symbolism. After liberation, Siniavsky himself felt like a specter issuing from the camp: "Leaving prison is like being re-born after death. . . . All that remains is a naked point of view, so you feel like a ghost visiting this world."[22]

These ghostly feelings match the worldview of another ex-prisoner whose art had prepared Siniavsky for the camp, Boris Sveshnikov (see chapter 5). As Siniavsky noted, "Sveshnikov's drawings have a reversible meaning. Anyone who didn't know this was a camp would never guess it. . . . Those who are in the know (I almost said, the initiated) . . . would make out [the telltale signs] here and there: a stockade, rubbish-dumps, barracks, a prison. Someone has only just hanged himself, someone else is just sitting and waiting out his term."[23] The favorite subjects of Siniavsky's studies—Pushkin, Gogol, and sectarians—were also, at their best and most creative moments, suspended in this intermediary, reversible state between life and death. Sveshnikov portrayed this condition in his memorable images; Siniavsky depicted it in *In the Shadow of Gogol*:

In the "transitory condition," as Gogol put it (and all his work was like a transitory, loose swing between life and death) . . . his personality split into some kind of multitude, which existed on different levels of being and consciousness, dying and resurrecting itself daily, and even from somewhere beyond the grave still reaching back to life, and weeping, and threatening, and arguing with compatriots. (2:189)

Gogol "was dying all his life"; Gogol "encompassed within himself the impassable gap between the living and the dead"; Gogol lived "in the coffin of his tired, almost unresponsive flesh." Such was also the life of the typical inmates of the camps, the goners. Siniavsky escaped their fate, but Sveshnikov had been one of these soon-to-be-dead before the camp doctor saved him. It was in their shadow—in the shadow of Gogol—that Siniavsky wrote the camp letters that contained his future books. From the vanguard position of the goner, Gogol manifested "a striking ability to reason and control . . . seeing more and farther than normal vision can see."[24]

Siniavsky started to write *Strolls with Pushkin* in August 1966, five months after his term began. He wrote to his wife that he wanted to compose something "non-academic . . . cheerful, light" about Pushkin. While working on *Strolls*, Siniavsky read Osip Mandelstam's *Conversation about Dante* (see chapter 4).[25] He immediately felt its affinity to his own project and in a letter to his wife revealed Mandelstam's "historical method." Like no other poet, Mandelstam had "an immediate, intrinsic sense of history," and his historical writing was "not a restoration but a daring intimization of remote centuries." He approached the past with an attitude of "respectful familiarity," like that of a "loving son" toward his father.[26] These were all features of Siniavsky's own historicism, which combined the self-conscious modernization of the past with its "daring intimization."

A Theory of Metaphor

Siniavsky was an ironist, and both his historicism and his mysticism were often parodical. A combination of self-mocking irony and deadly seriousness was a Russian tradition that he appreciated in both Pushkin and Gogol. It is ironical that philosopher Richard Rorty formulated his ideal of combining irony with heroism while reading Vladimir Nabokov, who, while definitely an ironist, was no hero;[27] in fact, Siniavsky would fit Rorty's description much better. Always eager to reveal and mock the internal contradictions within his favorite texts, Siniavsky combined his irony with an unusually serious attitude toward literature. He elaborated his own theory of metaphor that fitted his textual practice. Metaphors (which in his extended use of the term also include allegories and parables) have their own life, flesh, and blood, but these are different from the factual realities that they describe. Good metaphors produce "a piercing physical sensation." They do not belong to mere literature; they acquire their own being, "as if growing into the physical body." While Russian romanticism just mentioned the devils and the dead as "pure literature," its re-visionary, Gogol, "responded to these stories with his very blood" and presented them as "the terrifying truth." Gogol had seen "the country of the dead"; it had been revealed to him "first-hand." His most hazardous and shocking metaphors were not blasphemy; they were testimony.

When metaphors are translated into real life, the consequences are disastrous. According to Siniavsky, the overflow of metaphors into history brings catastrophe. "Not communism but literalism is a mortal threat to the world."[28] Realized metaphors are monsters. More precisely, when metaphors are realized, the sublime turns into the monstrous. *The Sleep of Reason Produces Monsters* is the title of Francisco Goya's series of tragic sketches that Sveshnikov loved and emulated. In Siniavsky's version, it is not the sleep of reason but rather its incomplete awakening—its inability to differentiate between nightmare and sober reality—that produces monsters.

In Siniavsky's letters and studies, specters and monsters are organic for literature, which cannot do without them: "Take the shadow of [Hamlet's] father out of *Hamlet*, and immediately the play withers away into nothing" (3:140). Maeterlinck suggested a more thorough discussion that touched upon the very essence of the monstrous:

Another question—who depends on whom: the people on the ghosts, or the ghosts on the people. . . . People do not think what their "uninvited guests" are doing in their homes. . . . [The ghosts], in contrast, cling to the people, stare into their eyes, initiate conversations . . . with an unconscious envy for the destiny of man. (1:118)

Siniavsky's wife sent him a book about vampires and a collection of gothic novels in Russian translation. Sectarians in the camp gave him mystical manuscripts to read. But none of this was ever enough; Siniavsky's "dream of reading about ghosts" (2:165) remained unsatisfied, and he asked for more. Calling the time of his youth "the period of late, mature, and blooming Stalinism," he remembered "craziness, plots, horrors . . . ghouls, vampires, which still do not let me sleep," and also the "atmosphere of the black mass, a dog's wedding, and howling from beyond the grave."[29] These youthful motifs would often find a place in Siniavsky's texts. Their poetics is monstrous, but the author saw it as resulting from the historical reality in which he lived and worked. "Monsters are just as universal as the little devils that alcoholics see in their dreams," Siniavsky wrote (1:356–357)—in other words, not universal at all, but rather specific to the sinner and his sins. Besides this clinical awareness, there was not much to rely on for a child of Stalinism who wanted to stroll with the ghosts.

In his closing speech to the court in 1966, before being sent off to the camp, Siniavsky said: "Frightening passages of the indictment . . . have grown in a monstrous atmosphere . . . in which the real ends and the monstrous starts."[30] Thus at this decisive moment of his life he operated with the category of the monstrous. He did not define it, and his judges were not interested in asking him to do so. Let me try. In Siniavsky's idiosyncratic vision, the "monstrous" is the Hegelian antithesis of the "sublime." If the sublime pulls apart the different levels of reality, the monstrous merges them. Combining the human with the inhuman, the monstrous is hybrid; it is supernatural and countercultural. Humans have "always" loved monsters, stated Siniavsky, "for the sake of higher potencies." Pagan religions portrayed deities as monsters, and Gothic architecture with its chimeras did the same.[31] This was the context in which Siniavsky likened Pushkin to a ghoul and Gogol to a tarantula. Metaphors can be monstrous; moreover, in this textual practice, they usually are. Textual games keep monstrous metaphors within the boundaries of speech and prevent them from breaking through into real life. But once they get out of discursive control and materialize in the interplay of human bodies, the monstrous threaten revolution, prison, and death. Here Siniavsky is not far from his beloved Pasternak. At the end of *Doctor Zhivago*, Pasternak inserted into the conversation between characters from a new generation of Muscovites an astonishing statement:

Take Blok's line, "We, children of Russia's terrible years," and you'll immediately see the difference between the epochs. When Blok said this, it had to be understood in an extended sense, figuratively. . . . But now everything figurative has become literal; the children are children, and the fears are terrible, that's the difference here.[32]

At the trial in 1966, responding to the charges laid against him, Siniavsky said: "Here, really very strangely and unexpectedly, an artistic image is losing its conventionality. The prosecution has taken it literally, so literally that the whole judicial procedure is becoming plugged into the text, as though it were its natural extension."[33] He interpreted the trial not as a punishment for his texts but as their monstrous continuation by other means. In his later novel *Goodnight!* (1983), Siniavsky confirmed that in his trial and imprisonment, "everything was correct, as it had to be . . . as it had happened many times before in literature—in following through to the conclusion, to the truth, the comparisons and metaphors for which the author, of course, must pay with his head."[34]

This formula—overflowing of text into life, with monstrous results—defined the core of Siniavsky's idea of literature. Siniavsky saw this overflowing in all three of his scholarly subjects, Pushkin, Gogol, and Rozanov. "Or were it the machinations of an ancient literary law according to which fate dealt mysteriously with the author, using the texts of his works for a crib-sheet?"[35] The author's texts predict his life, and this is what people call fate. In the case of writers, fate is comprehensible. One can read and grasp it, though one cannot edit it. Siniavsky's camp writings are full of these literary games with fate, also a major interest for other intellectual survivors of the camps such as Dmitry Likhachev (see chapter 4). This wisdom works well with Pushkin, who wrote stories about dueling and met his own end in a duel. Responsibility for one's destiny should be accepted because it has been made by one's own hands, or rather written by one's own pen. "Humility and liberty are one when we recognize fate as home," wrote Siniavsky in *Strolls with Pushkin*.[36]

Pushkin the Vampire

Reading the short and striking *Strolls with Pushkin*, we learn astonishing news: Pushkin was a vampire. In Siniavsky's treatise, this was illustrated by many examples in which Pushkin's characters (Don Juan, Godunov, Aleko, Marko) expressed a peculiar interest in the dead, particularly the unburied dead. All of Siniavsky's examples were drawn from the lives of Pushkin's characters, not Pushkin himself. This is the very same logic that the Soviet court applied to Siniavsky. Then, he protested with such energy that even his judge agreed that the author could not be tried for the crimes of his characters. This is the logic of literalism, which according to Siniavsky, is the source and the nature of the monstrous. It was also the logic of the gulag. After reading *Strolls with Pushkin*, Dmitry Likhachev, also an ex-prisoner, commented in his memoirs: "This was fiction of a kind that was typical for camps and prisons."[37]

In a later essay, "Journey to the Black Stream," Siniavsky returned to the idea of the writer as vampire. "Probably every self-respecting writer is by nature a vampire.... In the allegorical sense, of course.... He operates in a spectral world but pretends that it is real." The self-respecting writer is a vampire because "he wants to multiply," and this is why he must bite. In Lermontov's romantic poem of 1839, Demon—probably the most spectacular beast in Russian literature—fell in love with a human female and killed her with his kiss. In contrast to Demon, the vampire would turn her into a vampire, his equal. The vampire's nature is vicious but open and productive, and in this it resembles the nature of the poet. Just as love for a vampire produces new vampires, so love for a poet creates new poets.[38]

Siniavsky never repudiated this monstrous language. In 1989, a Soviet journal asked him to choose a text for his first posttrial publication. Of all that he had published in emigration Siniavsky chose that very section that compared Pushkin to a vampire.[39] This publication caused a scandal. One Soviet writer declaimed that Siniavsky was worse than the officer who killed Pushkin in a duel; another suggested that Siniavsky would be better off strolling not with Pushkin but with Shalom Aleichem, the Yiddish writer. A sensible critic, Sergei Bocharov, commented that the real author of *Strolls with Pushkin* was the camp.[40]

Siniavsky's *Soviet Civilization*, an academic treatise based on his course at the Sorbonne, features the key word on the very first page: Soviet civilization is not just "extraordinary," it is "a monstrosity."[41] A heart-breaking episode from Siniavsky's *Goodnight!* in which he learns, after meeting with his father upon his release from prison, that his father is suffering from paranoid delusions (see chapter 3) combines two key words, "fantastic" and "monstrous."[42] A persistent horror fueled both the prose and the criticism that Siniavsky produced. What he called "fantastic realism" was not a philosophical statement about the fantastic nature of reality, but a historical testimony about the monstrous quality of Soviet reality, as the author knew it. His generation, the people who saw Stalin's death and brought about the Thaw and then perestroika, experienced a "rapture in the face of the metamorphoses of God." In one of his delightful metaphors that are worthy of Bakhtin or Sveshnikov, Siniavsky described this ecstatic feeling as something that was summoned up by "the monstrous peristalsis of God's guts, the convolutions of our brains' grey matter."[43]

A doyen of the gulag ex-prisoners, Varlam Shalamov, admired the courage of Daniel and Siniavsky and rejected the accusation that in their writings they had "slandered" the Stalinist past: "I assert that the concept of libel is inapplicable to the time of Stalin. The human mind is incapable of imagining those crimes that were committed during this period." The horror of the historical past was so extreme that it was impossible to overstate, claimed Shalamov. But then, could it be represented? Though Shalamov and Siniavsky were close in their political ideas, their textual practices were so far apart as to be polar opposites, and they knew it. In the same letter to a fellow ex-prisoner, Shalamov disagreed with Siniavsky's idea of fantastic realism and criticized the rampant experiments with the narrative form that were characteristic of both Daniel and Siniavsky. Shalamov specifically questioned the use of what he called "satire" and "the grotesque" in the literature about the past: "our experience categorically rules out the use of the genres of the grotesque or the fantastic. But neither Siniavsky nor Daniel has seen those rivers of blood that we saw. Both of them, of course, can use the grotesque and the fantastic."[44]

However, Siniavsky continued his work with history, satire, and magic well after he received his immediate experience of the camps. Combining political pessimism with a sort of cultural optimism, he believed in the relevance of the camp experience for the twentieth century. "The Russian camps will still generate, and have already generated, an amazing kind of literature . . . none of us can escape it, can run from it . . . because we all live in the 20th century—behind the wire."[45]

Siniavsky hoped that by returning his books to Russia he would "call forth hosts of vampires, ready to fly through the night."[46] He was right about this. There is a straight route from Siniavsky's image of Pushkin the vampire to the vampiric novels by Viktor Pelevin, which also experimented with the conjunction between creativity, eroticism, and bloodsucking about forty years after Siniavsky. Even though almost none of the post-Soviet generation of Russian writers has had firsthand experience of living on the wrong side of barbed wire, this generation has filled the literary space with a multitude of haunting and mourning creatures—ghosts, monsters, hybrids, and clones (see chapter 11).[47] As Shalamov predicted, this generation of writers, who have never seen the camps themselves, have been increasingly engaged in "the grotesque." In a recent piece of literary criticism, Dmitry Bykov traced his genealogy of the post-Soviet authors not to Shalamov, but to Siniavsky.[48]

Uninvited Guests

Siniavsky's conclusions had always been extreme, but it was the brutal experience of the camp that prompted him to produce a more literal interpretation of the heretical and monstrous than either the Russian symbolist poets or their scholarly heirs, the Soviet semioticians, ever dared to perform. In a way that resembled Walter Benjamin, whom he never read, Siniavsky interpreted the great texts of the Russian poetic tradition—Pushkin's "Prophet," Lermontov's "Demon," Gogol's *A Terrible Vengeance*—as memories of religious rituals. "Telling fairytales required dedication and extreme caution. . . . Violating these conditions brought disaster in its wake, even the death of the storyteller. . . . The figure of the storyteller was surrounded by mystery, suffering, and omniscience" (2:385).

The camp experience stimulated the writing of ghost stories and helped to make visible the monstrous aspects of classical texts. In Siniavsky's camp and postcamp writings, Pushkin was a vampire; the romantic Russian troika was harnessed to the devil; Gogol oscillated between a goner and a revenant; and Soviet civilization was monstrous. There in the camp Siniavsky also developed an unusual version of Russian ethnography, which was focused on the non-Orthodox folk beliefs. In his *Ivan the Fool*, a book on Russian religiosity, a cursory account of the history of the Russian church gives way to a detailed analysis of heresies, schisms, and sects that occupies the larger part of the book. In this revisionist narrative, a direct line of succession runs from the classical Russian fairy tale to the schismatic priest Avvakum, to the leader of the Skoptsy (castrates) sect Kondraty Selivanov, and then to the sectarian-socialist prophet Vasily Siutaev (who was also a major influence on Lev Tolstoy), and further, to those sectarians whom Siniavsky met in the camp. Expanding on these variegated themes, Siniavsky developed his method that I would define as a playful combination of historicism, mysticism, and ironism. This combination characterized his writings from the precamp *Liubimov* up to the Parisian treatises, but it grew into a full-fledged method in the camp. In one letter from there, he formulated this method as "twisting the primitive into surrealism." This method should be different from "the intellectual-modernist formation" because Siniavsky preferred the "ancient, age-old forms of expression that are close to the elemental nature of magical thinking." After the disappointments of the Thaw, ethnography and folklore were coming into fashion among the intelligentsia. "Demonstration of eternal dreams, fears, and desires . . . [t]he totemic principle . . . [t]he resurgence of the myth . . . [a] deep, unfathomable connection to the folk beliefs" (1:356–357).

From this program of "twisting the primitive into surrealism" followed Siniavsky's mystical readings of Pushkin and Gogol as well as the interpretations of Communism as a religion and revolution as apocalypse, which organize his Parisian books and essays. Sometimes Siniavsky was perceived as a Slavophile, a word that he eagerly applied to himself.[49] What distinguished him from the nineteenth-century Slavophiles was his longing for Russian sects rather than for Orthodox religion. He shared this predilection with one of his heroes, Rozanov, but even for the latter the sects were largely a bookish fantasy.[50] After meeting sectarians in the camp and taking part in their secret liturgies, Siniavsky had planned to write a full-scale novel about these sectarians, but completed only a course of lectures on the subject.[51] "The Khlysty are the most interesting sect in Russia,"[52] Siniavsky told his Parisian students, who surely must have found it difficult to follow him into this territory. He probably inherited a general interest in popular sects and cults from his father; this interest fueled his early, precamp preoccupation with Gorky, also a lay expert in the Khlysty. However, this interest acquired historical grounding, ethnographic material, and intellectual confidence in the camp. Then, he saw the Khlysty everywhere, particularly in his favorite books. After rereading *The Brothers Karamazov* in the camp, Siniavsky wrote that Dostoevsky was "definitely close to the Khlysty," in contrast to Tolstoy, who gravitated toward rationalistic sects. Gogol in his later years also "revealed his Khlysty motifs" (3:390). On himself, Siniavsky tried out another sectarian theme: "If I were a Skopets—how much more I could have done!"[53]

Occupying about half of *Ivan the Fool* and a part of *Soviet Civilization*, these sectarian motifs were fed by Siniavsky's camp experience. The conclusion to *Ivan the Fool* describes his sectarian friends in the camp. One was the leader of the *Skrytniki* (Hiders), another an Adventist, and still another a follower of the nineteenth-century prophet Captain Ilyin. A group of Orthodox believers met regularly to recite the Apocalypse by heart. Ecstatic Pentecostals prayed in tongues. "I thought lightning would strike me in the back of the head.... They proclaimed to the whole world—in all its languages at once—what it meant to talk to God in a torture chamber."[54] This was Siniavsky's spiritual home: a coal pit where semiliterate convicts prayed in invented languages and recited the Apocalypse by heart. This mysticism was hidden deep beneath the Soviet soil. It took a stouthearted author to descend to hell to discover it.

Croaking

Siniavsky's wife made a distinction between death in the camp and death in civil life: in civil life people die, in the camp they croak (*dokhnut*). Osip Mandelstam, for example, croaked, she said.[55] Since life in the camp was not human life, death there was not human death. The difference was social and also temporal. In civil life death is a boundary, an instantaneous turn from one condition to another. There is no gray zone here. It is different in the camp, where there is nothing but the gray zone. "Dying alive is worse than death," writes Siniavsky in his essay on Shalamov. "Death in Kolyma was dispersed in time and space. Here death was drawn out over many years and thousands of kilometers." A gradual loss of life turned people into "building material with which the builders could do whatever they liked." Whether this was life or death, it was not a human condition. "Shalamov writes as though he were dead," states Siniavsky.[56] In his Siberian servitude, Dostoevsky experienced the same "passage through death."[57] Life in the camp was worse than death for two reasons, writes Siniavsky. The first reason was the victim's pain, the second was survivor's guilt: "in the condition of Kolyma, every life was egotism, a sin, the murder of one's neighbor."[58] People create art, wrote Siniavsky from the camp, "for the sake of overcoming death, but also in rapt anticipation of death" (1:64). Art is "just a histrionic one-man-show in the face of death" (2:377). Or—for the unluckiest—of croaking.

In light of Shalamov's and Siniavsky's witnessing, bare life of the goners should more properly be called monstrous life. Life in the camp—monstrous life between life and death—knows only the movement toward death. This is why, in the camp, Pushkin was construed as a ghoul, Gogol was imagined alive in his coffin, and the neighbors looked like ghosts: it was the camp. In 1974 in Paris, Siniavsky claimed that the camp was the most important theme of Russian literature of the time. "The Russian writer's heart doesn't burn . . . for agricultural or industrial themes right now. He is concerned with other themes: how people get put away, where they're sent into exile, how exactly (it's interesting, after all!) they're shot in the back of the head."[59] Russian books have always been written in blood. An author is the writing dead. The literary form has a shape of a coffin. This is how Siniavsky distributed his monstrous metaphors. His picture of "the literary process in Russia" built on his recent strolls with ghosts:

"The camp theme is leading and central today.... Now all of Russia is howling in the House of the Dead."[60] In this focus, Siniavsky was different even from his beloved Rozanov. A model for modern Russian writers, Rozanov was always eager to explain human actions as manifestations of sexuality. In contrast, Siniavsky understood even the sexual act itself in the context of death and memory. Describing the annual visits his wife made to the camp, he rendered the rhythm and meaning of the sex act as an act of memory: "Remember before the end. Until the end. Remember. Remember. Understand and remember."[61]

The voices of the dead speaking through the lips of the half-dead—this is how Siniavsky saw the Russian literature of his time. "And they're moving, they're on the move now. As long as I live, as long as we all live—they will go on and on."[62] They were prisoners at the gates of the camp, and they were either leaving the camp or trying to find their way back to it, we never know which. For Siniavsky, the author is a medium who speaks with both the dead and the living, on behalf of both. "The living owe a debt to the dead." This is why the Russian author feels most at home in a prison or a madhouse, said Siniavsky. "He sits there quietly ... and he rejoices: here is my story!" Like Gogol to the cemetery, Siniavsky was drawn to the camp.

7

The Cosmopolitan Way

In 1939, the famous filmmaker Grigory Kozintsev started work on a biographical film about Karl Marx. Eloquently and sincerely, he expressed his admiration for Marx, a prophet of the victorious revolution. But the film was never realized. There were rumors that Kozintsev fainted while giving a progress report on this film project to Joseph Stalin.[1] An experimental, futurist filmmaker in the 1920s, a leader of the "cheerful generation that created the Soviet cinema,"[2] Kozintsev embraced the theory and practice of the Marxist revolution in Russia. However, his disenchantment grew steadily over the subsequent decades. Like his Marxist beliefs in Stalin's presence, Kozintsev's early support for the socialist experiment did not survive the long decades of Soviet rule. In this chapter, I argue that mourning for the victims of the regime *and* mourning for revolutionary ideas were both crucial for the films that Kozintsev directed during the late-Soviet period. The next generation of intellectuals and filmmakers, who came of age during the Thaw, would go on to subvert this complex condition of *double mourning*.

Local Victims

Kozintsev is known most widely for his screen versions of *Hamlet* (1964) and *King Lear* (1970). These austere, black-and-white versions of Shakespeare in Boris Pasternak's translation and with scores by Dmitry Shostakovich have been recognized as major cultural achievements of the

Soviet period. At the end of his career, Kozintsev, a laureate of two Stalin Prizes and one Lenin Prize, was the most important filmmaker in Leningrad. By all indications, this success was genuine. While Kozintsev's films were screened at Shakespeare events in England, a Tajik film studio produced a documentary about screening his *Hamlet* for mountaineers in Pamir.[3] Clearly, Kozintsev had succeeded in finding a language that was comprehensible to various audiences on both sides of the Iron Curtain. He was a hugely influential figure in Soviet cinema, teaching the leading filmmakers of the later period, Eldar Riazanov and Aleksei German, and inspiring others such as Andrei Tarkovsky and Aleksandr Sokurov.[4]

From his eccentric experiments that made him famous in the 1920s, Kozintsev turned to ironic films in the 1930s and then to insipid biopics in the 1950s. Up to this point, the trajectory of Kozinstev's career is unsurprising for the historian of Soviet film, but his Shakespearean turn in the 1960s was unique. Kozinstev was also unusual in that, apart from his lifelong filmmaking, he was a prolific scholar and author who wrote many volumes of essays and memoirs. While some of his books were published in the Soviet period and some were translated into English, many additional writings have been published after his death and some only after the collapse of the Soviet Union.[5] In important ways, Kozintsev's thoughts and feelings were parallel to those that were documented in the letters and conversations of his friend and associate Dmitry Shostakovich. Both managed to combine success in the Soviet artistic world with a consistent, self-conscious protest against the Soviet oppression, and both revealed their political sentiments within the established conventions of their arts. While the credibility of some of the Shostakovich reminiscences is controversial, the authenticity of the Kozintsev notes has never been questioned. Apart from the editors who assiduously prepared these documents for publication, scholars have paid little attention to these materials, a striking contrast with the furious debates generated by Shostakovich's "Testimony."[6]

Like Shostakovich, Kozintsev was not "repressed" himself, but was witness to many campaigns of Soviet terror and their impact on his family and friends. Kozintsev's childhood friend and scriptwriter Aleksei Kapler was arrested for courting Stalin's daughter, Svetlana, and spent eleven years in the camps. Kozintsev's mother-in-law, Olga Ivanovna, a longtime secretary to Viktor Shklovsky, was arrested in 1937 and spent ten years in the camps. She was arrested again in 1949 and spent seven more years in the Arctic, near Vorkuta. As in myriad other cases, the circumstances of her second arrest were routine: "They called [Kozintsev] and said, pick up your child. We are coming after your mother-in-law."[7] For years, the family received two letters a year from her. At one point Kapler, who happened to be serving his second term in the same camp, saved her life by helping her to get an office job working for the camp administration.

Kozintsev was also friends with Solomon Mikhoels, an actor and theater director who shared Kozintsev's interest in Shakespeare and was famous for his staging of *King Lear*. Mikhoels founded and led the Jewish Anti-Fascist Committee, an organization that helped Stalin to attract worldwide sympathy during World War II.[8] Mikhoels's assassination by the secret police in 1948 signaled the start of a major anti-Semitic campaign waged during Stalin's last years. Kozintsev was also close to Ilya Ehrenburg, a charismatic writer who was married to Kozintsev's sister. It was Ehrenburg who coined the term "Thaw" for Russia's post-Stalinist condition.[9]

Born in Kiev in 1905, Kozintsev entered an elite gymnasium under the Jewish quota system; in his notes, he richly documented his hatred toward this school, which haunted him for many decades. A leader of the Soviet avant-garde, Nathan Altman, trained him as an artist. After the revolution of 1917, Kozintsev met Vsevolod Meyerhold and Sergei Eisenstein, the towering figures of the Soviet theater and cinema, respectively. Kozintsev adored Meyerhold, who was arrested and killed in 1940, and used to say that Meyerhold would have been the best person to play King Lear. In his memoir about Eisenstein, Kozintsev called him a friend rather than a teacher. Only seven years younger than Eisenstein, Kozintsev lived significantly longer and now seems more like our contemporary. He watched the ideological campaign against Eisenstein with disgust and took a risk by writing encouraging letters to him. Kozintsev was equally compassionate when another brilliant friend, Shostakovich, became a target of ideological attacks.

Throughout his life, Kozintsev was close to the leading Soviet literary scholars, whom he recruited to write screenplays for his films. Some of these people were arrested; the survivors were targets of ideological campaigns. Adrian Piotrovsky, a charismatic classicist who wrote screenplays for Kozintsev's films, died in jail. The philologist Matvei Gukovsky,

Kozintsev's close friend, also died in jail. Yulian Oksman, another philologist who wrote scripts for Kozintsev, served ten years in the Kolyma camps. Yet another friend from the world of literary scholarship, the Renaissance scholar Leonid Pinsky, served five years. Kozintsev survived the successive waves of terror in 1937 and again in the campaign against the Jewish "cosmopolitans" in 1949, when many in his circle were arrested, hounded, or sacked. On dozens of films Kozintsev worked with the same cameraman, artist, composer, and even fencing instructor. Some of them world-famous and others unknown, they were randomly cut down by the terror along with the rest of the Soviet elite. Yevgeny Yenei, the artist who worked for Kozintsev on many films, was arrested in 1938 and also served years in the camps. Kozintsev saw his longtime friend and coauthor Leonid Trauberg scapegoated and sacked; Shostakovich, Ehrenburg, Tynianov, and many others were all under threat, until they were saved by Stalin's death. When Kozintsev's mother-in-law finally returned home in 1956, Kozintsev told his wife that they should never argue with her, given how much she had suffered.[10] Observing the amazing events that followed Stalin's death, Kozintsev wrote to his student in May 1956, after one of the chiefs of Stalinist culture, Aleksandr Fadeev, committed suicide: "An era of shame has started in the arts."[11]

Kozintsev shunned official titles and never led a Soviet organization larger than his filmmaking workshop in Leningrad. At the peak of the Thaw, in June 1960, Shostakovich experienced a crisis when offered a position as chairman of the Union of Composers, on condition that he also enter the Communist Party. After desperate resistance, Shostakovich accepted the offer.[12] Luckily, Kozintsev escaped making such a choice.

The Overcoat

Writing in the 1950s, a friend noted that the 1920s had endowed Kozintsev with his "snobbish, aristocratic nature": in the disillusioned world of post-Stalinism, maintaining the values of the revolutionary years was perceived as personal vanity.[13] But Kozintsev's continued identification with that time was central to his artistic life. Many of his coauthors, such as Shostakovich, and his literary friends, the formalists like Yury Tynianov, were also "people of the twenties."[14]

The most successful among Kozintsev's early films, *The Overcoat* (1926), ridiculed the social hierarchy of the old regime. The film was based on Nikolai Gogol's short story; Tynianov, an expert in Gogol who had authored pioneering studies of prototype and parody in the 1920s, wrote the script.[15] In the film, as in the story, the protagonist cherishes a new coat, which is then stolen by thieves. Played by Aleksei Kapler, a Very Important Person refuses to investigate the crime. Deprived of his coat and illusions, the protagonist dies of sorrow. A hapless Oedipus who fails to resolve the puzzle of power, he is portrayed questioning the enormous Sphinx of St. Petersburg in one of the most expressive scenes of early Soviet cinema. With its obvious dependence on Weimar film, *The Overcoat* is human and funny. In the end, however, something shocking happens or rather, does not happen. The powerful ending of Gogol's story is entirely omitted. At the end of Gogol's *The Overcoat*, the protagonist rises from the dead and, as a gigantic specter, roams the streets of St. Petersburg, taking revenge on the city's inhabitants. This wandering specter steals one overcoat after another and disappears only after he scares and robs the very same official who refused to help the protagonist in his last struggle. This scene, sentimental but subversive, contributed to the incredible popularity of *The Overcoat* in the Russian literary tradition. A Gogolian premonition of the revolution, the specter from *The Overcoat* (1842) has an organic place among the other great ghosts of world literature, from the ghost of Hamlet's father to the specter of Communism haunting Europe in the *Communist Manifesto* (1848). The difference is, however, that Gogol's ghost is not tragic or threatening but rather ironic, maybe even parodic. With subtle humor, Gogol presaged Marx's image of the wandering specter of Communism by demonstrating the futility of this hope.

The 1926 film replaced Gogol's public apparition, which is visible to the whole city, with the clerk's private deathbed visions that have nothing to do with retribution. Whether the reason was technical limitations or ideological self-restrictions, the eccentric hallucinations of Kozintsev's dying clerk were far inferior to Gogol's unbridled imagery. Interestingly, Kozintsev's friend, the literary scholar Boris Eikhenbaum, in his famous essay on Gogol's *The Overcoat* (1919), also chose to omit its final scene from his analysis. The consistency of this postrevolutionary misreading of *The Overcoat* is striking.[16] After the long-awaited revolution came to pass, it wiped out this last refuge of utopian hope, effectively rendering this key scene from Gogol off-limits. From now on, an overly faithful reading of Gogol's story ran the risk of parodying the revolution itself.

Gogol's imagery haunted Kozintsev for decades. In his later productions, he substituted Gogol's self-mocking fantasy of ultimate retribution with Shakespearean tragic, self-sacrificial justice. However, at the end of his life, Kozintsev was preoccupied with plans for a new film, *Gogoliada*. In his later notes, Kozintsev returned to *The Overcoat* again and again, as if he thought that his debt to Gogol had not been paid: "It was difficult to think about the past as reality: the past felt like a mirage.... These [Gogol] stories strike us with their combination of plausibility and nightmare.... It was evident: the social structure resembles a nightmare, the state is dead." When Solzhenitsyn's famous story about a small man in the gulag first came out in a Soviet journal, Kozintsev compared it, as "equal in scale," to Gogol's *The Overcoat*.[17]

In several volumes of his published notes, Kozintsev was absorbed in classical Russian authors from Gogol to Tolstoy. In an entry from 1971, he acknowledged his increasing alienation from the contemporary cinema, both in the USSR and the West, and continued:

One day, and after much sorrow, I realized that I have inherited not the American 20th century, with comic characters fighting policemen and escaping across rooftops, but the Russian 19th century, with the unbearably sick conscience of its art, with the martyrdom of Gogol and Dostoevsky... with its feeling of co-responsibility, its enormous bleeding wounds.[18]

In the 1960s, Kozintsev's project consisted of "re-reading Shakespeare after Dostoevsky" and not after Marx. He believed that Russian classical literature helped him to represent the scenes of suffering and desolation that were a major part of his Shakespearean films. Late in life, Kozintsev contemplated making a film about Lev Tolstoy's final flight, a tragic story of his terminal going-to-the-people. His Shakespearean films show kings and princes, not the masses; when we do see "the masses," the picture is usually a repulsive one. Disenchanted with the basic Marxist ideas such as class warfare or economic determinism, he did not use them in his essays and did not integrate them into his films. Arguably, there is more Marxism in John Madden's *Shakespeare in Love* than in Kozintsev's *Hamlet*.

The task that Kozintsev set for himself illuminated the ambiguous plotlines of the English Bard with the conscientious, guilt-ridden sensitivity of the Russian *intelligent*, who felt his responsibility for the suffering of millions of Soviets just as his nineteenth-century forebears felt their responsibility for the suffering of millions of serfs. However, Kozintsev did not repudiate the rationality and faith in historical progress that were intrinsic for Marxism. Like many of his friends, Kozintsev was a convinced atheist, a belief system that was necessitated not only by his Soviet allegiance but also by his hybrid Russian-Jewish experience. In its practical application, this post-Marxist but still secular framework resulted in a sublime understanding of high culture that was uniquely endowed with meaning that had previously been invested in religion and ideology. Secularizing both Shakespeare and Dostoevsky meant that their religious themes were interpreted in purely human ways, political and moral. In Kozintsev's *Hamlet* and *Lear*, famous scenes became unusually earthly: ghosts are full-bodied, hesitations are resolved, wars are bloody and dirty, life is bare and meaningless, and the division of the state is a utopian project doomed to meet an ignoble end.

We do not know much about the extent to which censorship restrained the mature Kozintsev, and whether he would have made similar films if he had been perfectly free to define them. One of his friends, a much-experienced playwright, believed that Kozintsev had never been able to do what he wanted.[19] Kozintsev's own private notes do not corroborate this statement. In fact, the scale and financing of his Shakespearian productions were generous, and his use of Shakespeare to formulate his feelings about his life and the world was his choice. Inside of this framework he was not particularly restricted.

In his writings on Shakespeare as well as in his films, Kozintsev insisted that his ideal was not historical accuracy but rather a self-conscious modernization of the classical text. Having found in Shakespeare an adequate cultural idiom—resonant, cosmopolitan, and ambitious—Kozintsev used every chance to tell his audiences that his interest in Shakespeare was not antiquarian. Shakespeare is our contemporary, he wrote; in *Hamlet* and *Lear*, Shakespeare had found solutions to the "most important issues of our time." These tragedies contain much that "resembles us" and much that does not; Kozintsev saw his task as highlighting the resemblances and downplaying the differences. After the success of *Hamlet*, Kozintsev was invited to spend a year in England to make another film. The trip never happened, but his widow remembers a revealing dialogue. Let's go to England, she said, at least we will spend a year in decent conditions. But Kozintsev responded that he could never have made such a *Hamlet* in England. His wife rendered his explanation: "Indeed, he could do it only here, because his *Hamlet* was a direct response to our life."[20] The next film, *Lear*, was also a success: "a bloody melodrama," Kozintsev wrote, in which blood poured "as if from a fireman's hose." This genre, melodrama, should return to the screen if cinema was to be true to the twentieth century: "Bloody melodrama has become routine; it has become our everyday existence; it is no more exceptional than drinking tea in Chekhov."[21]

Interestingly, at the end of his life Kozintsev still understood his method as the legacy of the revolution. It was the revolution in Russia that "violated, exploded, leveled" the boundary between life and art. "The spirit of the new art was in the perfect merger of these spheres," wrote Kozintsev; after the revolution, art and life were one.[22] This is a distant echo of a thesis of total art, which aspired to transform all aspects of life in an act of artistic theurgy. In Kozintsev's post-Stalinist version of this thesis, however, the focus shifted to the victims of this attempted transformation. "There should be no demarcation line between the people of Shakespeare and the people in our audience, between the suffering on the screen and the memory of suffering in life," wrote Kozintsev in 1971.

From Remembrance to Vengeance

Watching Kozintsev's *Hamlet*, one cannot fail to see the subversively ironic treatment of earthly power, embodied in Claudius. Living and dying among his portraits, Claudius is full of himself, always pompous and silly.[23] I see in this *Hamlet* not only an allegorical protest against a criminal state but also a mourning play for its victims.

Hamlet is unusually decisive in this film, and so is the ghost of his father. Kozintsev was critical of the many attempts to produce *Hamlet* without the ghost. Providing historical examples, he argued that Shakespeare's contemporaries understood the apparitions of ghosts as signs of coming catastrophes. "The ghost is the herald of national disasters.... Everything in Denmark is going to ruin." Like Jacques Derrida but much earlier,

Kozintsev connected the ghost of Hamlet's father with the specter from the *Communist Manifesto*: "Marx recalled Hamlet speaking to the specter and purposely made it an image of the continual, subterranean work of history." The ghost is memory, commented Kozintsev, and this "metaphor is literal": in *Hamlet*, he speculated, those who remembered the dead king saw his ghost, while those who had forgotten the king did not. Contrasting Hamlet's "spirit of Wittenberg" to Claudius's "spirit of Elsinore," Kozintsev espoused his own historical experience: "In many eras, the finest men knew despair and lofty dreams proved futile. The time came when the heavy cannon of Elsinore dispersed the ideas of Wittenberg." Now, he wrote, a modern Elsinore was once again eager to enclose "humanity into concentration camps."[24]

A political reading of the ghost of the father constituted the core of Kozintsev's version of *Hamlet*. Wanting revenge for himself and redemption for his country, this armored ghost with a doubling visor is a symptom of the crisis but also a promise of overcoming it. From the ghost, Hamlet learns the truth that every son of a catastrophe wants to learn about his dead father—and ideally, *from* him. "The ghost reveals for Hamlet the truth about life, as if he lifts the curtain over Denmark the prison, and everything becomes clearly visible."[25]

Like Derrida but much earlier, Kozintsev found it important that the ghost came to Hamlet in his combat armor. For Derrida, the ghost's armor is prosthetic: "We do not know whether it is or is not part of the spectral apparition. . . . The armor may be but the body of the spectral artifact, a kind of technical prosthesis." For Kozintsev's film, historical armor was borrowed from a museum. It was so heavy that a champion wrestler was recruited to carry it. Moreover, Kozintsev chose an unusual helmet, with an open visor that had the shape of a human face. Derrida wrote about the visor that "even when it is raised," it signifies "that someone, beneath the armor, can safely see without being seen," which for Derrida is "perhaps the supreme insignia of power." The visor that emulates a human face in Kozintsev's *Hamlet* deepens this paradoxical, prosthetic function of the ghost's armor even further. Again, this doubling of the face of the dead father matches Derrida's dictum that ghosts do not come alone and that by its nature, a specter is "more than one."[26]

Russian scholars deciphered Kozintsev's message immediately after the film's victorious premiere in Soviet and Western cinemas. "Life's

FIGURE 9. The ghost of the father in a helmet with a visor in *Hamlet* (1964), a film by Grigory Kozintsev.

pretexts fade away, but their spiritual consequences do not," wrote the aspiring film critic Maia Turovskaia. Appropriately called "Hamlet and Us," her review was published in the same issue of the *Novyi mir* that discussed, in glowing terms, Solzhenitsyn's *One Day in the Life of Ivan Denisovich*. According to Turovskaia's masterful analysis, different tragedies emerged on the Soviet stage at different moments. In the 1930s, the Soviet theater presented *Othello* as the symbol of "a bloody but fair retribution." At the time, Othello looked so wholesome that even the murder of Desdemona "did not look like a murder." Despite his blind mistake, this Othello demonstrated, as Turovskaia put it, "the splendor of simplicity and the innocence of greatness." While this Othello was the hero, Hamlet was accused of "Hamletism," a form of bad nerves combined with the inability to act. Turovskaia juxtaposed two plays of revenge, *Othello* and *Hamlet*, by connecting them with two Soviet eras, *Othello* with the 1930s and *Hamlet* with the 1960s.[27] "It was 1954," wrote Turovskaia, "that became a breakthrough in the stage history of *Hamlet*" in the USSR. She explored the decade after Stalin's death as the maturation of the Soviet *Hamlet*, from Kozintsev's theater version of 1954 to his film version of 1964. "This *Hamlet* does not require particular erudition or volumes of commentaries."[28]

Kozintsev imagined Hamlet as his compatriot who survived the terror to find himself a foreigner in his own country. "Hamlet is a pre-1937 man," he wrote, using this year to signify the Great Terror.[29] "Pre-1937 men" would also be a good description for the coauthors of this *Hamlet*, its director Kozintsev, translator Pasternak, and composer Shostakovich, all of whom miraculously survived the terror, physically and psychologically (the fourth member of their team, artist Yevgeny Yenei, had been arrested in 1938). Like Hamlet, they all had the energy to mourn their dead. As Turovskaia noted, Kozintsev was far from the Russian theatrical tradition of presenting Hamlet as a weak, hesitant embodiment of "Hamletism": Kozintsev "does not argue with the 19th century concept of hamletism—he ignores it."[30] Played by Innokenty Smoktunovsky, a veteran of World War II who marched from Kursk to Berlin, this Hamlet was not young.[31] In Shakespeare he is thirty years old, in some Soviet versions he looked eighteen, but Smoktunovsky was about forty and looked even older. In *Hamlet*, Smoktunovsky played himself—a survivor of the Great Terror, a soldier of a great war, a man who perceives his country as a prison though he does not know the reason or remedy for this state of affairs. He searches for both, and we watch this epistemological process, which is closer to a military reconnaissance than to a display of neurotic incapacity. This is a focused, intellectual Hamlet who creatively uses various tools, from the ghost to the theater, to crack the mystery of his fate. He does not hesitate to take revenge, but he wreaks it only after he accomplishes his task of learning. In Kozintsev's film, Hamlet's meditative monologues were largely omitted, a fact that surprised some critics. But the scenes of exploration and revenge were shown in detail, and with full sympathy.[32]

For Turovskaia, Hamlet lays claims to the "human right to spiritual complexity." The decade after the death of Stalin, which was also the decade when Kozintsev transferred his *Hamlet* from the stage to the screen, was a time of tremendous growth in the perceived complexity of the world. Acknowledgment of this complexity had nothing to do with indecisiveness. The opposite was true; after the Thaw was over, it was simple minds in the Soviet leadership that manifested hesitation and indecision. Understanding the crimes of the past was the purpose of the Thaw, a time of exploration and mourning. Turovskaia claimed that Kozintsev's Hamlet was neither a tragic hero nor a romantic one; he was an "*intelligent* hero." But of course this Hamlet was not a typical representative of the Soviet intelligentsia; he was rather its collective ego-ideal. Succeeding in his heroic, self-sacrificial act of revenge, he was not only a scholar but also a warrior. It was in the double nature of the scholar-warrior, which

Smoktunovsky rendered so beautifully, that the complexity of this Hamlet was rooted. Grieving the father and interrogating his ghost, Hamlet took revenge, an action that the Soviet intelligentsia was barely capable of contemplating in the 1960s. According to Stephen Greenblatt, generations of critics have observed the "startling Shakespearean shift from vengeance to remembrance" in *Hamlet*. Kozintsev's film puts this shift into reverse. In many details, it choreographs Hamlet's revenge against his uncle (revenge that, in the film as in the play, also destroys his mother, his beloved woman and her kin, his two friends, and the avenger himself) as a heroic but inescapable action, something that ought to happen in the given circumstances. It is in this call for remembrance *and* revenge that this Soviet *Hamlet* stands out in the long tradition of interpreting and performing the tragedy.[33]

Those who survive the bloody massacre, the local scholar who would tell the sad story and the foreign invader who would occupy the desolated land, seem to agree that this Hamlet is a hero and that his deed is justified. Together, they stage the high point of this *Hamlet*, its most successful scene, a funeral that lasts about ten minutes at the end of the film. Based on a one-line description in Shakespeare's tragedy, this funeral is a product of Kozintsev's fantasy. Fortinbras gives Hamlet military honors, as one soldier to another, and then the funeral starts, scored with Shostakovich's music, which reaches the peak of its unbearable intensity in the last moments of the film. Kozintsev had in mind an even better story:

I had a good alternative for *Hamlet's* finale: the wall of Elsinore . . . slowly, the ghost of the father is walking along and after him, proceeds Hamlet, i.e. the ghost of the son. Military patrols are saluting them.[34]

Even as staged, the final scene of Kozintsev's *Hamlet* was a powerful, sublime mourning ceremony. Posthumously, Hamlet completed his work of mourning, which had remained tragically unaccomplished while he was alive. With this powerful scene, Kozintsev transfigured a Shakespearean orgy of revenge into a Soviet dream of mourning. It was his personal desire but it was also a collective project, a drive to give a decent funeral to the unmourned Soviet dead, one generation deferred.

The World after Catastrophe

Eagerly historicizing his work, Kozintsev wrote in 1968: "the year in which I was working on *Lear*: there was war . . . people were killed . . . whole districts were burnt down . . . students revolted . . . the tanks rolled into the town." Responding with his *Lear* to the war in Vietnam, the Soviet invasion in Czechoslovakia, and the global student unrest, Kozintsev pursued the same strategy he had employed in *Hamlet*: the double movement of modernizing Shakespeare and interpreting the Soviet condition. In his private notes, Kozintsev also characterized his film as a new commentary on the Apocalypse. "The Sermon is over. What remains? The smell of ashes and the echo of crying." His anxiety and mourning were intense and unmistakable, his imagery shocking: "Lear and Cordelia in captivity: the terror and humiliation of a concentration camp. Barbed wire, dogs, machine guns. Humanity, herded like cattle."[35]

Kozintsev's *King Lear* had a powerful predecessor: the 1935 version by the State Jewish Theater, with his friend Solomon Mikhoels playing the king. Mikhoels reinterpreted *King Lear,* driven by his insight about the resemblance between Lear and Lev Tolstoy. Lear left his kingdom as Tolstoy left his house, stated Mikhoels. His tragic *Lear* was hugely successful and, in hindsight, prophetic. Mikhoels's murder on Stalin's orders in 1948 signaled the collapse of state-sponsored Jewish culture in the USSR. Many arrests of Jewish activists and cultural figures followed, and rumors about the imminent deportation of Soviet Jews to newly built camps near the Chinese border started to circulate right after Mikhoels's murder. When the news of Mikhoels's "sudden death" became public, Kozintsev was staying in Moscow with Ehrenburg, who was also a prominent member of the Jewish Anti-Fascist Committee. The two men remained silent at the news, but Valentina Kozintseva ran around the room in a panic. Ehrenburg quipped, "No Jews are more orthodox than these Russian wives."[36] Looking at the photographs of Mikhoels as Lear, one immediately detects a strong resemblance to the Lear in Kozintsev's film. Like Mikhoels, Kozintsev was fascinated by Tolstoy's departure from home; in fact, he abandoned a film project about this event to shoot *Lear* instead, effectively swapping one for the other. The 1968 film became a monument to Mikhoels, who saw in his performance a monument to Tolstoy.

Kozintsev's *Lear* continues the major themes of his *Hamlet*: the obscenity of power, the truth found in personal relations, and a finale starring a funeral of the central character. In *Lear*, this funeral became double, thus implementing Kozintsev's unrealized plan for *Hamlet*'s finale: slowly, ceremoniously, the dead bodies of the king and his daughter pass by the military patrols. The slow action of the film develops the idea of Lear's spiritual regeneration after his abdication, but then the focus shifts onto the broad picture of the collapse of the state and the catastrophe as experienced by the people. With his new experience of suffering, Lear starts to understand the world, the people, and his daughter. This is Shakespeare read after Dostoevsky, and also after Khrushchev.

The chain is broken, it could not be otherwise because order is already dead, an illusion. Underneath lies total collapse and everything is rolling, tumbling, turning to confusion. . . . Space and people are at one in this commotion.[37]

Combining *Lear* with Dostoevsky's *Notes from the House of the Dead*, Kozintsev wrote, "The King of Britain has ended up in a hut on a penal settlement." Unlike Hamlet, who dies as a prince, Lear suffers the full and complete collapse of his status. He descends from the very top to the very bottom of the social ladder, from king to pariah, from sovereign to bare life. This top-down transfiguration is symbolic: "Does it not happen in time of revolutions, coup d'etats, and wars, that those who held power find themselves behind barbed wire? . . . We can bear witness: this has happened . . . to many thousands." This *Lear* is unusually interested in the depiction of the bottom: the hapless Lear, the poor Thom, and the blind Gloucester merge with those who have always wandered across the miserable land. In these long, slow scenes, Kozintsev showed the meaningless life of the people. Treated like cattle, they live like cattle; they can be killed but not sacrificed. Having been reduced to this bare life, Lear has been transformed; in fact, he is unrecognizable. This is why at the end of the play, the soldiers cannot find Lear: "the difficulty was not in finding Lear but in recognizing him," Kozintsev wrote.

Here, at the very bottom of existence, the tempest has thrown one who was on the very top of the social pyramid. Here, in the midst of this miserable life that mixes dirt, straw, beggars and men, Lear asks his question, is it true that the bare man is just a bipedal animal?[38]

Kozintsev made a great deal of effort to modernize the action of *Lear* in line with his principle "Shakespeare is our contemporary," and to provide it with a catastrophic, apocalyptic, twentieth-century dimension. There are no ghosts in this film, but human transformations are dramatic, eerie, and unjustified. Some characters undergo the full-range transition from the highs of power to the lows of misery; some characters lift themselves from the very bottom to the very top, only to fall again. People are unhappy, Kozintsev speculated, not because of the fate of humankind, an idea that he associated with "citations from Kafka and Camus, the jeans and the black sweater," the symbols of existentialism. People are miserable because of the policies of the state, which he associated with barbed wire, handcuffs, and prison bars.[39] In his private notes, Kozintsev explicitly stated that the dynamic that he saw in *Lear* was typical of Soviet life, with its banal *and* extraordinary character: "Much of what we have seen with our own eyes, of what is taught in schools, of what people talk about in the subway, is similar to the tragedy of Lear."[40] Both a victim *and* an agent of the crime, Lear triggered the catastrophe with his own action. The film presents Lear's move to divide his kingdom as a well-meaning but ill-fated project, a study in the unintended consequences of utopian politics. In the course of the film, Lear comes to accept this responsibility, a lesson for the Soviet public.

"The world after catastrophe"—this is how Kozintsev described the physical setting where he wanted his *Lear* to be shot. He searched across the enormous Soviet space for this setting. Some scenes he shot on the wild rocks of the Crimea and others on the wasted mounds of shale in Estonia. In many ways, this Soviet *Lear* was an imperial production. Performed in Russian, the film featured very few Russian actors or landscapes. While scenes were shot in the exotic environments of Soviet colonial domains in the north and south, most members of the cast were Baltic—Lithuanian and Estonian—actors. Among those who played the central characters, only Lear's daughters and the Fool were ethnically Russian. Astonishingly, the actor who played Lear did not even speak Russian and was dubbed. The set designer was Georgian, and the cameraman was Lithuanian (the composer was, as always, Shostakovich). Prophetically, Kozintsev imagined Lear's decision to divide his kingdom as a premonition of the dividing of the Soviet Union, which he did not live to see. "The Duke of Cornwall and the Duke of Albany are rulers of particular, separate peoples, who resemble one another no more than the Georgians resemble the Lithuanians," he wrote.[41] In *Hamlet*, Kozintsev settled his accounts with the past; in *Lear*, he anticipated the future. As a result, we watch not only tragedies of mourning and revenge but also the drama of a changing political order, which leads to social catastrophe. But viewers associated Kozintsev's *Lear* with the Soviet past: "our recent past with its bloody, scary events, war, fire, destruction, and suffering."[42] The future was unknown, and though in retrospect mourning so often feels associated with warning, contemporaries tend to respond only to the first part of this equation.

Beware the Fool

Though the action of *Lear* is generally clear, there are moments of complete irrationality in the film, bizarre action that cannot be explained or justified. Such is the scene of the funeral of the Duke of Cornwall, when his wife unexpectedly kisses his dead lips with an open mouth, as if she were a vampire from the Weimar films that Kozintsev adored in his youth. Paradoxically, Kozintsev believed that this subtle play on the edge of reality brings the action closer to the contemporary world.

I often see my task as transforming some consistent, logical scenes into nightmares. The meaning of these dreams is found not in their distortion of reality. This is the way to approach modern reality: the delusions of coup d'états, mass repressions, murders, and the degeneration of beliefs.[43]

Kozintsev appreciated Bakhtin's idea of carnival, but in his Shakespearean films he created an atmosphere of misery and mourning that had nothing to do with humor. Hamlet's jokes are never funny in Kozintsev's film, and Lear's Fool is sad. "The cry of grief reaches us through time. Grief integrated the people, kept them together. This is why we are making the film, to hear this cry." The overwhelming atmosphere of Kozintsev's versions of Shakespeare is one of sadness. With approval, he described how Shostakovich kept rewriting some of the music for his films so that "it would be even sadder." In this he saw his poetic license: his right to screen this tragedy had been authorized by "the people's misery," he wrote. He wanted to show Lear's tragedy, an extraordinary story by any criteria, in such a way that "everyone would understand: the same or something similar has also happened to me." He wanted to immerse the action of *Lear* not in the beauty of decorations but in "the midst of the people's misery." The proper form of compassion, he said in the spirit of the Soviet 1920s, "means feeling hatred towards the source of misery." But it was grief that he saw in all his favorite authors, in Dostoevsky as well as in Shakespeare: "I do not know what color grief is, or what shades suffering has," wrote Kozintsev. "No matter where man goes, grief is bound to him. . . . The tragic power of history and the grief of everyday life are always inseparable."[44]

This is why Kozintsev made his Shakespearean films black-and-white: the colors of mourning. These films are deadly serious, and even the Fool tells truths rather than jokes. The filmmaker's notes articulate an idea to present the Fool as Lear's hallucination, his exteriorized conscience; Kozintsev compares Lear's conversations with this Fool to Alyosha Karamazov's dialogues with the devil. Like the ghost of the father in *Hamlet*, sometimes this Fool is visible to everyone around and sometimes only to the king. He is a powerful performer, but he is never funny. Kozintsev wrote that this Fool was "a symbol of art under tyranny." The filmmaker acknowledged that his *Hamlet* departed from the classical Shakespearean proportions by "weakening, or even eliminating, everything comic" in the play; the same was true of his *Lear*. Citing Marx, Kozintsev stated that history repeats itself twice, first as tragedy, then as farce. Working on Shakespeare, he added, "in the twilight of civilization, tragedies and farces mix in such a way that they become indistinguishable."[45] Kozintsev was probably wrong about Shakespeare: his comedies are distinct from his tragedies. But perhaps more surprisingly, it turned out that Kozintsev was also wrong when it came to Soviet cinema.

One of his students reformed Kozintsev's mournful tradition and produced sparkling comedies, popular for their humor and clever in the ways they confront and reflect the Soviet twilight. This man was Eldar Riazanov.[46] An experienced teacher, Kozintsev developed a problematic relation with this talented but underperforming student. Riazanov's father was "repressed"; late in his life, Riazanov still talks about his own fear of "the Soviet authorities."[47] According to Riazanov's memoir, Kozintsev was supportive but never warm toward him; upon graduation, they parted ways, not without rivalry it seems. In the symbolic year of 1956—the year of Khrushchev's revelations—Riazanov screened his first commercial comedy, *Carnival Night* (1956).[48] The film celebrates the victory of a group of artistic young people, the emerging post-Stalinist generation with its newfound buoyancy, over a parochial bureaucrat who tries to censor their

New Year's Eve festivities. With a characteristic ambivalence, Riazanov decided against inviting Kozintsev to the premiere of this film, in the hope that the teacher would come of his own accord. When it became clear that Kozintsev was not going to show, Riazanov telephoned him at the last moment and then postponed the show's opening until Kozintsev arrived. When the screening was over, the master told Riazanov, "This is not what I taught you to do."[49]

Riazanov said nothing about Kozintsev's response to another very popular comedy, *Beware of the Car* (1966). He had good reason to be silent, as this film contains a parody of Kozintsev and, in particular, his *Hamlet*. The two films by teacher and student, *Hamlet* and *Beware of the Car*, share one actor, Innokenty Smoktunovsky, who plays Hamlet in both films, the first time as tragedy, the second time as farce. Throughout *Beware of the Car*, *Hamlet* is rehearsed and performed as a play within the play, a kind of latter-day Mousetrap in Shakespear's *Hamlet* that reveals the secret of the larger story.

Set in Moscow, *Beware of the Car* shows a corrupt society where almost everyone benefits from illegal networks of connection and distribution, with a private car being the highest symbol of success and prestige. Smoktunovsky plays the charming maverick and belated utopian, Detochkin. A character whose name connotes childishness, he struggles against corruption and disenchantment by tracking down corrupted functionaries, stealing their cars, selling them on the black market, and sending the money to orphanages. When his schemes are eventually exposed, some condemn him as a criminal, and others dismiss him as crazily naive. Refusing to accept the dystopian message of latter-day Soviet history, this noble savage pursues the radical agenda of the bygone revolutionary generation: expropriation of the expropriators. Like Kozintsev, Detochkin is a man of the 1920s living in the 1960s. He is an anachronism, which makes him funny; but he is also shown to be resourceful, loving, and loved. On top of his robbing and driving skills, he is a talented actor. His auto thefts are interspersed with scenes in which we watch him playing Hamlet as part of an amateur theatrical troupe. Finally, he receives a public trial, a sign of the new era in Soviet justice. A handful of older characters stand by him, the last keepers of the revolutionary flame. His mother is among these outdated supporters; meaningfully, we learn nothing about his absent father.

FIGURE 10. Hamlet and Laertes in *Hamlet* (1964), a film by Grigory Kozintsev. Innokenty Smoktunovsky is playing Hamlet.

A theme of friendship runs through the film. In a little episode, Detochkin asks for the Soviet cigarettes, Belomor, a popular brand whose name brought a lethal agglomeration of labor camps into everyday life. But the cheerful kiosk on a Moscow street has run out of Belomor, and Detochkin satisfies himself with cigarettes called simply Drug (Friend). Make friends, not camps—this could be the slogan of the Thaw, and Detochkin acquires friends even among the law enforcement officers who are investigating his crimes. In the end, of course, these friendships recede before the Soviet law, and Detochkin is sent to serve in the newest version of the gulag. But at the very end he returns to his friends.

Like Hamlet, Detochkin preserves the betrayed values of the generation of the fathers, which brings him into mortal conflict with his corrupted contemporaries. The play that the protagonists prepare, rehearse, and finally perform is *Hamlet*, which encapsulates the action of the film in miniature, just as the Mousetrap scene does in Shakespeare's *Hamlet*. In the amateur theater that is run by two trade unions, the militiamen and the taxi drivers, Detochkin, who plays Hamlet, meets his nemesis, the state investigator who plays Laertes. Together they listen to a long, funny speech in which the director of this theater echoes Detochkin's utopianism: is it not obvious, he asks the audience, that actors who are not paid for their performances do a better job than those who perform for money? Without further ado, the director announces his production of Shakespeare, whom he calls by his first name, just as Kozintsev did in

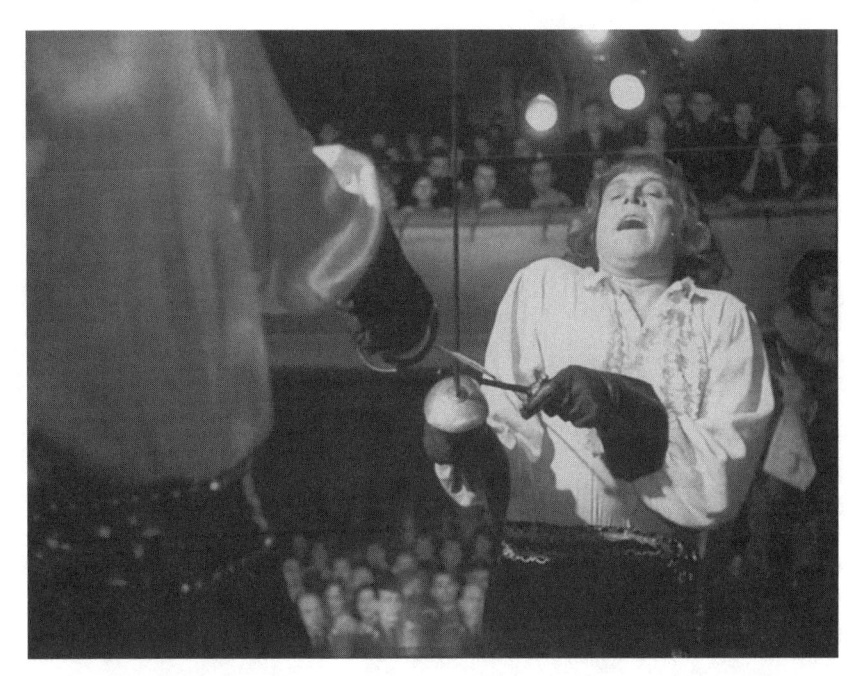

FIGURE 11. Hamlet and Laertes in *Beware of the Car* (1966), a film by Eldar Riazanov. Innokenty Smoktunovsky is playing Detochkin, who is playing Hamlet.

some of his letters. To add to the fun, the director mispronounces William in a very Russian way, starting with V and stressing the second syllable. With his high-pitched voice and the aura of a pompous cultural manager, this director looks and sounds like Riazanov's caricature of Kozintsev. The fact that Smoktunovsky, the actor who played Hamlet for Kozintsev, also played Detochkin playing Hamlet in *Beware of the Car* deepens the feeling of a blasphemous, even cruel parody on Kozintsev's *Hamlet*.

At the end, the film shows an on-stage duel between Hamlet and Laertes, accompanied by a loud, pathetically out-of-tune amateur orchestra—a truly vicious mockery of Shostakovich's music in *Hamlet*. Then, we see a court trial in which the two duelists fight again, one as the suspect and another as the investigator. The latter gives a speech in which he acknowledges the complexity of the world in Hamletian terms that were remarkably different from the Soviet tradition: "He is guilty," the

FIGURE 12. "I have returned": the final scene of *Beware of the Car* (1966).

investigator says about Detochkin, "but he is not guilty." After deliberation, the court convicts Detochkin. But in place of Hamlet's funeral in Kozintsev's film, *Beware of the Car* features a happy ending. The aged, shaved, but recognizable hero returns from a camp and is reunited with his fiancée, who is waiting, unchanged. "I have returned"—these are Detochkin's final words. Illuminated by Smoktunovsky's beaming face, this iconic scene is an epitaph to the saga of the gulag returnees and to the decades of the Soviet experience.

The film feels conciliatory. Though it exposes the endemic corruption of late-Soviet society, it also condemns Detochkin's attempt to solve this problem using force. Even the punishment that this noble criminal receives from the Soviet court looks mild and fair. With its focus on an admirable but half-deranged avenger of social ills, the film shows the problems of late-Soviet society without offering easy solutions. In its creative mockery of *Hamlet*, the film singles out only one symbolic scene, Hamlet's and Laertes's mutual murder; we do not know how the trade-union theater performed other parts of *Hamlet*, such as the scene with the ghost. Apart from its passing reference to Belomor, the film does not mention and, in a sense, does not remember the victims of the Soviet state. Detochkin and several other characters mourn the lost Soviet ideals, but to many other Muscovites these ideals mean nothing, and the film presents this indifference as a sign of hope. It is the ability to enjoy the petit-bourgeois values—cars, friendship, loyalty, unchangeability—that the film celebrates as a fresh and promising, though contested, achievement.

Waiting for Goga

Everything would have flowed on as usual, but a huge barge is blocking the Moscow River from bank to bank, and a queue of vessels is waiting up the river. This is the first frame of the most popular production of the late-Soviet cinema, *Moscow Does Not Believe in Tears*.[50] As we hear a sentimental song that plays with the odd title of the film without ever explaining it, the barge makes a slow, tortured U-turn, unblocking the river, history, and tears.

Starting in 1958 and ending sixteen years later, the action of this film presents a sad picture of late socialism. Three provincial young women come to Moscow in search of a better life. Moscow is bursting with newfound energy, and the women wander through some fascinating scenes. Playing himself, the leading poet of the Thaw, Andrei Voznesensky reads a poem to a crowd under the monument to the leading poet of the revolution, Vladimir Mayakovsky. Then, the three women come across an even larger crowd at the entrance to the first Moscow festival of French films, and Innokenty Smoktunovsky, also playing himself, tells them, "My name will tell you nothing. I am Smoktunovsky": the joke here is that though the actor was a household name in the 1980s when the film was screened, he was still an unknown in 1958. Hosting a party, the women listen to a conversation typical for the intelligentsia "companies" at the time. An older man tells a group of youngsters, "It is easy to criticize now. Where were these critics in my time?" and a younger man responds, "We would not have kept silent," while the women (and the audience) dislike them both. The film preserves our sympathies for another person, who will arrive on the scene much later.

The Moscow of 1958 is a place where three adventurous women invent false identities for themselves in their efforts to overcome the massive social inequality that they confront there—not exactly a picture of victorious socialism. Jumping forward to 1974, that social inequality turns into a reversed gender disparity. Watching the Muscovites who still do not believe in tears, we find males weak, despicable, or absent, and females taking the leading roles but feeling lonely and unhappy. Analyzing Moscow in gender terms, this melodrama even shows a dating agency that has stopped accepting women because there are so few men available. One of the three women, Katerina, is now a single mother and successful career woman. Craving a "real man," she finds him, at the very end of the story, in Goga. Different from the other male characters in the film, he combines rare talents: he can win a street fight, cook a good square meal, and keep his word. He seems to have come to Moscow out of nowhere. He detests the authorities but cannot escape them, and when he leaves his fiancée at one point, her friend from the police tracks him down and brings him back. He has no name but Goga, and the characters play with this name as if it were a criminal alias ("This is Goga, also known as Gosha, etc."). In contrast to the overachieving female protagonist, whom the film follows through decades and presents in exhaustive biographical and psychological detail, we know almost nothing about Goga's past. Building on its persistent vision of Moscow as a world of suffering, strong women and incapacitated men, the film concludes with a clash between the realistic story of the female protagonist and an ur-romantic, dreamlike plotline centered on Goga, a clash that concludes with Goga's flight and return. Goga is not ghostly; he is just unreal, a fact that is noted and discussed by several characters of the film.

Aleksei Batalov, the actor who played Goga, had a heroic aura; he previously played fearless soldiers and scientists. But this portrait of an urban noble savage, an embodiment of the intelligentsia's fantasy of living through the Soviet system unscathed, was Batalov's biggest success.[51] Though it is probably true that this film is "the closest that Soviet cinema came to Hollywood,"[52] Batalov made Goga more human, seasoned, and worldly than the conventional Soviet or Hollywood hero. Batalov said recently that he knew that the film needed Goga for an American-style happy ending; but, continued Batalov, the role of Goga also included certain "unhealthy deviations" that opened up a crucial space for the actor to inject life into his character.[53] Raised among the Moscow intelligentsia, Batalov emphasizes the formative influence that his conversations with the returnees of the 1950s had on his worldview. All of his grandparents were imprisoned; his grandmother returned to Moscow after ten years in the camps. He was also connected to some of the celebrated survivors of the gulag, such as the World War II hero General Vladimir Kriukov and his wife, folksinger Lidia Ruslanova. In an interview, Batalov has said that he hated the Soviet state and realized early on that it was "a band of scoundrels and murderers."[54] His Goga emanates some of these feelings, and when the film won an Oscar in 1981, the Soviet state did not allow its authors and actors to attend the awards ceremony.[55]

Goga is loved but remains unrecognized. With all her connections in high places, Katerina could find out Goga's whereabouts, but she could learn nothing about his past, and neither can the public. If we are to understand him as more than a dream of the frustrated heroine, where might such a Goga have come from? Under the romantic conventions of late-Soviet cinema, the most obvious answer would be: from the front of World War II. But Goga is too young for this. A distant relative of Hamlet, Goga keeps his secrets undisclosed, though we see how alcohol helps him to control his melancholy. Like a prince, he inherits Moscow but cannot escape its surveillance, which is presented as a parody of well-worn KGB techniques. Instead of fighting like Hamlet, Goga succumbs. "Does Katerina's triumph mean that the USSR is officially feminist?" asked *New York Magazine*; the reviewer was surprised to find that the Soviets in this film looked so much like Americans, but seemed to make different choices.[56]

My hypothesis is that Goga came from the same place that Detochkin did at the end of *Beware of the Car*—from the Soviet prison. These two characters, late-Soviet machos who wage their hapless crusades against duplicitous Moscow, have much in common. Both films show their male protagonists endowed with similar qualities—shrewdness and naïveté, love of justice, working-class dexterity, and contempt for the rich and powerful. These qualities endear them to the Moscow women, but still, the two characters have no equals in their respective films. Though they do not look like probable friends, it is easy to imagine them as one and the same person. Indeed, Goga could easily be seen as Detochkin several years after his return from the camp to post-Stalinist, but still

Soviet, Moscow. Both characters are Soviet survivors, the soloists of the long tragedy in which the chorus has perished. Apart from its title, however, *Moscow Does Not Believe in Tears* does not send this message with the clarity of the earlier *Beware of the Car*, with its homecoming scene, or of the later 500-ruble note. It is precisely this ambiguity that makes Goga such a wonderful character.[57]

For the generation that came of age during the Thaw, the Shakespearean way of mourning—one of the highest manifestations of the "longing for world culture," a cosmopolitan key to the emotional makeup of the Soviet intelligentsia—seemed incapable of reflecting the historical process that had led to the deaths of their grandparents and parents and then to the disenchanted and merciless Moscow that was awaiting its perestroika. Now, Shakespeare seemed too earnest, austere, stiff; his gravity seemed laughable. Pragmatic, worldly success rather than the mythical world culture now became the magnet for creative efforts and energies, and exoticizing Moscow was a shorter route to this end than domesticating Shakespeare. History had to be grasped locally, by looking at mundane characters in their indigenous environment, and allowing these characters to reveal their routinely incredible stories through satire rather than tragedy.

In late-Soviet film, mourning for the lives, ideas, and energies that had been lost in the catastrophic past took comic and melodramatic forms. Riazanov's long and productive career, which featured the most popular Soviet-style Christmas story, *Irony and Fate* (1975), and a forward-looking analysis of the complexity of social change, *Garage* (1979), proved that this comedian had mastered an art that he could not learn from his sublime teacher. But it was the dry-eyed and subtly absurdist film about waiting for Goga that won the cosmopolitan Oscar.

8

The Tale of Two Turns

In what is arguably the most important film of post-Soviet memory, *Khrustalev, My Car!* by Aleksei German (1998), the military surgeon Klensky is arrested and then raped on his way to the gulag. Suddenly, his tormentors dress him in a pristine uniform, sprinkle him with perfume, and take him to the ailing Stalin. As Klensky regains his military posture and clinical focus, Stalin dies in his arms, producing a final expulsion of flatulence. At one stroke, Klensky reverts from the stinking, bare life of a prisoner to the sublime condition of a professional, dutiful citizen. In the same X-shaped movement, the dictator departs from his duty and, quickly passing through the stage of stinking, bare life, is annihilated forever. The central scene of the film occurs when the sovereign and the abject meet and their positions swap.

A disciple of Grigory Kozintsev, the author of the Soviet *Hamlet* (see chapter 7), Aleksei German based his previous film, *My Friend Ivan Lapshin* (1984), on novels that were written by his father, the writer Yury German, who glorified the secret police and survived the terror untouched. *Khrustalev* was a fantasy, said German, about what would have happened to his father if he had been arrested. "It all comes from my childhood—the faces, the feelings, everything."[1] A son narrates both films, but *Lapshin* presents a father who admires the Soviet regime and glorifies its police, while *Khrustalev* mourns a father who became a victim of that same police. Working through these Hamletian themes, German's films also borrowed their sharp movements across the social space from the picaresque novel, in which both Mikhail Bakhtin and Walter Benjamin noted a capacity to change statuses, unsettle the routine, and mourn the victims of history. Thinking about the connection between Stalin's gulag and Bakhtin's carnival, I began to notice these picaresque constructions in other Russian films about the Soviet past. Like *Khrustalev*, some of these films, probably the most remarkable ones, also develop in two turns: the first from citizen into victim, the second from victim into citizen.

. . . but not sacrificed

A remarkable example of these two turns is the story of General Kotov in Nikita Mikhalkov's epic trilogy, *Burnt by the Sun* (1994, 2010, 2011). The first and most successful episode ends when Kotov, a dashing Red Army commander played by Mikhalkov himself, is arrested and beaten by agents who, in an instant, turn him into a bleeding, bare-living body. Fifteen years later, the Russian public watched the opening of the second episode in which the same Kotov, featuring his gleaming parade uniform and triumphant smile, greets Stalin at his stately dacha. Kotov is still played by the tireless Mikhalkov, but a different actress has been brought in to play Kotov's wife, as handsome as she was sixteen years earlier. She has baked a huge cake for Stalin: a chocolate Stalin face floats on top of white cream. Stalin is eager to taste it, but nobody dares to cut into his chocolate portrait. Finally, Stalin moves to cut the cake himself; but then Kotov suddenly shoves Stalin's face into the cake. Humiliating the adored tyrant, Kotov yells hysterically. He wakes up in a barrack and we realize that the scene was Kotov's dream, and Kotov is now a convict in the gulag. In this brief and drastic dream, we watch the X-shaped movement of Stalin, who falls from his heavenly stature into the sticky mess of the cake, and Kotov, who leaps out of his prisoner's existence back to his uniform and status.

In Aleksandr Proshkin's film *The Cold Summer of 1953* (1987), the central character is a captain of military intelligence who, after many battles with the enemy, finds himself in the gulag. In 1953, after Stalin's death, the former captain is living in exile in a northern village, refusing to work and barely surviving on the leftovers that some of the locals give him out of pity. Everyone calls him by his nickname, Luzga; his actual name and his past are irrelevant. Still alive, he is a goner, exhausted, apathetic, and silent. But when a gang of former prisoners, released from the camps during the chaotic amnesty of 1953, come to the village intent on rape and plunder, Luzga comes back to life and saves the village.[2] The captain gives the lie to external definitions. He was judged as a dying object of power; actually, he is the heroic subject of his own life. Again, this is an X-shaped movement across the political space. Those who held power turn into slaves of the gang; the lowest of the low becomes the embodiment of power.

Luzga is bitter but complacent. Relying on the popular conventions of British and American spy films, *The Cold Summer* presents a central character who demonstrates perfect integrity and is essentially foreign to his environment. But unlike his luckier colleague James Bond, Luzga belongs to the same political community as the villagers and the bandits. His difference from them is presented as moral, not political. In Proshkin's film, there is no symmetry between the soon-to-be-dead Luzga and those who personify the Soviet regime in the village. But in the state of emergency that is depicted in the film, it is Luzga who puts a stop to random acts of violence and restores legal order. In the micropolitics of this story, the goner becomes the sovereign of the domain that he pacifies by killing his enemies and sacrificing his friends.

It is not quite plausible that an exhausted, chronically underfed man could defeat a gang of armed bandits. However, it is true that thousands of World War II combat officers ended up in the gulag. Like so many other stories of Stalinism, Luzga's situation is incomprehensible and unthinkable, but we know that it occurred on a mass scale. Along with the film's dynamic plot, this clash between the fundamental improbability of the gulag and the public knowledge of its historical reality secured the film's success.

Thus the victims—Klensky, Kotov, and Luzga—all turn into heroes. This transformation is the gulag version of old tales about Brer Rabbit, Ivan the Fool, and the Prince and the Pauper, which show the magical ascendance of the lowest of the low to the highest of the high. Anthropologists interpret such folk stories as mental "weapons of the weak," hidden transcripts that the oppressed compose to disavow their dependencies and to produce mental drafts for future rebellions.[3] However, we do not see rebellions in these films. The travels and transfigurations of their picaresque characters occur in a moral rather than in a political universe.

The difference is made clear in Pavel Lungin's *Island* (2006). The film was shot in Kem, which is mainly known as the transit hub for the nearby Solovetsky camp. However, there are surprisingly few references to the gulag, Stalinism, or other recognizable features of the Soviet period in this film. The action starts with a wartime scene in 1942, when the protagonist, Anatoly, appears as a pathetic coward, a sailor who betrays his captain to a Nazi and then kills the captain in exchange for his own life. Since the film begins in the familiar black-and-white idiom of Soviet war movies, this betrayal provokes a well-conditioned disgust. Then we leap to 1974, the screen obtains color, and we recognize the same Anatoly as an ascetic, pious, and witty elder of an Orthodox monastery who works miracles, speaks truth to power, and inspires awe among his fellow monks. Both the script and the director heavily emphasize this transfiguration.

The central scene of the film presents both of the characters, Anatoly and his former captain, encountering each other once again. The captain, now an admiral, delivers his hysterical daughter to the famous elder for healing. After a successful exorcism, the two men, Anatoly and Tikhon, recognize one another, though neither in the least resembles his former self. The actors who play these two old men are deliberately chosen to look the opposite of those who played the same men in their youth. Two life trajectories have crossed and all but swapped. The traitor has turned into a saint; the hero who met his death with a cigarette in his lips has evolved into a suffering father and nervous bureaucrat. "Do not be afraid," says Anatoly, the former coward, to Tikhon, the former hero.

Thus Anatoly learns that he did not kill his captain after all. Having committed no mortal sin, he is ready to die, and he dies without fear. The film follows the trajectory from the lowest to the highest, from bare life to sovereign, but in a spiritual disguise. At the same time, the film skips over the entire world in between these two poles. When it turns up somewhat unexpectedly in a commercially successful product of contemporary cinema, this picaresque plotline needs an explanation. The commonality of this self-refashioning in post-Soviet films about the past, which occurs in religious as well as in secular contexts, leads me to suggest that these miraculous transformations are not only part of a new Russian piety, but belong to a broader pattern of memory.[4]

... this is me

Khrustalev also tells the improbable story of a citizen who is first turned into an outcast and then elevated to the very summit of power. However, in this film, the two turns of the story are performed in a different context from the one described above. This is a context that is more plausible historically, and more satisfying aesthetically: the context of a personal story of mourning. Critics have argued that German's film possesses a "dreamlike" and "disorientating quality" and that its different parts work in different ways.[5] I submit that the film is a coherent narrative of mourning that makes perfect sense when read as such.

Aleksei Klensky, a man who lost his father in his adolescence, tells the story from off-screen. He mourns his late father, confesses his guilt toward him, and fantasizes about his return. Aleksei is twelve years old when the action of the film starts, but he narrates the story as an old man. On screen, we see Aleksei as a boy, never as an adult. Throughout the film, however, we hear his aged voice sporadically commenting on the film's action. The gap between two stages of one person, which in *Island* is represented by two remarkably different actors, is suggested here via the unbridgeable difference between *the face* of a boy and *the voice* of the same man forty-five years later.

The story as Aleksei tells it is a mixture of reminiscence, conjecture, and fantasy.[6] The film is grainy black-and-white with a barely audible soundtrack. Its narrative gaps and allegoric sidesteps require interpretation, like a dream. The distance between Aleksei Klensky, the narrator of the film, and Aleksei German, its creator, is intentionally short. Klensky bears German's first name and matches his age. He also shares German's fascination with the father figure. However, Aleksei is the narrator of the story and not its witness or cameraman. We see him and his family in 1953; we also see large chunks of the action that Aleksei could not possibly have seen. Like narrators of modern novels (by Vladimir Nabokov, say, or Philip Roth), Aleksei Klensky realizes his power to combine what he has seen and what he has imagined in one complex narrative, which is now unfolding before our eyes. From this distance in time, memory is not precise, but neither is it arbitrary. It is not innocent either. At the very start of the film, we observe a scene in which the twelve-year-old Aleksei has apparently had a wet dream; having soiled his underpants, he rinses them, looks in the mirror, and spits at his reflection. "This is me," comments his voice forty-five years later. For the next couple of hours, we watch his father enjoying himself with power, cognac, and physical exercise. This father is a dazzling general, military neurosurgeon, and cheerful alcoholic. His huge body, beautiful uniform, funny tricks, and success among women provide a striking contrast to his son's adolescent ordeals.

But the film is the story of the father's arrest. It is set in 1953, immediately before and after Stalin's death. Running his military hospital at the time of the "Doctors' plot," General Klensky foresees disaster.[7] In an attempt to help him, a foreign journalist in Moscow passes Klensky a message from his relatives in Stockholm. After receiving it, Klensky flees, leaving his wife a note. The agents search his apartment. One of them asks Klensky's son, Aleksei, to report on his father if he comes home.

Soon, the agents capture Klensky and put him into a covered truck with other prisoners, who gang rape him anally and orally. The rape scene is unbearably long and horrifying; it evokes a visceral response of disgust and fear. This scene reduces a suave general to a bleeding, vomiting, and weeping victim, an ordinary goner who can be killed but not sacrificed because his life is not worth living. By the force of art, after watching the scene we feel something similar about ourselves. With unprecedented power, this scene embodies the fear that the Stalinist regime provoked among its actual and potential victims.

Homosexual gang rape as an emblem of the horror of the gulag merges two literary traditions of representing Communism. The anti-utopian oeuvres of Yevgeny Zamiatin, Aldous Huxley, and many others have connected the idea of Communism with the dissolution of marriage, the family, and traditional ways of love. A different but interdependent tradition connects the twentieth-century totalitarian dictatorships with homosexual violence. Influential in Russian literature, this tradition merges, in a peculiar way, homophobia with liberalism.[8] But Klensky's story does not end in the torture wagon. A new group of officials abduct him, bleeding and stinking. They wash Klensky, dress him in uniform, and bring him to Stalin. The soon-to-be-dead dictator is dirty, unconscious, and pitiful. Administering medical help, Klensky soon finds Stalin dying in his arms. In gratitude, Lavrenty Beria releases Klensky, who returns home to his family.[9] But upon seeing his father, Aleksei calls the police to denounce him, as he had promised the agent he would. After a heart-breaking scene,

Klensky leaves his family forever. "I never saw my father again," reports the voice of the aged Aleksei from beyond the screen.

Klensky's suffering at the hands of the state is senseless in the most profound, existential meaning of the word. Like Benjamin's "radical stoics,"[10] Soviet victims lived and died with the sense of the absurd; but for those who loved them, this senselessness is unbearable, second only to the loss itself. Their work of mourning invests the loss with reversibility and the absurd with meaning. The second, ascending line of the X-shaped tale emerges out of this tension. In the final frames, we see Klensky as a train conductor. Drinking, working out, and joking around, Klensky seems as comfortable in his new circle of drivers and prostitutes as he was among generals and academicians. His new job is no less important than his former one, operating on brains. His train transports those who have been released from the dissolved camps back to their homes.

There are three axes in this film. The psychological axis is formed by the disparity between the father and the son and the son's tortured feelings. The historical axis is shaped by the representation of the Stalinist terror, which deprived millions of sons of their fathers, and imbues the idiosyncratic events on the screen with broader meaning and verisimilitude. The narratological axis is defined by the relations between the narrated reality (what the viewer perceives as representing the actual life-world of the narrator) and the narrated fantasy (what the narrator and viewer agree to accept as fantasy). There are also zones of indistinction, in which reality claims are dubious or contested. These axes structure Aleksei's lifelong melancholia, an incomplete and never-to-be-completed mourning for his father, which mixes love, guilt, and self-hatred. The son remembers his father and also imagines his ordeal, his grandeur, and, most important, his survival. The father's return would mean the redemption of the son's guilt. The son is melancholic, but he is not mad. He knows (and he tells us) that his father has not returned; but the passing decades have not eased his loss, guilt, and fantasy. The son's guilt is the central point of these three axes. In Aleksei's case, the universal guilt of the son merges with the historically specific guilt of the survivor and, moreover, the traitor. In this hyperemotional film, the highest tension follows Aleksei's denunciation, when the son and the father weep together before the father leaves the son forever. Psychologically, Aleksei's feelings are structurally similar to Anatoly's in *Island*. Both men feel remorse for their betrayal of the paternal figure. Both men live on the hope that actually, their victims survived their ordeal and will come back, bringing mercy by the very fact of their survival and also by their forgiveness. Anatoly attains this mercy, Aleksei does not; but Aleksei keeps his father alive for as long as he tells his story.

Historically, Aleksei German reconstructs the misery and chaos of life in the Soviet Union in the 1950s. A large part of the film documents seemingly unmotivated outbursts of aggression, which the exhausted, frightened adults direct at each other and Aleksei. His mother participates in this; his father does not. In the hysterical world of late Stalinism, Aleksei remembers his father as the embodiment of sanity and masculinity. In a long close-up at the beginning of the film, we watch the tense face of General Klensky upside-down, as he performs a gymnastic exercise. In the last frame of the film, we see him, also in a long close-up, balancing a glass of liqueur on the top of his head. Performed by the extraordinary actor Yury Tsurillo, who combines physical power with inexhaustible irony, this memorial image of the father is highly unusual, tragicomic, and subtly uncanny.

Though the historical background and the psychological conflict are the most remarkable features of this film, they are both incomprehensible without a careful analysis of the narrative structure. Since we watch and hear the first-person narration, we assume that only those events in which the narrator participated as a witness, and those events about which he could have heard from other credible witnesses, constitute his memory. The other events that he narrates—though he could not possibly have seen or heard about them—constitute his imagination. While the memory parts of the film feel plausible, detailed, and even precise, the imaginary parts are weird and outlandish. These boundaries between memory and imagination are sometimes evident and sometimes vague. It is up to the critic to map them.

. . . a tear as hot as fire

Aleksei could not possibly have seen the scene in which his father attends to the dying Stalin. Nor could he have heard about this scene from his father, because they did not talk after his father's return. Immediately following the scene in which he remembers how he denounced his father, he says, "I never saw my father again." In doing so, he reveals to the viewer that his father's visit to Stalin's dacha never really happened. Now, is the rape of the father also a fantasy of the son? This scene is Aleksei's answer to the inescapable question that, for many years, Nadezhda Mandelstam asked her husband in a persistent nightmare: "What are they doing to you 'there'?"[11] Aleksei could not possibly have witnessed or heard about this scene, but he imagines it in a desperate act of mimetic mourning. Horrifying as it is, Aleksei's fantasy is no crueler or no more senseless than myriad real-life Soviet stories of investigative or transformative torture. The nightmarish scene of the gang rape in the paddy wagon destroys the father's dignity precisely in the area in which the son admired and envied him most of all, the area of masculinity. The more guilt the son feels, the more remarkable an image of his father he produces.

Four uncoordinated phantasms accompany the father's disappearance. First, the father is doubled, producing a man who looks, smokes, and performs tricks like the father, but is not the father. We see Klensky's double at the crucial moments of the film, first in Klensky's hospital, where he is kept as a privileged patient, and then after the rape, when this double, with other uniformed officials, escorts Klensky to Stalin. One could speculate that the production of doubles and clones is the imminent result of the Soviet-style process of leveling differences.[12] Since we do not see Aleksei in either of the scenes with the double, we should treat this double as Aleksei's fantasy rather than his testimony.

Freud believed that the image of the double, originally invented in myth or delusion as "an insurance against the extinction of the self," becomes "the uncanny harbinger of death."[13] One of many reasons for the horror that doubles evoke stems from the fact that they obstruct the processes of recognition (see chapter 3). If Aleksei should see Klensky again, how could he be sure it was his father? Multiplying Aleksei's uncertainty, his father's double works as a powerful trope that suggests the incomprehensibility of terror. Alluding to the uncanny doubles of Gogol's and Dostoevsky's stories, who subverted the sacred order of the bureaucratic world, Klensky's double plays an entirely different role. The existence of the double casts into doubt any possible evidence of Klensky's survival that might come from the elusive world of the gulag. It also undercuts any rational effort to understand what happened to Aleksei's father.[14]

Second, the father spends a night with a woman who wants to have a child with him, thus promising Aleksei a chance to have and find a brother. This and other erotic scenes in the film belong to the sphere of imagination as opposed to memory. Throughout the film, the aged Aleksei juxtaposes his father's potency with his own sexually deprived youth. In this spirit, after the meeting with General Klensky, the Scandinavian socialist recites cryptic lines from Lermontov's "Demon," a parable of superhuman masculinity that is fatal to the female: "By a tear as hot as fire, / An inhuman tear!" In the crucial scene in which Klensky departs, a Jewish boy sings the folk song "Tumbalalaika": "One night a young lad could not sleep / And he thought and thought / How to marry and not be shamed." The father is lost not only because of the son's political betrayal but also because of the son's sexual maturation. As we saw in other stories of children's guilt (see chapter 3), the power of the narrative comes from the confluence of these two strands, one historically specific and the other psychologically universal.

Third, Aleksei's memory breaks out of the cinematic duality of the visual and the acoustic and absorbs another sensory domain that is unusual for film: the olfactory. Beginning with Aleksei's memory of his wet dream, the film culminates in his intense fantasies of the pains, sounds, and smells of his father (and of Stalin, the father of the people). The anal processes in this film include a fascinating demonstration of the logistics of toilet usage in a communal apartment; the sounds of farting that many characters produce in their constant attempts to threaten and humiliate others; Stalin's bloated stomach and terminal fart, which is shown in detail as Klensky's therapeutic success; the violation of Klensky's anus and his subsequent bleeding, suffering, and futile self-help; and the repetitive complaints of Stalin's internal security at Klensky's offensive smell after the rape. The sensory intimacy of Aleksei's fantasy brings him into closer contact with the memory of his father than any other detail could. Exploring sensory domains that are new to Russian cinema, German forcefully provokes in his viewers responses of unusual intensity, from fear to revulsion to the feeling of the dense reality of the represented life-world. Precisely because a large part of this film is introduced as the self-conscious fantasy of the narrator, it is elaborated with naturalist detail and sensory power.

Fourth, after the rape scene the father is turned into a semihuman, half-animal monster. Though the rapists call him "a cockerel" he behaves like a dog. He drinks from a puddle and paws at a pile of snow to cool his bleeding mouth and anus. Like a dog, he sniffs the dying Stalin. For a long time, cultural critics have speculated on monsters and doubles as two major types of the uncanny. "There is no monster who does not tend to duplicate himself . . . no double who does not yield a monstrous aspect on closer scrutiny," said René Girard.[15] The reduction of a human person to bare life inevitably leaves an uncanny trace, an irreducible leftover of the dear and familiar that has become foreign and then horrifying. Agamben, in his own fantasy of the bare life in the camp, described transformation as the "lupization of man and humanization of wolf."[16] In a more general perspective, we are dealing with another manifestation of the Clorinda effect, a compulsive process that transfigures the object of mimetic mourning into a monstrous form. As in some other post-Soviet film tragedies such as *4* (see chapters 10 and 11), dogs accompany human characters throughout German's film. Responding to the image of the dog at the very start of the film, the final hint at this transformation of the father into a beaten-up dog, a parody of the werewolf, is bizarre and bitter; but it also bears hope for the father's viability and return.

Using a different artistic language, Aleksei reproduces the ordeal of Fyodor from Nabokov's *The Gift,* a novel of the son's mourning for his murdered father, who keeps returning to the son in night dreams.[17] Adoring their lost fathers, both sons desperately believe in their survival. Construing their fathers' fate as uncertain, the sons engage in unbridled fantasies about their fathers' heroic adventures that would bring about their salvation and return. Starting the narrative with the pedantic reconstruction of his youth in the shadow of his father, Aleksei shifts into sheer fantasy. The task of a filmmaker, as German understands it, is to depict his dreams as though they were real. "The boy fantasized or dreamed about the general. But we had to show it in such a way that the viewer would believe us," said German.[18]

The film ends with a cheerful picture of Klensky balancing a glass of wine on the top of his head while standing on the roof of a moving train. If, after all, Klensky is still eager to perform his tricks, then Aleksei can keep waiting for him to come back. But actually, what the viewers believe is not that the image of the living and playful Klensky is true, but that Aleksei, now in his sixties, cherishes this image as the dearest part of his inner life. In Aleksei's melancholic fantasy, which contrasts with

Hamlet's, the father survives betrayal by the son to return with unusual powers. Emerging from his bare, doglike life, he performs his final service to Stalin and brings the prisoners of the gulag home.

. . . two symmetrical figures

First, a citizen turns into a victim. Second, a victim turns into a hero. As we have seen, a number of Russian films about Stalinism play out this masterplot of mimetic mourning. Historically, perpetrators often became victims, though for a victim to become a perpetrator was less common. Theorizing the Nazi camps, Giorgio Agamben argues that the sovereign and its victims both mark limits of the juridical order. "The camp is thus a structure in which the state of exception . . . is realized *normally*." Since the tyrant and the camp are both states of exception, they are intrinsically connected; they both live in the Hobbesian state of nature. Using an archaic terminology in which *homo sacer* is another name for a goner, Agamben formulates: "As the two extreme limits of the order, the sovereign and *homo sacer* present two symmetrical figures: the sovereign is the one with respect to whom all men are potentially *homines sacri*, and *homo sacer* is the one in respect to whom all men act as sovereigns."[19]

But thinking about the Holocaust and the gulag, is there any way in which it makes sense to talk about a symmetry between the victim and the tyrant? The films under consideration operate not through a philosophical construction but through a dynamic plotline. A protagonist first is lowered into the hell of political victimization and second, reshapes himself into the position of a sovereign of his life-world. Like a werewolf, this accursed character transgresses the very borders that define him, demolishing the hierarchy of power along with his acquired stigmata. A similar process happens to sovereigns. As German said in an interview, summarizing ages of Russian political myth-making, "The Russian mentality is such that everyone is longing to be someone else. One tsar became a wanderer, another one became a monk. . . . To go and hide is an important component of the Russian mentality."[20]

No symmetry mysteriously spreads from the tyrant to the victim and back to the tyrant, equalizing them in a manner that is entirely foreign to a totalitarian regime. Agamben vastly exaggerates when he says,

"The state of exception and the state of nature are nothing but two sides of a single topological process . . . as in a Möbius strip." Postcatastrophic memory constructs this Möbius strip, which Agamben attributes to the very functioning of the state. In a belated attempt at justice, the mourning memory constructs the symmetry between the sovereign and the victim. This posthumous mechanism elevates the sick, weak, soon-to-be-dead victim to the level of the tyrant. In a reciprocal move, it brings the tyrant down to the level of a victim. This symmetry and this mobility are fantasies, but not random ones. On the contrary, in the works of post-Soviet filmmakers they appear recurrently, maybe even obsessively. They form a systemic allegory that shapes cultural memory in its desperate search to imagine the unrepresentable and to make sense of the meaningless. While the historical processes of victimization had no understandable meaning for either the victims or the perpetrators, cultural memory tends to redeem these processes in hindsight by turning victims into sacrifices and even more, into self-sacrificial heroes who earn leadership and sovereignty in exchange for their losses. Arguably, this redemptive mimesis is an operating mechanism of melancholy.

By its very nature, this work of mourning employs allegories that are, as Walter Benjamin put it, "the only pleasure the melancholic permits himself, and a powerful one."[21] The severe truth of the pathetic, stinking goner who does not know why he suffers because no such reason exists is redeemed by a gigantic transformation of historical reality. At each end of this eerie equation between the superior perpetrator and the lowest of his victims, the work of memory transgresses the frame of history.

9

The Hard and the Soft

In 1997, independent researchers uncovered a large mass grave close to the Belomor Canal, in the northwestern corner of Russia. The site, called Sandarmokh after the closest village, is a pine forest in which about 9,000 people were shot in 1937 and 1938. The victims were men and women of sixty ethnicities and nine religions, with an unusually high proportion from the political and academic elites. More than 1,000 of the murdered were delivered here from many hundreds of miles away, from the Solovetsky camp. For unknown reasons, they were brought here alive, forced to dig their own graves, and then shot on the spot. The site was discovered in 1997 by Veniamin Iofe and Irina Flige, leaders of the Memorial Society in St. Petersburg, together with a local enthusiast, Yury Dmitriev, from Petrozavodsk. None of these three researchers was trained as a historian, though Iofe was a political prisoner (1965–1968)—good training in itself.

Energy of the Remnant

The discovery was based on the testimony of Captain Matveev, who was sent by the NKVD to Karelia in 1937, shot thousands in Sandormokh, and was arrested by the same commissariat in 1939. This Matveev died an old man in 1981. His evidence has also survived in the archives, and led to the discovery of the remains of his victims. The excavations at the site recovered bones and skulls, many marked by a bullet hole.

Decomposing under a thin layer of soil, the corpses of the people whom Matveev executed on each of his daily missions form separate depressions in the ground.

Today, humble wooden poles or stakes mark every mass grave. Specially designed as a local symbol of mourning, these poles, with their sharply angled roofs, vaguely remind the viewer of either a peasant cross or a human figure with hands raised in prayer. Scattered among the pines, they make an impressive image. The complex also includes a figurative sculpture that represents the falling prisoners and an angel. The angel's hands are bound; he uses his wings to protect the prisoners. On the top of a stone obelisk, an inscription says, "People, do not kill each other." This monument was created by Grigory Saltup, an artist and writer from Petrozavodsk. After taking part in the excavations at the site, Saltup applied to the Karelian Republic's Ministry of Culture with a project for a monument. The government promised funding, but the money never materialized; Saltup believes that the ministry wanted a kickback. Saltup went ahead regardless. He built a three-meter model in his workshop, mortgaged his apartment, eventually scaled down the project, and completed it in a local factory.[1] Today, the memorial in Sandarmokh is one of the most important, and best developed, of the secular sites of memory of the Soviet victims. After this memorial was opened, different religious communities erected their specific crosses here, and now these crosses compete with the "poles" and with each other. The Russian Orthodox Church has built a chapel nearby. The visual structure of the Sandarmokh memorial is effective, but information on the site is completely absent. There is no museum here, no information board, and the directions on the highway indicate the "Sandarmokh Cemetery" rather than a historical memorial.

I interviewed Yury Dmitriev, a slight man with a sailor's mustache and unusual energy. He is obsessed with the duty of memory, which he feels as his personal responsibility. His father served in the Soviet military; his own family's connection to the Soviet terror seems to be irrelevant.[2] Among his discoveries is the largest known burial ground in the area of the Belomor Canal, the notorious construction site of the gulag that connected the Baltic and White Seas. Dmitriev knew that in 1933, the hectic race to beat the spring floods killed about 10,000 of the prisoners who dug the ten-kilometer-long rocky, frozen terrain of Canal No. 165, which connects the northern and the southern parts of the Belomor Canal.

Wandering in the woods with a local hunter, Dmitriev found a deep hole made by a raccoon that had dug up human remains from under a layer of stones. Nearby, Dmitriev identified about 100 depressions in the moss floor. In this marshy land, the victims had dug deep holes, in which they were shot and covered with stones in a futile attempt to prevent animals from digging them up. There is no monument there.[3] In 1997, Dmitriev found another mass grave in Krasny Bor, twenty kilometers from Petrozavodsk. He identified and marked about forty "shooting holes," and then started excavations. After months of work with a shovel and a computer, Dmitriev identified the names of 1,193 victims and two executioners. Having failed to convince the authorities to allocate money for a memorial, Dmitriev erected a self-made one. Two rocks stand vertically like strange teeth pointing to the skies.

Simultaneously, Dmitriev was working on *The Karelian Book of Memory*, which he published in 2002, after many years of assiduous research and dogged fund-raising. This 1,000-page volume lists more than 13,000 biographical entries for those who were murdered in Karelia in 1937–1938.[4] In this work, Dmitriev was supported by Ivan Chukhin, whose father was an NKVD officer who was implicated in the terror, and Pertti Vuori, whose father was murdered in 1936 by the same NKVD in Karelia. It was a remarkable team: a descendant of a victim, a descendant of a perpetrator, and a third party, as neutral to the subject as it is possible to be. Before their *Book of Memory* was completed, however, Chukhin and Vuori both died young men. Having survived them, Dmitriev publicly stated that his coauthors had been killed by "the black energy of crimes and murders which were committed decades before." Using his own words, the local newspaper described Dmitriev's ordeal:

After many months, which Dmitriev spent in the archive reading the files of those who were exiled or shot, he lost his appetite, could not sleep. . . . There is a black energy; it leaks into everyone who touches the yellowish pages of interrogations, denunciations, and shooting protocols. But Dmitriev continued his work on the Book of Names. He ran out of money. His friends died. His nerves betrayed him. His relationships were destroyed. He lapsed into months of heavy drinking.[7]

On the central square of the northern city of Vologda, a supply hub of the Belomor Canal, there are monuments to the Soviet heroes of the revolution, to the Soviet heroes of World War II, and to the Orthodox cathedral that was destroyed by those same Soviets. The fourth corner of this square is still empty, as if in anticipation of another monument: one to the victims of the Soviet terror, who died in and around Vologda in huge numbers. "There is nothing more inconspicuous than a monument," said the writer Robert Musil after the collapse of the Austro-Hungarian Empire. Looking at the ruins of the Soviet empire, I would add: there is nothing more conspicuous than an absent monument.

But Aleksandr Lukichev, the Speaker of the Vologda Municipal Council, told me that there were other forms of keeping memory of the victims, which were proper to this special subject. "We know about them from literature," said Lukichev. His grandfather, a peasant, was accused of anti-Soviet conspiracy in 1931 and died in a camp. Concerned about his grandfather's memory, Lukichev obtained archival documents to produce a book and a documentary film that tells the story of his grandfather. But creating a monument to the millions of other, similar cases was not on his agenda, Lukichev asserted. He advised me to visit a memorial stone on the place of a mass grave near the former KGB building, where relatives and descendants of the victims of Soviet murder on this and other sites gather once a year. There, on a piece of granite, one can read: "To the memory of the victims of political repressions. We love. We remember. We mourn." No further information about the "political repressions" is available at the site. "How do people understand what it is all about?" I asked. Once again, Lukichev referred to "literature." After seven years of work as an elected official, Lukichev is now writing historical books.

Solution of Memory

In a work that has become exemplary, in the 1980s-1990s a group of French historians led by Pierre Nora produced an eight-volume study of French monuments and other sites of historical memory.[5] Shifting the emphasis from the content and functions of cultural memory to its forms and "sites," Nora interpreted monuments belonging to several epochs of French history as representations of the changing national identity. Erecting these monuments, he argues, the state imprints its own self-representations as they were shaped in time, and constructs its own grandeur. This is memory as Pantheon: the selective representation of great personalities and events of the past. For a modern nation-state, immortalizing the memory of its victories and great leaders becomes not only an indispensable instrument but, moreover, a part of its internal structure.[6] Such monuments demonstrate the continuity of the political tradition of a nation-state from its great founders.

Nora's volumes presented cultural memory as a number of spatially organized sites, which are static, self-contained, and unconnected. These volumes contrasted memory and history as if they belonged to two different worlds: memory vanishing and romanticized, and history modernizing, trivializing, and all but colonizing. They overemphasized the spatial structures of cultural memory and underestimated its temporal dynamics. They focused on monuments, memorials, and museums, and deprecated the historical controversies and competing narratives that fuel imaginative novels and alternative histories. As Pierre Nora's phenomenal success in the France of the 1990s showed, this shift of balance responded to the needs of that society. In his subtle analysis, Tony Judt connected Nora's volumes with François Mitterand's monumental constructions that were erected during the same decade. I would add that both were created when France shunned the Internet, the deterritorialized and increasingly language-neutral space of memory, and chose instead Minitel, a closed network bound by French language and fixed terminals.[7] France is special, but in many ways it is also typical, and Judt generalized: "The Western solution to the problem of Europe's troublesome memories has been to fix them, quite literally, in stone."[8] It was indeed a Franco-German solution, but in eastern Europe and Russia, it did not translate into anything close in scale either to German memorials or to French historiography. In these eastern parts of the West, the cultural memory is out of balance, but its trajectory moves in the opposite direction. In Russia and eastern Europe, novels, films, and debates about the past vastly outpace and overshadow monuments, memorials, and museums.

I like to compare monuments to crystals that settle in a solution of memory, provided that this solution is strong and stable. But in the east of Europe, cultural memory is hot and liquid rather than cool and crystallized.[9] Its structures are temporal rather than spatial. Its units are memory events rather than sites of memory. Contemporary Russian memory barely approaches the minimal conditions of crystallization. Its important condition, analogous to the temperature of the solution, is social consensus. High social consensus encourages the proliferation of monuments, but since there is not much to debate if everyone agrees, it discourages public debates; we see such a situation in contemporary Germany. In contrast, low consensus suppresses public memory, but can intensify its manifestations among the remembering minority. The enthusiastic efforts of solitary individuals, veritable heroes of memory like Dmitriev or Iofe, are vital in this situation. Like catalyzers, they help the solution of memory to shape the crystallike monuments.

This intuitive model allows for a range of possible imbalances and imperfections, and in the east of Europe these shifts are the opposite of those that Judt noticed in France. Studies of Russian memory and mourning should take full account of the proliferation of cultural texts, from memoirs to novels to films, and the lack of monuments in the region. Monuments are inconspicuous if people are not talking and writing about them; mourning rites are incomplete if they do not crystallize in monuments. The interaction between texts and monuments makes the core of cultural memory, but this interaction has not been adequately explored in memory studies.

The arts of memory are diverse. Awareness of the past may be achieved by the publication of a document or by the erection of an obelisk; by writing a memoir or by creating a memorial; by launching a discussion or by opening a museum. In culture, as in a computer, there are two forms of memory, which might be likened to hardware and software. Soft memory consists primarily of texts (including literary, historical, and other narratives), while hard memory consists primarily of monuments. Of course, the soft and the hard are interdependent. Monuments without inscriptions are mute, while texts without monuments are ephemeral. The monumental hardware of cultural memory does not function unless it interacts with its discursive software. On the other hand, the software—public opinion, historical debates, literary imagery—would pass away with every subsequent generation or even fashion if it were not anchored by monuments, memorials, and museums. The hardening of memory is a cultural process with specific functions, conditions, and thresholds. It is not the mere existence of the hardware and the software but their interaction, transparency, and conflicts that give cultural memory life. Like a computer, culture does not work if either the software or the hardware does not work, or if there is no proper interaction between the two. The Holocaust survivor and writer Primo Levi wrote that if he had been asked right after his emancipation what to do with the camp where he was imprisoned, he would have said, "Destroy it forever along with the Nazi and the Germans." But forty years later, he would prefer to see on this place a "warning monument."[10]

Printing and digital technologies have largely de-territorialized cultural memory. Texts such as the Jewish Torah or medieval manuscripts are singular. Located in sacred spaces, they function as hardware monuments as well as software texts. In contrast, the modern arts of memory, from memoir to film to the Internet, are neutral to space. Often describing specific sites, they do not have location themselves: mechanically or electronically reproduced, they are available in many places at once. Still dependent on space and its sites, modern memory is structured by time. Its temporal units are *memory events*, which I define as acts of revisiting the past that create ruptures with its established cultural meanings.[11] Memory events are secondary to the historical events that they interpret, usually taking place many years or decades later. Sometimes a memory event attains the significance of a historical event, therefore blurring the distinction between the two. But there are also a number of differences.

Memory events unfold in many cultural genres, from funerals to historical debates, from museum openings to court proceedings, from the erection or the destruction of a monument to archival findings, films, novels, exhibitions, and websites. Historical events tend to be singular while memory events rarely are. They repeat themselves in new, creative but recognizable forms, which circulate in cultural space and reverberate in time. Like waves, these events move across cultural spaces, and they are indeed often carried by waves.

Sites of memory structure its cultural hardware; memory events structure its software. Memory events are simultaneously acts and products of memory. They have their authors and agents—initiators and enthusiasts of memory—who lead the production of these collective events in the same way as film directors make their films. Memory also has its promoters, as surely as it has its censors and foes. As multimedia products, memory events feature a permanent interaction between "hardware" (sites, monuments, and so forth) and their "software" (historical, literary, and other texts). Like a computer, cultural memory is dependent on the balance between hardware and software—sites and events, monuments and texts, traces of the past and stories about it, hardware and software.

Memory events change how people remember, imagine, and talk about the past. They are performatives, and we can apply to memory events some ideas from Habermas's theory of communicative action.[12] In my adjusted version, the power of a memory event depends on its truth claims, that is, whether the community perceives it as a true description of the past; on its originality claims, that is, whether the community perceives it as new and different from the accepted version of the past; and on its identity claims, that is, whether the community perceives the changing vision of the past as central to its identity.

Texts and Monuments

The Russian-American scholar Roman Jakobson noted that in celebrated poems by Pushkin (*The Bronze Horseman, The Stone Guest*, and so forth), a statue comes to life and confronts a human character, who in effect loses his memory, mind, or life.[13] More recently, another Russian-American scholar, Mikhail Yampolsky, formulated a contrasting idea. He believes that a monument creates a "mystical protective zone," a sacral space around the monument that stops the flow of time.[14] Precisely because monuments freeze history, their rare moments of dynamism are imbued with uncanny effects, which are associated with an exchange between the living and the dead.

Contemplation of the future monument to the poet is a leitmotif of some spectacular pieces of Russian poetry, from the eighteenth-century Derzhavin to the twentieth-century Akhmatova. In 1836, Pushkin wrote, "I have erected a monument to myself, not made by human hands"; in 1962, Brodsky responded, "I have erected a different monument to myself! Its back is turned to the shameful century." Reportedly, these latter verses inspired the sculptor to erect Brodsky's monument in Moscow, which shows its back to the Kremlin.[15] The real and practical events that happen to monuments, such as their removal, destruction, vandalism, or renaming, tend to provoke strong responses in their observers. Transformations of monuments are memory events, and they necessarily entail productive interactions with texts. When monuments move in Pushkin's stories, they create uncanny effects; when texts penetrate the monumental space, they are able to vitalize monuments. It is the combination of stones and texts that makes monuments work; without words, the meaning of these stones would be undecipherable. For example, the Solovetsky stone in St. Petersburg is complemented with strong inscriptions, such as "To the victims of Communism." Such a monument can also be vandalized by words. In 2002, I witnessed the results of one such attempt, in which unknown vandals wrote on the Solovetsky stone in St. Petersburg in red oil, "Too few were shot."

According to Yampolsky, a monument creates a mystical zone in which time stops its flow, as in a snapshot, and space is transfigured from its neutral, dispersed condition into one that radially focuses on the monument. Do such monuments need to physically exist, to be made of stone or bronze? Or can they be textual but still produce the same effects? Mourning texts of various genres—poems, memoirs, novels, and even scholarly treatises—have an ability to memorialize the horror of the past by emulating the same petrifying effect by purely textual means. The effect comes from an unusual, unexpected stoppage of the narrative flow, creating a static image that becomes memorable and mournful precisely because of this contrast between its frozen, petrified fabric and the flow of the story that encircles it. I will give several examples of this effect of the *textual monument*, as I call it, and will then turn to the important Soviet poetic text of mourning, Akhmatova's *Requiem*, which presents such a monument in the process of petrifying.

An exciting example of the textual monument stands out in the middle of Khrushchev's memoir. He remembers how at the peak of the Stalingrad battle, he could not find the headquarters of one of the armies that took part in encircling the enemy. It was a dark night near the frontline, and Khrushchev and his entourage lost their way. Rockets illuminated the terrain, but they saw only three dead bodies on the ground, two naked German soldiers and a gray horse. "Naked corpses are very visible at nighttime," Khrushchev says. He made circles around these corpses, and time and again returned to them. "No matter which way we went, we kept returning to the same corpses. It was simply some kind of enchanted place! Without end, we kept meeting the corpses of the two naked soldiers and the gray horse. What kind of bewitchment was this? Like something out of Gogol! A devil was leading us around this place."[16] Khrushchev said to his companion, a general, that they would remember these two Germans and the horse. Indeed, twenty-something years later, when he dictated this memoir, he mentioned these dead bodies five times. The reader also remembers them. Contrasting with the lively flow of Khrushchev's memoir, this expressionist scene concentrates the tension and anxiety of an organizer of the Stalingrad triumph. Static and repetitive, it embodies the death wish at the center of the life-affirming victory.

In Bakhtin's book on the carnival, there is a similar scene, horrifying, central, and petrified: "the Crimean sculptures" of pregnant, smiling old women. "This is an expressive and characteristic grotesque. It is ambivalent: pregnant death, death that is giving birth." For generations of readers, these eternally smiling, eternally pregnant sculptures symbolize both the laughter and horror of Bakhtin's text.[17] In Dmitry Likhachev's memoir, one of the most striking pages describes an open car that removed the frozen corpses from the Leningrad streets during the siege of the city in 1942. "The car that stuck in my memory was loaded with corpses, frozen into the most fantastic positions. It was as if they had been frozen in the act of giving speeches, screaming, grimacing, prancing. Raised hands, open glassy eyes. Some of the corpses were naked. One female corpse stuck in my memory, she was naked, brown, skinny, she was standing up in the car like a pillar, propping up the other corpses."[18] The description goes on and on, and it erects a memorable, horrible monument to the victims of the siege, one that would make a fine subject for future sculptors.

In her *Requiem*, a cycle that Akhmatova passed to the underground circulation in 1961 (it was published in the USSR only in 1987), she describes her experience of standing in line at the Crosses prison in 1938 with the purpose of passing food to her son, Lev Gumilev, who was held for investigation there before serving in the gulag for the next six years. She reports in rhymes that over seventeen months, she spent 300 hours in these lines. "We were all in a torpor there," Akhmatova says. Only the dead were smiling then, says Akhmatova, in a trope that is as grotesque as Bakhtin's. Through the poem, she describes the steady, frozen, and petrified character of the torpid line. She also depicts the internal change that she underwent because of her fear for her son and her compassion for him, and this change she also describes as petrifying. "I have a lot of work to do today; / I need to slaughter memory, / Turn my living soul into stone." Indeed, petrification is a process that she describes throughout the poem; in some lines the son turns into stone, in another line apostle Peter does, then the mother. In the last and culminating poem of the cycle, Akhmatova develops this theme by describing her desire that a future monument be erected to her on the place where she stood in line at the Crosses. At the end of the poem, the narrator is already a monument: "Let the thawing ice flow like tears / From my immovable bronze eyelids."

In this poem, Akhmatova predicted important phenomena of the subsequent development of Russian memory: "I'd like to name them all by name, / But the list has been confiscated." From this desire to list the victims she turns to another impossible desire, to erect a monument to one of them, herself: "if ever in this country / They decide to erect a monument to me," she writes, it should be located at the Crosses prison where her son was kept.[19] Akhmatova speaks about this monument not metaphorically (text as monument) but literally, as a man-made monument. She does not specify any feature of this monument but its location. This is an essential feature of the postcatastrophic monument: it rarely has a visual concreteness, since any such concreteness would reduce the catastrophic experience to a human routine, but it memorializes the fact and location of the catastrophe.

There is no monument to Akhmatova at the Crosses prison in St. Petersburg.[20]

Memorials of Guilt

Looking at monuments in Paris, Washington, D.C., or St. Petersburg, we see the body of the nation on display. Monuments represent its continuing identity as a desired and often mythical unity between the state, the people, and their common history. They work as materialized forms of patriotic sentiment: sites of historical memory, of course, but first and foremost visible and touchable bodies of nationalism, which has created the present by distorting the past.

States do not eagerly erect monuments that memorialize their guilt. Some of their crimes were committed in colonial territories, and the burden of memory is placed upon those former colonies. The memory of the "collateral damage" that resulted from national glory is more often preserved in oral or written texts than in monuments. Monuments to revolutions and internal conflicts glorify those who won them and tend to ignore those who lost them. In times of revolution, monuments become one of the first, and certainly the most visible, targets for overthrow; their unexpected movements create memory events. In the Iraq war we saw how the self-celebrating monuments of power became stages for the most dramatic shows. Similar acts of foundational violence against monuments were important in the American, French, and Russian revolutions.[21]

By building monuments to its former enemies and victims, the state asserts its own transformation. This deconstructive mode tends to go along with military failure, decolonization, or revolution. Memorials at the sites of mass terror usually consist of two parts, a museum and a monument. The museum tells the story and displays the material traces of the events. Producing a coherent narrative, a museum is available to discursive analysis and rational criticism, like a lecture or a book. In contrast to a historical museum, a monument should not be judged by rational criteria. Generating emotional responses, monuments are close to rituals. While museums embody historical knowledge, monuments are pieces of art, and they do not make truth claims. The typical monument is usually a tower, obelisk, or another secular, abstract symbol, visible from all around. In contrast to the museum component, the monument usually does not have a figurative, historical meaning. In the museum portion, reconstructions of a gas chamber, a barrack, or a cell refer to their historical prototypes and aspire to reproduce them as closely as possible. In contrast, obelisks were not present in the camps when they functioned as camps. Monuments do not reproduce historical reality but rather comment upon it, emotionally and judgmentally. Maybe one way to interpret the vertical shape and central location of such monuments is to imagine a wooden stake that nails a mythological vampire to the ground.

In Russia, such stakes do not nail, and vampires are always ready to fly. Lack of social consensus blocks the crystallization of memory. Its solution remains oversaturated and volatile. Left in solution or locked in software, memory creates virtual circles. In contrast, in Germany, the first monuments to the dead were erected inside the camps right after the victims' liberation. The conversion of camp into museum demonstrated that it was not to be used in its former, frightening function by the new powers; it also informed the population about the methods of the defeated regime. This process was initiated by the former prisoners, who erected the first primitive signs of their mourning right after their emancipation in the form of wooden obelisks, grave markers, and so forth. In different sectors of the occupation, the processes of memorialization developed in different ways. In the eastern sector, the management of the camps was led by the changing ideological prescriptions of the Soviet and GDR governments. From 1945 to 1951, the Soviet troops and police used ten former Nazi camps on the territory of the GDR to house German prisoners of war. Later, some of these sites were transformed into museums, but the Soviet part of these camps' history was carefully omitted.[22]

Victims into Sacrifices

In Russia, the Memorial Society was founded in 1987 by enthusiasts of memory who started a campaign for a national monument to the victims of repressions. There was a foundational energy in this initiative, an identity claim that aspired to break the continuity with the Soviet past and to create a new, nonrepressive nation. In 1989, Veniamin Iofe and a group of activists from the Memorial Society erected their first memorial, a simple granite stone, in the cemetery on Solovetsky Island. Ten years later, speaking near this stone, Iofe said that it was created as a "question mark that asked about the meaning of this tragedy. We wanted to understand why all these millions were sacrificed, if they were indeed sacrificed? What was the supreme value which demanded these sacrifices?"[23] Iofe's doubt regarding the idea of sacrifice parallels Giorgio Agamben's ambigious concept of *homo sacer*, which describes the victims of the Nazi camps as those who could be killed but not sacrificed.[24]

As often happens in mundane situations of violent or premature death, the victims and, even more so, their peers and their descendants want to find meaning in their suffering. If meaning can be discovered, then death becomes a sacrifice, rather than just a loss or a murder. Mass murders can be sacrificially interpreted in religious terms, as punishment for sins, or in political terms, as the cost of nation-building, modernization, or similar causes. The Russian language adds to the possible confusion: the Russian word "*zhertva*" has two meanings, "victim" and "sacrifice," and Iofe explicitly played with this double meaning. He motivated his choice of the simple local stone, an empty signifier or "question mark," by his refusal to interpret victimization as sacrifice: "an ordinary natural stone which, with time, could probably take on a more definite contour, but this will happen only with time, when we reach a new understanding."[25]

What is truly important for this memorial practice is location. In 1990, a stone from the Solovetsky camp was erected near the headquarters of the Soviet secret police, NKVD-KGB, where the FSB (Federal Security Service), its post-Soviet reincarnation, still resides. This monument to the victims of the Solovetsky camp marks the square where the statue to its founder, Felix Dzerzhinsky, was demolished in 1991. In 2002, another Solovetsky stone was erected in St. Petersburg across the Neva River from the KGB residence, where the FSB is working now. Why did huge boulders have to be transported for thousands of miles, from the Solovetsky Islands to Moscow and St. Petersburg? Does a spirit of place travel with them? The idea of the spirit of place feels pre-Christian. However, in 2007 the Russian Orthodox Church reproduced the same logic of transporting spirits: carved in the Solovetsky Islands, a gigantic cross was ceremonially brought to Butovo near Moscow, a mass grave that the church has made into its official site of memory. But in Moscow, the former mayor Yury Luzhkov proposed reinstating the statue to Dzerzhinsky. Various compromises have been discussed, one of them being the replacement of the Solovetsky stone with a gigantic water clock. Two symbolic visions compete at this site: one of historical time, which changes by unpredictable leaps from the old condition (a monument to the executioner) to a new and radically different one (a monument to his victims); another of circular time, which always returns to the starting point, like a water clock. Brought from afar and converted into monuments, even boulders acquire political lives.

The sculpture of previous ages had greater narrative capacity. Russian official monuments of the nineteenth century told long, complex, horizontally developing narratives, much as comics and graphic novels do today. Soviet and Russian monuments to victories and victims of World War II were also multifigured and descriptive. Traveling in European Russia today, one cannot miss the huge memorial complexes to the "Great Patriotic War" with monuments showing armed soldiers in the moment of self-sacrifice. They contain lists of the heroes and the ubiquitous but not always true inscription, "Nothing is forgotten, nobody is forgotten."

According to an exhibition of monuments to the victims of the gulag staged in 2007, there were 1,140 such monuments and memorial plaques currently in place on the territory of the former Soviet Union: stones, crosses, obelisks, bells, bas-reliefs, and angels. Among these monuments, there are very few realistic sculptures that depict an actual prisoner in a moment of suffering. Interestingly, if anthropomorphic sculptures are found at all, they are usually erected in places like Ukraine, Kazakhstan, or Tuva, where a bare, senseless life in the camp is easier to reimagine as a sacrifice to the nationalist cause. For example, in the Tuva Republic in southeastern Siberia, a huge bronze man in national clothing was erected in 1989 with the inscription, "The Untamed. To the victims of political repressions in Tuva." The general rule seems to be that guilt monuments are nonfigurative, while pride monuments tend to depict people, on horseback or otherwise. It is easier for postcolonial memory to construct meaning for losses and revolutions than it is for postsocialist memory. The imagining of meaningless suffering requires nonhuman, abstract or monstrous symbols. These monstrous monuments feel strange and sometimes shocking, but the most important memorials to the victims of the Soviet terror belong to this category.[26] Fascinating examples include a monument in St. Petersburg by Mikhail Shamiakin, which represents two sphinxes across the Neva River from the infamous Crosses prison, with Akhmatova's verses on their pedestals; *Moloch of Totalitarianism* in Levashovo by N. Galitskaia and V. Gambarov, which shows a robotic cannibal who is devouring or raping a human figure; and what is probably the largest and most successful among the post-Soviet monuments, the *Mask of Sorrow* in Magadan by Ernst Neizvestny, which represents a concrete Leviathan, composed of multiple human faces, with a cross in place of the nose.

Sculptor Ernst Neizvestny became known in 1962 when he confronted Khrushchev during the latter's notorious attack on the artists and poets of the Thaw, whom Khrushchev called "abstractionists" and "homosexuals," two words that he believed to be derogatory. During that meeting, Khrushchev and other members of the Politburo openly threatened to shoot some Moscow artists or to send them to a lumberjack camp.[27] In response, Neizvestny, a former World War II combat officer, offered to prove his macho sexuality with any woman nearby, and said that he would commit suicide before "they" would arrest him. Years later, the dying Khrushchev asked his wife to commission Neizvestny to create

FIGURE 13. *Moloch of Totalitarianism* (1996), a memorial at the Levashovo Cemetery near St. Petersburg. Photo by the author.

his grave monument, which she did. Made of black and white pieces of marble, the monument symbolized Khrushchev's internal contradictions. In his memoirs, published after his emigration to the United States, Neizvestny expressed his feelings toward the Soviet officials by calling them "cannibals who were scared of their own wives"; he also gave a brilliant psychological analysis of his former friends in the party apparatus. Playing with the doubling idea that he used for Khrushchev's monument, he created two similar monuments for two opposite occasions, one celebrating Soviet power and another condemning it. The fifteen-meter high *Mask of Sorrow* (1996), a concrete sculpture in Kolyma, is a genuinely impressive monument to the victims of the Soviet terror. It obviously refers to Abraham Bosse's image of Leviathan on the frontispiece of Thomas Hobbes's book of 1651. It has not been noticed, however, that in a warped way this monument also refers to an equally huge bas-relief on the facade of the headquarters of the Central Committee of the Communist Party of the Turkmen Soviet Republic, in Ashkhabad, which Neizvestny created in 1975. Both pieces present a Hobbesian image of a monstrous state that consists of its miniscule subjects who are also its victims, and a cross that is cutting this total space apart, in a visual revenge and spiritual redemption. If this anti-utopian, Christian image of political mourning was appealing to the pious Russian officials of the 1990s, one can only guess what it meant for their Turkmen colleagues in the 1970s.

In the current practice, stones and monsters comprise two types of monuments that express the political nature of life and death in the camps. Bare stones convey the memory of bare life, construed from the perspective of the victims. Monster monuments express the unimaginable quality of the experience of the millions of goners. When trying to create a monument to the victims of the Great Terror, Russian artists also produce anthropomorphic or zoomorphic images such as a crying woman (the monument in Abakan), a man on his knees (Tver), or a wounded bird (Astrakhan). In almost all these projects, "victims" are represented as passive sufferers, deprived of any capacity for resistance. This imagery is very different from the contemporary German, and especially Israeli, representations of the Holocaust, which search for heroes of the resistance rather than for passive sufferers.[28] Russian monuments do not give any hint of the solidarity of political prisoners, their fights with criminals and with the administration, their numerous camp rebellions and escapes. Other than the usual image of prison bars and barbed wire, these monuments do not tell us much about techniques of torture, incarceration, or execution. These depoliticized images avoid Soviet emblems and say nothing about the ideology that determined all of these murders. A basic lack of information is typical for all of these monuments, including the most sophisticated ones. The director of the local museum in Medvezhiegorsk told me that it was easier to open a whole exhibition about "political repressions" inside museum walls than to put up a single information board on a site of mass murders. Information boards seem more vulnerable to criticism than highly abstract monuments, and the initiators of memory tend to reserve their knowledge for their books, most of which have tiny print-runs. It is lack of information that makes post-Soviet monuments inconspicuous. In 2000, on a highway from St. Petersburg to Pskov I visited a small café, which had on its wall a memorial board, carefully crafted in metal. It said that victims of the Stalinist repressions had been murdered here. It did not say who the victims were; nor did it say who hung the board, or when. The owners of the café knew nothing. No wonder that when I passed through again a few years later, the board had simply disappeared.

Monuments to the Soviet victims have been built by civil society, but the resources that are necessary for these monuments, starting with their sites, are controlled by the state. The only trustworthy feature of the memorialized event seems to be the location of the murders—Butovo, Sandarmokh, Levashovo... Interestingly, the most important monuments are erected not on the sites of the former camps or prisons, as is true in many German cases, but near them. This out-sitedness features the most important of these monuments, such as the boulder on Lubianka Square in Moscow, which abuts the edifice of the NKVD-KGB-FSB, or Shemiakin's two sphinxes and the nearby monument to Akhmatova in St. Petersburg, which looks at the Crosses prison across the wide Neva. This pattern demonstrates not the replacement of the old regime by a new one, but rather manifests their quiet coexistence. In a comparative perspective, such localization is not necessarily exceptional. The obvious analogy is the Berlin Holocaust Memorial near the Reichstag. On the other hand, even such proximate location of memory is far from being the rule in Russia. Near the horrifying building of the Leningrad KGB, there is not a single monument, plaque, or inscription commemorating the millions of its victims. Such a monument is notably absent from the vicinity of the Kremlin as well.

Near the Solovetsky stone in Moscow, since 2007 the Memorial Society has organized annual commemorations of the Great Terror on the eve of October 30, the Day of Memory of Victims of Political Repressions, instituted by President Yeltsin in 1991. For hours, volunteers read aloud thousands of names, and some spontaneously add, "my grandfather," "my uncle . . ." In provincial centers such as Vologda, descendants of the victims come annually, on October 30, to the local memorials. In these commemorations, the monument becomes a center of a social ritual, which integrates this hardware construction with ceremonial texts and performative acts in an organized, politically meaningful spectacle of memory. Commemoration of October 30 was initiated in 1974 in Soviet prisons as Political Prisoners' Day. In 1991, when this date was adopted by the Yeltsin government as an official memorial day, its title was changed to the Day of Memory of Victims of Political Repressions, a change that, as one observer notes, effectively prevents the commemoration of current, post-Soviet political prisoners.[29]

According to the Memorial Society, there were about 400 fully deployed camps that comprised the system of the gulag. But only two of the gulag sites, in the Solovetsky Islands and in Perm, house small museums (or dedicated departments of museum) that show the conditions in the camps, the techniques of torture and murder, the documents, and the portraits. These two camps are bookends marking the very beginning (Solovetsky) and the very end (Perm) of the system of the gulag. There are no memorials or museums on the sites of many significant camps, which contained dozens or hundreds of thousands of prisoners. However, in some centers of the northern gulag, the modest objects on display at local museums are fascinating. In a small exhibit in the Kargopol museum there is a clay pitcher. As the detailed plaque says, this pitcher was presented to the museum by the descendants of a camp guard, who, sometime in the 1930s, appropriated a package that was sent to a prisoner, a pitcher full of honey. The family of the guard preserved the legend of this pitcher. In such exhibits, however, it is practically impossible to find answers to the most obvious questions: How many prisoners went through this camp? How many died here, and when? Who were the founders of this camp, its administrators, guards, executioners?

The monument at the Perm camp consists of a concrete construction resembling an observation tower, which is not fitted with a machine gun, the central attribute of such towers in the times of the gulag, but instead supports two objects that are rarely combined: a church bell and a hunk of barbed wire. This monument is located at the only gulag site that has been converted into a museum. One can visit barracks and the administration building, look at many historical exponents, and even sample authentic prisoner fare in the prison mess. The creators of this museum hope to attract tourists. Its advertisement in a commercial newspaper specifically said that the museum would be attractive to "children and foreigners." In Novgorod, not far from the ancient city wall, there is a Soviet-looking park with a monument to the Bolshevik Revolution, which presents two hands clutching a globe. One hundred meters away there is a monument to this revolution's victims. It depicts a candle made of granite, with a metallic wick at the top. The inscription addresses the visitor on behalf of the victims of the Soviet terror, "Do not allow our fate to become your fate." As in so many other cases, texts prove stronger than monuments.

On Solovetsky Island, in 1992, the Russian Orthodox Church erected a cross at the entrance to Sekirnaia Mountain, an infamous site of mass murders. The cross bears a long, elaborate text devoted to the memory of the victims, formulated in archaic but strong and clear language. While the cross itself is noticeable from far away, the inscription can be seen and read only in the closest proximity. Numerous tourists overlook this inscription, perceiving this monument as just another cross, one of many in the monastery. On a mass grave on Solovetsky Island two monuments visibly compete with each other: an Orthodox cross and a granite stone erected by the Memorial Society. Neither of them contains information about those who are buried there. In 2002, the Moscow Academy of Art, Sculpture and Architecture, in collaboration with the Memorial Society, held a contest for designs for a future monument "to the victims of political repressions" on Solovetsky Island. Out of fifty entries, twenty proposed Orthodox chapels as monuments. Crosses, angels, and bells played the central part in nine designs. In eleven projects, memory was represented by secular symbols, such as obelisks or ruins. Seriously developed museum space was proposed only in five projects. Only two proposed reconstructing parts of the camp.

The Solovetsky camp, the first and "model" camp of the gulag, functioned for about twenty years, and hundreds of thousands of people were incarcerated there through the years. The buildings of the monastery have now been returned to the church and are used according to their original function. One memorial plaque on the buildings that surround this enormous site of mass murder is heartbreakingly simple. It reads, "The Children's Barrack of the Solovetsky Camp." However, in 2011 the Russian government, led by Prime Minister Vladimir Putin, decided to move the historical museum from the island to the mainland. This probably means that soon there will be nothing on the island but the monastery, and no memory of the camp and its secular prisoners will be preserved locally.

In the case of the gulag, the return to the religious symbolism of memory denies its historical specificity. Many of those who perished there were not Christians, but Jews or Muslims, and many were atheists. Canonical Orthodox crosses are different in shape not only from Catholic and Lutheran crosses but also from the Old Believer crosses. Therefore, on sites such as Sandarmokh, one can see a number of different crosses, which have been erected by non-Orthodox religious minorities. The secular, political character of the Soviet terror makes its religious interpretation highly questionable. Mourning senseless loss on such a catastrophic scale is an impossible task. Though this unrepresentability has been theorized less in the case of the gulag than in the Holocaust, many heirs of the gulag's victims have intuitively chosen nonsacrificial monuments to commemorate their dead.

The Virtual Gulag

Almost all projects of memorialization in Russia, the soft and the hard, have been initiated by private persons. On the other hand, private individuals and voluntary associations cannot erect monuments without the collaboration of the state. Access to archives is controlled by the state (specifically the FSB, the descendant of the KGB), and this access has been diminishing throughout the last decade. Financial resources and land property, which are required for any memorial, are also controlled by the state. If writing memoirs is predominantly an individual activity, constructing memorials is a collective one. Moreover, because of the large scale and public nature of memorials, their construction generally requires the participation of the state. Hard memory is usually the responsibility of the state, while soft memory is the domain of society.

The German art of memory is richer in experiments, both successful and failed. Among the successes is the Monument to the Burned Books on Bebelplatz in Berlin. Created in 1996, the monument is a semitransparent window in the pavement, through which pedestrians can see many empty bookshelves, an underground library without books. Another interesting example is the "Warm Monument" in Buchenwald, erected in 1995 on the site where fifty years earlier, prisoners erected the first monument to the murdered. The sculptor has placed at the site a rectangular stone that is heated to human body temperature, giving it a kind of living energy. Tourists love to touch it in the wintertime.[30] Recent memorials to the victims of the Holocaust in Berlin caused furious debates in Germany. One could probably measure the success of a monument not by its aesthetic appreciation by the critics or even by the public, but by the amount of discursive responses generated by it. What is important for the memorial function of the stone-made hardware is its debate-provoking capacity. Complaining of "Holocaust fatigue," some critics are concerned that the German audience is growing immune to Holocaust monuments, even to the new ones, and that without social debate these monuments fail to realize their supposed functions. This was the point of an important discussion launched in the late 1990s by the writer Martin Walser, who accused the German state of "instrumentalization of the Holocaust."[31] According to Walser, it is senseless to repeat the same project of memory, converting it into a "compulsory exercise," while the public progressively loses interest in it. One might suggest that the way to return the intrinsic value to the monuments would be to initiate a political debate that would make meaningful symbols of these monuments once again. In an unexpected way, Walser's controversy produced precisely such a result.

As vehicles of cultural memory, texts and monuments differ in their relation to the public sphere. In a democratic society, the public sphere strives to realize its ideals of inclusivity, free speech, and competition. Fully applicable to texts about the past, this vision does not work with monuments. The Habermasian public sphere is a textual domain; public monuments do not comply with its laws but instead remain outside of it.

Monuments are monological; they usually stand on their sites with no rivals to challenge them; they do not debate and compete. Though two different opinions on the same historical subject are perfectly legitimate, there cannot be two monuments on the same spot. Intellectual debate about the past is pluralistic, but monuments are singular. A historical debate cannot provide a final conclusion to the question of memory—a monument does. There are exceptions, of course; American Civil War memorials, which in some cases feature monuments to each side of the war in close proximity, are one such exception.

However, no memory is absolutely hard. Physical preservation of monuments, cemeteries, and other sites of memory take titanic efforts. Renaming and reframing can change the meaning and destiny even of those places that are well preserved. St. Petersburg was renamed four times in one century, and this process reflected major transformations of its role and meaning despite the relative intransigence of its historical center. Monuments can move back and forth. Russians have seen some bronze czars removed and returned to their places, and the same may still happen to some of the remaining or removed stone dictators.

During vague discussions of a "third de-Stalinization" under President Medvedev (the first two having taken place under Khrushchev and Gorbachev), the Memorial Society in Moscow produced a pioneering plan for establishing memorial museums of Stalinist terror in Moscow and in St. Petersburg. As an alternative to this dream, the Memorial Society in St. Petersburg has developed the *Virtual Gulag*, a web-based project that acknowledges the political limits of the situation and uses digital, largely cosmopolitan means for dealing with them. *Virtual Gulag* combines the features of an online exhibition of the nationwide memorabilia of the gulag with a catalog of the actual sites of memory, the local monuments and museums, that have emerged during the fifty years of de-Stalinization.[32] Independently of local politics, an ever-larger part of our memory now resides online, and post-Soviet Russia, with its high proportion of Internet users, is no exception. Readable and visible from anywhere and to some extent bilingual, this virtual and cosmopolitan memorial has many advantages. However, it is decisively de-territorialized. The continuity of place is a universal and potent weapon of humans' struggle with relentless time. The idea of the sacred is often connected to the place where the dead are buried, and even more so to the place where they were murdered and left unburied. Cemeteries and monuments materialize a belief in a spirit of place, which remains on the site of death through years and, as an article of faith, forever. No such spirits inhabit the Internet, but the memory it preserves may turn out to have a longer life.

10

Post-Soviet Hauntology

From German memorials to Russian memoirs, one can trace a continuum of the cultural genres of mourning, but the contrasts are remarkably sharp. Though terror in Nazi Germany and Communist Russia both resulted in many millions of victims, their memories are different. The popular memory of the Holocaust boomed in the last years of the twentieth century on an industrial scale, but the popular memory of the Soviet terror has been cyclically returning to the insights and taboos that were first established in the times of the *Gulag Archipelago*. This double standard operates in various contexts, not only in post-Soviet Russia. The idea of a Holocaust denier lecturing at a Western university is now unimaginable, but that same university might well manifest tolerance toward a gulag denier. A writer or professor who claimed that fighting the Nazis in World War II was unnecessary or harmful would be ostracized, but it is far from unusual to hear similar doubts expressed in respect to fighting the Cold War against the Soviet Union.

The debate over the relationship between German Nazism and Soviet Communism has been a long and fierce one. Hannah Arendt's Cold War–era concept of totalitarianism, positing a metaphorical "common denominator" shared by the two regimes, was largely rejected by Western academics in the 1960s-1980s, was embraced enthusiastically in Russia in the 1990s, and has been largely resurrected in the Western scholarship of the new century. However, many Western thinkers, from Freud to Habermas, have emphatically rejected the notion that these two regimes should be viewed as symmetrical.[1] Their methods may have been similar but their purposes were fundamentally different, they say; the Soviet project was at least congruent with the Enlightenment tradition and based on admirable ideals. Historians have often challenged this philosophical argument. From Ernst Nolte, who launched the German "Historians' Dispute" in 1986, to Timothy Snyder's *Bloodlands* (2010), historians demonstrate the comparable scale and mutual dependency of the lethal policies pursued by the Soviet and Nazi regimes. In this chapter, I look at the response that one of the most important Western philosophers, Jacques Derrida, gave to this problem, and then proceed to the Russian cultural scene that looks different, I believe, after reading Derrida.

Derrida's Silence

The rise of poststructuralism has been explained by the legacy of the Holocaust and postcolonial struggles, which were all pertinent for the Jewish, Algerian-born Derrida.[2] However, in his late works, which often sound like memoirs, Derrida defines his deconstruction in its relation to Marxism, as at once its radicalization and a product of disenchantment. Insisting that he learned "early" about the "totalitarian terror in all the Eastern countries," he derives the genealogy of his central ideas from these early impressions, which he describes clearly and powerfully:

From the Moscow trials [1936–1938] to the repression in Hungary [1956] . . . such was no doubt the element in which what is called deconstruction developed—and one can understand nothing of this period of deconstruction, notably in France, unless one takes this historical entanglement into account.[3]

It seems unlikely that Derrida's disillusionment could have occurred earlier than Khrushchev's revelatory speech of 1956, which caused the first anti-Stalinist debates within the French Communist Party.[4] Then, he writes, talk about the "end of history" and the "ends of man" was his "daily bread." In the 1990s, these terms circulated because of the collapse of the Soviet Union and the end of the Cold War, but Derrida remembers them from the late 1950s, when they connoted the end of Stalinism, the collapse of the gulag, and the first revelations of the "cult of personality." In the 1990s, Derrida viewed the debates that accompanied the end of the Soviet Union through these old lenses, and they seemed a revival of the debates that accompanied the end of Stalinism. In that crucial moment in the 1950s, Derrida had "indissociably" connected the readings of the philosophical "classics of the end" (he gives a long list of names, from Hegel to Heidegger) with the news about "the totalitarian terror in all the Eastern countries . . . the Stalinism in the past and neo-Stalinism in the process." It was precisely from this combined knowledge that he derived his "apocalyptic tone in philosophy," a catchphrase that he coined retrospectively, in 1980.

In 1981, Derrida was arrested in socialist Prague and spent two days in jail. Horrified by the experience, he saw no end to the Soviet domination of eastern and central Europe: "this barbarism could last for centuries."[5] He used the same popular label for the Soviet gulag, which he said was "at least equal to the Nazi barbarity."[6] However, Derrida remained faithful to the "specters of Marx"; crucially, he has described this faithfulness as a kind of grieving and haunting. In this respect, Derrida felt an affinity with his bereaved colleagues in post-Soviet Russia, an emotional identification that he translated into intellectual terms, noting in 1993 that he had been told by colleagues in Moscow—he does not mention their names but he anachronistically calls them "Soviet"—that the best translation for "perestroika" was not "reconstruction" but "deconstruction."[7] In *Specters of Marx*, he presents this mourning for the spirit of Communism as global and interminable, so that it amounts to what he calls a "geopolitical melancholy."

"We are heirs of Marxism, even before wanting or refusing to be, and like all inheritors, we are in mourning."[8] How can we understand this chain of metaphors? If it is true that we are heirs of Marxism, what are we mourning for? As Derrida repeatedly showed, metaphors are pregnant with meaning, whether they work or not. Derrida's statement may refer to victims of Marxism, who are not mentioned here though "we are in mourning," or, alternatively, it might mean that he is mourning the loss of his belief in Marxism, which is also not mentioned here, because "we are heirs." Derrida's statement could also combine both meanings, which corresponds to the condition of double mourning that I described in chapters 1 and 7. This uneasy alternative finds illumination in Derrida's reminiscences about the leading Marxist philosopher, Louis Althusser. A tragic figure whose mature life started with imprisonment in a German POW camp and led to psychotic delusion and murder, Althusser was a longtime member of the French Communist Party. In his angry response to the Twentieth Congress of the Soviet Communists, Althusser attacked Khrushchev for using a non-Marxist concept, "the cult of personality," and reproached Stalin, of all things, for an "excessive economism."[9] It was precisely in 1980—the year to which Derrida dates his own "apocalyptic" turn—that Althusser strangled his wife and was found mentally unfit to stand trial. Althusser would never recover his sanity, and Derrida has described his experience as he tried to care for his friend.[10]

The historian and psychoanalyst Elisabeth Roudinesco gives a striking interpretation of Althusser's ailment as "the melancholy of revolution."[11] She believes it to be similar to "a subjective collapse, a plunge into madness" that many went through, she states, after the French Revolution and its Terror. Conversing with Derrida about their mutual friend, Althusser, Roudinesco presents melancholy as an "invariant" of postrevolutionary situations. Following this logic, Roudinesco explains that "when an entire generation of communists were faced with the disaster of real socialism," they were "forced to mourn" their ideal, or "succumb to melancholy."[12]

Explicating the spirit of postrevolutionary melancholia, Derrida substitutes "ontology," a central term of traditional philosophy, with "hauntology," a science of specters and an art of talking to them. He believes that hauntology is the proper approach to Marxism, a ghost that was exorcized after the fall of the Soviet Union and the Berlin Wall, but continues its stalking and warning; he also emphasizes the ghostly metaphors of some crucial texts by Marx, most importantly the *Communist Manifesto* (1848) with its opening line, "A specter is haunting Europe—the specter of Communism. All the powers of old Europe have entered into a holy alliance to exorcise this specter."[13] An inheritor, Derrida speaks more often about specters of Marx than about the ghosts of those who died for or because of Marxism; however, his hauntology embraces all these multinatural spirits. In Colin Davis's formula, "hauntology is part of an endeavor to keep raising the stakes of literary study, to make it a place where we can interrogate our relation to the dead, examine the elusive identities of the living, and explore the boundaries between the thought and the unthought."[14] This ambitious endeavor also entails new ways of exploring the relations between the past, the present, and the future.

Throughout his book Derrida presents *Hamlet*, and specifically the scenes between the prince and the ghost, as the key to the fate and memory of Communism. The tripartite construction of *Specters of Marx* starts with Hamlet as the paradigm of mourning and haunting; moves on to Marx, who envisioned Communism as a specter; and ends with a picture of the late twentieth century that Derrida sees as haunted, like Hamlet, by the betrayed and revengeful spirit of Marxism, still in full armor. Persistent references to Hamlet are to Derrida's hauntology what references to Oedipus are to Freud's psychoanalysis. By replacing the tragedy of misrecognition and murder of the father with the tragedy of mourning and revenge for the father, Derrida shifts his central concern from the revolutionary, patricidal Oedipus to the postrevolutionary, melancholic Hamlet. Eloquent as it is, this analogy between the stories of Marx and *Hamlet* does not always work very well: in contrast to Shakespeare, Marx scornfully eschewed ghosts. According to Derrida, Marx "does not want to believe in them. But he thinks of nothing else."[15] It is precisely here that Derrida gains the upper hand over his precursor, and reproaches Marx for his "terrified hostility" toward ghosts and his "fear of spectrality," which betray a dependence on these hauntological beasts.[16]

Using Arendt's concept of totalitarianism but rejecting the idea of "symmetry" between the two totalitarian regimes, the founder of deconstruction demonstrates his eagerness to combine these contradictory ideas, sometimes in a single sentence.[17] "I constantly refused to posit a symmetry between Nazi totalitarianism and Soviet totalitarianism," he says in a phrase that provocatively rejects and embraces the same idea.[18] Indeed, Nazism and Stalinism are "inseparable adversaries" for Derrida.[19] In one of the most obscure and inspired parts of *Specters of Marx,* Derrida combines magic, history, and politics in an original master plot. The specter of Communism, he writes, terrified both the Nazis and the Bolsheviks out of their wits, and this fear is key to explaining the outbreaks of terror in both cases. In these speculations, specter turns into spirit, haunting into hunting, and enemies into mirrors, but their "symmetry" is still emphatically denied. Derrida was careful to defend himself against charges of "revisionism," whether in the sense of defending Nazism or denouncing Marxism. "There is nothing 'revisionist,'" he wrote, "about interpreting the genesis of totalitarianisms as reciprocal reactions to the fear of the ghost [of] communism." "Revisionism" is a slippery term, but Derrida's point here is that both the Nazi and the Soviet totalitarianisms were equally hostile to the specter and spirit of

Communism. The Nazi socialists responded to this noble ghost from the outside and the Soviet socialists from the inside, but their responses were similar. Derrida would never run out of strong words while explicating the internal fear of Communism among the Communists as well as among their enemies, "the terror that [Communism] inspired in its adversaries but . . . felt sufficiently within itself to precipitate the monstrous realization, the magical effectuation, the animistic incorporation of an emancipatory eschatology."[20] This is, in the final account, Derrida's explanation for the Soviet Union's collapse and his method of rescuing Marx from under the rubble.

Derrida presented *Specters of Marx* as the book that broke the long years of his self-imposed silence—silence about Althusser, Marxism, and Communism. "For a long time," he said in what I see as a crucial statement, "I was virtually reduced to silence, a silence that was also assumed, almost chosen, but also somewhat painful with regard to what was happening right in front of me."[21] I believe that with this figure—silence about Communism—Derrida is alluding, consciously and with a healthy dose of self-irony, to a historical model that was all too well known to him: Heidegger's silence about the Holocaust.

Derrida's chosen teacher in philosophy, Heidegger is a dubious model. Having built his university career on collaboration with the Nazis, Heidegger kept a conspicuous silence about their crimes even after the war. In 1988, when Derrida was contemplating *Specters of Marx*, he gave a talk about Heidegger's silence. Since the early 1960s, Derrida said, he had been struggling to understand how Heidegger's "difficult work could fit together with what we knew of his political engagement," and he proposed to distinguish between two aspects of this engagement. While Derrida saw in Heidegger's prewar career with the Nazis a complicated problem that "could be understood, explained, and excused," he deemed Heidegger's silence after the war to be "wounding" and "inexcusable." Heidegger's silence, Derrida said, "leaves us a commandment to think what he did not think" and moreover, to "approach what we condemn and to know what it is that we condemn."[22]

Heidegger did not break his silence about Nazism; Derrida did break his silence about Communism. His self-ironical idea of his own long-term silence about Communism affirmed the symbolic equivalence between Nazism and Communism, on the one hand, and Heidegger and

Derrida, on the other. Having refused to posit "symmetrical" relations between Nazism and Communism, Derrida produced a striking figure of these relations.

Inabilities to Mourn

In the 1980s, the question of the incomparability of the Nazi crimes launched a fierce discussion in Germany, which is remembered as the "*Historikerstreit,*" or "Historians' Dispute." The dispute was sparked by a controversial statement by the philosopher Ernst Nolte, in which he emphasized the historical fact that the practices of state terror, such as concentration camps, had been developed in the Soviet Union earlier than in Germany and that German socialists knew of them well before the Nazis came to power, thus suggesting the direct influence of the Soviets upon the Nazis. The philosopher Jürgen Habermas found that these arguments entailed an unacceptable "historicization of the Holocaust," which, he argued, served to relieve the burden of historical guilt. The ensuing controversy demonstrated the strength of the taboo governing the topic of the comparability of fascism and Communism. Even in 1998, François Furet characterized this comparison as a "taboo subject."[23]

In Russia, this has not always been the case. While any comparison between the Soviet Union and Nazi Germany was prohibited during the Soviet period, Vasily Grossman, in his *Life and Fate*, produced a convincing analysis of resemblances, differences, and interactions between these two regimes. Written in the 1950s but read in Russia only in the 1990s, this monumental novel unfolded, along with Solzhenitsyn's *The Gulag Archipelago*, a credible and responsible history decades before academic historians approached the subject. After the collapse of the Soviet Union, a former member of the Politburo of its Communist Party, Aleksandr Yakovlev, characterized the Soviet regime in terms that alluded to the German parallel: "It was full-scale fascism of the Russian type. Our tragedy is that we have not repented." Yakovlev chaired the Presidential Commission for the Rehabilitation of the Victims of Political Repressions; as he knew well, "rehabilitation" was far from being synonymous with repentance. A founder of the Memorial Society, Veniamin Iofe wrote that the "chaos of speculations" about the Soviet past works like "a smoke-screen" that masks the problem of "evaluating the Soviet period of Russian history in terms as clear as those used for evaluating Nazi Germany."[24] Iofe obviously wanted the Russia of the 1990s to produce as "clear" a vision of its violent past as Germany had managed to do.

Recent scholarship has returned to the question of mutual Nazi-Soviet influences. Indeed, the institutions of state and terror in Nazi Germany and Communist Russia featured multiple interactions before and after Molotov and Ribbentrop signed their pact in 1939. At crucial moments of their histories, these two regimes selectively emulated one another, and this reciprocal mimesis continued even at the peak of the confrontation. The history of the bloodiest lands and events of the twentieth century can be presented as a chain of imitations and confrontations, a sort of mimesis that can often be found at the core of rivalry.[25] In the recent historiography, the intricate timeline of these reciprocal influences—trade, emulations, deceptions, disenchantments, conflicts, and new imitations—have overshadowed the old-style "typological" speculations about resemblances and differences between the two totalitarianisms.

Several major factors should be taken into account in comparing the state of the German memory of National Socialism to the Russian memory of Soviet socialism. First, the Communist regime in Russia lasted much longer than the Nazi regime in Germany. Repairing the damage will probably require more time. In addition, Russia is less distant from the collapse of its Soviet state than Germany is from the collapse of its Nazi state. Since the Soviet regime lasted for seven decades, including at least three decades of terror, the concept of generation is less useful here than in the studies of the Holocaust survivors and their descendants. In post-Stalinist Russia, historical debates were suspended for several decades after an abortive mourning period during Khrushchev's Thaw. Second, the Soviet victims were significantly more diverse than the Nazi victims; their descendants are more dispersed and, in some cases, have competing interests, which creates multiple memory conflicts in the post-Soviet space. Third, Germany's postwar transformation was forced upon it by military defeat and occupation, while Russia's post-Soviet transformation was a political choice. No occupation force ruled Russia; it has continuously ruled itself. Instead of a Marshall Plan, the international support for the post-Soviet transition was remarkably inconsistent. Finally, there are substantial differences when it comes to the subjective experiences of victimization and mourning among the victims of both regimes and their descendants.

Decades ago, the French-Russian historian Mikhail Geller pinpointed the crucial difference here in a strong statement from his introduction to the first edition of Varlam Shalamov's *Kolyma Tales*:

Kolyma is a twin of Hitler's death camps. But it is also different. . . . The difference is that in Hitler's death camps, the victims knew why they were killed. . . . Those who died in the Kolyma or other Soviet camps, died bewildered.[26]

If the Nazi theory of racial purity was implemented with consistency, the application of the Soviet theory of class warfare was more arbitrary. Most of those Jews and Gypsies who died in the Nazi camps agreed with their jailers that they were Jews or Gypsies (though of course they did not agree that this should be cause to kill them). In contrast, most of those kulaks, saboteurs, and enemies of the people who died in the Soviet camps disagreed with their jailers that they were kulaks, saboteurs, and enemies of the people. Some of them hated "enemies of the people" just as much as their jailers did. In the Stalinist camps, many political prisoners shared the principles of their perpetrators but clung to the belief that in their personal cases, they had been mistakenly identified. In Nazi camps, on the other hand, the typical victim did not question his or her identification (for example, as a Jew), but objected to the general reasons for his or her persecution. Equally monstrous, the Soviet and Nazi regimes manifested different structures of disagreement between those in power and those who became their victims. These two structures of disagreement gave rise to two deeply different sentiments on the part of the victims, which in turn had different consequences: a strong and coherent anti-Fascist and Zionist movement in one case, and a chaotic and often painful mix of misplaced loyalty, escapism, and resistance to the Soviet state in the other.

Comparing the Russian and German memory of terror is like comparing two individuals at divergent points in the life cycle: an adolescent and an old man. In order to grasp their actual difference, one needs to imagine the old man in his younger years. Marking the end of the Nazi regime in 1945 and the end of the Soviet regime in 1991, we must judge the current state of Russian memory against German memory as it was documented in the 1960s. Germans had already experienced the Nuremberg trials (1945–46) and the Frankfurt Auschwitz trials (1963–1965). In Russia, an attempt to try the Communist Party failed in 1992. Germans began to open memorials and museums on the sites of camps in the 1960s; Russians started opening memorials in the 1990s. But in the 1960s, complaints about "collective amnesia" and "silencing the catastrophe" were probably as typical in Germany as they were in Russia over the last two decades.

The first study of German memory, *The Inability to Mourn* by Alexander and Margaret Mitscherlich, documents the situation in 1967. In their cultural critique of German society of the 1960s, the Mitscherlichs identified a syndrome that consisted of an "unconscious fixation on the past" whose consequences included what they called "collective ego depletion" and the "blockage of social imagination," and which was both enabled and masked by the conditions of material prosperity experienced by German society at the time. Germany had failed to produce the required "political working-through of the past." Historians, public intellectuals, and politicians had failed to "master the past" in which millions had been murdered. "After the enormity of the catastrophe that lay behind them . . . the country seems to have exhausted its capacity to produce politically effective ideas"; as a result, political life had frozen into "mere administrative routine." Atypically for psychologists, the Mitscherlichs blamed the political system rather than specific individuals. They also drew a connection to economic developments, arguing that "hard work and its success soon covered up the open wounds left by the past. . . . Economic restoration was accompanied by the growth of a new self-esteem." In the case of post-Soviet Russia, the rise in the standard of living has not been achieved through hard work, but is rather the result of pure luck, a combination of natural resource endowment and the vicissitudes of energy prices. But in all other respects, this diagnosis of 1960s Germany holds equally true for post-Soviet Russia. Like German society of the 1960s, Russian society of the 2000s is cushioned by a newfound prosperity; it is "at least materially, on the whole better off than ever before. . . . [I]t [feels] no incentive to expose its interpretation of the recent past to the inconvenient questioning of others." Like German society of the 1960s, Russian society today has no reason to overcome its "affective isolation . . . from the rest of the world." The working hypothesis of these German psychologists is still relevant, though in a context that its authors would find hard to imagine: "Our hypothesis views the political and social sterility of present-day Germany as being brought about by a denial of the past."[27]

The picture presented in *The Inability to Mourn* bears a strong, sometimes striking resemblance to the Russia of the 2010s. But this German-Russian comparison is less gloomy than it might appear; in fact, it gives a modest hope for the future, particularly if viewed in the light of Germany's subsequent development. A number of studies demonstrate that the transformation of German memory has both reflected and led the broader development of culture, society, and politics.[28] If German memory and German political life have changed so dramatically since the time analyzed by the Mitscherlichs, then this reinforces the possibilities for similar transformations in Russia in the near future.[29]

The Electorate in the Graves

According to some calculations, the total number of victims of internal violence in the twentieth century was larger than the number of victims of all international wars, including the two world wars.[30] Politics is about distinguishing between friends and foes, but the new data on "democides" supplement Carl Schmitt's tradition of political theory by asserting that this political differentiation took place not only in the noble domain of international relations but also—in the twentieth century, predominantly—in the dirty internal policies of the emerging nation-states, declining empires, and insecure dictatorships. Both the Nazis and the Soviets murdered many millions of those whom they doctrinally defined as their enemies with the help of various means of othering. However, it is also true that many millions were victimized before the process of their discursive excision from the political body had been completed, or even started.

A political theory of mourning might be built upon the famous dictum of Edmund Burke, who in his polemics against the ideas of the French Revolution claimed that the social contract "becomes a partnership not only between those who are living, but between those who are living, those who are dead, and those who are to be born." Different generations, living and dead, are partners in this contract, which links "lower with higher natures, . . . the visible and invisible world." This idea of a "great primeval contract" was conservative, but at the same time innovative and globalizing. A nation-state in this contract, wrote Burke, is "not but a clause."[31] More common in mystical contexts than in political ones, these concerns with the past and the dead were similarly theorized by Walter Benjamin, who wrote, "There is a secret agreement between past generations and the present one."[32] Disappointed with both the failure of revolution in Germany and its success in Russia, Benjamin revived Burke's ideas. The same postrevolutionary formula inspired Derrida in his *Specters of Marx*, though Burke does not feature in its index: no ethics or politics, writes Derrida, is just that does not recognize respect for those others who "are already dead or not yet born," and no justice is possible without responsibility "before the ghosts of those who are not yet born or who are already dead." Like Burke 200 years before him, Derrida does not posit his ghostly ideas as a metaphysical speculation about the nature of politics, but addresses them to the historical situation in which he lives, in the wake of "the oppressions of imperial capitalism or any other forms of totalitarianism."[33]

In the 1990s, when the Memorial Society discussed the forms of its political involvement in Russia's tortured transformation, one of its leaders, Veniamin Iofe, used to repeat: "Our electorate is there, in the graves."[34] Rejecting the direct participation of the Memorial Society in political elections, Iofe proclaimed the unique role of the past in the post-catastrophic politics. He was a physicist by training and probably never read Burke, but he knew the relevance of the "contract with the dead." A Soviet-era dissident and ex-prisoner, he also knew the affinity between memory and power.

Scholars tend to grumble about the condition of memory in contemporary Russia. Many speculate about collective nostalgia and cultural amnesia, or observe the "cold" character of the memory of Soviet terror.[35] Yet this notion of a deficit or crisis of popular historical knowledge in Russia does not reflect the current state of affairs and needs qualification. In fact, far from demonstrating an outright denial or forgetting of the Soviet catastrophe, the vast majority of Russians are well aware of their country's recent history. It is not historical knowledge that is at issue but its interpretation. Sociological surveys reveal a complex picture of a people who retain a vivid memory of the Soviet terror but are divided in their interpretation of this memory. This interpretation inevitably depends upon the schemas, theories, narratives, and myths that people receive from their scholars, artists, and politicians. Many Russians explain the Soviet terror as an exaggerated but rational response to actual problems that confronted the country at the time. These people believe that the terror was necessary for the survival of the nation, its modernization, industrialization, victory in World War II, and so forth. In Holocaust studies, interpretations of this kind are called "redemptive narrative"; as Lawrence Langer has shown convincingly, such redemption obstructs a sensible, "deep" connection to the catastrophic past.[36] Sociological polls reflect the massive spread of the need for a redemptive understanding of the past in contemporary Russia. However, the same polls say that the overwhelming majority of Russians and other post-Soviets are well aware of the crimes, misery, and "repressions" that remain memorable parts of the Soviet period. The polls, however, do not tell us about the substance of the historical truths and myths in which the public believes. Nor do they tell us why the public believes in the truth of some myths. They do not tell us who creates myths, mixes them with truths, and defines their changing boundaries.

In a popular post-Soviet Russian film, *The Peculiarities of National Hunting* (1995), a Finnish student is writing a dissertation about the history of Russian hunting.[37] During his field trip to Russia, he falls into the company of a group of drunken and bumbling Russian men on an amateur hunting trip. While they go about their drinking and shooting, the student visualizes gorgeous scenes of prerevolutionary aristocratic hunting with Borzoi dogs and mounted beauties. The comic effect of the film is based on the interpenetration of a pathetic present and an extraordinary but irrelevant past. Indeed, historical memory in Russia is a living, de-centered combination of symbols and judgments, which are experienced simultaneously, all at once, responding to various political needs and cultural desires. Because of the de-centered nature of this construction, deprived of consensual anchors or reference points, the public does not perceive the inconsistencies or logical conflicts between its different parts. In contrast to the multiculturalism that is actively promoted by American society, Russians live in and promote a condition I would call multihistorical.

There are university professors in Russia who explain Lenin or Gorbachev by the "fact" that they were Freemasons. There are influential churchmen who want to canonize Ivan the Terrible and Grigory Rasputin. There are authors who have written volumes on "the New Chronology," a popular alternative history penned mainly by astronomers, who dispute the Mongol occupation of Russia and claim that, in fact, Russia occupied Europe in the Middle Ages; some go so far in their revisionist efforts as to claim Slavic origins for Jesus Christ. There are academics and officials of law-enforcement agencies who believe that the years of Stalinism were the best time for Russia. In popular culture, manifestations of this multihistoricism border on kitsch. In 2002, I visited a fancy St. Petersburg restaurant called Russian Kitsch: Cafe of the Transitional Period, which featured grand frescos executed in the manner of socialist realism. In these images, Soviet collective farmers dance with American Indians, and Leonid Brezhnev, looking strangely similar to Frank Sinatra, gives a speech to a Stone Age tribe. In a similar spirit, artist Andrei Budaev, who is popular in the Moscow of the 2010's, depicts a fictional encounter between Putin and Brezhnev. In the scene, Brezhnev and Putin are shaking hands, to the applause of members of their respective contemporary entourages, such as Mikhail Suslov and Vladislav Surkov—a gathering that could never have taken place in real life. The anachronistic character of this painting does not obscure its critical message: the happy confluence of two corrupt and cynical cliques and the historical regress of Putin's rule to the Brezhnev template. In another series of large-scale works, Budaev reproduces the classical canvases by Bosch, Breughel, and Rubens, with the faces of their characters substituted by those of Russian political leaders and oligarchs. In this newest version of the Russian longing for world culture, hilarious combinations of persons and situations fit the classical patterns of corruption and decadence, barbarian invasions, the end of empire, and the descent into hell.

In 2008, many millions were invested, and probably earned, on the show "The Name of Russia," which TV-Russia declared "our most significant project of the year." On the program, the leading filmmaker, Nikita Mikhalkov, the celebrated director of *Burnt by the Sun* (1994) and many other films, presided over a jury of twelve VIPs who were supposed to guide the public in electing the greatest figure in Russian history. From the Speaker of the Russian parliament to the metropolitan (and future patriarch) of the Russian Orthodox Church, all the jury members were male; all were ethnically Russian; all of them were, and looked, aged. Without any doubt, they represented the ruling group.

According to the promotional blurb, TV-Russia asked unnamed historians to produce an initial list of 500 candidates, which was then published for an online vote. The vote produced a landslide victory for Stalin. Surprised but not discouraged, TV-Russia explained this as the result of an attack by hackers. This vote was annulled, the technology was improved, and a fresh vote produced a new short list of medieval warriors, czars, nineteenth-century writers, and Bolshevik leaders, with one scientist thrown in for good measure. In the weekly sessions of the show, the twelve dignitaries discussed each of these figures, from Tolstoy to Stalin. The jury voted in-house; the public voted online or by telephone. As a result, Russia would learn who was its greatest personage, or rather personification. The segment dealing with Alexander Nevsky, a thirteenth-century Russian prince, began with fragments of the eponymous 1938 film by Sergei Eisenstein, which was commissioned by Stalin to showcase Russia's historical victory over the Germans. A historian expressed doubts about the film's truth-value. The chairman, Nikita Mikhalkov, made a spirited rebuttal, arguing that the jury was interested not so much in verifying historical facts as in identifying inspiring and legendary images, which the new Russia might profitably use. But if this self-conscious mythmaking worked smoothly when it came to the ancient Alexander Nevsky, it produced new questions when applied to Stalin. Even a veteran general who praised Stalin on the show admitted that his own father had been imprisoned during the repressions, though "only" for six months. But although the jury ultimately substituted the cultish Stalin with the legendary Alexander Nevsky in the role of "the name of Russia," their sympathies for Stalin were evident. Despite the undisputed knowledge of Stalin's "repressions," the viability of Stalin's cult is remarkable. Nationalism requires sacrifices as much as socialism did: the number of victims also makes Russia great.

The show included footage from the new film by Mikhalkov, *Burnt by the Sun-2*, which was released later, in 2010. The central character, Commander Kotov, who is played by Mikhalkov, has survived the gulag and is now talking to Stalin, who is instructing Kotov on how to attack the enemy. Usually suave and ironic, Kotov loses his cool when he sees Stalin. The scene is full of admiration and awe, though the dialogue verges on the absurd; with no attempt at analysis, Mikhalkov affirms the irresistible impact of Stalin. Essentially, he reproduces here the same phenomenon that was dubbed the "cult of personality" fifty years earlier. In this vision, Kotov and millions of others were "burnt by the Sun," but one can neither deny the force of the sun nor turn it off. Stalin's "charisma" is ineffable, beyond human communication.

After Repentance

Reflecting the moving equilibrium between the competing forces of politics, culture, and time, accepted definitions of what is "right" and "healthy" in the memory of the Soviet past shift with every new generation. But no consensus on the crucial issues of historical memory has been reached in twenty-first-century Russia. While the state is led by former KGB officers who are no more interested in apologizing for the past than they are in fair elections in the present, the struggling civil society and the intrepid reading public are possessed by the unquiet ghosts of the Soviet era. But the circular time of postcatastrophic experience conflates uneasily with the linear time of history.[38] Whatever the scale of victimization, mourning remains a personal matter, but collective rituals and cultural artifacts are critical for the process. Sharing sorrow with the community, burial rituals prevent mourning from developing into melancholy. Crystals of memory, monuments keep the uncanny where it belongs, in the grave. The anthropologist Katherine Verdery asserts that "in many human communities, to set up right relations between living human communities and their ancestors depends critically on proper burials." Though it is never easy to learn which relations are "right," wrong relations are universally believed to be unfair to the dead and dangerous to the living.[39] In the post-Soviet economy of memory, where the losses are massive and the monuments in short supply, the dead return as the undead. The innocent victims turn into uncanny monsters. Locked in various but usually monstrous bodies and speaking in various but usually fictional tongues, post-Soviet Clorindas are bearing witness to their Tancreds about war and peace, life and fate, violence and the sacred.

Having distinguished between two forms of cultural memory, the hardware and the software, in Russian memory and mourning, I see the proliferation of a third form, which is impossible to reduce to the first two. I am referring to ghosts, spirits, vampires, dolls, and other simulacra that carry the memory of the dead.[40] Usually, ghosts live in texts; sometimes they inhabit cemeteries and emerge from monuments. Most often, ghosts visit those whose dead have not been properly buried. Three elements of cultural memory—its software, hardware, and ghostware—are intimately connected. Texts are symbolic, while ghosts are iconic: as signs, ghosts possess a visual resemblance to the signified; in contrast to monuments, texts and ghosts are ephemeral; and in contrast to texts and monuments, ghosts are uncanny. These ghostly components of memory deserve a detailed analysis and close reading. One scholar of German memory confronting similar problems has devised an approach that he calls "spectral materialism"; I have used the concept of "ghostware" to indicate this new and challenging domain.[41]

One can feel the swift evolution of the popular style of historicizing by watching and comparing several Russian films, starting from the pre-post-Soviet *Zero City* (1988). In the course of the film, the narrative gradually shifts from an antibureaucratic comedy to a fable about the grasping power of the past. The protagonist is a typical Soviet man, an unambitious engineer who comes from Moscow to a provincial factory on a business trip. Screened as a drama of misrecognition, the story focuses on the investigation of a local scandal that was suppressed in the 1960s but leads to a suicide in the 1980s. Irresistibly drawn into this provincial story, the protagonist finds himself unable to escape. A key setting for this imprisonment is the local historical museum, where the engineer is presented with a past that feels more lively and consequential than his present has ever been. He ends up stuck in the museum, under the sway of a monotonous, pedantic historian who presents this Soviet Everyman with an astonishing panoply of pictures of the past in the form of group statues composed of living people. Full of tricks, conspiracies, and outright hallucinations that are all presented as apparitions of the past, the film leaves the aftertaste of a mystery that has not been resolved by its creators.

In the spirit of melancholy, *Zero City* combines an ecstatic fascination with the great but horrible past with a vague anxiety about the future. Conveying expert knowledge but zero sympathy for the late-Soviet present, this film still lacked the staple feature of post-Soviet cinema: hostile, mystical beasts that operate among humans and interfere with their present. In contrast to the hyperhistorical *Zero City*, *Night Watch* (2004) and its sequel, *Day Watch* (2006), demonstrate the post-Soviet infatuation with magic in a deliberately abstract, ahistorical context.[42] Based on the bestselling trilogy by Sergei Lukianenko, a psychiatrist from Kazakhstan who has made himself into one of the most popular post-Soviet authors, these films present an enormous taxonomy of immortal creatures. Vampires and other supernatural beasts rule over Russians and live in their midst. Humans are entirely deprived of self-control, autonomy, and political life in this world. As in a camp, these Muscovites have been reduced to bare life, and essentially fulfill the role of the vampires' cattle (the vampires in the film prefer human blood but will settle for pigs' blood if necessary). But actual politics are deployed by creatures of a higher order than vampires and humans. These creatures are immortal and powerful though otherwise look like humans. Like Americans, they are divided into two equally powerful parties, an achievement that has never been accomplished by Muscovites. The origins of their conflict are projected back to medieval Europe in one episode, and to the Asia of Genghis Khan in another. As in historical debates between contemporary Russian intellectuals, the roots of the current problems are presented as lost and found in the most distant time and spaces, but not in current or recent Russian politics. There is not a word in this movie about Stalin or the Soviet Union. The contemporary commoners, all of whom are potential victims of vampires, are juxtaposed against noble warriors whose moments of glory and sources of conflicts are all in the past. What matters is not happening here and now; it all happened in the past. The past, which is imagined as grand and foreign, determines the actual, dismal present. While the contemporary rulers are of alien and metaphysical origins, the vampires are local and earthly. Curiously, the most important of these vampires is played by the only actor in this young, all-star cast who was famous in the Soviet era, Valery Zolotukhin. The vampires represent, as they do in Slavic folklore, the unburied dead, while the remarkable face of their leader reflects a free play of Soviet shadows.[43] These films convey a static, irresolvable melancholy that risks slipping into paranoia. If vampires really ruled Russia, this is the worldview that they would disseminate among their human chattel to keep them subdued and passive. In the battle between light and dark forces, what is at stake is probably not the right to license vampires' bloodsucking activities, as *Night Watch* suggests. Inverting the film's metaphor, the only means of preventing the reproduction of vampires is to bury, acknowledge, and remember the dead.

Some other post-Soviet blockbusters produce a deeper analysis of the changing relations between the past and the present. The action of *Terra*

Nova takes place in 2013.[44] Prisons are overfilled worldwide, and the global society now exports its outcasts to Russia, where the international inmates reproduce the mores of the gulag. Left to fend for themselves on an Arctic island, the prisoners reinvent administrative corruption, ethnic hatred, and cannibalism. When the global overseers arrive at the scene they are horrified by what they find, though it remains an open question whether it was their stupidity or greed that has caused this disastrous result of social engineering. The message is that despite its part in globalization, Russia is still living by the rules of the gulag, and these rules are powerful enough to spread throughout the global community. A somewhat more parochial thriller under the challenging title *Death to the Soviet Children*[45] chronicles a reality TV show that a Moscow television company is shooting at the site of a former pioneer camp, where Soviet children spent their summers as part of their Communist upbringing. While young, attractive, and well-dressed volunteers rehearse their show, a mysterious killer begins to murder them, one by one. The murderer turns out to be the producer of the show, who was a pioneer and spent childhood summers in this camp about thirty years earlier. Possessed by the memories of his youth, he takes revenge on it by sacrificing about a dozen young bodies in a bloody ritual whose meaning remains unexplored. The film plays out a clash of civilizations, the Soviet and the new Russian, which are deeply incompatible but are forced to exist on the same sites and puncture the same people. Reinventing a sacrificial ritual that is even older and less familiar to his victims than Soviet life, the middle-aged murderer plays out a conflict that is known to many of his peers. While killing his victims, the murderer reads and sometimes writes with their blood the long-forgotten horror doggerels (*uzhastiki*) that were popular in the 1980s (see chapter 5), hence bridging the epochs and presenting his post-Soviet murders as a resurgence of the Soviet terror.

One of the best Russian films, *4*, illustrates the spectral dynamics of a postcatastrophic memory that produces the undead, cherishes and holds on to them, and, in rare acts of heroism, buries them.[46] One of the male characters, a Moscow manager, trades in frozen meat that has been preserved since Soviet times and still feeds Russia's capital. A huge pile of frozen meat bearing the label "1969" is the opening image of this film, which is set in the recognizable landscape of twenty-first-century Russia's capital and provinces. The fifty-year-old meat is a metaphor for the

Russian culture and economy, which despite all the dramatic changes of the past decades, continues to depend on the legacy of its long-dead Soviet predecessor. Another male character, a musician, is sent to a labor camp after he runs into trouble with the Moscow police. In the camp, he is reduced to the lowest caste of the physically and sexually abused prisoners; in the end of the film we see him convoyed, among hundreds of fellow prisoners, to a distant "hot spot," a front of the civil war. The female protagonist, a Moscow prostitute, travels deep into the countryside to attend the funeral of her sister. This sister had lived in a community of abandoned females who manufacture dolls made of bread. These women use their yeasty dolls as substitutes for partners; they play, drink alcohol, and have sex with these dolls. Creating a world of simulacra, this melancholic substitution protects the villagers from their pathetic reality. The dolls and the meat of the past must be buried in order to let the people live in their present. In a climactic moment, the only vital character of the film, the prostitute, burns the bread dolls on the grave of her sister in a gesture of despair and triumph. With its panoramic survey of social reality; a bizarre obsession with quadruplets and mutations; a ceaseless exchange between humans, dogs, and dolls; and a persistent deconstruction of folkloric and populist themes, this film works as a veritable encyclopedia of post-Soviet culture. Its authors, Vladimir Sorokin and Ilia Khrzhanovsky, have since gone on to direct an ambitious new film, *Dau*, a filmic biography of the Soviet physicist Lev Landau, who spent a year in prison in 1938–1939 and received the Nobel Prize in 1962. Reportedly, the setting of *Dau* reproduces the Moscow lifestyle of the late 1950s in an unprecedented and extreme level of detail, which includes exact replicas of Soviet-style underclothing for hundreds of actors and extras. Adherence to the rules of this simulated world is compulsory, and strictly enforced on the set. Crew members are fined for using ahistorical words, pieces of clothing, or cell phones.[47]

In Tengiz Abuladze's film *Repentance*,[48] which is now a Soviet classic, the daughter of a victim digs up the corpse of the dictator. She goes on trial but does not repent: she would do it 300 times over, she declares. It is not the corpse of the dictator that is uncanny in this film but the living dictator, as he is remembered or imagined by his former subjects. As in Sophocles's *Antigone*, the perpetually moving corpse begets new tragedies; in *Repentance*, it brings about the suicide of the dictator's grandson.[49] In *The Living*, a Russian soldier of the Chechen War, Kir, is rescued by his comrades, who are then themselves killed in action.[50] On his way home from the war, Kir murders his officer and cheats on his fiancée. He does not care; he is possessed by the ghosts of his lost comrades, who come to him alive though other people do not see them. When Kir and his ghostly companions travel to Moscow, what they (and the viewers) actually see is the burial monument to Stalin near the Kremlin Wall. The movie ends with Kir's visit to an abandoned cemetery, where he hopes to find his friends buried like heroes. While trying to find these graves, Kir dies; immediately, he joins the company of his ghostly fellows. The multiple tricks that the undead play with the living in this film force the viewer to suspect that the soldier was probably dead from the very beginning; perhaps all or a large part of what we see actually happened to his ghost.

These two films, *Repentance* and *The Living*, mark the start and the possible end of the post-Soviet transition, which may yet turn out to have been a false start and a dead end. In the 1980s, it seemed that the most important goal was to punish the dead dictator and, in this way, to restore justice posthumously; twenty years later, the living were still struggling with the authorities, but their unburied dead were friends, not foes. There are enemies who are alive and deserve death, but there are also friends who are dead and need to be buried. Both films play on the uncanny effects of communication between the living and the dead; but while *Repentance* celebrates the change of generations, the trial of memory, and historical time, *The Living* deconstructs the meaning of death in an obsessive way that makes time cyclical and history irrelevant. Still hopeful for the future, *Repentance* argues for a new ethical order that would include dead corpses in its scope. Self-censoring any sign of hope, *The Living* shows the ghostly nature of postcatastrophic consciousness, which obscures the very difference between the living and the dead. Here, the post-Soviet trial of the dead gives way to a new Russian communion and mingling with the dead.

A scene from a historical film, *Tsar* (2009), returns this post-Soviet metaphor to its medieval roots. Based on a novel by a major writer, Aleksei Ivanov, and directed by a major filmmaker, Pavel Lungin, both of whom have vast experience with historical fictions, the film presents an episode from the reign of Ivan the Terrible. Engaged in an explicit polemical relation with Eisenstein's Soviet classic *Ivan the Terrible* (1944–1946), this post-Soviet film represents Ivan as a cruel tyrant, deluded millenarian, and self-destructive coward. In one scene, the czar pardons his prisoner, a prince who, during torture that is shown in bloody detail, admits to high treason. His torturer understands the czar's granting of mercy as an order to kill the prince instead of continuing the torture. Before the execution, the perpetrator asks the prince to give his word that he will not haunt the czar after his death. Begging for death, the prince makes the promise on behalf of his ghost, and the satisfied executioner hangs him. Consciously and purposefully, the film transcends the boundaries between the mystical and the political. Exemplifying the unity of mourning and warning (see chapter 2), it merges three epochs: Ivan the Terrible's Russia of the mid-sixteenth century; Stalin's Russia of the mid-twentieth century; and Putin's Russia of the present day.

The scholars of the European Enlightenment observe how its rational ordering of the world, which was still full of unpredictable suffering, led to the invention of the uncanny, "a new human experience of strangeness, anxiety, bafflement, and intellectual impasse."[51] By analogy I argue that Soviet culture, with its combination of bellicose rationalism and absurd violence, generated a veritable explosion of figurative and mystical ways in which people responded to their world. Official culture locked these ghostly ways in the underground of everyday life with its rumors, legends, and anecdotes, and also in low genres of art and literature that were less susceptible to censorship. Released by the glasnost of the late twentieth century, repressed figures of this Soviet underground returned to their place of origin, high culture, where they became dominant ways of representing history and even politics. Slavoj Žižek suggests that the return of the dead has become "a fundamental fantasy of contemporary mass culture."[52] Defeating the ideals of the Enlightenment, this process seems to be especially prominent in Russia, which has inherited and rejected the ideals of the Enlightenment in their perverted Soviet forms. Postsecular politics entails a transformation of "the state's secularist self-understanding" in various parts of the world, and its historical mechanisms and manifestations are different everywhere.[53] In the global world of the twenty-first century, mourning and warning are developing their dual alliance, but their proportions and relations within this alliance differ in different cultures. Some authors and cultures proliferate their ghosts, vampires, and zombies in response to the catastrophes of the past; others generate this imagery in anticipation of the catastrophes of the future. Either way, this ghostly perspective on world affairs—hauntological worldliness, I would say—is both realist and humanist. It is only on the hauntic level that Edmund Burke's "great primeval contract" between the living, the dead, and the unborn can be imagined or, for that matter, observed.

Having taught the relevance of ghosts to the interpretative community of his readers, Derrida does not offer much help in understanding their nature, taxonomy, or life cycle. As some critics have mentioned, his ghosts are not the same as the sophisticated phantoms of Nicolas Abraham and Maria Torok, which keep the secrets of the past and transmit them, in eternally encrypted form, from generation to generation. Derrida's ghosts could reveal a secret if they wanted to, but they do not necessarily do that, and the reason behind their existence is different from this conspiratorial knowledge. "It is in the name of *justice*" that Derrida speaks about the ghosts, and not in the name of knowledge. But this is a special kind of justice, one that brings the living and the dead together in a single ghostly equation. As for Burke, for Derrida "present existence . . . has never been the condition . . . of justice." Theirs is the justice of relations between the living and the dead. It needs to be established "*through* but also *beyond* right and law,"[54] though not beyond human comprehension, with its rhetorical devices such as ghosts. Practically speaking, this particular "justice," one of the most frequent concepts in Derrida's late writings, is the debt owed to the dead (see chapter 6). As far as I know, Derrida and Siniavsky never met and never read one another, though they easily might have. Despite the fact that their experiences differ dramatically, their conclusions are similar: the living owe a debt to the dead, and this debt must be returned. Otherwise, the dead will continue to return to life in disguised forms, like Clorinda, presenting their claims and preventing the Tancreds from continuing their crusades.

But it is also true that these debts before the dead can never be returned, and this justice can never be established. I am sure that all our philosophers of mourning, from Tasso to Burke to Freud to Siniavsky to Derrida, would agree with this thesis, which gives postcatastrophic mourning its interminable, melancholic character. Having granted these images—ghosts, debts, posthumous justice—all the metaphorical relevance they deserve, one still feels puzzled by them. How can we the living redeem our debt to the dead? What kind of justice are we talking about? Can we repay the ghosts? Do we have a currency that is convertible for this task? Can this toolkit of legal and financial metaphors provide any help in carrying out the work of mourning?

Derrida links his hauntology with the idea of retributive justice. In a postcatastrophic situation, we mourners live lives and die deaths that are incomparably better than those of our precursors. This is why to live with ghosts means "to live otherwise, and better. No, not better, but more justly."[55] This kind of justice does not require judiciary power, but it does need scholars, as Hamlet needed Horatio. As the living and the undead grow more accustomed to each other, they develop an uneasy friendship that needs to be noticed, articulated, and recognized. As Derrida urged, the ghostly dimension of our lifeworld is permanent; we must "learn to live with ghosts." This is a departure from a folklore understanding of ghostly apparitions as consequences of improper burial rites, with the implicit promise that reburial would send the ghosts safely back to their graves. Derrida does not want this to happen as a general case, and I do not see it happening in Russia. In contrast to laying them to rest, learning to live with ghosts is an open-ended process, which generates the unpredictable and rich variety of Victims' Balls, memory events, and cultural innovations.

These mournful experiences need to be summarized, but justice is a poor concept for doing this work. Ghosts need recognition rather than justice. There is no way to redistribute anything of value between the dead and the living; but there is a very real sense in which unjustifiable deaths can be recognized by the living. Like Clorinda in her tree, or Hamlet's father in his armor, or Siniavsky's marching convicts who "are on the move . . . as long as I live, as long as we all live,"[56] ghosts demand recognition.

11

Magical Historicism

Strange creatures have permeated the cultural representation of the gulag. Solzhenitsyn's *The Gulag Archipelago* starts with the story of Siberian convicts coming across a triton, a kind of prehistoric newt that has been preserved by chance under the ice, a frozen monstrosity. The convicts immediately fall upon it and consume it greedily, and Solzhenitsyn reflects: "I have absorbed into myself my own eleven years there [in the camp] not as something shameful nor as a nightmare to be cursed: I have come almost to love that monstrous world." Solzhenitsyn had cartloads of material on hand, even without that grisly triton. But in a strange yet convincing way, Solzhenitsyn contrived to make precisely that monster into an all-encompassing symbol of terror. Convicts were "the only people who could devour a prehistoric salamander *with relish*." They were a "tribe," he said, and the frozen monster was their totemic father. Freud would have appreciated this image.

We could picture the entire scene right down to the smallest details: how those present broke up the ice in frenzied haste; how, flouting the higher claims of ichthyology and elbowing each other to be first, they tore off chunks of the prehistoric flesh and hauled them over to the bonfire to thaw them out and bolt them down.

In his work on the uncanny, Freud asserts that whatever (and Solzhenitsyn would add, whoever) is repressed returns in distorted, fragmented, or monstrous forms. The postcatastrophic memory carries within itself elements of the uncanny—the familiar and the forgotten, the restored and the unrecognized, the never-experienced and the well-masticated. When the gulag prisoners tear the prehistoric monster apart and consume it in the light of the bonfire, it feels like a scene not from Solzhenitsyn's *Gulag Archipelago* but rather from Freud's *Totem and Taboo*. The devoured monster is immortal, of course; a memorial symbol of pain, fear, and guilt, it devours those who have tasted it. Indeed, Solzhenitsyn introduced his great book as an attempt "to give some account of the bones and flesh of that salamander—which, incidentally, is still alive."[1]

Shades We No Longer Call Back

As Tancred learned from Clorinda imprisoned in her tree, the spirits of the dead do not just pass away over the years; their return in new forms feels dangerous to the living. Akhmatova's verses of 1945 analyze this posthumous transformation, a crucial part of the work of mourning, in bitter and sober words. She describes three stages of memory: the warm and immediate feeling of the fresh loss that retains the image of the lost; ritualized, compulsive visits to the sites and images of memory that emancipate the subject by making the remembrance routine and aseptic; and finally, the eventual acceptance of the loss. With the passing of time, human memory defamiliarizes the dead. The dead become alien and frightening, and this third, shameful stage of memory is the bitterest.

> And there are no remaining witnesses to the events . . .
> And slowly the shades withdraw from us,
> Shades we no longer call back
> Whose return would be too terrible for us.[2]

For this last and "bitterest" stage, the most characteristic is the mutual misrecognition between the dead and the living. In her beautiful elegy, probably the best analysis of mourning in Russian poetry, Akhmatova repeats the theme of misrecognition twice, applying it first to the self, then to the other: if we could descend into the past, it would have been futile, because the past changes in its own way:

> Nobody knows us: we are foreign . . .
> And this is when the bitterest comes: . . .
> We understand that those who died we would not recognize.[3]

Akhmatova's husband, Nikolai Gumilev, was incarcerated in the Crosses prison in the center of Petrograd and then shot at a still unknown site in 1921.[4] Their son, Lev Gumilev, was imprisoned in the Crosses in 1938–1939. It was there that Akhmatova spent "seventeen months" trying to pass food to her son and to obtain information about him, and where she wanted to be commemorated by a monument, though all this proved to be equally futile. Joseph Brodsky, who was imprisoned in the same prison in 1964, says that "the main thing in [Akhmatova's] *Requiem* is the theme of splitting, the theme of the author's inability to have an adequate reaction. . . . The theme of *Requiem* is not the perishing of millions but the impossibility of the survivor coming to terms with this perishing."[5] Depicting her experience at the gates of the Crosses, Akhmatova "is constantly talking about how close she is to madness," notes Brodsky. He quotes from *Requiem*:

> Already madness dips its wings
> And cuts a shade across my heart . . .
> I realize that . . . I must yield,
> Listening closely to my own
> Delirium, however strange.

"These last two lines pronounce the greatest truth," says Brodsky. He might have continued this thought by quoting from Akhmatova's *Poem Without a Hero*, about the call of memory that interpellates the narrator:

> . . . from afar, responding to this appeal,
> Come the terrible sounds—
> Of gurgling, groans and screams.[6]

Akhmatova scholars and translators have had a difficult time interpreting these lines. Classical Russian literature is a treasure house of the uncanny. Its most memorable monsters include the "thoughtful vampire" in Pushkin's *Onegin*, Lermontov's "Demon," Gogol's horrifying visions, and a panoply of Russian symbolists' beasts.[7] Aleksandr Blok even called the nineteenth century a "vampiric century." Intertextually, Akhmatova might be referring to any or all of these predecessors. More important, however, is her general intuition, which tells us the poetic truth about memory and mourning after catastrophe: "Delirium, however strange."

Snake Charmers

Vampire stories were also popular in Soviet culture and specifically in the gulag. In Shalamov's story "The Snake Charmer," prisoners force a writer in their midst, Platonov, to entertain them with "stories." Platonov's favorite is Bram Stoker's *Dracula*, but the prisoners prefer pulp fiction.[8] Even though the prisoners are captivated by his storytelling, there is a sense of menace and violence hanging over the scene; his survival depends on his ability to keep them pacified with his stories. This is how Shalamov saw the Soviet writer: as a doomed snake charmer, a magician who mesmerizes the public because if he fails to do so, the public will beat him to death.

I see a lineage that runs from this fictional Platonov, who is not too distant from the real-life postrevolutionary writer Andrei Platonov, to a hermetic pioneer of the snake-charming genre in the late-Soviet period, Yury Mamleev. His first novel, *Shatuny* (written in 1966, published in 1988 in the West and in 1996 in Russia), presents the sleepy central character, Sonnov, who is able to talk only to corpses, preferably to those whom he has killed himself. Sonnov is not interested in women, work, or anything else but the dead. The peak of his life is the random murder of a student with whose corpse he establishes an inspired, sublime dialogue. In his intuitive but pretentious prose, Mamleev depicts a crucial paradox of the postcatastrophic culture: its obsessive interest in the dead, which obstructs its ability to communicate with the living. In the dacha community in which Mamleev sets this novel, a professor is dying; after his death, or instead of it, he turns into a half-bird, half-human monster whom other characters call the "chicken-corpse"—a caricature of the intelligentsia. Written with multiple allusions to symbolist and early Soviet prose, this bizarre fiction was one of the first exemplars of the emerging genre, which Mamleev's critics of the 1990s labeled, not without reason, necrophilic.

The son of a professor of psychiatry who studied Freud and died in the gulag in the 1940s, Mamleev became a leader of the "mystical underground" in the Moscow of the Thaw.[9] He emigrated to the United States in 1975, wrote *Shatuny* in Paris, and returned to Russia after 1991. There he befriended Aleksandr Dugin, the leader of the pro-Kremlin "Eurasian movement," which combines an obscure mysticism with nationalist politics. In his comment on *Shatuny*, Dugin wrote that Sonnov "uses the soul of every victim as a streetcar which brings him to the afterworld" and that he represents "the uncanny truth" about "the Russian people who are pregnant with metaphysical rebellion."[10] I believe that Sonnov's "uncanny truth" is about the enormity of the Soviet losses. His compulsive desire to talk to the dead is, simply, a Hamlet-like obsession with their parental spirits. Longing for the dead, Sonnov and his author are possessed by the memory of their fathers. To be sure, Mamleev's eerie, semiconscious mourning is different from the factual, righteous witnessing exemplified by Solzhenitsyn's account of the Soviet past. Both versions of mourning are mimetic, but the difference between them might be compared to the difference between the genres of the documentary film, which represents a catastrophe by striving to reconstruct its facts, scale, and causes, and the horror movie, which reenacts the catastrophe, distorting all its features but actualizing the most important one—its horror.[11]

In 1992, Yefim Etkind wrote: "The reality of devils in our time is incomparably higher than it was in the past epochs."[12] Indeed, post-Soviet devils seem more real and also even more frequent than their predecessors in the classical Russian and Soviet literatures; but in contrast to the unfading interest in the gothic motifs of Russian and European letters, critics and scholars have barely noticed the uncanny in the post-Soviet literature.[13] However, this theme has a generally acclaimed leader, Viktor Pelevin. In contrast to the warped and nationalist Mamleev, the younger Viktor Pelevin is highly successful both in Russia and abroad. His works present a panoply of monsters, which like their ancient precursors combine human and nonhuman features, though sometimes the nonhuman part is high-tech rather than beastly. In his early essay "Comparative Anthropology," Pelevin interpreted the Soviet experience as zombification. Basing his ideas on *The Serpent and the Rainbow* by American anthropologist Wade Davis (1985), Pelevin describes how Haitian secret societies converted humans into zombies by burying them, digging them up the next day, and then selling them on as farmhands to plantation owners. Those who lived through the Soviet period went through something similar to this, speculates Pelevin. He imagines a person who, "after reading some brochures," attempts to initiate perestroika in a typical Soviet town. Unexpectedly, the would-be reformer falls "into an incomprehensible pit. There are half-rotten logs, skeletons of horses and humans, pieces of ceramics and ruined metal around. He is in a grave." He is a zombie who returns to the grave where he came from. The Soviet town rests on the remains of a camp: try to change it, and you are pulled into the gulag below. Its population is made up of zombies; "many zombies were members of the Soviet Union of Writers and therefore, zombies were described from the inside as well as from the outside."[14] In a more serious way, the ex-prisoner Veniamin Iofe wrote that surviving a Soviet camp was a symbolic death that always threatened to become real. Every personal survival was a return from the land of the dead, and, like Pelevin, Iofe imagined the whole nation returning to the new life from the state of frozen nonbeing.[15] This is the reason for the specifically post-Soviet usage of prosopopoeia, a classical trope that enables poets to speak with and for the dead by lending voice to "an absent, deceased, or voiceless entity."[16] In the post-Soviet revival of this archaic tradition, these fictional but indispensable voices are lent to revenants, hybrids, and monsters.

In Pelevin's *Life of Insects* (1993), the characters are talking insects who sound like the confused Soviet subjects struggling to find their way in the new era; in his *Sacred Book of the Werewolf* (2004), the characters are revenants of the canine variety; and in *Empire V* (2006), they are vampires who reign over Russia. At one level all this adds up to a caricature of the greedy and ambitious, but still awkward and stumbling Muscovite elite; but there is also a deeper message. In *The Sacred Book*, the narrator, an immortal fox, turns into a woman at will. Working as a prostitute in Moscow, she meets a werewolf who works there as a general of the secret service, the heir to the KGB. From time to time, this wolf-general travels to the north where, among the abandoned camps, he growls at the exhausted oil wells, begging them to produce oil.[17] In *Empire V*, vampires are not the ancient parasites who sucked human bodies, but modern ones who milk their cattle, humans, and take care of them like dairy farmers. A Muscovite-turned-vampire, the protagonist finds consolation in the idea that his new identity is no more surprising than his earlier transfiguration from a Soviet child into a post-Soviet man: "It was really strange when the epoch ended but the people stayed where they were. . . . The world became entirely different. There was something insane in it."[18] Vampires teach the two arts that are central to the new Russians, "glamour and discourse." Unfortunately, these arts help vampires to establish their power over humans, but do not help humans banish vampires.

Pelevin's swinging between werewolves and vampires is understandable. In Slavic folklore, dogs, wolves, and werewolves were believed to be the worst enemies of vampires. Left unburied, a corpse turns into a vampire unless it is eaten by wolves.[19] Rivals of the uncanny, canines play a large part in the cultural memory of the Soviet past. One of the early realistic narratives of the gulag, *Faithful Ruslan* by Georgy Vladimov (published in the West in 1975 and in Russia in 1989), focused on a camp guard dog that is presented as a more reliable witness than either the prisoners or their jailors. Vladimir Vysotsky, who celebrated the collective voice of ex-prisoners, presented himself as a cornered wolf in one of his famous songs, "The Wolf Hunt." Stray dogs start and end Ilya Khrzhanovsky's film *4* (2005), which is based on Vladimir Sorokin's screenplay; they guard some humans, kill others, devour their uncanny effigies, and seem to be on the brink of taking over Moscow. The strange success of the Russian artist Oleg Kulik, who plays a barking and biting dog in his performances, can be understood in the same context.[20]

Justification

For reasons that the reader will grasp easily by this stage, the late-Soviet and post-Soviet novel has been overpopulated by historians as its central protagonists. In the novel *Justification* (2001), Dmitry Bykov presents the young Moscow historian, Rogov, the grandson of a victim who was arrested in 1938. Obsessed with the grandfather he never knew, Rogov develops an ingenious theory of Stalinism. Those "repressions," he thinks, could not be "unjustified"; they must have had an interpretable meaning. Rogov theorizes that people were subjected to unbearable suffering in order to select out those few who were fit to survive it all. Those who gave up under torture and confessed to invented crimes betrayed Stalin and had to perish; those who resisted to the end were secretly preserved, healed, and trained.[21] As operatives and leaders, these people changed the course of World War II and the Cold War, Rogov believes. Inspired by this theory, he travels to Siberia in the hope of finding his grandfather still alive and residing in a secret Soviet-style reservation. On his journey, Rogov discovers a clandestine community of religious sectarians and a sadomasochist resort where new Russians torture their peers for pleasure.

Finally, Rogov drowns himself in a Siberian marsh. Starting as melancholy (a failure to separate from the lost object), the doomed longing for the grandfather ends by taking the form of paranoia (an obsession that is manifested in delusions).

Bykov is one of the most popular Russian intellectuals of the new century—writer, poet, media anchor, and biographer. In *Justification*, his first novel, he touched a nerve of post-Soviet memory.[22] By creating a direct connection between grandsons and grandfathers, the fictional post-Soviet family renders the last Soviet generation irrelevant.[23] Andrei Bitov should be credited with the invention of this motif; in his pre-post-Soviet novel *Pushkin House*, Odoevtsev, a young historian of literature, wants to undo the Soviet experience by rejecting his father and worshipping his grandfather, the gulag survivor. In contrast to Rogov who was born too late, Odoevtsev does find his grandfather, though the damaged returnee expresses little interest in his grandson (see chapter 3). Both novels confront Soviet history as part of a desperate quest for its meaning. Importantly, central characters in both novels are historians, professionals of memory. Odoevtsev survives his heavy drinking to become an established scholar at the Soviet Academy of Sciences; Rogov commits suicide. In comparing these texts, one observes that the pain of memory for the lost grandfathers has not been much alleviated during the last thirty years. But we can make out a certain narrowing of focus: in the 1970s Odoevtsev addressed his speculations to mid-nineteenth-century poetry, something that was irrelevant to his grandfather's or his own life; in the 2000s Rogov concentrates on Stalinism, which everyone—the protagonist, the author, and the reader—identifies as the source of his inherited suffering.

For the reader of Russian historical fiction, it has been entertaining to see how some professional historians have joined their fictional colleagues in their self-destructive musings. In 2007, Vladimir Putin's administration approved a new textbook on Soviet history. Describing Stalin's terror as "the price of the great achievements of the Soviet Union," the textbook presents "the utmost efficiency of the ruling elite" as a result of this terror. Stalin's purges shaped "the new managerial class which was adequate to the tasks of modernization. . . . This class was unconditionally loyal to those in power. Its executive discipline was irreproachable."[24] No grand total of victims could ever be impressive enough to overshadow these fabulous results. This official textbook does not deny the mass violence of Stalin's era, but it does entertain the radical transformation of the meaning of that violence. Essentially, the history textbook for Russian high schools presents as truth the same idea that Bykov's novel explored as a paranoiac delusion: that the mass violence of the early Soviet era helped to shape the "New Soviet Man," the tortured Bolshevik version of the Übermensch.

Among the current generation of Russian writers, one of the most passionate about the past is Vladimir Sorokin, a prolific novelist, poet, and artist who was trained as an engineer. In *Marina's Thirtieth Love* (1999), Sorokin drew an ironic picture of a young Muscovite who vacillates in her commitment to political dissidents and Soviet true believers. Marina's loves, male and female, defy novelistic convention by their very multitude. Like many post-Soviet novels, this is a story of a community rather than an individual. In her dissident phase, Marina imagines underground Moscow in a typically post-Soviet manner:

Under Stalin's skyscrapers, under the puppet-like Kremlin, under modern constructions lie the pressed bones of millions of the tortured, murdered by the scary machinery of the gulag. . . . Nothing has changed here. It seemed that time ossified or maybe was canceled by decree. The hands of the Kremlin chimes turn in vain, like a wind-up doll without a spring.[25]

Paradoxically, since there are so few monuments on the former sites of the gulag, these sites are imagined to be everywhere. Mourning, writes Derrida, "consists always in attempts to ontologize the remains, to make them present."[26] In Sorokin's fantasy, Marina fools around Moscow without an orgasm, like a wind-up doll without a spring, until her thirtieth love, a Communist leader, satisfies her by retrapping her mind in Soviet discourse. This erotic novel effectively predicted the political events of the subsequent decade, when Putin built up his popularity on two elements, Soviet retro-style and primitive masculinity. Among many possible readings of Sorokin's novel, I propose to understand Marina's thirtieth love and first orgasm as a feat of mimetic mourning. Like intercourse on the grave, a favorite scene of the late nineteenth-century decadent novel, Marina's satisfaction comes out of the reproduction of her loss. Living in the shadow of the puppetlike Kremlin, she repeats the frightening discourse of the gulag in the orgasm of repetition compulsion. This is why her act of mourning has worked for the art of warning.

In Sorokin's *Ice* (2002), we read the story of Snegirev, not a historian but a student of astronomy, which he understands as "the history of the universe." At the start of the terror, in 1928, Snegirev goes to Siberia. He is about to die there in a marsh, like Bykov's character, but instead he comes across a fragment of magic ice, which changes his nature. From then on, Snegirev has special powers and is, on top of that, unusually communitarian, but only with his own kind. Instead of making love with his words and genitals, he can speak straight from his heart, and his peers respond by using the same organ. Born again through this ice, Snegirev recruits his fellowship by hammering humans with sacred ice. A few are fully transformed, but many are killed in the process. The People of the Ice make their way into the core of the Soviet system, which they exploit for their benefit. They infiltrate the NKVD and take part in building a gulag system, which they use as a plantation for selecting and cultivating their fellowship. Performing sacral manipulations on human bodies, the People of the Ice strive to reach a magic number of their fellowship, which will instigate the desired end of the world.[27] They produce their alternative histories in intonations that are reminiscent of some Russian religious narratives, starting from the great writer of the Russian schism, Avvakum. Like many of their precursors, Sorokin's sectarians struggle to overcome history but inevitably return to it. Though Sorokin's apocalyptic fantasy is very different from Pelevin's, they converge in depicting their protagonists as superhumans who parasitize humans. Unlike Pelevin's vampires, the People of the Ice do not suck blood; in fact, they are vegetarians. In its own way, Sorokin's fantasy responds to the same desperate quest for meaning that inspired Bykov's *Justification*.

I take another example from the works of Vladimir Sharov, author of seven novels and a trained historian with an advanced degree. In his first novel, *Rehearsals* (1992), the narrator is a historian who is working in Tomsk, in Siberia, in 1965. His dissertation subject is the seventeenth-century schism of the Russian church (Sharov himself defended his dissertation on a slightly earlier period, the Time of Troubles). There are some indications that what we are reading is a fictional dissertation, though of course there was no chance that the narrator could ever have defended this work in the Soviet Union in 1965, or even much later. From his friend, a survivor of the gulag, the narrator acquires a manuscript, which was written in the seventeenth century by the founder of a mysterious sect. This author happens to be a French theater director, Jacques de Certan. Captured by Russian troops in Livonia, Certan lived at the court of Czar Alexei and worked with Patriarch Nikon in his monastery. He documented his Russian travels and exploits in Breton, and the narrator now translates and updates Certan's story in the form of the current book. The action starts in New Jerusalem, an amateurish copy of the Holy Land that Patriarch Nikon built in the countryside near Moscow. Nikon renamed every river and village after their Palestinian originals and built churches as copies of their Jerusalem models; started in 1658, the Cathedral of Resurrection was erected as a full-size replica of the Church of the Holy Sepulcher in Jerusalem, built where Jesus met his end. In the Soviet period, there was a labor camp there, which was also called New Jerusalem; Solzhenitsyn spent many months in this camp after his arrest in 1945. The monastery was reopened in 1994, and many pilgrims and tourists have since visited Nikon's (and Solzhenitsyn's) Jerusalem on the banks of the Istra River.

Sharov bases his story of New Jerusalem on established fact, but the narrator then takes a few steps beyond it. We learn that while building his Holy Land, Nikon asked Certan to rehearse a full-scale mystery play there, a theatrical reenactment of Christ's words and passions and everything that is described in the four Gospels, plus some apocrypha. Everyone would be depicted in these rehearsals but Christ, since the *mysterium* itself was aimed at bringing about the Second Coming by luring Christ to come forth as the real-life Messiah. Then Nikon falls into disgrace, which did happen in 1666, and the hundreds of peasants who have been taking part in the rehearsals are exiled to Siberia. Certan dies on the road, but his actors remain faithful to his teaching, form a sectarian community, and continue the rehearsals in hope of the imminent arrival of Christ. Surrounded by Siberian marshes, they rehearse for generations, but then something unplanned happens to them. A quarrel breaks out between those playing Christians in these scenes from the Gospels and those playing Jews. The conflict escalates to the point where the former start to exterminate the latter, by which stage a gulag has already been established in their village. The apostles become the commandants of the camp, and they continue their rehearsals as their chosen method of atheist propaganda. The only Jewish survivor of this holocaust, a little boy, supplies the narrator with Certan's manuscript.

Sharov's grandfather and grandmother were lost to the Stalinist terror, and he remembers his father, also a writer, as "a very sad man."[28] Despite his academic training, Sharov believes that his real university was his experience as a child in the late 1950s, when friends and colleagues of his father were returning from the camps and telling their stories.[29] The central character of Sharov's novel *Before and Then* (1993) is Madame de Staël, the French romantic author who was once influential in nineteenth-century Russia. In Sharov's novel, de Staël is immortal. She has moved to Russia and sleeps with its luminaries, including her own son, Stalin. The narrator meets her in a Soviet madhouse where she keeps company with the Russian fin-de-siècle mystical philosopher, a theorist of immortality and resurrection of the dead, Nikolai Fedorov, and a covey of old Bolsheviks. While the narrator is recording the oral history of these survivors, an apocalyptic flood drowns Moscow.

The author of these historical fantasies, Sharov describes his credo: "The history which I learned was not the history of humans. It was the history of hectares, crops, financial flows. . . . It was entirely foreign to me. . . . I am trying to understand what the revolution was . . . why the people who had beautiful dreams committed monstrous crimes."[30] In his *Resurrection of Lazar* (2002), Sharov writes in the first person and delineates in minute detail his dream of the physical resurrection of his father. Preparing this resurrection in the cemetery where his father was buried, the narrator uses techniques mostly borrowed from the writings of Fedorov. This project brings him back to the archives, where he produces a reinterpretation of the early Soviet period as Fedorovian resurrection in disguise, with a Bolshevik leader, Lazar Kaganovich, the builder of the Moscow metropolitan, as the chief executor of resurrection.[31]

Sharov's gentle, melancholic writing combines with his unbridled historical fantasy in a consistent way that has yet to be adequately explored by literary scholars. His last novel, *Be Like Children* (2009), presents a broad panorama of the revolution of 1917. As clues to understanding this event, Sharov depicts the legendary thirteenth-century Children's Crusade and the millenarian expectations shared by Russian medieval and modern sects. An amazing cast of characters, from Siberian shamans to Bolshevik leaders, play out this millenarian impulse in their different ways. "The revolution of 1917 was passionately awaited by a huge number of very different persons, parties, and religious groups," says Sharov, and his list of these groups starts with the Old Believers and sectarians.[32]

Drunk Reality, Sober Observer

In post-Soviet Russian literature, there are stories about werewolves and werefoxes; about sectarians who copulate with the soil, and bio-philologists who clone the great Russian writers to extract the essence of immortality (Vladimir Sorokin's *Blue Lard*); about the revival of the medieval Vikings and the Khazars and the civil war in Russia that follows the collapse of oil prices in the wake of a techno-magic invention that makes traditional energy sources redundant (Dmitry Bykov's *ZhD*); about a global dictator of mixed Russian-Chinese origins, whose teacher, a sectarian Old Believer, educates him by citing Sigmund Freud (Pavel Krusanov's *Angel's Bite*); about the restoration of the monarchy and public executions in twenty-first-century Russia (Sorokin's *Day of the Oprichnik*); about the survival of the old Finnish tribe Meria as a kind of religious sect among contemporary Russians, with the most bizarre sexual and funeral rites (Denis Osokin's *Finches*); and about vampires in disguise who secretly rule over the Russians in the manner of the Soviet Communists or the post-Soviet oligarchs (Sergei Lukianenko's multiple novels, Viktor Pelevin's *Empire V*). These stories do not necessarily belong to "popular literature" but rather cover the whole range from the low- to the high-brow. One can safely say that these writers are successful with Russian readers. They publish their novels with mainstream commercial publishers, enjoy celebrity status, produce literary scandals, and receive national prizes. Whatever these authors imagine in the past or in the future, the goal is usually the understanding of the central trauma, or rather the catastrophe, of the Soviet period.

Though the fantasy of post-Soviet authors seems unlimited, their actual themes overlap. They seem to be mostly interested in two areas of human experience, religion and history, which they combine in rich and shocking ways. At the same time, they are not concerned with other traditional areas of literary interest, such as psychology, or the realistic analysis of social issues. They tend to go deep into the past in order to contextualize the present. Sometimes they construct a future that looks frighteningly like the past. Then, it becomes difficult to distinguish between mourning and warning (see chapter 2); this conflation is exactly what the authors intend to accomplish.

Several authors have argued that the concept of magical realism would work in application to the east European literatures that have recently been emancipated from Soviet domination. Examples offered in this connection have generally comprised the works of non-Russian writers: Ukrainians, Kirgiz, Abkhazians.[33] Coined in Weimar Germany and applied to Latin American and then African fiction, the concept of magical realism made almost a full circle before it arrived in the post-Soviet space.[34] The anthropologist Michael Taussig explores the connection between the internationally renowned prose of the magical realists and native practices of healing and sorcery; he concludes that the literary elaborations of popular magic stand as a counterhegemonic force.[35] But does "magical realism" capture the unbridled peculiarity of post-Soviet Russian fiction?

Salman Rushdie famously described magical realism as "the commingling of the improbable and the mundane."[36] Improbable as they are, Sorokin's, Sharov's, or Pelevin's novels do not have much of what could plausibly be characterized as mundane. They involve plenty of magic, but to describe them as "realistic" would plainly be wrong. I believe that the application of the concept of magical realism to recent Russian fiction requires a major theoretical revision. These narratives are similar to and different from magical realist ones in several important respects. They are similar because they make extensive use of magic in full-scale novelistic constructions. They also present an implicit critique of contemporary society by revising its historical foundations. They are different because they are self-consciously distanced from the traditions of the realist novel that are so critical to magical realism. The post-Soviet novel does not emulate social reality and does not compete with the psychological novel; what it emulates and struggles with is history. However unrecognizable, its allegoric images retain their dependency upon the past, but this relationship cannot be described in the customary terms of Russian cultural criticism. I coin the concept of "magical historicism" to define the bizarre but instructive imagery that has evolved out of postcatastrophic, post-Soviet culture.

History and magic are strange bedfellows. The life of ghosts is ahistorical, wrote Benjamin, but this is only a partial truth. Witches are ahistorical, but witch hunts and hunters embody their historical moment. Ghosts, vampires, werewolves, and other beasts help authors and readers to discuss their own history, which is not comprehensible by other means. Such was the Soviet period with its "unjustified repressions." The uncanny scenery of post-Soviet literature signals the failure of other, more conventional ways of understanding social reality. It is not the pointed clarity of social and cultural criticism that attracts readers, but the inexhaustible fantasy of creators of alternative pasts. Often, these stories present manipulations on human bodies, which allow for supernatural warmth and an immediacy of contact between the manipulated. After being hammered by ice, Sorokin's sectarians can talk to each other with their hearts. After being bitten by a vampire, Pelevin's characters comprehend other creatures, human or vampiric, by biting them. Sharov's characters acquire similar powers after having sex with Madame de Staël. In the post-Soviet condition, the antimodern fantasy of immediate, extralinguistic communication becomes a popular refuge. In most of these stories, immediate knowledge leads to unlimited power. These are stories of super-communes, not supermen.

In the philosophical tradition, historicism strives to understand the current state of the world as the result of its development in the past. It also denies other ways of understanding the present, such as the concept of free will that shapes the present without being predetermined by the past. Ironically, magical historicism shares this belief in the explanatory power of the past with rational versions of historicism. In the melancholic visions of Bykov, Sharov, Sorokin, and their colleagues, the past is perceived as not just "another country" but an exotic and unexplored one, still pregnant with unborn alternatives and imminent miracles. Arguably, the expanded use of the subjunctive tense characterizes postrevolutionary periods. The feeling of loss opens up questions of what might have been.[37] Haunted by the past and unable to withdraw from its repetitive contemplation, post-Soviet writers find themselves trapped in a state of melancholia. Their time is "out of joint," like Hamlet's, and with or without awareness, they realize Derrida's dictum: "One never inherits without coming to terms with some specter, and therefore with more than one specter."[38] Celebrating an unprecedented consumer boom, their readers feel the loss of the political opportunities they recently enjoyed. Writing in a glossy men's journal, the cultural critic Grigory Revzin described the situation in political rather than clinical terms: "The past does not know the subjunctive mood only if the present knows it.... If the present is what you cannot change at all, the past becomes what you can change in every possible way."[39] When politics does not provide alternatives, historiography offers them in abundance. The hauntological idea of justice becomes relevant when the real courts deny hope; in a similar way, allegories bloom when other ways of constructing truth and memory betray the storyteller. Combining catastrophic past, pathetic present, and dangerous future, early twenty-first-century Russia is a greenhouse for ghosts, revenants, and other spectral bodies.

Michael Wood's twin concepts of drunk reality and sober observer help us understand the post-Soviet fantasies. Writing about magical realism, Wood distinguishes between two strands, one that is magic in material and realist in style ("as if the author were reciting a telephone book"), and another that is realist in material and magic in style ("the facts . . . are given to us as if they are fables"). Wood seems to be mostly interested in the first kind of narratives, which he suggests are written as if the reporter is sober and reality is drunk.[40] Famous Latin American examples such as Márquez's *One Hundred Years of Solitude*, which clearly belong to Wood's first kind of magical realism, deconstruct nationalist historiographies by telling the fantastic stories of the past impartially, as if the history were drunk but the historian sober. Recruiting popular magic and multiplying its use in the most unbridled ways, these stories disavow the official narrative of the people's suffering in the past as necessary, justifiable sacrifices for the sake of the people's present. Projecting magic into history, these novels subvert scholarly discourses of historiography with their habitual emphasis on rational choices and social forces. These novels tend to follow some of the stylistic conventions of historical writing, such as impartiality and what Wood aptly calls sobriety. Rarely, if ever, do the narrators of these novels play Nabokovian games with their readers by actualizing the presence of the narrator in the course of the action. They boost their readers' understanding of the relational, constructed nature of the narrated reality with genealogical rather than narratological experiments.

This is where post-Soviet Russian fiction converges with that of postcolonial Latin America.[41] In reality, there is no border between the past and the present; this is even more the case in the realm of magic. Correspondingly, the border between magical realism and magical historicism is a matter of focus or emphasis rather than one of definitions or boundaries. In the final account, the popularity of magical historicism among post-Soviet writers and readers realizes the "compromise by which the command of reality is carried out piecemeal" that Freud ascribed to melancholia.[42] Psychologically, the inability to differentiate oneself from the lost object prevents the individual from living in the present, from love and work. Politically, the reverse is probably equally important: when there is no choice in the present, the historical past unfolds into a cyclical narrative that obscures the present rather than explains it. Poetically, Freud's observation about the "piecemeal" character of the melancholic compromise with reality provides an instructive perspective on the nature of postcatastrophic writing. Literature has a mystical license that would not be recognized in other domains of human experience, such as religion, politics, or "real life":

> We adapt our judgments to the conditions of the writer's fictional reality and treat souls, spirits, and ghosts as if they are fully entitled to exist, just as we are in our material reality. . . . Whatever has an uncanny effect in real life has the same in literature. But the writer can intensify and multiply this effect far beyond what is available in normal experience.[43]

Allegorical constructions of the uncanny, the monstrous, and the corporeal are all metonymical; these constructions take parts for the whole, *pars pro toto*, and combine them in creative combinations. Producing its own range of readers' responses, this rhetorical convention is different from a more traditional, metaphorical poetics, which compares distant realms without dissecting them, focusing on the parts, and mingling them together. In this process, the metonymical poetics of magical historicism emulate the "piecemeal" logic of torture, which also manipulates parts of the body with the aim of changing the whole of truth, integrity, and history.

Close to Zero

The intermingling of the political and the literary in high quarters found its culmination in the 2009 novel *Close to Zero*. Published under a pseudonym, the novel is unanimously attributed to Vladislav Surkov, deputy chief of Russia's presidential administration who defined Russia's internal politics since his appointment to this position in 1999 until his scandalous removal after the forged elections of 2011, which he oversaw. Half-Chechen and half-Russian, Surkov was trained as a theater director. He has a reputation as an "effective manager" who has presided over the concerted and purposeful degradation of Russia's politics and public sphere.[44] Under his own name, Surkov has published an elusive review of *Close to Zero*; the review neither confirms nor denies his authorship.[45] The author's hostility toward the writing, reading, and thinking part of the Russian Federation is quite obvious from this novel; these are people who are "close to zero." The protagonist of the novel is a professional writer and editor. However, this innocent profession is described as a dirty activity in which bloodthirsty gangsters force drug-addicted storytellers to mock the undiscerning public, the newest reincarnation of the snake-charming activity that Shalamov ascribed to the storytellers of the gulag. After committing several murders for the sake of his publishing business, the protagonist loses his love to the related genre of post-Soviet film. A certain studio in the Caucasus makes snuff films for the Moscow club of millionaires that feature real-life scenes of rape and murder. This studio, Kafka Pictures, has even made a version of *Hamlet* in which the protagonists actually die of wounds and poison. After watching his girlfriend die on screen, the protagonist contemplates revenge. He goes to the Caucasus to find the filmmaker responsible, but ends up being tortured and mutilated himself by Kafka Pictures in an ordeal that is then screened for the viewing pleasure of the Moscow connoisseurs. At the end of the novel, he has most of his fingers and an ear cut off, which is indeed a popular form of torture in the Caucasus that was used by both sides during the Russian-Chechen wars. Finally, the protagonist finds the film director and kills him, though this final scene reads as his delusion rather than reality.

Medialization of violence is a crucial feature of this sadomasochist story, but its geography is also meaningful. The place for torturing, killing, and screening is the Caucasus, the most recent setting for Russian state violence and the birthplace of Surkov's father. The pleasurable contemplation of these acts takes place in Moscow, among the circles where the author lives and works. Whatever the authorial intentions of the individual or team that wrote *Close to Zero*, the cultural meaning of this fantasy is familiar: this is the high-tech version of the Victims' Ball, mimetic mourning for the losses of mass violence that emulates, in this fantasy very literally, the details of this violence. The novel depicts the Moscow club of sadistic millionaires, most of them corrupted officials with their glamorous women, as the proxy for its own readership.

Playing with classical texts, *Close to Zero* leaps from one text to another: the beginning rewrites Chekhov's *Seagull*, the film studio is named after Kafka, and the finale repeats the conclusion of Nabokov's *Lolita*. Curiously, in his review, Surkov insists that among these and other intertextual connections, the most important is *Hamlet*. However, it is not clear where this Hamletian connection is actually situated in the novel. There is no ghost in the narrative, and no lost father, but I find it meaningful that Surkov still insists that it follows *Hamlet*, a universal template for mourning and revenge. In his review, he claims that by crossing Shakespeare and Quentin Tarantino, *Close to Zero* reveals the moral vacuum of post-Soviet society. I would rather state that this novel creates a sense of vacuum by satirizing the reckless protagonist, bloodthirsty Moscow, and the violent Caucasus without exploring the historical processes of victimization that brought them all into being. Cutting history away from this medialized picture is like amputating limbs from a human body, a process that this novel depicts in many details. As in many other cases, ignoring the Soviet roots of the post-Soviet problems leads to their essentializing in terms of "postmodernity" or, alternatively, ethnic "psychology." Surkov's purpose is to present Russia's people of all classes and ethnicities as intrinsically violent and ultimately incapable of democratic self-rule, and to present the twenty-first-century's modernity as the rule of secret conspiracies and managed simulacra. This is the image that justifies the Kremlin's take on power, as implemented by Surkov and his colleagues.

Precisely because of its deliberately short historical perspective, *Close to Zero* does not belong to magical historicism even though it employs its techniques. Magical historicism does have critical potential. Though the political boundaries in Russia tend to blur, magical historicists are recognizably different from those authors who use realistic methods for spreading their pro-Soviet nostalgia. Organized by Surkov in 2002, the pro-Putin youth movement Marching Together (*Idushchie vmeste*) publicly destroyed copies of Vladimir Sorokin's *Blue Lard* by disposing of them in a giant commode in the center of Moscow (a performance that in its turn recalls Marcel Duchamp). Set in the future, *Blue Lard* tells the story of an elixir that the monstrous clones of great Russian writers, from Tolstoy to Nabokov, produce when writing. Turned into this "blue lard," their writings promise immortality. Exotic Russian sectarians from the future steal this substance from the Russian-Chinese scientists who produce the clones. Using a time machine, sectarians send this elixir to Stalin, who is presented here as the lover of Khrushchev. Finally, we see the immortal Stalin as a servant to one of the pathetic masters of the future. The final pages hint that Stalin is, in fact, the narrator of the story. Changing its focus from invented communities to pseudo-historical personalities and back to communities, this exemplary novel combines many features of magical historicism: unmotivated distortions of history, semihuman monsters, manipulations of the body, fantastic cults, circular time, and the resulting interpenetration of epochs. The Marching Together movement deciphered the political message sent by this novel—a message that was aggressively critical toward Putin's Russia.

As Russia approached its 2011 crisis, I observed peculiar manifestations of the magical-historical way of understanding contemporary reality, not only in post-Soviet fiction but in nonfiction as well. Let me share with you, as this book about the past and the past representations of the past reaches its conclusion, some brief observations on the curious kind of nonfiction that Russia's high officials, or people very close to them, are writing in this present moment of despair. At the end of 2010, the chairman of the Constitutional Court of the Russian Federation, Valery Zorkin, published an essay, "The Constitution against Crime," in an official newspaper of the Russian Federation. In this essay, Zorkin makes a subtle distinction between a criminalized state, which the Russian Federation (he admits) has become, and a criminal state, which the Russian Federation risks becoming. Amazingly, in formulating his warning, Zorkin chose not the language of the constitution, but the language of Pelevin, from *Empire V*:

> In a criminal state, our citizens will divide into predators, who will feel very free in the criminal jungles, and subhumans, who will understand that they are just food for these predators. The predators will be in the minority, the "walking beefsteaks" among the majority. The gap between the former and the latter will constantly expand.[46]

Zorkin uses a citation from Pushkin's ironic verses of 1823 to describe his attitude toward this subhuman majority: "they should be either slaughtered or shorn," he quotes bitterly. He further speculates that these subhumans are longing for a "savior" who can only take the form of a dictator and super-predator. This is not an anti-utopia, claims Zorkin, but a "negative scenario." It is instructive to see that while we literary scholars agonize over whether our soft language is appropriate to describe legal or political phenomena, the top lawyer of the Russian Federation embraces this language.

During the debates on President Medvedev's "modernization" project, one of the most skeptical voices belonged to Simon Kordonsky, a former official and a well-informed, very conservative thinker.[47] In the address that Kordonsky gave at a Moscow meeting of pro-Kremlin intellectuals, "Onwards, Russia!" in January 2011, Kordonsky offered a systematic analogy between plans to build a new scientific center near Moscow and the Soviet *sharashka*, a type of fenced, secret laboratory in the gulag in which the researchers were prisoners and the bosses were officers of the NKVD. Arguing his point, Kordonsky cites Stalin's letter of 1930, which launched the notorious trial of the "Industrial Party" and then, the first *sharashka* of the gulag. Bridging the historical gap of eighty years, Kordonsky draws an analogy between Leonid Ramzin, the engineer and chief victim of that trial, and Mikhail Khodorkovsky, the businessman who has been in prison since 2003. The speaker explicitly suggested creating a *sharashka* in which Khodorkovsky could realize his talent for modernization without doing any political damage. "Halfway to the *Sharashka*"—this is the title that Kordonsky gave to the published version of his talk.[48]

Gleb Pavlovsky had been a long-standing ally of the Kremlin administration, before this administration ostracized him in 2011. A one-time Soviet dissident who was imprisoned from 1982 until 1985, Pavlovsky went on to become the leader of the post-Soviet "political technologists," a term that he created and that has since passed into everyday usage. Sometimes officially and sometimes informally, he served as adviser to Presidents Yeltsin and Putin, and as a prototype for Tatarsky from Pelevin's novel, *Generation P*. In an essay that he published as an op-ed in the journal that he owns, Pavlovsky says that Russia had entered a "period of turbulence." He attributes this to what he calls the Russian people's dysfunctional relationship to reality. No matter what we try to do, it never turns out that way, he confesses in despair. To quote Pavlovsky's characteristic muttering:

It turns out that one of the most incomprehensible aspects of contemporary Russia are the powers-that-be. . . . The Russian state officials are conducting a kind of guerrilla warfare. They are worming their way into the places that have been privatized by "the regime" . . . but they never know for sure where they have a chance of succeeding in consolidating their grip, and where they should avoid even dipping their toe in the water. So, for example, a regiment of "state guerrillas" led by the Justice Minister . . . has managed to skulk its way into the gulag jungles of GUIN [the state prison administration], where they are trying to rationalize and humanize the world of the zone.[49]

According to this insider, state prisons in Russia are still a gulag, fifty years after this institution was officially disbanded. Russian officials with all their bureaucracies, bodyguards, and budgets are guerrillas who operate in the jungles of uncertainty and danger. Engaged in this unbounded mythologizing, Pavlovsky transfers responsibility from these hapless or corrupt officials onto anonymous, fantastic forces. Speaking of the Internet and the alleged danger that it poses for Russian sovereignty, Pavlovsky laments: "There are half-natural creatures operating in this world, with their inhuman politics." He compares these harmful forces disturbing the work of Russian officials and political technologists to sharks and volcanoes. Finally, he reveals the source of his inspiration: the current situation in Russia, he says, is like "pictures in certain novels: it is a gloomy morning, and there are swollen, incomprehensible people coming out of the woods, gathering in clusters. To what end is unclear." Pavlovsky does not name these novels, but they definitely belong to the magical historicist variety, starting with Mamleev and ending with Pelevin and Bykov.

In 2011, after it became clear that Putin would return to the Russian presidency, the prominent journalist Oleg Kashin said that in his view, journalism in Russia had shifted toward literature and to some extent had effectively been replaced by fiction. News has lost its value, he said, and this is not a result of censorship but rather of the impoverishment of the political process. But literature and even poetry have stepped into the role of investigative journalism: "one single poem by Dmitry Bykov is able to represent and explicate Russian politics in terms that are more adequate than any essay in a newspaper." In the spirit of magical historicism, Kashin took part in a collective experiment: several Moscow authors wrote fictional memoirs from the perspective of the leading Russian politicians and media moguls about twenty years into the future: "only in this way, by poems, fairytales, or devil knows what, can one continue a meaningful dialogue with the reader today."[50]

Imagining humans as animals, monsters, or walking beefsteaks renders both shame for the past and fear of the future—mourning and warning. Practicing senseless violence that eludes any functional interpretation, the Soviet system effectively reduced humans to working animals. Starting with Solzhenitsyn's triton and Vladimov's guard dog, literature has used humanized animals to tell the story of inhuman suffering. In the later spirit of magical historicism, these characters have developed into monsters that embody the horror, not the truth, of the Soviet period better than either humans or animals. This memorial culture is not so much postmodern as it is, precisely, post-Soviet. Many classical figures and motifs resurge here: monsters like the Sphinx, Moloch, Leviathan, and Triton; Antigone, who wanted to bury her brother; Dante's infernal adventures and Hamlet's possession and revenge; Clorinda's posthumous transformation; Dracula, to be sure; and also Bulgakov's stray dog with the glands of a Communist. Probably the most pertinent master-plot is that of Little Red Riding Hood: the wolf ate the granny, and now he looks like the granny—or maybe it is the murdered granny who looks like a wolf?

Conclusion

Mourning is work and like any work has its pace, stages, and instruments. There are latent periods when intellectuals, the conscience of the nation, talk about the inability to mourn. There are also periods of hectic activity when it seems that no other concern is more relevant; then, intellectuals talk about mourning fatigue. The longest are the periods of slow, blurred, but persistent remorse, when reminiscences of the past shape warnings about the future and compete with concerns about the present. Melancholic as they are, these periods are unavoidable. In a post-catastrophic nation, which suffers not only from the loss of people but also from the destruction of cultural symbols, social networks, and spiritual or ideological beliefs, the work of mourning re-creates and replenishes a wellspring of solidarity and coherence. Then, work of mourning becomes "action," as Hannah Arendt calls the free, essentially political manifestations of human plurality. Because of human vulnerability and violence, and also because of human solidarity and love, mourning is an essential part of Arendt's *vita activa*.[1] This book has presented many examples of acts and deeds of mourning, which are also actions of ethical choice, political resistance, and aesthetic self-expression.

I have looked at the Russian memory of the Soviet terror as an enormous cultural formation that encompasses different media and genres, incompatible versions of history, and various rituals of mourning. In the late-Soviet period, the work of mourning did see its moments of explosive release, but for the most part, it was blocked. Post-Soviet Russia, by contrast, has turned its tortured process of mastering the past into an important part of the political present. At the start of the twenty-first century, political opponents in Russia differed most dramatically not in their understanding of social issues or international relations, but in their interpretations of history. The present felt oversaturated with the past, and this solution refused to produce any sediment. With my concept of magical historicism, I have tried to embrace the particularity of this postcatastrophic moment.

Uncomfortably for the historian, postcatastrophic memory often entails allegories rather than facts and imaginative fiction rather than archival documentation. As we have seen, in the post-Soviet condition, narrative genres of high culture such as the novel and film play the central role in the double-edged processes of mourning and warning. Like posttraumatic consciousness, the postcatastrophic culture cyclically returns to the overwhelming events of the past. It returns there both willingly and unwillingly, sometimes even unconsciously, without reflection or acknowledgment. These reenactments are cyclical, but they are not, of course, eternal. Like all memory, intergenerational memory has its limits. But we do not know when the process of mourning will be over.

Putin's authoritarian regime has now controlled this country for over half of the post-Soviet period, and its oily grip has choked the newborn century in Russia. If the collapse of the Soviet state in 1991 was a revolution, a claim that has been passionately defended by some experts but is largely distrusted by the post-Soviet public, much of the subsequent two decades has been its "Thermidor," a dark and oppressive period of political restoration and cultural despair. A concept that was widely used by historians to denote the French Revolution's self-annihilation, this idea was used in the 1930s by Leon Trotsky, who interpreted Stalinism as a postrevolutionary Thermidor. In such periods, a victorious revolution suffocates in its own violence, and the unlimited, revolutionary power slides from the idealists to the oppressors. Trotsky defined the "Soviet Thermidor" as "a triumph of the bureaucracy over the masses," a definition that applies all too well to the post-Soviet condition. According to these revelations of the leading Russian revolutionary, "Nobody who has wealth to distribute ever omits himself." At the opposite end of the political spectrum, Trotsky's contemporary Carl Schmitt formulated the same truth as the fundamental law of political theory: "The *protego ergo obligo* is the *cogito ergo sum* of the state," he wrote.[2]

Redistributing the wealth, bureaucrats become oligarchs and oligarchs, bureaucrats. "The deposed and abused bureaucracy, from being a servant of society, has again become its lord," Trotsky lamented. With all his understandable bitterness (writing his *Revolution Betrayed* in exile, he anticipated his death at the hands of Stalin's assassins), Trotsky did not assert that the situation he observed in the 1930s was a resurrection of the ancien régime of czarist Russia; he saw the logic of Stalinism as belonging to the present and not to the past. For Trotsky, the "Soviet Thermidor" was a question "not of specters of the past, not of the remnants of what no longer exists . . . but of new, mighty, and continually reborn tendencies to personal accumulation."[3]

Abiding with these speculations that originate from Hobbes rather than from Marx, Russian politics shows little regret for the millions who perished in the Soviet terror. However, post-Soviet culture has produced unusual, maybe even perverted, forms of memory. As we have seen, two processes come together on this stage of postcatastrophic mourning: the defamiliarization of the past and the return of the repressed. Excavating the past buried in the present, the scholar of postcatastrophic culture watches memory turning into imagination. In Russia, many authors and readers seem to share a desire for a poetic reenactment of the catastrophic past. My point is that this is melancholy rather than nostalgia. Famously contrasted by Sigmund Freud against "healthy mourning," the logic of melancholy embraces the confusion between the present and the past, the obsessive reenactment of the loss, and the interruption of the relationship to the present. "The inhibition of the melancholic seems puzzling to us because we cannot see what it is that is absorbing him so entirely," Freud writes.[4] The dialectic of reenactment and defamiliarization produces a rich but puzzling imagery, which absorbs the melancholic, post-Soviet subjectivity.

The ghostly visions of Russian writers, filmmakers, critics, and even politicians extend the work of mourning into those spaces that defeat more rational ways of understanding the past. In a land where millions remain unburied, the dead return as the undead. They do so in novels, films, and other forms of culture that reflect, shape, and possess people's memory. We have seen that the atrocities of German Nazism and Soviet

Communism have left profoundly different memories in their respective countries. Due to unique combinations of political circumstances, these two cultures elaborated different forms of dealing with the past. German memory crystallized its "hardware" in the form of monuments and museums, with a consequent cultural debate over the need to revive and reinspire this memory, to rescue it from complete petrification. The hardening of memory is a cultural process with specific functions, conditions, and thresholds. It promises that the events themselves will not return, that the demons of the past have been exorcised, that the present exists and prevails. In a democratic society, it requires a relative degree of consensus in the public sphere. Such consensus follows after, and because, the intensity of the "soft" debates has reached a certain threshold.

In Russia, consensus about the past has not developed, and memory without memorials is vulnerable to a cyclical, recurrent process of refutations and denials. Feelings of guilt can be assuaged and soothed by new voices, and even the most influential texts can be challenged by new texts. Ghosts, vampires, monsters, and other species of the undead hover in the public space, available for observation by and conversation with any pedestrian consumer. They refuse to leave the living until the unlawfully killed have been remembered by culture high and low, official and popular, nationalist and cosmopolitan. Only with these multiple, infinitely numerous acts of recognizing and remembering will the new Russian culture regain its coherence and vitality.

It so happens that I am completing my book at a moment when Russia has entered another political crisis. The presidential term of Dmitry Medvedev (2008–2012) was wasted through his halfhearted attempts at changing the economic and political system in the spirit of what one observer has called "nostalgic modernization": depressingly, the template for Medvedev's reform project was still the Soviet Union.[5] But after the parliamentary elections of December 2011, with their massive fraud for the benefit of the ruling party, a series of large-scale protests struck the country, which had been deprived of an autonomous public life for more than a decade. It is much too early to evaluate the depth of this crisis or to predict its future development, but there has been no lack of historicizing metaphors in the public responses to the events. Many commentators in the Russian press and online media are talking about an imminent "revolution" in Russia and predicting "repressions" by the authorities.

One comparison that has become particularly popular in the Russian and Western press alike is between Putin and Brezhnev, the unchangeable general secretary of the ruling party and a symbol of the sclerosis of power. But the analogies run deeper. As the *Herald Tribune* reported with some irony, even President Medvedev used the language of memory when, in the midst of this electoral crisis, he issued a warning about Russia's future. "It is categorically inadmissible that the political system be delegitimized," Medvedev said. "What Russia is without government is something that everyone remembers from history books: it is 1917."[6]

But there was much that is new and encouraging in the public responses to the December 2011 election fraud. Many of these responses draw parallels between current events in Russia and recent events in foreign and culturally distant countries. The Arab Spring, a series of mass protests and revolutions in northern Africa that occurred in 2011, is a particularly salient source for symbolic borrowings. I find these comparisons important not only because Putin resembles Colonel Gaddafi more than he resembles Brezhnev but also because such cross-cultural identifications have hitherto been rare in Russia's political debates. The most popular way of explicating political and cultural events in the Russia of the twenty-first century derives these events from the preceding Soviet history, the situation that has been rendered by the sticky and now obsolete concept of the "post-Soviet." This feeling of continuity belongs to the ongoing condition of melancholia, the inability to attain distance from the violent, catastrophic past. Believing in their uniqueness, post-Soviet Russians did not want to compare themselves with other cultures, and least of all with the "backward" countries of the East that have been perceived in conservative and orientalist ways. With its allusions to the Arab Spring and laments about Russia's political backwardness in comparison to both the West and the East, the public sphere of 2011 has manifested a breakthrough. Future histories of the new Russia may well take as their starting point the year 2012, when, after a long and complicated pregnancy, the country finally gave birth to an open present. But the story told in these future history books may also turn out to be a sad story of regression and collapse, and such a story will no doubt overflow with historicizing allegories.

Indeed, many problems of post-Soviet Russia—its one-party system, state-supported corruption, ethnic conflicts, selective justice, unchangeable leadership, dependence on natural resources, and the miserable condition of the poor—do show strong continuities with the Soviet era. But the central issue of 2011, the forged elections, constitutes a break with the Soviet tradition, which made elections, and electoral manipulations, entirely irrelevant. Twenty years after the collapse of the Soviet regime, elections in Russia are still far from meeting democratic norms of transparency and fairness, but they have finally met a deeper and, in a sense, more important criterion that distinguishes an electoral (though always imperfect) democracy from tyranny: elections in Russia have become relevant. The passionate speeches at the rallies in Moscow and St. Petersburg at the end of 2011 attacked Putin and his regime rather than Soviet traditions and institutions. Even when the enormous crowd in the center of Moscow chanted, "We Won't Forget! We Won't Forgive!" they referred to the crimes of Putinism and not the crimes of Stalinism. In this crisis, the Russian public sphere turned to the present, not the past. Maybe it will pull the country out of the post-Soviet era, into the open future.

Notes

INTRODUCTION

1. Ronald Schechter, "Gothic Thermidor: The Bals des victimes, the Fantastic, and the Production of Historical Knowledge in Post-Terror France," *Representations* 61 (Winter 1998): 78–94; Joseph Clarke, *Commemorating the Dead in Revolutionary France: Revolution and Remembrance, 1789–1799* (Cambridge: Cambridge University Press, 2007). See also an intellectual history of the post-Terror France: Andrew Jainchill, *Reimagining Politics after the Terror: The Republican Origins of French Liberalism* (Ithaca, N.Y.: Cornell University Press, 2008), chap. 2. For a broader perspective on the body, performance, and mourning, see Paul Connerton, *The Spirit of Mourning: History, Memory and the Body* (Cambridge: Cambridge University Press, 2011).

2. Ruth Leys, in her *Trauma: A Genealogy* (Chicago: Chicago University Press 2000), distinguishes between mimetic and antimimetic theories of trauma, and argues that mimetic theories of trauma do not stand up to critical analysis. As I argue throughout this book, mourning for the other cannot be reduced to trauma, though elements of trauma theory help to understand mourning. Emphasizing mourning rather than trauma and performativity rather than realism, my concept of "mimetic mourning" is both similar to and different from Michael Rothberg's "traumatic realism"; see his *Traumatic Realism: The Demands of Holocaust Representation* (Minneapolis: University of Minnesota Press, 2000).

3. Stephen Kotkin, *Armageddon Averted: The Soviet Collapse, 1970–2000* (Oxford: Oxford University Press, 2003), 182.

4. Stephen Greenblatt, *Hamlet in Purgatory* (Princeton, N.J.: Princeton University Press, 2001), 248.

5. Dmitry Bykov, *Kalendar' 2: Spory o bespornom* (Moscow: Astrel, 2012), 133–134.

CHAPTER I

1. Old and new photos of the Solovetsky cathedral with onion-shaped cupolas are available in many tourist guidebooks and on Internet sites. For documentary

footage (1927–1928) of the Solovetsky camp, as it functioned in the former monastery with pyramidal towers, see the film by Marina Goldovskaia, *Vlast' Solovetskaia* (1988).

2. See Aleksandr Zolotorev, "Novye 500 rublei: Ispravlena sushchestvennaia oshibka," *F5 Blog*, November 19, 2011, http://f5.ru/zolotorev/post/378446.

3. Yurii Brodskii, *"Solovki": Dvadtsat' let osobogo naznacheniia* (Moscow: ROSSPEN, 2002), 3; see also Aleksei Laushkin, "500 rublei s oshibkami," *Rodina* 6 (2004) and http://www.solovki.ca/vsiako-razno/money.php (this site mentions debates about this banknote, starting from 1997). In 2004, I popularized Brodsky's discovery in the newspapers in eight languages: A. Etkind, "Remembering the Gulag," *Project Syndicate*, June 17, 2004, http://www.project-syndicate.org/commentary/etkind2/English.

4. Pavel Nerler, *Slovo i "delo" Osipa Mandel'shtama: Kniga donosov, doprosov i obvinitel'nykh zakliuchenii* (Moscow: Petrovskii Park, 2010), 29.

5. The leading Russian expert on the economic history of the gulag asserts that in terms of mortality rates and overall "catastrophic" conditions, a village undergoing collectivization was a worse place to be than a gulag camp. See A. K. Sokolov, "Prinuzhdenie k trudu v sovetskoi ekonomike," in *Gulag: Ekonomika prinuditel'nogo truda* (Moscow: ROSSPEN, 2005).

6. Cristina Vatulescu suggests that general concepts of Western origin, "police" and "police state," could perform this function. See Cristina Vatulescu, *Police Aesthetics: Literature, Film, and the Secret Police in Soviet Times* (Stanford, Calif.: Stanford University Press, 2010), 3. The use of "gulag" in its broad meaning has an opposite function; it emphasizes the singularity of the Soviet catastrophe.

7. Veniamin Iofe, *Granitsy smysla* (St. Petersburg: Memorial, 2002), 17. The Memorial Society is a nongovernmental organization that collects oral histories of the survivors of the gulag, publishes lists of the victims, and keeps track of local attempts to mark gulag sites with monuments and museums; it has also become a major human rights watchdog. The Memorial Society has had complex, ambivalent to hostile relationships with the Russian state. For Western histories of the Memorial Society, see Nanci Adler, *Victims of Soviet Terror: The Story of the Memorial Movement* (Westport, Colo.: Praeger 1993); Anne White, "The Memorial Society in the Russian Provinces," *Europe-Asia Studies* 47, no. 8 (December 1995): 1343–1366; and Kathleen E. Smith, *Remembering Stalin's Victims: Popular Memory and the End of the USSR* (New Haven, Conn.: Yale University Press, 1996).

8. Karl Jaspers, *Die Schuldfrage: Von der politischen Haftung Deutschlands* (Munich: Piper, 1965).

9. See Svetlana Boym, *The Future of Nostalgia* (New York: Basic Books, 2001).

10. Oleg Kashin and Zakhar Prilepin, "Ad i progressivnye tendentsii v nem," *Russkii zhurnal*, September 11, 2011, http://www.russ.ru/pole/Ad-i-progressivnye-tendencii-v-nem.

11. Tony Judt, "The Past Is Another Country: Myth and Memory in Postwar Europe," *Daedalus* 21, no. 4 (1992): 99; see also Richard S. Esbenshade, "Remembering to Forget: Memory, History, National Identity in Postwar East-Central Europe," *Representations* 49 (1995): 72–96.

12. Genocide is mass murder of an ethnic, racial, or religious group by another group or by the government; democide is a mass murder of *any* group by the government. For the history of the concept of genocide, see Anson Rabinbach, "The Challenge of the Unprecedented: Raphael Lemkin and the Concept of Genocide," *Simon Dubnow Institute Yearbook* 4 (2005): 397–420; and Natan Sznaider, *Jewish Memory and the Cosmopolitan Order* (Cambridge: Polity Press, 2011), chap. 6. For a survey of the Soviet genocides, see Norman M. Naimark, *Stalin's Genocides* (Princeton, N.J.: Princeton University Press, 2010). For the concept and statistics of democide, see Rudolf J. Rummel, *Democide: Nazi Genocide and Mass Murder* (New York: Transaction Publishers, 1992); and Rudolf J. Rummel, *Lethal Politics: Soviet Genocide and Mass Murder since 1917* (New York: Transaction Publishers, 1996).

13. For criticism of redemptive narratives of the Holocaust, see Lawrence Langer, *Holocaust Testimonies: The Ruins of Memory* (New Haven, Conn.: Yale University Press, 1991); and Dominick LaCapra, *Writing History, Writing Trauma* (Baltimore: Johns Hopkins University Press, 2001).

14. Saul Friedlander, *The Years of Extermination: Nazi Germany and the Jews* (New York: HarperCollins, 2007), xxvi.

15. Nadezhda Mandel'shtam, *Vospominaniia* (New York: Izdatel'stvo imeni Chekhova 1970), 386.

16. For the distinction between communicative and cultural memory, see Aleida Assmann, "Texts, Traces, Trash: The Changing Media of Cultural Memory," *Representations* 56 (1996): 123–134; and Aleida Assmann, "Transformations between History and Memory," *Social Research* 75, no. 1 (2008): 49–72.

17. Walter Benjamin, "Berlin Chronicle," in *One-Way Street and Other Writings* (London: Verso, 1979), 314.

18. I benefited a great deal from reading, among other studies of mourning, Jay Winter, *Sites of Memory, Sites of Mourning: The Great War in European Cultural History* (Cambridge: Cambridge University Press, 2005); Peter Homans, ed., *Symbolic Loss: The Ambiguity of Mourning and Memory at Century's End* (Charlottesville: University Press of Virginia, 2000); Darian Leader, *The New Black: Mourning, Melancholia, and Depression* (New York: Penguin, 2008); and Judith Butler, *Precarious Life: The Power of Mourning and Violence* (London: Verso, 2004).

252   Notes

19. See Shoshana Felman and Dori Laub, *Testimony: Crises of Witnessing in Literature, Psychoanalysis and History* (New York: Routledge, 1992); Cathy Caruth, *Unclaimed Experience: Trauma, Narrative, and History* (Baltimore: Johns Hopkins University Press, 1996); Michael Lambek and Paul Antze, eds., *Tense Past: Cultural Essays in Trauma and Memory* (London: Routledge, 1996); Leys, *Trauma*; E. Ann Kaplan, *Trauma Culture: The Politics of Terror and Loss in Media and Literature* (New Brunswick, N.J.: Rutgers University Press, 2005); Karyn Ball, *Traumatizing Theory: The Cultural Politics of Affect in and beyond Psychoanalysis* (New York: Other Press, 2007); and Ruth Leys, *From Guilt to Shame: Auschwitz and After* (Princeton, N.J.: Princeton University Press, 2009).

20. Marianne Hirsch, "The Generation of Postmemory," *Poetics Today* 29, no. 1 (Spring 2008): 103–128; Marianne Hirsch, *The Generation of Postmemory: Visual Culture after the Holocaust* (New York: Columbia University Press, 2012).

21. Sigmund Freud, "Beyond the Pleasure Principle," in *The Standard Edition of the Complete Psychological Works of Sigmund Freud* (London: Vintage 1975), 18:18–20; Michael Taussig, *Walter Benjamin's Grave* (Chicago: University of Chicago Press, 2006), 63; see also Todd Dufresne, *Tales from the Freudian Crypt: The Death Drive in Text and Context* (Stanford, Calif.: Stanford University Press, 2000); and Colin Davis, *Haunted Subjects: Deconstruction, Psychoanalysis and the Return of the Dead* (London: Palgrave Macmillan, 2007).

22. Sigmund Freud, "Dostoevsky and Parricide," in *Art and Literature*: *The Pelican Freud Library* (New York: Penguin, 1990), 14:447. I am using the idea of mimesis in the broad Aristotelian sense specified by two French theorists, René Girard and Mikkel Borch-Jacobsen. For a genealogy of the concept that leads to Girard, see Gunter Gebauer and Christoph Wulf, *Mimesis*, trans. Don Reneau (Berkeley: University of California Press, 1995). For my reading of Girard, see A. Etkind, *Internal Colonization: Russia's Imperial Experience* (Cambridge: Polity, 2011), chap. 12. Borch-Jacobsen has shown that the idea of mimesis structured many of Freud's texts, even if Freud never acknowledged it. According to Borch-Jacobsen, mimesis is rooted in Freud's intuition of sympathy or identification with other people. This is probably a reason why Freud did not feel the need to explain mourning, which figures in some of his texts as a primary motivation. See Mikkel Borch-Jacobsen, *The Emotional Tie: Psychoanalysis, Mimesis, and Affect* (Stanford, Calif.: Stanford University Press, 1993). On mimesis and antimimesis as conceptual dimensions in trauma theory, see Leys, *Trauma*.

23. Sigmund Freud, "Remembering, Repeating, and Working Through," in *Standard Edition of the Complete Psychological Works of Sigmund Freud*, 12:151.

24. Sigmund Freud, "The Uncanny," in *The Uncanny*, trans. David McLintock (New York: Penguin, 1984), 147–148; for analyses, see Jacques Derrida, *The Post Card: From Socrates to Freud and Beyond* (Chicago: University of Chicago Press, 1987); Jonathan Dollimore, *Death, Desire, and Loss in Western*

Culture (London: Penguin, 1998); Anthony Vidler, *Warped Space. Art, Architecture, and Anxiety in Modern Culture* (Cambridge, Mass.: MIT Press, 2001; Nicholas Royle, *The Uncanny* (Manchester: Manchester University Press, 2003); and Mikhail Epstein, "Zhutkoe i strannoe: O teoreticheskoi vstreche S. Freuda i V. Shklovskogo," in *Iz Ameriki*, vol. 2 (Yekaterinburg: U-Faktoriia, 2005); also http://old.russ.ru/krug/razbor/20030314_ep.html.

25. Misinforming the relatives of victims was a policy that was consistently pursued by the bureaucracy of terror. In December 1962, the head of the KGB, Vladimir Semichastnyi, reported to the Central Committee that the majority of relatives were given false information regarding their relatives' deaths. Introduced when rehabilitation began in 1955, this procedure was no longer necessary, wrote Semichastnyi. He proposed that relatives would be told by word of mouth the true circumstances of the death, and the death certificate would show the true date of death. However, on the certificate the cause of death would be left blank. The truth would not be told to relatives of those who had been rehabilitated before this new procedure. If information about rehabilitation was sent abroad, the procedure of falsifying the date and cause of death would continue. R. W. Davies, *Soviet History in the Yeltsin Era* (Houndmills, Basingstoke, and London: Macmillan, 1997), 160–161.

26. In psychoanalytic terms, this situation of mourning is analyzed in Maria Lucila Pelento, "Mourning for 'Missing People,'" in *On Freud's "Mourning and Melancholia,"* ed. Leticia Glocer Fiorini, Thierry Bokanowski, and Sergio Lewkowicz (London: Karnac, 2009), 56–70. Revisionist readings of Freud's works on mourning and melancholia emphasize the nonpathological character of interminable mourning or, as Jacques Derrida called it, "midmourning." See Jacques Derrida, *Specters of Marx: The State of the Debt, the Work of Mourning, and the New International*, trans. Peggy Kamuf (New York: Routledge, 1994); Tammy Clewell, "Mourning beyond Melancholia: Freud's Psychoanalysis of Loss," *Journal of the American Psychoanalytic Association* 52, no. 1 (2004): 43–67; David L. Eng and David Kazanjian, eds., *Loss: The Politics of Mourning* (Berkeley: University of California Press, 2003); and Alessia Ricciardi, *The Ends of Mourning: Psychoanalysis, Literature, Film* (Stanford, Calif.: Stanford University Press, 2003). However, important works follow Freud's conceptual distinction. See, for example, Paul Gilroy, *After Empire: Melancholia or Convivial Culture* (London: Routledge, 2004); Jean-Philippe Mathy, *Melancholy Politics: Loss, Mournng, and Politics in Late Modern France* (Philadelphia: Penn State University Press, 2011).

27. See Vamik D. Volkan, Gabriele Ast, and William Greer, *The Third Reich in the Unconscious: Transgenerational Transmission and Its Consequences* (New York: Brunner, 2002); and Gabriele Schwab, *Haunting Legacies: Violent Histories and Transgenerational Trauma* (New York: Columbia University Press, 2010).

28. See Nicolas Abraham and Maria Torok, *The Wolf Man's Magic Word: A Cryptonymy* (Minneapolis: University of Minnesota Press, 1986); and Nicolas Abraham and Maria Torok, *The Shell and the Kernel* (Chicago: University of Chicago Press, 1994). For criticism, see Colin Davis, "Hauntology, Spectres and Phantoms," *French Studies* 59, no. 3 (July 2005): 373–379.

29. For a psychological approach that emphasizes intergenerational negotiations and the agency of the younger generation, see Karoline Tschuggnall and Harald Welzer, "Rewriting Memories: Family Recollections of the National Socialist Past in Germany," *Culture & Psychology* 8, no. 1 (March 2002): 130–145; and Hans J. Markowitsch and Harald Welzer, *The Development of Autobiographical Memory* (New York: Psychology Press, 2010).

30. Walter Benjamin, *The Origin of German Tragic Drama*, trans. John Osborne (London: Verso, 1998), 138.

31. Sigmund Freud, "Mourning and Melancholia," in *Pelican Freud Library*, 11:245–268.

32. Benjamin, *Origin of German Tragic Drama*, 139, 189, 185.

33. Freud, "Beyond the Pleasure Principle," 22.

34. Torquato Tasso, *The Liberation of Jerusalem*, trans. Max Wickert (New York: Oxford University Press 2009), 247.

35. Cathy Caruth, in her (now classic) study of trauma, enriches Freud's reading of Tasso by important details, highlighting, for example, the Greek meaning of "trauma" as wound. In a critical response, Ruth Leys notes that the wound in this story is Clorinda's, while the trauma is Tancred's. I believe that this debate can be illuminated by the concept of mourning. Mourning evolves in the relation of one subject to another, while trauma develops within the experience of one and the same subject. The language of trauma blurs a crucial difference between its agent (Tancred) and subject (Clorinda); the language of mourning preserves this distinction. See Caruth, *Unclaimed Experience*, 2–9; and Leys, *Trauma*, 292–297.

36. Born as Christian and raised as Muslim, this white Ethiopian and female warrior is a wonderful character, "a mass of overlapping and contradictory identities." See David Quint, *Epic and Empire: Politics and Generic Form from Virgil to Milton* (Princeton, N.J.: Princeton University Press, 1993), 244.

37. Joseph Brodsky, "Uncommon Visage" (Nobel Lecture), in *On Grief and Reason: Essays* (New York: Farrar, Straus and Giroux, 1995), 48.

38. Quoted from Greenblatt, *Hamlet in Purgatory*, 207.

39. Benjamin, *Origin of German Tragic Drama*, 126.

40. For a similar intuition, see Svetlana Boym, *Death in Quotation Marks: Cultural Myths of a Modern Poet* (Cambridge, Mass.: Harvard University Press, 1991).

41. Freud, "Beyond the Pleasure Principle," 22.

42. In her research on the "post-memory" of the Holocaust, Marianne Hirsch emphasizes the relevance of personal artifacts, such as photographs and family albums, for the experience of the generation that did not see the catastrophe. Marianne Hirsch, *Family Frames: Photography, Narrative, and Post-Memory* (Cambridge, Mass.: Harvard University Press, 1997).

43. On cosmopolitan memory, see Daniel Levy and Natan Sznaider, *Holocaust Memory in the Global Age* (Philadelphia: Temple University Press, 2006); and Natan Sznaider, *Jewish Memory and Cosmopolitan Order* (Cambridge: Polity 2011). For a similar concept of multidirectional memory, *see* Michael Rothberg, *Multidirectional Memory (*Stanford, Calif.: Stanford University Press, 2009). On generations in the twentieth century, see Mark Roseman, ed., *Generations in Conflict* (Cambridge: Cambridge University Press, 1995); Stephen Lovell, ed., *Generation in Twentieth-Century Europe* (Basingstoke: Palgrave, 2007); and Mary Fulbrook, *Dissonant Lives: Generations and Violence through the German Dictatorships* (Oxford: Oxford University Press, 2011).

CHAPTER 2

1. A subtle reader, Joseph Brodsky believed that this ode was "the grandest poem Mandelstam ever wrote" and also the most significant piece ever written about Stalin: "After the 'Ode', if I were Stalin, I would have slit Mandelstam's throat immediately." See Solomon Volkov, *Conversations with Joseph Brodsky: A Poet's Journey through the Twentieth Century*, trans. Marian Schwartz (New York: Free Press, 1998), 31. For a close reading of this "Ode," see Mikhail Gasparov, *O. Mandel'shtam: Grazhdanskaia lirika 1937 goda* (Moscow: RGGU, 1996); and Svetlana Boym, *Another Freedom: The Alternative History of an Idea* (Chicago: University of Chicago Press, 2010), 70–73.

2. The evidence is collected and analyzed by Pavel Nerler in his *Slovo i "delo" Osipa Mandel'shtama* (Moscow: Petrovskii Park, 2010).

3. "Iz arkhiva Guverovskogo instituta: Pis'ma Iu. G. Oksmana k G. P. Struve," publication by Lazar Fleishman, *Stanford Slavic Studies* 1 (1987): 24. For the full account of Mandelstam's arrests, trials, and death, see Nerler, *Slovo i delo*. In comparison to other witnesses, Oksman dramatized Mandelstam's ordeal, but essential details of his letter match the information that we know from others.

4. Giorgio Agamben, *Homo Sacer, Sovereign Power and Bare Life* (Stanford, Calif.: Stanford University Press, 1995), 83; Giorgio Agamben, *Remnants of Auschwitz: The Witness and the Archive*, trans. Daniel Heller-Roazen (New York: Zone Books, 1999).

5. Alexander Solzhenitsyn, *The Gulag Archipelago, 1918–1956: An Experiment in Literary Investigation*, trans. Thomas P. Whitney (London: Collins and Harvill, 1978), part 3, chap. 7.

6. From 1948 onward, convicts working in the gulag were entitled to receive wages, which were set at 30 percent of the current salaries in the equivalent industries. However, in 1953 only 61.8 percent of convicts actually obtained these wages; the remainder were either too ill or physically incapacitated to perform the work required, or refused to work for religious or other reasons. See Sokolov, "Prinuzhdenie k trudu v sovetskoi ekonomike," 63–64.

7. According to the numbers that were collected by the central administration of the gulag, mortality in the camps was generally four times higher than for the civilian population, but sometimes ten times higher. S. G. Wheatcroft, "The Scale and Nature of Stalinist Repression and Its Demographic Significance," *Europe-Asia Studies* 52, no. 6 (2000): 1143–1159. During the construction of the Belomor Canal (1931–1933), mortality increased sixfold. Sokolov, "Prinuzhdenie k trudu v sovetskoi ekonomike," 22.

8. Julia Kristeva, *Powers of Horror: An Essay in Abjection*, trans. Leon S. Roudiez (New York: Columbia University Press, 1982), 2. Goners were not the only category that was perceived as disgusting in the camps. See Adi Kuntsman, "'With a Shade of Disgust': Affective Politics of Sexuality and Class in Memoirs of the Stalinist Gulag," *Slavic Review* 68, no. 2 (Summer 2009): 308–328.

9. "I menia tol'ko ravnyi ub'et," a line from Mandelstam's poem, "Za gremuchuiu doblest' griadushchikh vekov."

10. Solzhenitsyn, *Gulag Archipelago*, part 3, 208.

11. Hannah Arendt, "Social Science Techniques and the Study of Concentration Camps" [1950], in *Essays in Understanding* (New York: Schocken, 1994), 233, 240–241.

12. Elaine Scarry, *The Body in Pain: The Making and Unmaking of the World* (New York: Oxford University Press, 1985), 56; see also Harriet Murav, *Russia's Legal Fictions* (Ann Arbor: University of Michigan Press, 1998), 172. The torturer usually perceives torture as a means and not an end, but the tortured, and her friends and descendants, may have the opposite opinion. My definition of torture camps attempts to formulate the victims' perspective. It does not, however, deny the perpetrators' perceptions of the economic, political, and psychological purposes of the gulag.

13. Sokolov, "Prinuzhdenie k trudu v sovetskoi ekonomike"; Oleg Khlevniuk, *The History of the Gulag: From Collectivization to the Great Terror* (New Haven, Conn.: Yale University Press, 2004). For an extreme example of the inefficiency of the gulag, see Nicolas Werth, *Cannibal Island: Death in a Siberian Gulag* (Princeton, N.J.: Princeton University Press, 2007). For a fresh study of violence in the camps, see Golfo Alexopulos, "A Torture Memo: Reading Violence in the Gulag," in Golfo Alexopulos, Julie Hessler, and Kiril Tomoff, *Writing the Stalin Era: Sheila Fitzpatrick and Soviet Historiography* (New York: Palgrave, 2011), 157–176.

14. See Il'ia Gerasimov, "Pered prikhodom t'my: (Pere)kovka novogo sovetskogo cheloveka v 1920–kh godakh: Svidetel'stva uchastnikov," *Ab Imperio* 3 (2002): 297–320; Anne Applebaum, *Gulag: A History of the Soviet Camps* (London: Allen Lane, 2003), 23; Steven A. Barnes, *Death and Redemption: The GULAG and the Shaping of Soviet Society* (Princeton, N.J.: Princeton University Press, 2011), 36–41; and Julie Draskoczy, "The 'Put' of Perekovka: Transforming Lives at Stalin's White Sea-Baltic Canal," *Russian Review* 71 (2012): 30–48. For other methods of psychological transformation, see Igal Halfin, *From Darkness to Light: Class, Consciousness, and Salvation in Revolutionary Russia* (Pittsburgh: University of Pittsburgh Press, 2000); Vadim Volkov, "The Concept of Kul'turnost': Notes on the Stalinist Civilizing Process," in *Stalinism: New Directions*, ed. Sheila Fitzpatrick (London: Routledge, 2000), 210–230; and Jochen Hellbeck, *Revolution on My Mind: Writing a Diary under Stalin* (Cambridge, Mass.: Harvard University Press, 2006). On the instrumental use of state violence as a means for ideological and aesthetic transformation of the population, see Amir Weiner, *Making Sense of War: The Second World War and the Fate of the Bolshevik Revolution* (Princeton, N.J.: Princeton University Press, 2001), 26–30, 82–126; Peter Holquist, "State Violence as Technique: The Logic of Violence in Soviet Totalitarianism," in *Landscaping the Human Garden*, ed. Amir Weiner (Stanford, Calif.: Stanford University Press, 2003), 19–45; and Christian Gerlach and Nicolas Werth, "State Violence—Violent Societies," in *Beyond Totalitarianism: Stalinism and Nazism Compared*, ed. Michael Geyer and Sheila Fitzpatrick (Cambridge: Cambridge University Press, 2009), 133–179. On the underappreciated depths of the Soviet transformation of humans, see A. Etkind, *Eros of the Impossible: The History of Psychoanalysis in Russia*, trans. Noah Rubens and Maria Rubens (Boulder, Colo.: Westview Press, 1996); for a particularly bizarre project, see A. Etkind, "Beyond Eugenics: The Forgotten Scandal of Hybridizing Humans and Apes," *Studies in History and Philosophy of Biological and Biomedical Sciences* 39 (2008): 205–210.

15. Agamben, *Homo Sacer*, 83; Agamben, *Remnants of Auschwitz*. For criticisms of Agamben's analysis of the *Muselmann*, bare life, and witnessing, see Dominick LaCapra, "Approaching Limit Events: Siting Agamben," in *Giorgio Agamben: Sovereignty and Life*, ed. Matthew Calarco and Steven DeCaroli (Stanford, Calif.: Stanford University Press, 2007), 126–162; Davis, *Haunted Subjects*, 119–126; and Mark Mazower, "Foucault, Agamben: Theory and the Nazis," *boundary 2* 35, no. 1 (Spring 2008): 23–34.

16. On sacrifice and its modern repercussions, see Boym, *Another Freedom*.

17. Eric L. Santner, *The Royal Remains: The People's Two Bodies and the Endgames of Sovereignty* (Chicago: University of Chicago Press, 2011), 6.

18. Igal Halfin, ed., *Language and Revolution: Making Modern Political Identities* (London: Frank Cass, 2002); Jochen Hellbeck, *Revolution on My Mind:*

Writing a Diary under Stalin (Cambridge, Mass.: Harvard University Press, 2006); A. Etkind, "Soviet Subjectivity: Torture for the Sake of Salvation?" *Kritika* 6, no. 1 (2005): 171–186; Choi Chatterjee and Karen Petrone, "Models of Selfhood and Subjectivity: The Soviet Case in Historical Perspective," *Slavic Review* 67, no. 4 (Winter 2008): 967–986.

19. See Hannah Arendt, *Origins of Totalitarianism* (New York: Harcourt, 1966); and Tzvetan Todorov, *Facing the Extreme: Moral Life in Concentration Camps* (New York: Holt, 1996), 28.

20. Jan Plamper, "Foucault's Gulag," *Kritika* 3, no. 2 (2002): 255–280. For a perspective on the anthropology of violence, see Veena Das, ed., *Violence and Subjectivity* (Berkeley: University of California Press, 2000); and Veena Das, *Life and Words: Violence and Descent into the Ordinary* (Berkeley: University of California Press, 2007).

21. Alexei Yurchak, *Everything Was Forever, Until It Was No More: The Last Soviet Generation* (Princeton, N.J.: Princeton University Press, 2006), 40.

22. *Istoriia Grazhdanskoi voiny v SSSR* (Moscow: OGIZ, 1936).

23. Hannah Arendt, *On Violence* (Orlando, Fla.: Harcourt, 1970).

24. Arendt, *Origins of Totalitarianism*, 54; for analyses of Arendt's "boomerang effect," see Michael Rothberg, *Multidirectional Memory* (Stanford, Calif.: Stanford University Press, 2009); and Etkind, *Internal Colonization*, chap. 1.

25. Ann Laura Stoler, *Race and Education of Sexuality* (Durham, N.C.: Duke University Press, 1995), 17.

26. Vasilii Grossman, *Everything Flows*, trans. Robert Chandler and Elizabeth Chandler (London: Harvill, 2010), 51.

27. In a parallel way, Friedrich Hayek called his classic book, which defended liberalism against the twentieth-century proponents of state property, *The Road to Serfdom*. By using the historical term "serfdom" (not slavery or servitude), Hayek derived a genealogy of Soviet-style socialism from the Russian imperial order. See Friedrich Hayek, *The Road to Serfdom* (London: Routledge 1944).

28. For this concept, see Timothy Snyder, *Bloodlands: Europe between Hitler and Stalin* (New York: Basic Books, 2010).

29. Rebellions in the gulag, which started in 1953, could also convince Khrushchev that the system was not sustainable. See Anne Appelbaum, *Gulag: A History* (London: Doubleday 2003), 484–507; and Igor Chubais, "Reformator ponevole," *Nezavisimaia gazeta*, April 21, 2009.

30. Sokolov, "Prinuzhdenie k trudu v sovetskoi ekonomike," 65.

31. Sergei Khrushchev, *Nikita Khrushchev* (Moscow: Novosti, 1994), chap. 4.

32. Sigmund Freud, "The Uncanny," in *Standard Edition of the Complete Works of Sigmund Freud* (London: Hogarth, 1968), 17:245.

33. The term "contact zone" has been developed in postcolonial studies, where it describe exchanges and conflicts between the colonizers and the colonized.

See Mary Louise Pratt, *Imperial Eyes: Travel Writing and Acculturation* (London: Routledge, 1992).

34. Akhmatova said this on March 4, 1956, a week after the Twentieth Congress of the Communist Party. See Lidiia Chukovskaia, *Zapiski ob Akhmatovoi* (Moscow: Soglasie, 1997), 2:190; quoted here in the translation by Applebaum, *Gulag*, 463.

35. Ludmila Alexeyeva and Paul Goldberg, *The Thaw Generation: Coming of Age in the Post-Stalin Era* (Boston: Little Brown, 1990), 71.

36. Aimé Césaire, "Lettre à Maurice Thorez," trans. Chike Jeffers, *Social Text* 28, no. 2 (2010): 145–152; I am grateful to Nancy Condee for introducing me to this document.

37. Aleksandr Tvardovsky's ghostly poem that he wrote from 1954 to 1963, "Tyorkin in the Other World", illustrates the surreal imagination of the period. On the culture of the Thaw, see Nancy Condee, "Cultural Codes of the Thaw," in *Nikita Khrushchev*, ed. William Taubman et al. (New Haven, Conn.: Yale University Press, 2000), 160–176; Jan Plamper, "Cultural Production, Cultural Consumption: Post-Stalin Hybrids," *Kritika* 6, no. 4 (2005): 755–762; Susan Reid, "The Soviet Art World in the Early Thaw," *Third Text* 20, no. 2 (March 2006): 161–175; Polly Jones, ed., *The Dilemmas of De-Stalinization: Negotiating Cultural and Social Change in the Khrushchev Era* (London: Routledge, 2006); Aleksandr Prokhorov, *Unasledovannyi diskurs: Paradigmy stalinskoi kul'tury v literature i kinematografe ottepeli* (St. Petersburg: Akademicheskii proekt, 2008); Polly Jones, "Memories of Terror or Terrorizing Memories?" *Slavic and East European Journal* 86, no. 2 (2008): 346–371; Vladislav Zubok, *Zhivago's Children: The Last Russian Intelligentsia* (Cambridge, Mass.: Belknap 2009).

38. Dan Diner, *Beyond the Conceivable: Studies on Germany, Nazism, and the Holocaust* (Berkeley: University of California Press, 2000), 191–192.

39. On associations and democracy in Alexis de Tocqueville's work, see Theda Skocpol and Morris P. Fiorina, eds., *Civic Engagement in American Democracy* (Washington, D.C.: Brookings Institution Press, 1999); Robert D. Putnam, *Bowling Alone: The Collapse and Revival of American Community* (New York: Simon and Schuster, 2000); and Mark E. Warren, *Democracy and Association* (Princeton, N.J.: Princeton University Press, 2001), 29–30.

40. See Aleida Assmann, *Cultural Memory and Western Civilization: Functions, Media, Archives* (Cambridge: Cambridge University Press, 2011).

41. Wulf Kansteiner, "Finding Meaning in Memory: A Methodological Critique of Collective Memory Studies," *History and Theory* 41 (2002): 179–197.

42. See Kathleen E. Smith, *Remembering Stalin's Victims: Popular Memory and the End of the USSR* (Ithaca, N.Y.: Cornell University Press, 1996); Leona Toker, *Return from the Archipelago: Narratives of GULAG Survivors* (Bloomington: Indiana University Press, 2000); and Catherine Merridale, *Night of Stone: Death and*

Memory in Twentieth-Century Russia (London: Granta, 2000). In recent years, autobiographical accounts have received more attention than other forms of memory. See Veronique Garros, Natalia Korenevskaya, and Thomas Lahusen, eds., *Intimacy and Terror: Soviet Diaries of the 1930s* (New York: New Press, 1995); Irina Paperno, "Personal Accounts of the Soviet Experience," *Kritika* 3–4 (Fall 2002): 577–610; and Jochen Hellbeck, ed., *Autobiographical Practices in Russia/Autobiographische Praktiken in Russland* (Göttingen: Vandenhoeck & Ruprecht, 2004).

43. Marietta Chudakova, "Pod skrip ukliuchin," *Novyi mir* 4 (1993): 136.

44. For a critical theory of nostalgia, see Svetlana Boym, *The Future of Nostalgia* (New York: Basic Books, 2001).

45. Alexis de Tocqueville, *Democracy in America*, book 2 (Boston: Palgrave, 2009), chap. 5.

46. Since 2001, a small Museum of the History of Gulag has been working in Moscow on Petrovka. The exposition shows photos of prominent prisoners, the interior of a typical barrack, a model of the observation tower in the yard, and some interesting pieces of art created by the former convicts.

CHAPTER 3

1. "*Nepmen*" were small entrepreneurs who benefited from the Soviet government's New Economic Policy (1921–1928), which allowed for some forms of private enterprise to be resumed.

2. "My father told me: crowds of prisoners were rounded up and driven into small cells where it was so crowded that it was impossible to sit down and where [we were confronted with] constant heat, intensified day and night by the blinding glare of the revolving floodlight." Yefim Etkind, *Zapiski nezagovorshchika: Barselonskaia proza* (St. Petersburg: Akademicheskii proekt, 2001), 315.

3. Grigory Etkind died of starvation twelve years later during the siege of Leningrad.

4. Etkind, *Zapiski nezagovorshchika*, 316.

5. During the decades of Stalin's rule, about 20 million people returned from the gulag alive; in 1954–1957, 2.5 million people were released from the system of the camps, prisons, and settlements. Sokolov, "Prinuzhdenie k trudu v sovetskoi ekonomike," 38, 65.

6. The memoirs of gulag survivors have been explored in Merridale, *Night of Stone*; Toker, *Return from the Archipelago*; and Orlando Figes, *The Whisperers: Private Life in Stalin's Russia* (New York: Metropolitan Books, 2007). The Sakharov Museum in Moscow has published 1,505 memoirs of the gulag at http://www.sakharov-center.ru/asfcd/auth/list.xtmpl. On the post-Soviet memoirs as a genre, see Irina Paperno, *Stories of the Soviet Experience: Memoirs, Diaries, Dreams* (Ithaca, N.Y.: Cornell University Press, 2009); see also my review of this book in the *Times Literary Supplement*, June 11, 2010.

7. Charles Taylor, *Multiculturalism: Examining the Politics of Recognition* (Princeton, N.J.: Princeton University Press, 1994); Pierre Bourdieu, "Marginalia: Some Additional Notes on the Gift," in *The Logic of the Gift: Toward an Ethic of Generosity* (London: Routledge, 1997), 231–241; Paul Ricoeur, *The Course of Recognition* (Cambridge, Mass.: Harvard University Press, 2005). For a critical analysis, see Patchen Markell, *Bound by Recognition* (Princeton, N.J.: Princeton University Press, 2003).

8. Nancy Fraser, *Justice Interruptus* (London: Routledge, 1997); Nancy Fraser and Axel Honneth, *Redistribution or Recognition? A Political-Philosophical Exchange* (London: Verso, 2003). For criticism, see Simon Thompson, *The Political Theory of Recognition: A Critical Introduction* (London: Polity, 2006); Lois McNay, *Against Recognition* (London: Polity, 2008); and Terry Lovell, ed., *(Mis)recognition, Social Inequality and Social Justice: Nancy Fraser and Pierre Bourdieu* (London: Routledge, 2007).

9. Aristotle, *Poetics*, ed. and trans. Gerald F. Else (Ann Arbor: University of Michigan Press, 1970), 1452a29–32; for exemplary analysis, see Terence Cave, *Recognitions: A Study in Poetics* (Oxford: Clarendon Press, 1988). On the affinity between situations of misrecognition and ghostly apparitions in Shakespeare's comedies, see Greenblatt, *Hamlet in Purgatory*, 159–162.

10. In Soviet film, the most popular comedies such as *The Diamond Hand* (dir. Leonid Gaidai, 1968) or *The Irony of Fate* (dir. El'dar Riazanov, 1975) were stories of misrecognition.

11. Sheila Fitzpatrick, *Tear Off the Masks! Identity and Imposture in Twentieth-Century Russia* (Princeton, N.J.: Princeton University Press, 2005).

12. Nadezhda Mandel'shtam, *Vtoraia kniga* (Paris: IMCA-Press, 1972), 22. On the arrest of Osip Mandelstam and his wife's search for him, see Vitalii Shentalinskii, *Raby svobody: V literaturnykh arkhivakh KGB* (Moscow: Parus, 1995), 222–256; and Pavel Nerler, introduction to Nadezhda Mandel'shtam, *Ob Akhmatovoi*, ed. Pavel Nerler (Moscow: Novoe izdatel'stvo, 2007).

13. Mandel'shtam, *Vtoraia kniga*, 208.

14. See Nanci Adler, *The Gulag Survivor: Beyond the Soviet System* (New Brunswick, N.J.: Transaction Publishers, 2002); and Stephen F. Cohen, *The Victims Return: Survivors of the Gulag after Stalin* (New York: Tauris, 2011).

15. Inga Clendinnen, *Reading the Holocaust* (Cambridge: Cambridge University Press, 1999), 36.

16. B. Okudzhava, *Devushka moei mechty: Avtobiograficheskie povestvovaniia* (Moscow: Moskovskii rabochii, 1988). Though the described events are similar to the actual life of Okudzhava, this is a fictional tale written as a first-person narrative. However, Okudzhava included the story in his "Autobiographical Stories"; as a result, we are entitled to read it as a memoir.

17. In the real-life story of Varlen Riabokon and his mother, Anna Abrukina, we find a similar combination of the son's longing for his mother and his anxiety

that he does not "know" her after the many years that she spent in the camp. Varlen was twelve years old when his mother was arrested in 1937. Like the mother of Okudzhava's character, Abrukina was held in Kazakhstan, in the Karaganda women's camp. She was released in 1946 and met her son, who was serving in the army, in 1949. Varlen wrote to his mother: "Can you imagine me, if only vaguely? I do not have a single photograph of you." Having received such a photo in September 1947 ("you are really young and look good"), he wrote her: "it is still the same: I cannot imagine you as you really are. In any photograph, I can only guess and remember the old, now erased, features of my mama as you were in 1937. But you know me even less." Ye. V. Riabokon', "Pis'ma izdaleka," available at the Sakharov Museum's website *Vospominaniia o GULAGe*, http://www.sakharov-center.ru/asfcd/auth/auth_pages.xtmpl?Key=23975&page=0.

18. This film was produced in Berlin in 1944 under Joseph Goebbels's supervision and was a wartime hit. It featured Marika Rökk, "the undisputed prima ballerina of National-Socialist cinema." See Klaus Kreimeier, *The Ufa Story: A History of Germany's Greatest Film Company 1918–1945* (New York: Hill, 1996), 234. Decades later, Okudzhava remembered Marika Rökk's name and mentioned it in his story.

19. While his family's history served Okudzhava as a source of inspiration for his historical novels and memoirs, his mother's years in the camp remained untouchable. In his nonfictional study "Uprazdnennyi teatr" (1995), Okudzhava describes events that preceded the arrest of his parents in 1937, including his mother's visit to Beria. Okudzhava's mother returned from the Karaganda camps to Tbilisi only in 1955. See also Dmitrii Bykov, *Bulat Okudzhava* (Moscow: Molodaia gvardiia 2011), 142–143.

20. Yevgeniia Ginzburg, *Krutoi marshrut* (Moscow: Sovetskii pisatel', 1990), 219.

21. Vasilii Grossman, *Vse techet: Pozdniaia proza* (Moscow: Slovo, 1994), 283.

22. Ibid., 328, 284–285, 295.

23. Joseph Brodsky, "Three Poems by Joseph Brodsky," trans. George L. Kline, *Russian Review* 25, no. 2 (April 1966): 131–134.

24. The life-story of the poet Nikolai Zabolotsky features a similar event. In the early 1950s, the former chief of the unit in eastern Siberia, in which Zabolotsky spent a large part of his gulag term (he served from 1938 to 1945), visited him in Moscow, drank vodka with him, and even spent nights in his apartment. Moreover, in 1946 Zabolotsky met in a restaurant that very critic, N. V. Lesiuchevsky, whose denunciation was the main reason for his arrest; the two men recognized each other and dined together. Telling this story to his friends, Zabolotsky said: "this is a psychological problem: why did Lesiuchevsky join my table? Do you want to resolve it? Perhaps he needed to make sure that I am not a ghost, that I am real, that I am eating soup." See Nikita Zabolotsky, *Zhizn' N. A. Zabolotskogo* (Moscow: Soglasie 1998), 321, 361. Bitov

writes about Zabolotsky as his "favorite poet." Bitov, "O literaturnykh reputatsiiakh," *Oktiabr'* (2006): 8.

25. A. Bitov, *Pushkinskii dom* (Ann Arbor, Mich.: Ardis, 1978), 49.

26. In his auto-commentary, Bitov states that he was inspired by the first rumors about Bakhtin's life and work. See A. Bitov, "Pushkinskii dom: Kommentarii," in *Blizkoe retro* (Yekaterinburg: U-Faktoriia, 2004), 472. He also knew about the repressed historians of literature from Pushkinskii dom (the Institute of Russian Literature of Academy of Sciences in Leningrad), such as Dmitry Likhachev and Yulian Oksman (see chapter 4), and also about the brothers Grigory and Matvei Gukovsky, two prominent scholars who worked at Pushkinskii dom. They were arrested in 1949. Grigory died in prison in 1950; Matvei survived.

27. Abram Tertz, *Spokoinoi nochi* (Paris: Sintaksis, 1984), 260.

28. In 1944, Kazarnovsky came to Tashkent to live with Nadezhda for a while and tell her his untrustworthy stories about Osip, whom he claimed to have seen in a camp near Vladivostok. On Kazarnovsky as a flamboyant poet in the Solovetsky camp in 1930, see Dmitry Likhachev, *Vospominaniia* (St. Petersburg: Logos, 2005), 254; on Kazarnovsky as a beggar and drug addict in the 1950s, see Gleb Vasil'ev, "Vstrechi s Iuriem Kazarnovskim," *Grani*, 182 (1996); and Eduard Babaev, *Vospominaniia* (St. Petersburg: Inapress, 2000), 180. Babaev remembers Kazarnovsky as a ghostly figure: "Yurochka the ghost." A leading expert on Mandelstam, Pavel Nerler believes that Nadezhda actually learned about Osip's death from Varlam Shalamov, who received reliable information about the poet from a camp doctor, Nina Savoeva. See Pavel Nerler, "Ot zimy k vesne: Na poliakh perepiski Nadezhdy Mandel'shtam i Varlama Shalamova," *polit.ru*, June 22, 2007, www.polit.ru/analytics/2007/06/22/mandelshtam.html.

29. Mandel'shtam, *Vospominaniia*, 397.

30. The 1918 constitution of the Russian Socialist Federative Soviet Republic used the formula of "the complete elimination of class divisions in society" (Article 3). The Soviet constitution of 1936 softened the formula to "equal rights of all the citizens of the USSR" (Article 123); a similar formula appears in Article 34 of the Soviet constitution of 1977.

CHAPTER 4

1. Matvei Liubavskii, *Obzor istorii russkoi kolonizatsii* (Moscow: MGU, 1996); Evgenii Tarle, *Napoleon* (Moscow: Molodaia gvardiia 1936).

2. Complaints of chronic overcrowding are universal in the Soviet memoir literature. All the social engineering of the period—from collective farms to communal apartments to prison cells to the gulag—featured enforced sociality, the essential mechanism of Soviet disciplinary practices.

3. N. M. Druzhinin, *Izbrannye trudy. Vospominaniia. Mysli. Opyt istorika* (Moscow: Nauka, 1990), 102.

4. N. M. Druzhinin, *Gosudarstvennye krest'iane i reforma Kiseleva* (Moscow: Akademiia nauk SSSR, 1946), 1:81.

5. See Moshe Lewin, *Russian Peasants and Soviet Power: A Study of Civilization* (Evanston, Ill.: Northwestern University Press, 1968); James C. Scott, *Seeing Like a State: How Certain Schemes to Improve the Human Condition Have Failed* (New Haven, Conn.: Yale University Press, 1998); and Lynn Viola, *The War Against the Peasantry, 1927–1930: The Tragedy of the Soviet Countryside* (New Haven, Conn.: Yale University Press, 2005).

6. See Kathleen F. Parthé, *Russian Village Prose: The Radiant Past* (Princeton, N.J.: Princeton University Press, 1992); and Yitzhak M. Brudny, *Reinventing Russia: Russian Nationalism and the Soviet State, 1953–1991* (Cambridge, Mass.: Harvard University Press, 2000).

7. Dmitry Likhachev (1906–1999) was the founder (in 1986) and the head (until 1993) of the Soviet (later Russian) Cultural Fund. Until his death, he was believed to be the personal friend of Mikhail and Raisa Gorbachev and their adviser on cultural and historical issues. I can imagine that among many other issues, his influence was crucial for choosing the image of the Solovetsky camp for the 500-ruble note, which was issued in 1995 (see chapter 1).

8. There is a large and growing literature on the Solovetsky camp. See Applebaum, *Gulag*, 40–58; Roy R. Robson, *Solovki: The Story of Russia Told through Its Most Remarkable Islands* (New Haven, Conn.: Yale University Press, 2004); Yury Brodsky, *Solovki: Dvadtsat' let osobogo naznacheniia* (Moscow: Mir iskusstv 2008); and Michael David-Fox, *Showcasting the Great Experiment: Cultural Diplomacy and Western Visitors to Soviet Russia, 1921–1941* (New York: Oxford University Press, 2012), 142–175. There is also an excellent bilingual site, http://www.solovki.ca/.

9. Dmitry Likhachev, *Zametki i nabliudeniia* (Leningrad: Sovetskii pisatel', 1989).

10. Dmitry Likhachev, "Kartezhnye igry ugolovnikov (iz kriminologicheskogo kabineta)," *Solovetskie ostrova* 1 (1930): 32–35; Dmitry Likhachev, "Cherty pervobytnogo primitivizma vorovskoi rechi," *Iazyk i myshlenie*, vols. 3–4 (Moscow-Leningrad: Institut imeni N. Ia. Marra, 1935), 47–100; Dmitry Likhachev, "Argoticheskie slova professional'noi rechi" [1938], in *Razvitie grammatiki i leksiki sovremennogo russkogo iazyka* (Moscow: Nauka, 1964), 311–359.

11. See James C. Scott, *Domination and the Arts of Resistance: Hidden Transcripts* (New Haven, Conn.: Yale University Press, 1990); and Etkind, *Internal Colonization*, chap. 8.

12. Viktor Paneiakh, *Tvorchestvo i sud'ba istorika: Boris Aleksandrovich Romanov* (St. Petersburg: Bulanin, 2000), 138–146. These survivors routinely

used the idea of "psychic trauma." In 1946, shortly before the end of his ten-year-long term, Yulian Oksman wrote his wife from a Kolyma camp: "A feeling of large-scale confusion, lack of confidence, doubt in everything and everyone has mastered me, and I do not recognize and understand myself. Of course, this is a psychic trauma that is common for such conditions." M. O. Chudakova and Ie. A. Toddes, "Iz perepiski Iu. G. Oksmana," in *Chetvertye Tynianovskie chteniia: Tezisy dokladov i materialy dlia obsuzhdeniia* (Riga: Zinatne, 1988), 153.

13. Boris Romanov, *Liudi i nravy drevnei Rusi*, 2nd ed. (Moscow-Leningrad: Nauka, 1966), 23–45, 216.

14. Likhachev, *Vospominaniia*, 171.

15. Ibid., 137–139.

16. Ol'ga Berggol'ts, *Zapretnyi dnevnik* (St. Petersburg: Azbuka, 2010), 26, 31.

17. Katerina Clark and Michael Holquist, *Mikhail Bakhtin* (Cambridge, Mass.: Harvard University Press, 1984), 142; V. V. Duvakin, *Besedy V. V. Duvakina s M. M. Bakhtinym* (Moscow: Progress, 1996), 205.

18. On Medvedev and Liubov' Mendeleeva-Blok, the addressee of many celebrated poems by Aleksandr Blok, see Duvakin, *Besedy V. V. Duvakina s M. M. Bakhtinym*, 196–197.

19. The best Russian biographies of Bakhtin state that Sukhanov was Bakhtin's only interlocutor during the Kustanai exile. See S. S. Konkin and L. S. Konkina, *Mikhail Bakhtin* (Saransk: Mordovskoe knizhnoe izdatel'stvo, 1993), 209–210; and N. A. Pan'kov, *Voprosy biografii i nauchnogo tvorchestva M. M. Bakhtina* (Moscow: MGU, 2011), 427. Sukhanov's biography, however, does not contain any mention of Sukhanov ever having been exiled to Kazakhstan. See Israel Getzler, *Nikolai Sukhanov: Chronicler of the Russian Revolution* (Basingstoke: Palgrave, 2002). The foremost Russian expert on Sukhanov, A. A. Kornikov, responded to my query with a very informative letter in which he also stated that Sukhanov and Flakserman had never been in Kazakhstan exile. They lived in Moscow until Sukhanov was arrested in July 1930, before being sent to the Urals and Siberia, and shot in 1940. My conjecture is that Bakhtin and Sukhanov conversed in Moscow before their arrests but that decades later, Bakhtin wrongly located their meetings in Kustanai.

20. See Duvakin, *Besedy V. V. Duvakina s M. M. Bakhtinym*.

21. On Bakhtin's interest in Russian sects, see A. Etkind, *Khlyst: Sekty, literature i revoliutsiia* (Moscow: NLO, 1998), 155–159.

22. Nadezhda Mandel'shtam, *Vospominaniia*, ed. Iurii Freidin (Moscow: Soglasie, 1999), 1:296.

23. Osip Mandel'shtam, *Sobranie sochinenii*, ed. Sergei Averintsev and Pavel Nerler (Moscow: 1999), 2:221. The first edition of Mandelstam's *Conversation about Dante* was published in 1967 with an afterword by Leonid Pinsky, a historian of literature and survivor of the gulag. Having read this edition in the

camp, Andrei Siniavsky wrote that Pinsky strove in vain to find a place for Mandelstam's treatise in the literature on Dante, whereas in fact the right approach would be to read it in terms of Mandelstam's "personal experience." Andrei Siniavskii, *127 pisem o liubvi*, 3 vols., ed. Mariia Rozanova (Moscow: Agraf, 2004), 1:356. Indeed, in other Soviet biographies of Dante we find a different portrait from Mandelstam's; Aleksei Dzhivilegov presented Dante as a gallant knight in his youth, and then a proud statesman and a stoic wanderer—a far cry from Mandelstam's tortured man. Aleksei Dzhivilegov, *Dante* (Moscow: OGIZ, 1933).

24. Mikhail Bakhtin, "François Rabelais v istorii realizma," in *Sobranie sochinenii* (Moscow: Iazyki slavianskikh kul'tur, 2008), 4:26–27, 43–45, 112. For a history of this text, see N. A. Pan'kov, "N. N. Bakhtin: Ranniaia versiia kontseptsii karnavala," *Voprosy literatury* 5 (1997): 87–122; Pan'kov, *Voprosy biografii*.

25. Benjamin, *Origin of German Tragic Drama*, 53–56, 66, 119, 135–136; see also Max Pensky, *Melancholy Dialectics: Walter Benjamin and the Play of Mourning* (Amherst: University of Massachusetts Press, 2001); Eric Santner, *On Creaturely Life: Rilke, Benjamin, Sebald* (Chicago: University of Chicago Press, 2006); Tim Beasley-Murray, *Mikhail Bakhtin and Walter Benjamin: Experience and Form* (Basingstoke: Palgrave Macmillan, 2007); Jonathan Flatley, *Affective Mapping: Melancholia and the Politics of Modernism* (Cambridge, Mass.: Harvard University Press, 2008); and T. Bubnova, "Bakhtin i Benjamin (po povodu Gete)," in *Khronotop i okrestnosti: Festschrift for Nikolai Pan'kov* (Ufa: Vagant, 2011), 54–67.

26. In the 1960s, the word "grotesque" became a cliché for describing Soviet life; shortly after her emigration, Stalin's daughter wrote that "the history of Russia resembles the sad and uncanny grotesque." Svetlana Allilueva, *Tol'ko odin god* (New York: Harper, 1969), 247.

27. A. Anikst, "L. E. Pinskii," in L. E. Pinskii, *Magistral'nyi siuzhet* (Moscow: Sovetskii pisatel', 1989), 5. The essay was published as L. E. Pinskii, "Tragicheskoe u Shekspira," *Voprosy literatury* 2 (1958).

28. Chudakova and Toddes, "Iz perepiski Iu. G. Oksmana," 104, 112; G. M. Frolov, "K istorii aresta, zakliucheniia i reabilitatsii Iu. G. Oksmana," *Voprosy literatury* 2 (2011): 431–473. Unfortunately, these memoirs and letters do not clarify the philosophical substance of Oksman's new ideas, apart from their anti-Stalinist and probably anti-Marxist character.

29. Belinsky is referring to Gogol's *Selected Passages from Correspondence with Friends* (1847). Belinsky's letter is quoted from *V. G. Belinsky: Selected Philosophical Works* (Moscow: Foreign Languages Publishing House, 1948).

30. On the other side of the Iron Curtain, Isaiah Berlin also singled out Belinsky as one of his favorite Russian thinkers. See Isaiah Berlin, *Russian Thinkers* (London: Penguin 1978).

31. A. L. Grishunin, ed., *Iu. G. Oksman-K. I. Chukovskii: Perepiska 1949–1969* (Moscow: Iazyki slavianskoi kul'tury, 2001), 38, 72, 115. The study was published

as Yulian Oksman, "Pis'mo Belinskogo k Gogoliu kak istoricheskii document," *Uchenye zapiski Saratovskogo universiteta* 31 (1952): 111–205, and in a shorter version in Yulian Oksman, *Ot "Kapitanskoi dochki" k "Zapiskam okhotnika"* (Saratov: Knizhnoe izdatel'stvo, 1959), 203–245.

32. "Donoschiki i predateli sredi sovetskikh pisatelei i uchenykh," *Sotsialisticheskii vestnik* 5, no. 6 (1963): 74—76, republished in M. D. El'zon, "Iskrenne Vash Iulian Oksman," *Russkaia literatura* 1 (2004): 161–163; see also Lazar Fleishman, "Iz archiva Guverovskogo instituta: Pis'ma Iu. G. Oksmana k G. P. Struve," *Stanford Slavonic Papers* 1 (1987): 70.

33. Kathryn B. Feuer and Martin Malia took part in this endeavor. See A. B. Gribanov, "Iu. G. Oksman v perepiske G. P. Struve 1963 goda," in *Sed'mye Tynianovskie chteniia: Materialy dlia obsuzhdeniia* (Riga: 1995), 495–505.

34. Dmitrii Zubarev, "Iz zhizni literaturovedov," *Novoe literaturnoe obozrenie* 20 (1996): 145–177, quote from 146–147.

35. Chudakova and Toddes, "Iz perepiski," 115.

36. Meletinsky's memoirs are published in his *Izbrannye stat'i, vospominaniia* (Moscow: RGGU, 1998). One of his major books is available in English: *The Poetics of Myth*, trans. Gue Lanoue and Alexandre Sadetsky (New York: Routledge, 2000). On Lev Gumilev, see Viktor Shnirelman, *The Myth of the Khazars and Intellectual Anti-Semitism in Russia, 1970s-1990s* (Jerusalem: Hebrew University 2002); and Serguei Oushakine, *The Patriotism of Despair: Nation, War, and Loss in Russia* (Ithaca, N.Y.: Cornell University Press, 2009).

37. Lev Samoilov [Lev Klein], *Perevernutyi mir* (Berlin: Taschenbuch, 1991) (later, the book was republished in Russia); Lev Klein, "Etnografiia lageria," *Sovetskaia ethnografiia* 1 (1990): 96–108. See also his huge and informative book of memoirs: Lev Klein, *Trudno byt' Kleinom* (St. Petersburg: Nestor, 2010).

38. Vladimir Kabo, "Struktura lageria i arkhetipy soznaniia," *Sovetskaia ethnografiia* 1 (1990): 108–113; Vladimir Kabo, *Doroga v Avstraliiu. Vospominaniia* (New York: Effect Publishing, 1995). For an eloquent picture of the Russian penitentiary system in the 2000s, see a fresh collection of prison memoirs, Zakhar Prilepin, ed., *Limonka v tiur'mu* (Moscow: Tsentrpoligraph, 2012).

39. Likhachev, *Vospominaniia*, 142, 171, 217.

CHAPTER 5

1. Yefim Etkind, *Zapiski nezagovorchshika: Barselonskaia proza* (St. Petersburg: Akademicheskii proekt, 2001), 383.

2. Ibid., 385.

3. Mikhail Gronas collected many examples of gulag prisoners who remembered and daily repeated poetic texts, classical or original. He argues that the rhythm and rhymes of Russian poetry helped the prisoners to memorize these texts and rely on them for ordering their mental life. Gronas believes that these

"mnemonic and therapeutic" functions of poetic speech explain its significance for the Soviet convicts. See Mikhail Gronas, *Cognitive Poetics and Cultural Memory: Russian Literary Mnemonics* (New York: Routledge 2011).

4. Nadezhda Mandel'shtam, *Vospominaniia* (Moscow: Soglasie, 1991), 1:296.

5. Henry Orlov, "A Link in the Chain," in *A Shostakovich Casebook*, ed. Malcolm Hamrick Brown (Bloomington: Indiana University Press, 2004), 194–195.

6. Hannah Arendt, *Men in Dark Times* (San Diego, Calif.: Harcourt, 1968), 4–6, 10, 13, 30.

7. Paperno, *Stories of the Soviet Experience*, 24.

8. Sergei Averintsev, "Sud'ba i vest' Osipa Mandel'shtama," in O. E. Mandel'shtam, *Sobranie sochinenii* (Moscow: Khudozhestvennaia literatura, 1990), 1:5–64.

9. Agamben, *Remnants of Auschwitz*.

10. Nanci Adler, *The Communist Within: Narratives of Loyalty to the Party before, during, and after the Gulag* (Bloomington: Indiana University Press, 2012).

11. Nadezhda Mandel'shtam, *Vtoraia kniga* (Moscow: Soglasie, 1999), 495.

12. See Valerii Yesipov, *Varlam Shalamov i ego sovremenniki* (Vologda: Knizhnoe nasledie, 2007).

13. V. T. Shalamov, "Tishina" (1966), in *Sobranie sochinenii v chetyrekh tomakh* (Moscow: Khudozhestvennaia literatura, Vagrius, 1998), 2:111–117.

14. For contextual readings of Shalamov, see Toker, *Return from the Archipelago*, chap. 6 (on "belletrization," 150); Svetlana Boym, "Banality of Evil, Mimicry, and the Soviet Subject," *Slavic Review* 67, no. 2 (Summer 2008): 342–363; and Sarah Young, "The Convict Unbound: The Body of Identity in GULAG Narratives," *GULAG Studies* 1 (2008): 57–76.

15. Benjamin, *Origin of German Tragic Drama*, 73.

16. Lawrence Langer introduced the concept of redemptive narrative in Holocaust studies; see his *Using and Abusing the Holocaust* (Bloomington: Indiana University Press, 2006).

17. Tat'iana Leonova, "Shalamov: Put' v bessmertie (zapis' O. Isaevoi)," *Novyi zhurnal* 245 (2006); http://magazines.russ.ru/nj/2006/245/le17.html.

18. LaCapra, *Writing History, Writing Trauma*.

19. Georges Nivat, *Solzhenitsyn* (London: Overseas Publications Interchange, 1984), 62.

20. Walter Benjamin, "Theses on the Philosophy of History" (1940), in *Illuminations*, trans. Harry Zohn (New York: Schocken, 1968), 257–258.

21. Yurii Lotman and Boris Uspenskii, "Rol' dual'nykh modelei v dinamike russkoi kul'tury," in *Trudy po russkoi i slavianskoi fililologii* (Tartu: TGU, 1977), 28:3–37; on the importance of purgatory for ghost stories, see Greenblatt, *Hamlet in Purgatory*.

22. Art Spiegelman, *Maus: A Survivor's Tale* (Harmondsworth: Penguin Books, 1987).

23. In Grossman's *Life and Fate*, a prisoner kills a camp doctor, who is also a convict, because the doctor has identified him as a malingerer and refused to prescribe him a day of leave for health reasons. There is no doubt that Grossman had a real-life prototype for this doctor.

24. Sveshnikov told the story of his rescue by Steinberg to their mutual friend, the artist Dmitrii Plavinsky. See Dmitrii Plavinsky, "Zapiski o proshlom," *Novyi zhurnal* 179 (1990): 127.

25. Walter Benjamin, "Surrealism," in *Selected Writings*, trans. Rodney Livingstone, vol. 2, part 1 (Cambridge, Mass.: Belknap, 1999), 190.

26. Alexander Glezer, "The Knight of the Sad Countenance," in *Painting for the Grave: The Early Work of Boris Sveshnikov*, ed. Norton T. Dodge and Jane A. Sharp (New Brunswick, N.J.: Zimmerli Art Museum, 2008), 44.

27. In one of the very first Western responses to Sveshnikov, Matthew Baigell noted some features of resemblance between Sveshnikov and Bakhtin. See Matthew Baigell, "Boris Sveshnikov," in Dodge and Sharp, *Painting for the Grave*, 43.

28. Hal Foster explicated the similar dynamics in postwar west European art as an anthropological turn, which focuses on "traumatized subjects" and "sited communities." See Hal Foster, "The Artist as Ethnographer," in *The Return of the Real* (Cambridge, Mass.: MIT Press, 1996), 171–204. For a relevant analysis of "unwanted beauty" in artitsic responses to the Holocaust, see Brett Ashley Kaplan, *Unwanted Beauty: Aesthetic Pleasure in Holocaust Representation* (Urbana: University of Illinois Press, 2007)

29. Igor' Golomshtok, "Vospominaniia starogo pessimista," *Znamia* 2 (2011): 139–166.

30. G. Anisimov, "Snovideniia vechnosti: Lagernaia grafika Borisa Sveshnikova," *Kul'tura* 15 (7423) (April 2004).

31. Golomstok, "Vospominaniia starogo pessimista."

32. Alexei Yurchak, "Necro-Utopia: The Politics of Indistinction and the Aesthetics of the Non-Soviet," *Current Anthropology* 49, no. 2 (April 2008): 212. See also Yurchak, *Everything Was Forever*, chap. 7.

33. As cited by Yurchak, "Necro-Utopia," 208, n.15.

34. Ibid., 207.

35. Agamben, *Remnants of Auschwitz*, 120.

36. Yurchak, "Necro-Utopia," 211.

37. Volkov, *Conversations with Joseph Brodsky*, 25.

38. Ibid.

39. Interestingly, the future filmmaker and émigré Andrei Tarkovsky also spent about a year in eastern Siberia as a part of the geological expedition,

starting from the spring of 1953. See P. D. Volkova, *Andrei Tarkovsky* (Moscow: EKSMO, 2002).

40. Brodsky, "Three Poems by Joseph Brodsky," 131–134.

41. Ibid., 26.

42. Joseph Brodsky, "Uncommon Visage. Nobel Lecture," in *On Grief and Reason: Essays* (New York: Farrar, Straus and Giroux, 1993), 54–55. Andrei Siniavsky, in his *Voice from the Chorus*, written in the camp, realized a similar reversal of the classical relations between the hero and the chorus (see chapter 6).

43. This essay, "The Writer in Prison," was the last written by Brodsky (*New York Times*, October 13, 1996).

44. The only job that Oskar Rabin could find in Lianozovo was in the camp that was still functioning nearby. From 1950 to 1956, he worked as a *desiatnik*, a manager who organized the work of a team of convicts on the railway. At the same time, he started an artistic career, which led to his stellar exhibitions in Paris, New York, and Moscow. See Arkadii Nedel' and Oskar Rabin, *Narisovannaia zhizn'* (Moscow: Novoe literaturnoe obozrenie, 2012), 67–69.

45. Igor Kholin, "Weeping," in *A Night in the Nabokov Hotel: 20 Contemporary Poets from Russia*, trans. Anatoly Kudryavitsky (Dublin: Daedalus Press, 2006).

46. For interesting speculations on the Lianozovo school as "deconstruction" of the idea of "world culture," see Vladislav Kulakov, *Poeziia kak fakt: Stat'i o stikhakh* (Moscow: Novoe literaturnoe obozrenie, 1999), 226–230.

47. Chertkov's verses were published in Leonid Chertkov, *Ognepark* (Köln, 1987), and are available on the *Russkaia Virtual'naia Biblioteka* website, http://www.rvb.ru/np/publication/05supp/chertkov/ognepark.htm#verse1. For the quoted obituary, see Roman Timenchik, "Lionia Chertkov," *Novoe literaturnoe obozrenie* 47 (2001): 128–131; for analysis, see Kulakov, *Poeziia kak fakt*, 134–137; and Il'ia Kukulin, "Istoriia pogranichnogo iazyka: Vladimir Narbut, Leonid Chertkov i kontrkul'turnaia funktsiia," *Novoe literaturnoe obozrenie* 72 (2005): 207–223.

48. N. Tamruchi, "Iz istorii moskovskogo avangarda," *Znanie—sila* 5 (1991).

49. Il'ia Kukulin, "Razvitie besposhchadnogo pokaza," interview with Genrikh Sapgir (1999), http://sapgir.narod.ru/talks/with/with02.htm.

50. For the concept of grievability, see Judith Butler, *Frames of War: When Is Life Grievable?* (Brooklyn, N.Y.: Verso, 2009).

51. I translated this couplet, which I remember from my Leningrad youth; with some credibility, similar couplets and quatrains are attributed to Oleg Grigoriev, a leader of the Mitki. Several dozen of these verses have been collected by Aleksandr Belousov, though his structuralist approach to this folklore is different from mine. See A. F. Belousov, "Sadistskie stishki," in *Russkii shkol'ny fol'klor* (Moscow: Ladomir, 1998), 545–558; see also Mikhail Lur'e, "Sadistskii stishok

v kontekste gorodskoi fol'klornoi traditsii," *Antropologicheskii forum* 6 (2007): 287–313.

52. Benjamin, "Berlin Chronicle," 314.

CHAPTER 6

1. Tertz, *Spokoinoi nochi*, 43.
2. Western works on Siniavsky tend to read him as an author of philosophical prose who was able to transcend his cultural context. See Margaret Dalton, *Andrei Siniavskii and Julii Daniel': Two Soviet "Heretical" Writers* (Wurzburg: Jal-Verlag, 1973); Olga Matich, "Spokojnoj noci: Andrej Sinjavskij's Rebirth as Abram Terc," *Slavic and East European Journal* 33, no. 1 (Spring 1989): 50–63; Stephanie Sandler, "Sex, Death, and Nation in the *Strolls with Pushkin* Controversy," *Slavic Review* 51, no. 2 (Summer 1992): 294–308; Catharine Theimer Nepomnyashchy, *Abram Tertz and the Poetics of Crime* (New Haven, Conn.: Yale University Press, 1995); Catharine Theimer Nepomnyashchy, "Andrei Donatovich Siniavsky (1925–1997)," *Slavic and East European Journal* 42, no. 3 (1998): 368; Harriet Murav, *Russia's Legal Fictions* (Ann Arbor: University of Michigan Press, 1998); Walter F. Kolonosky, *Literary Insinuations: Sorting Out Siniavsky's Irreverence* (Lanham, Md.: Lexington Books, 2003). Beth Holmgren was specifically interested in the pretexts and contexts of Siniavsky's fiction; see her "The Transfiguring of Context in the Work of Abram Tertz," *Slavic Review* 50, no. 4 (Winter 1991): 965–977. On Siniavsky's nonfiction, see Tat'iana Ratkina, *Nikomu ne zadolzhav: Literaturnaia kritika i esseistika A. D. Siniavskogo* (Moscow: Sovpadenie, 2010). The recently published massive collection of Siniavsky's camp letters provides new material for analysis: Siniavskii, *127 pisem o liubvi* (hereafter cited in the text by volume and page number). See also Yulii Daniel', *"Ya vse sbivaius' na literaturu": Pism'a iz zakliucheniia. Stikhi* (Moscow: Memorial-Zven'ia, 2000).
3. Likhachev, *Vospominaniia*, 142.
4. On their relations as classmates, see Stalin's daughter's memoirs: Svetlana Allilueva, *Tol'ko odin god* (New York: Harper, 1969), 242–249.
5. Galina Belaia, "Ya rodom iz shestidesiatykh," *Novoe literaturnoe obozrenie* 70 (2004).
6. On *Klim Samgin* and Gorky's interest in sects, see Etkind, *Khlyst*, 496–520.
7. Alexeyeva and Goldberg, *Thaw Generation*.
8. Igor' Golomstok, "Vospominaniia starogo pessimista," *Znamia* 3 (2011): 155.
9. These songs include "The Tattoo," "Bodaibo," "The Convict Petrov and the Convict Vasil'iev," and "Wolf Hunt." Vysotsky's brutality was matched by an overwhelming sense of tragedy and folkish mysticism, all familiar features of post-Stalinism. See Mark Tsybul'skii, "Vladimir Vysotsky i Andrei Siniavsky' (2004), http://www.liveinternet.ru/community/vladimir_vysotsky/

post36284769/; Richard Stites, *Russian Popular Culture: Entertainment and Society since 1900* (Cambridge: Cambridge University Press, 1992), 157–160; Christopher Lazarsky, "Vladimir Vysotsky and His Cult," *Russian Review* 51, no. 1 (1992): 58–71; and *Russian Bards*, a volume of *Russian Studies in Literature* 41 (2005).

10. When the KGB arrested Siniavsky, agents found in his home Vysotsky's tapes and confiscated them. See Valerii Perevozchikov, *Vladimir Vysotskii: Pravda smertnogo chasa. Posmertnaia sud'ba* (Moscow: Vagrius, 2003), 69–70.

11. Vadim Tumanov, *Vse poteriat' i vnov' nachat's mechty* (Moscow: Novosti, 2004), 97, 279. Marianne Hirsch and Leo Spitzer provide a revealing self-analysis of a similar act: they took stones from an abandoned camp, in their case the Romanian concentration camp, Vapniarka. "This physical testimonial fragment reflects our transformation into co-witnesses, carriers of a memory we have adopted." Marianne Hirsch and Leo Spitzer, *Ghosts of Home* (Berkeley: University of California Press, 2010), 231.

12. Vladimir Vysotskii and Leonid Monchinskii, *Chernaia svecha* (Moscow: AST, 1999).

13. Igor Golomstock, *Totalitarian Art in the Soviet Union, the Third Reich, Fascist Italy and the People's Republic of China* (London: Collins Harvill, 1991).

14. S. I. Simonova, "'Maska skorbi' Ernsta Neizvestnogo v Magadane: Istoriia stroitel'stva," http://mounb.maglan.ru/index.php?option=com_content&task=view&id=128&Itemid=240.

15. From the introduction to Yuly Daniel, *Govorit Moskva* (Moscow: 1997).

16. Arendt, *On Violence*, 54.

17. Tertz, *Spokoinoi nochi*, 43.

18. Ibid., 30, 40.

19. Mariia Rozanova, "Neskol'ko slov ot adresata etikh pisem," in Siniavskii, *127 pisem o liubvi*, 14.

20. Siniavskii, *Spokoinoi nochi*, 119.

21. Abram Tertz, *Progulki s Pushkinym* (Paris: Sintaksis 1989), 83.

22. Abram Tertz, *Golos iz khora*, in *Sobranie sochinenii* (Moscow: Start, 1991), 1:664.

23. Quoted from G. Anisimov, "Snovideniia vechnosti: Lagernaia grafika Borisa Sveshnikova," *Kul'tura* 15 (7423) (April 2004).

24. Abram Tertz, *V teni Gogolia* (Moscow: KoLibri, 2009), 1:8, 17, 19, 106.

25. Ibid., 1:356. Mandelstam's *Conversation* was written in 1933 but published only in 1967. The afterword to *Conversation* was written by Leonid Pinsky who, despite or because of his own five years in the gulag, had the courage in 1966 to sign a collective letter that called upon the authorities to release Daniel and Siniavsky on bail.

26. Tertz, *Golos iz khora*, 1:647.

27. Richard Rorty, *Contingency, Irony, and Solidarity* (Cambridge: Cambridge University Press, 1989).
28. Andrei Siniavskii, "V noch' posle bitvy," *Sintaksis* 3 (1979): 45.
29. Tertz, *Spokoinoi nochi*, 323, 325–326.
30. *Siniavskii i Daniel' na skam'e podsudimykh* (New York: Inter-Language Literary Associate, 1966), 107–108.
31. Tertz, *Golos iz khora*, 1:583.
32. Boris Pasternak, *Doktor Zhivago* (Moscow: EKMSO, 2007), 606.
33. *Siniavskii i Daniel' na skam'e podsudimykh*, 107–108.
34. Tertz, *Spokoinoi nochi*, 19; for analysis, see Murav, *Russia's Legal Fictions*, 208–212.
35. Tertz, *Progulki s Pushkinym*, 53.
36. Ibid., 54.
37. Likhachev, *Vospominaniia*, 142.
38. Andrei Siniavskii, *Puteshestvie na Chernuiu rechku* (Moscow: Zakharov, 1999), 449–450.
39. This debate is published in *Oktiabr'* 4 (1989): 192.
40. *Voprosy literatury* 10 (1992): 80.
41. Andrei Siniavsky, *Soviet Civilization: A Cultural History*, trans. John Turnbull (New York: Arcade, 1988), xi.
42. Tertz, *Spokoinoi nochi*, 260.
43. Abram Tertz, "Chto takoe sotsialisticheskii realism?" in *Literaturnyi protsess v Rossii* (Moscow: RGGU, 2003), 139, 156, 173, 175.
44. V. Shalamov, "Pis'mo staromu drugu," in *Tsena metafory ili prestuplenie i nakazanie Siniavskogo i Danielia*, ed. E. M. Velikanova (Moscow: Kniga, 1989), 519. Nepomnyashchy, *Abram Tertz and the Poetics of Crime*, 179, and Toker, *Return from the Archipelago*, 229–240, emphasize the formative experience that Siniavsky underwent in the camps. Harriet Murav argues that the idea of the realized metaphor was the key to Siniavsky's understanding of the Stalinist epoch and of his own trial; see her "The Case against Andrei Siniavskii: The Letter and the Law," *Russian Review* 53, no. 4 (October 1994): 549–560. Stephanie Sandler has explored Siniavsky's controversial metaphor of Pushkin as vampire; see her "Sex, Death, and Nation."
45. Abram Tertz, "Liudi i zveri" (1975), in Siniavskii, *Puteshestvie na Chernuiu rechku*, 207.
46. Abram Tertz, "Puteshestvie na Chernuiu rechku," in Siniavskii, *Puteshestvie na Chernuiu rechku*, 450.
47. On the "unconscious" continuity between the leaders of post-Soviet literature (Pelevin, Shishkin, Petrushevskaia) and Siniavskii, see Dmitry Bykov, "Tertz i synov'ia," *Toronto Slavic Quarterly* 15 (Winter 2006), http://www.utoronto.ca/tsq/15/bykov15.shtml; see also Alexander Etkind and Mark Lipovetsky

"The Salamander's Return: The Soviet Catastrophe and the Post-Soviet Novel" *Russian Studies in Literature* 46, no. 4 (Fall 2010): 6–48.

48. Bykov, "Terts i synov'ia."

49. "Ya dazhe slyl slavianofilom," in *Siniavskii i Daniel' na skam'e podsudimykh*, 78.

50. Etkind, *Khlyst*, 179–189.

51. "In the camp I spent a lot of time with the representatives of various sects, and this was very interesting. I simply didn't think that these sects still existed. I had read about them in books, but I didn't think they had survived. . . . And for this reason this material is familiar and interesting for me to some degree. But so far I simply haven't had time to get around to it. Artistically speaking, this will also be rendered in the style of the fantastic, of course" (Kyoko and Mitsuyoshi Numano, "Beseda s Siniavskim," http://ci.nii.ac.jp/naid/110004837059/en/).

52. Andrei Siniavskii, *Ivan-durak, Ocherk russkoi narodnoi very* (Moscow: Agraf, 2001), 383.

53. Andrei Siniavskii, *Mysli vrasplokh* (New York: Izd-vo Rauzena, 1966), 48.

54. Siniavskii, *Ivan-durak*, 420. One memoirist, Lev Khurges, writes that he met sectarians in 1940 in a Kolyma camp. Calling themselves "little crosses," they developed an original theology that was appropriate for the torture camps. God loves human beings, but those sinful who deserve punishment, he sends to earth. They suffer here until God forgives them, makes them die, and brings them back to heaven. See Lev Khurges, *Moskva-Ispaniia-Kolyma: Iz zhizni radista i zeka*, ed. P. L. Polian and N. L. Pobol (Moscow: Vremia, 2012). I am grateful to Pavel Nerler (Polian) for sharing with me this source.

55. Mariia Rozanova, "K istorii i geografii etoi knigi," *Voprosy literatury* 10 (1992): 156.

56. Andrei Siniavskii, "O 'Kolymskikh rasskazakh' Varlama Shalamova: Srez materiala" (1980), in Tertz, *Literaturnyi protsess*, 341.

57. Siniavskii, "Dostoevskii i katorga" (1981), in Tertz, *Literaturnyi protsess*, 334.

58. Siniavskii, "O 'Kolymskikh rasskazakh,'" 339.

59. Siniavskii, "Literaturnyi protsess," in Tertz, *Literaturnyi protsess*, 179.

60. Ibid.

61. Tertz, *Spokoinoi nochi*, 192.

62. Tertz, *Golos iz khora*, 1:669.

CHAPTER 7

1. The source for this scene is the memoir of Kozintsev's friend, the playwright Yevgeny Shvarts. See Yevgeny Shvarts, *Pozvonki minuvshikh let (*Moscow:

Vagrius 2008), 394. Kozintsev's widow retold this story but expressed doubts in its validity. See Valentina Kozintseva, ed., *Vash Grigorii Kozintsev* (Moscow: Artist, 1996), 92, 241; see also Vera Kozintseva and Yakov Butovskii, "Karl Marks: Istoriia nepostavlennoi postanovki," *Kinovedcheskie zapiski* 18 (1993): 198–206.

2. From N. A. Kovarskii's letter to Kozintsev, March 30, 1961, in Vera Kozintseva and Yakov Butovskii, eds., *Perepiska G. M. Kozintseva* (Moscow: ART, 1998), 214.

3. This filmmaker was Vladimir Ervais. See L. P. Pogozheva, "On khotel byt' poniatym," in Kozintseva, *Vash Grigorii Kozintsev*, 96.

4. Kozintsev played a crucial role in the struggle for the release of Tarkovsky's *Andrei Rublev* (1966) to the Soviet public. In a letter to Kozintsev, Tarkovsky called Kozintsev "my only protector" (Kozintseva and Butovskii, *Perepiska*, 417). Sokurov expressed his gratitude to Kozintsev in a documentary film, *Peterburgskii dnevnik: Kvartira Kozintseva* (Nadezhda Studio, 1997).

5. Grigorii Kozintsev, *Shakespeare: Time and Conscience*, trans. Joyce Vining (London: Dobson, 1967); Grigorii Kozintsev, *King Lear: The Space of Tragedy*, trans. Mary Mackintosh (London: Heinemann, 1977); Grigorii Kozintsev, "Glubokii ekran," in *Sobranie sochinenii*, ed. Valentina Kozintseva and Yakov Butovskii (Leningrad: Iskusstvo, 1982), vol. 1; Grigorii Kozintsev, "Prostranstvo tragedii," in Kozintseva and Butovskii, *Sobranie sochinenii*, vol. 4; Grigorii Kozintsev, "Zapisi po fil'mu 'Korol' Lir'," in Kozintseva and Butovskii, *Sobranie sochinenii*, vol. 4; Grigorii Kozintsev, *Vremia tragedii* (Moskva: Vagrius, 2004). The last selection includes a separate collection of particularly frank and bitter notes that Kozintsev did not mean to publish; it was compiled by his widow under the title *The Black, Rakish Time* (363–443).

6. In 1979, musicologist Solomon Volkov published, in his transcription, a series of interviews with Shostakovich: *Testimony: The Memoirs of Dmitri Shostakovich*, trans. Antonina W. Bouis (New York: Harper & Row, 1979). Infused by protest against the Soviet regime, this book caused much controversy. See Laurel Fay, "Shostakovich versus Volkov: Whose Testimony?" *Russian Review* 39, no. 4 (1980): 484–493; Allan B. Ho and Dmitry Feofanov, eds., *Shostakovich Reconsidered* (London: Toccata Press, 1998); Malcolm Hamrick Brown, *A Shostakovich Casebook* (Bloomington: Indiana University Press, 2004); and Elizabeth Wilson: *Shostakovich: A Life Remembered* (New York: Faber, 2006). On Kozintsev and Shostakovich, see John Riley, *Dmitri Shostakovich: A Life in Film* (London: Tauris, 2005).

7. Kozintseva, *Vash Grigorii Kozintsev*, 117.

8. Benjamin Harshav, *The Moscow Yiddish Theater: Art on Stage in the Time of Revolution* (New Haven, Conn.: Yale University Press, 2008).

9. Ehrenburg launched the enormous stream of anti-Stalinist memoirs with his *People, Years, Life* (1961–1965).

10. Valentina Kozintseva, "Vspominaia Grigoriia Mikhailovicha," *Kinovedcheskie zapiski* 70 (2005), http://www.kinozapiski.ru/ru/article/sendvalues/225/.

11. Kozintsev to S. Rostotskii, May 13, 1956, in Kozintseva and Butovskii, *Perepiska*, 161.

12. According to his friend and correspondent Isaak Glikman, after receiving this offer Shostakovich was in a "deep hysteria," wept "in full voice," and lamented: "They have persecuted me, chased me for so long." Many times he told Glikman that he would never enter the Communist Party, which "wreaks violence." A few days later, he accepted both offers and wrote his *Eighth Quartet*, which he wanted to dedicate to his own memory. When he broke his leg a few months later, he said, "This is how God punishes me for entering the Party." Isaak Glikman, *Pis'ma k drugu: Dmitrii Shostakovich-Issaku Glikmanu* (St. Petersburg: Kompozitor, 1993), 160–163.

13. Yevgenii Shvarts in Kozintseva, *Vash Grigorii Kozintsev*, 91. The idea of generation was crucial for Kozintsev's literary friends, the formalist theorists Yury Tynianov and Boris Eikhenbaum. The leading image in Tynianov's major novel, *Death of Vazir Mukhtar* (1928), is the melancholy of a brilliant generation that has outlived its time. For Kozintsev's rendering of Tynianov's idea, see Kozintsev, *Vremia tragedii*, 376.

14. Kozintseva, *Vash Grigorii Kozintsev*, 91.

15. Yakov Butovskii, "Grigorii Kozintsev i zolotoi vek dovoennogo Lenfil'ma," *Kinovedcheskie zapiski* 70 (2005), and http://www.kinozapiski.ru/ru/article/sendvalues/227/.

16. Boris Eikhenbaum, "Kak sdelana 'Shinel'" Gogolia," in *O proze* (Leningrad: Khudozhestvennaia literatura, 1969); the vast literature on this classical study makes no mention of this omission. Barbara Leaming, in her *Grigorii Kozintsev* (Boston: Twayne, 1980), 42–48, likewise does not comment on this divergence between Gogol's story and the film. For comparison, see Andrei Siniavsky's perception of Gogol in his *V teni Gogolia* (1975) (Moscow: Agraf, 2001), discussed in chapter 6.

17. Kozintsev, *Vremia tragedii*, 433.

18. Ibid., 327.

19. Yevgenii Shvarts in Kozintseva, *Vash Grigorii Kozintsev*, 91.

20. Kozintseva, "Vspominaia Grigoriia Mikhailovicha," 109.

21. Kozintsev, "Zapisi po fil'mu 'Korol' Lir'," 178, 319; Kozintsev, "Prostranstvo tragedii," 40; Grigorii Kozintsev, *Nash sovremennik Vil'iam Shekspir* (Moscow: Iskusstvo, 1962).

22. Kozintsev, "Prostranstvo tragedii," 109; Kozintsev, *Vremia tragedii*, 327.

23. The historian of Soviet film Birgit Beumers discerns in this Claudius a portrait of Stalin. Birgit Beumers, *A History of Russian Cinema* (Oxford: Berg, 2009), 142.

24. Kozintsev, *Shakespeare*, 152–155, 166–168.

25. Kozintsev, *Vremia tragedii*, 205.
26. Derrida, *Specters of Marx*, 7–8, 24; for a different reading of this armor, see Leaming, *Grigori Kozintsev*, 114.
27. Interestingly, Richard III—according to Greenblatt, "a brilliant depiction of a radically illegitimate regime of terror"—did not receive comparable attention from the Soviet theater and film directors. Greenblatt, *Hamlet in Purgatory*, 167.
28. Maia Turovskaia, "Gamlet i my," *Novyi mir* 11 (1964): 216–230. However, Vladimir Turbin criticized Kozintsev's *Hamlet* precisely for the same "modernizing" that Turovskaia admired in the film. Vladimir Turbin, "Gamlet segodnia i zavtra," *Molodaia gvardiia* 9 (1964): 302–313. A junior friend of Mikhail Bakhtin, Turbin later became a prominent literary scholar.
29. Kozintsev, *Vremia tragedii*, 432.
30. Turovskaia, "Gamlet i my," 227
31. Smoktunovsky's story was characteristically complex. He was born in a Belarusian family that in the late 1920s fled to Siberia from collectivization. Drafted in 1943, he was captured by the Nazis near Kiev. After a month in a Nazi camp, he managed to flee and joined the partisans. Later, some of his comrades were arrested by the Soviets because they had been in German captivity; Smoktunovsky escaped this fate and took part in many battles. As he said later, "I lived in permanent fear that I would be arrested because I was in a German camp, and I decided to get lost." Therefore in 1946 he voluntarily moved to Norilsk, a center of the northern gulag. He acted in the theater there until a local convict, the actor Georgii Zhzhenov, recommended him to a Moscow colleague in 1954. In 1966, Smoktunovsky and Zhzhenov performed together in *Beware of the Car*. Elena Korenevskaia, "Innokentii Smoktunovskii: Korol', kotoryi vsiu zhizn' boialsia," *Argumenty i fakty*, August 23, 2004.
32. Interestingly, in the highly successful *Hamlet* of 1971, performed by the Taganka Theater in Moscow and staged by its dissident director, Yury Liubimov, Hamlet was also played by the energetic and even brutal actor Vladimir Vysotsky.
33. Greenblatt, *Hamlet in Purgatory*, 208, 229.
34. Kozintsev, *Vremia tragedii*, 327. Compare this unrealized project with Greenblatt's speculation that Hamlet's last words, "I am dead," would be appropriately "spoken by a ghost," as if the spirit of Hamlet's father had "been incorporated by his son." Greenblat, *Hamlet in Purgatory*, 229.
35. Kozintsev, *King Lear*, 124, 161; Kozintsev, *Vremia tragedii*, 366.
36. Kozintseva, "Vspominaia Grigoriia Mikhailovicha."
37. Kozintsev, *King Lear*, 113.
38. Ibid., 191–195, 46.

39. This distinction resembles one that Dominick LaCapra draws between absence and loss. Understanding a loss in existential terms, as absence, or in Lacanian terms, as the Real, "typically involves the tendency to avoid addressing historical problems." LaCapra, *Writing History, Writing Trauma*, 48.

40. Kozintsev, *Vremia tragedii*, 279, 295.

41. Kozintsev, *King Lear*, 129; Kozintsev, *Vremia tragedii*, 36.

42. N. N. Chushkin to Koziuntsev, in Kozintseva and Butovskii, *Perepiska*, 514.

43. Kozintsev, "Zapisi po fil'mu 'Korol' Lir'," 4:290.

44. Kozintsev, *Vremia tragedii*, 290, 261, 255, 436; Kozintsev "Glubokii ekran," 52–55; Kozintsev, *King Lear*, 37, 88–89.

45. Kozintsev, *Vremia tragedii*, 203, 436; Kozintsev, "Prostranstvo tragedii," 55.

46. On Riazanov in a different perspective, see David MacFadyen, *The Sad Comedy of El'dar Riazanov* (Montreal: McGill University Press, 2003).

47. Artur Mekhtiev, interview with Riazanov: "El'dar Riazanov: 'Kazhdaia kartina—chast' moei dushi'," *Narodnaia gazeta* (Belarus), November 28, 2008, http://www.ng.by/ru/issues?art_id=27637.

48. It is worth mentioning that Riazanov's *Carnival Night* was screened about ten years after Bahktin defended his dissertation on carnival, and about ten years before he published this study.

49. Eldar Riazanov in *Vash Grigorii Kozintsev*, 62.

50. *Moskva slezam ne verit* (1980), script by Valentin Chernykh, directed by Vladimir Men'shov. This film has received rich and diverse scholarly analysis; see Svetlana Boym, *Common Places: Mythologies of Everyday Life in Russia* (Cambridge, Mass.: Harvard University Press, 1994), 137–139; David MacFadyen, "Moscow Does Not Believe in Tears: From Oscar to Consolation Prize," *Studies in Russian and Soviet Cinema* 1, no. 1 (November 2006): 45–67; and Lilya Kaganovsky, "The Cultural Logic of Late Socialism," *Studies in Russian and Soviet Cinema* 3, no. 2 (August 2009): 185–199.

51. This actor, Aleksei Batalov, grew up in the house of his stepfather, the writer Viktor Ardov, who was close to Anna Akhmatova. In fact, as a young man, Batalov was so close to Akhmatova that her son, who was imprisoned at the time, was jealous of him. See Tat'iana Khroshilova, "Goga, on zhe Gosha, on zhe Aleksei Batalov," *Rossiiskaia gazeta*, no. 4025, March 24, 2006, http://www.rg.ru/2006/03/24/batalov.html.

52. Boym, *Common Places*, 137.

53. "Russkaia kinodvadtsatka," *Radio Svoboda*, n.d., http://archive.svoboda.org/programs/cicles/cinema/russian/MoscowDistrustsTears.asp.

54. Anna Veligzhanina, "Aleksei Batalov: 'Ia nikogda ne byl vernoi sobakoi partii,'" *Komsomol'skaia pravda*, November 13, 2008, http://nsk.kp.ru/daily/24197.3/402738/.

55. *Moscow Does Not Believe in Tears* won the Academy Award for the Best Foreign Film of 1980.

56. David Denby, "Letters from the Unknown Woman," *New York Magazine*, May 25, 1981, 93.

57. In 2004, the scriptwriter of *Moscow Does Not Believe in Tears*, Valentin Chernykh, published an eponymous novel. It does not explain Goga's origins, though the reader learns that Goga is a Muscovite and at some point served in the air force. Like the film, the novel emphasizes Goga's hatred of the authorities and his belief in male superiority. The novel ends like the film: the heroine's friends from the KGB (they are described in many details in the novel) find Goga and bring him back to the heroine. It happens precisely at the moment when a television broadcast announces the death of Leonid Brezhnev, signaling a new life for the protagonists, who anticipate it with fear. See Valentin Chernykh, *Moskva slezam ne verit* (Moscow: Amfora, 2004).

CHAPTER 8

1. *Aleksei German*, a documentary film directed by Petr Shepotinnik, "Rossiia" channel, 2005.

2. For the historical context, see Miriam Dobson, *Khrushchev's Cold Summer: Gulag Returnees, Crime, and the Fate of Reform after Stalin* (Ithaca, N.Y.: Cornell University Press, 2006).

3. James C. Scott, *Weapons of the Weak: Everyday Forms of Peasant Resistance* (New Haven, Conn.: Yale University Press, 1985); Lawrence W. Levine, *The Unpredictable Past: Explorations in American Cultural History* (Oxford: Oxford University Press, 1993).

4. For cinematic memory and mourning, see Eric Santner, *Stranded Objects: Mourning, Memory and Film in Postwar Germany* (Ithaca, N.Y.: Cornell University Press, 1990); Robert A. Rosenstone, ed., *Revisioning History: Film and the Construction of a New Past* (Princeton, N.J.: Princeton University Press, 1995); and Adam Lowenstein, *Shocking Representation: Historical Trauma, National Cinema, and the Modern Horror Film* (New York: Columbia University Press, 2005).

5. Anna Lawton, "Russian Cinema in Troubled Times," *New Cinemas: Journal of Contemporary Films* 1, no. 2 (2001): 98–112; Svetlana Vasil'eva, "A. German: Khrustalev, mashinu!" *Znamia* 12 (1999); Tony Wood, "Time Unfrozen: The Films of Aleksei German," *New Left Review* 7 (2001): 99–107.

6. Mikhail Yampol'skii has compared German's films *My Friend Ivan Lapshin* and *Khrustalev, My Car!* to Marcel Proust's *In Search of Lost Time*. In contrast, Valerii Podoroga emphasizes the dreamlike quality of the narration, ignoring the consistent voice of the mourner behind the screen. See Mikhail Yampol'skii, "Ischeznovenie kak forma sushchestvovaniia," *Kinovedcheskie zapiski* 44 (1999),

http://www.kinozapiski.ru/ru/article/sendvalues/656/; and Valerii Podoroga, "Moloch i Khrustalev," *Iskusstvo kino* 6 (2000), http://kinoart.ru/2000/n6–article12.html.

7. For a historical account of "the inverted world" of 1953, see Jonathan Brent and Vladimir P. Naumov, *Stalin's Last Crime: The Plot against the Jewish Doctors* (New York: HarperCollins, 2003). General Klensky has several historical prototypes; one is Professor Sergei Yudin (1891–1954), chief surgeon of the Sklifosofsky Institute in Moscow and the laureate of two Stalin Prizes who was arrested in 1948 and kept in prison and exile until 1953. More than once he was brought back to Moscow for secret tasks, such as the project of creating a store of blood for transfusions in the coming World War III; using Yudin's method, the blood was to be collected from the corpses of gulag victims. See Viktor Topolianskii, "Delo professor Yudina," *Kontinent* 147 (2011): 9–56.

8. Major examples are Vasily Rozanov's *The People of the Moon Light* (1911), Vladimir Nabokov's *Bend Sinister* (1947), and Vladimir Sorokin's *Day of the Oprichnik* (2006). Even Joseph Brodsky believed that "the support for Stalin among the intelligentsia in the West had to do with their latent homosexuality." Volkov, *Conversations with Brodsky*, 31.

9. The film's title comes from Stalin's daughter, Svetlana Allilueva's remembrance of Beria's words, which he addressed to his driver and assistant, Khrustalev, after Stalin's death was confirmed: "Khrustalev, my Car!" (this scene appears in the film). According to Allilueva, Beria said this in a "triumphant voice." Analyzing this and other circumstantial evidence, the writer Edward Radzinsky speculates that it was Khrustalev who administered poison to Stalin. By citing these words in the title of the film, German concurs in this apocryphal speculation. See Edward Radzinsky, *Stalin: The First In-Depth Biography Based on Explosive New Documents from Russia's Secret Archives* (London: Doubleday 1996), 577.

10. Benjamin, *Origin of German Tragic Drama*, 73.

11. Nadezhda Mandel'shtam, *Vospominaniia* (New York: 1970), 386.

12. See René Girard, *Violence and the Sacred* (New York: Continuum, 1995); and Etkind, *Internal Colonization*, 244–248.

13. Freud, "Uncanny," in *The Uncanny*, 142.

14. Researching camp legends about the death of her husband, Nadezhda Mandelstam struggled to distinguish the "truth" about him from the stories about his "double" in a different camp (Mandel'shtam, *Vospominaniia*, 406).

15. Girard, *Violence and the Sacred*, 160.

16. Agamben, *Homo Sacer*, 106.

17. Vladimir Nabokov's father was murdered in 1922 in Berlin, and *The Gift* documents Nabokov's work of mourning. For my reading of *The Gift* and other Nabokov's novels, see A. Etkind, *Tolkovanie puteshestvii: Rossiia i Amerika v travelogakh i intertekstakh* (Moscow: Novoe literaurnoe obozrenie, 2001).

18. Aleksei German, "Izgoniaiushchii diavola," http://kinoart.ru/1999/n6–article18.html#3.
19. Agamben, *Homo Sacer*, 84, 37, 27.
20. German, "Izgoniaiushchii diavola."
21. Benjamin, *Origin of German Tragic Drama*, 185.

CHAPTER 9

1. Grigorii Saltup, *Barak i sto deviatnadtsatyi* (Petrozavodsk: 2004).
2. In this, Yury Dmitriev resembles another enthusiast of memory, a leader of the Memorial Society, Dmitry Yurasov, who developed his interest in the repressions by reading Soviet encyclopedias. See Stephen Kotkin, "Terror, Rehabilitation, and Historical Memory: An Interview with Dmitrii Iurasov," *Russian Review* 51 (April 1992): 245. For another example of excavated remains and contested memories, see Irina Paperno, "Exhuming the Bodies of Soviet Terror," *Representations* 75 (2001): 89–118.
3. Yurii Dmitriev, "Belbaltlag otkryvaet tainy," *Kur'er Karelii*, November 12, 2003.
4. Yurii Dmitriev, ed., *Pominal'nye spiski Karelii, 1937–1938* (Petrozavodsk: 2002); see also Yurii Dmitriev, *Mesto rasstrela Sandarmokh* (Petrozavodsk: 1999); and Yurii Dmitriev, ed., *Bor krasnyi ot prolitoi krovi* (Petrozavodsk: 2000).
5. Pierre Nora, *Realms of Memory: Rethinking the French Past*, ed. Lawrence Kritzman (New York: Columbia University Press, 1996).
6. Contemporary theorists of nationalism are more interested in other forms of memory and imagination, such as newspapers (Benedict Anderson), education (Ernest Gellner), and invented traditions (Eric Hobsbawm). More sensitive to monuments is M. Hroch, *Social Preconditions of National Revival in Europe* (Cambridge: Cambridge University Press, 1985).
7. See Manuel Castells, *The Rise of the Network Society: The Information Age*, vol. 2 (New York: Blackwell, 1996).
8. Tony Judt, *Postwar: A History of Europe since 1945* (London: Vintage, 2010), 773, 826
9. On hot and cold memories, see Jan Assmann, *Das Kulturelle Gedächtnis: Schrift, Erinnerung und Politische Identität in frühen Hochkulturen* (Munich: Verlag C. H. Beck, 1992).
10. Primo Levi, "Revisiting the Camps," in *The Art of Memory: Holocaust Memorials in History*, ed. James Young (New York: Prestel, 1994), 185.
11. Alexander Etkind, "Mapping Memory Events in East European Space," *East European Memory Studies* (Cambridge) 1 (2010): 4–5; Alexander Etkind, Rory Finnin, Uilleam Blacker, Julie Fedor, Simon Lewis, Maria Mälksoo, and Matilda Mroz, *Remembering Katyn* (Cambridge: Polity, 2012).

12. Jürgen Habermas, *The Theory of Communicative Action*, trans. Thomas McCarthy (Cambridge: Polity, 1984–1987).

13. Roman Jakobson, *Pushkin and His Sculptural Myth* (The Hague: Mouton de Gruyter, 1975).

14. Mikhail Yampolsky, "In the Shadow of Monuments," in *Soviet Hieroglyphics: Visual Culture in Late Twentieth-Century Russia*, ed. Nancy Condee (Bloomington: Indiana University Press, 1995), 93–112.

15. The monument, by sculptor Georgy Frangulian, was unveiled on May 31, 2011.

16. Nikita Khrushchev, *Vospominaniia* (Moscow: Moskovskie novosti 1999), 432.

17. On these fourth-century B.C. terracotta sculptures and how Bakhtin knew about them, see Nikolai Pan'kov, "Kerchenskie terrakoty i problema antichnogo realizma," *Novoe literaturnoe obozrenie* 79 (2006).

18. Dmitrii Likhachev, *Vospominaniia*, 346–347.

19. Anna Akhmatova, *Requiem*, in *The Complete Poems*, trans. Judith Nemschemeyer and Roberta Reeder (Boston: Zephyr, 1992), 2:115. For analysis, see Susan Amert, *In a Shattered Mirror: The Later Poetry of Anna Akhmatova* (Stanford, Calif.: Stanford University Press, 1992), 58.

20. A monument to Akhmatova has been erected across the Neva River, about a mile from the Crosses prison.

21. One of the best films about the Russian Revolution, Sergei Eisenstein's *October* (1927), presented the destruction of a fictional monument as an all-embracing idiom of the revolution.

22. See Sara Farmer, "Symbols That Face Two Ways: Commemorating the Victims of Nazism and Stalinism at Buchenwald and Sachsenhausen," *Representations* 49 (1995): 97–119; and Gregory Wegner, "The Power of Selective Tradition: Buchenwald Concentration Camp and Holocaust Education for Youth in the New Germany," in *Censoring History: Citizenship and Memory in Japan, Germany, and the United States*, ed. Laura Hein and Mark Selden (Armonk, N.Y.: Sharpe, 1999), 227–243.

23. Veniamin Iofe, "Itogi veka," in Iofe, *Granitsy smysla*, 52.

24. Agamben, *Homo Sacer*, 83.

25. Iofe, "Itogi veka," 52.

26. On monsters, monuments, and representation in broader contexts, see Jeffrey J. Cohen, ed., *Monster Theory* (Minneapolis: University of Minnesota Press, 1996); and Bruce Grant, "New Moscow Monuments, or, States of Innocence," *American Ethnologist* 28, no. 2 (2001): 332–362.

27. Ernst Neizvestny, *Govorit Neizvestny* (Frankfurt: Posev, 1984), 5.

28. James E. Young, *At Memory's Edge: After-Images of the Holocaust in Contemporary Art and Architecture* (New Haven, Conn.: Yale University Press, 2000).

29. Aleksandr Podrabinek, "Razdvoenie dnia," *grani.ru*, October 31, 2011, http://www.grani.ru/opinion/podrabinek/m.192734.html.

30. Young, *Texture of Memory*; Andreas Huyssen, *Present Pasts: Urban Palimpsests and the Politics of Memory* (Stanford, Calif.: Stanford University Press, 2003).

31. Thomas A. Kovach and Martin Walser, *The Burden of the Past: Martin Walser on Modern German Identity* (Rochester, N.Y.: Camden House, 2008).

32. See http://gulagmuseum.org/start.do.

CHAPTER 10

1. On Freud's thinking about the changing regime in Russia, see Etkind, *Eros of the Impossible*, 225–227.

2. See, for example, Robert Eaglestone, *The Holocaust and the Postmodern* (New York: Oxford University Press, 2004).

3. Derrida, *Specters of Marx*, 16.

4. Interestingly, Derrida mentions Stalinism rather than Maoism, even though Maoism was widespread among his colleagues well after 1956. See Richard Wolin, *The Wind from the East: French Intellectuals, the Cultural Revolution, and the Legacy of the 1960s* (Princeton, N.J.: Princeton University Press 2010).

5. Derrida, *Specters of Marx*, 87. The site where the Communist illusions were finally buried in 1968 and the place of his own imprisonment, Prague retained a dark meaning for Derrida. Speaking about the death of Michel Foucault, he mentions that he and Foucault resolved their ten-year-long conflict after he "returned from a Czech prison" in 1982. Speaking about the death of Louis Althusser, Derrida says that he learned about this event upon his return from Prague in 1990—"and the very name of that city already strikes me as so violent, almost unpronounceable." Jacques Derrida, *The Work of Mourning*, ed. Pascale-Anne Brault and Michel Naas (Chicago: University of Chicago Press 2001), 80, 114.

6. Jacques Derrida and Elisabeth Roudinesco, *For What Tomorrow: A Dialogue*, trans. Jeff Rort (Stanford, Calif.: Stanford University Press, 2004), 82.

7. Derrida, *Specters of Marx*, 111.

8. Ibid., 126, 67.

9. Louis Althusser, "Response to John Lewis," in *Essays in Self-Criticism*, trans. Grahame Lock (London: NLB, 1976). Tony Judt wrote that Althusser's example "licensed a new generation of Communist philosophers to abandon *any* attempt at explaining the inexplicable." Tony Judt, *Marxism and the French Left* (New York: Oxford University Press, 1986), 228.

10. Derrida and Roudinesco, *For What Tomorrow*, 79.

11. Roudinesco compares Althusser to the protagonist of her book and a heroine of the French Revolution, Théroigne de Méricourt, whose descent into insanity coincided with the rise of the Terror that followed the revolution. Elisabeth Roudinesco, *Madness and Revolution: The Lives and Legends of Théroigne*

de Méricourt (London: Verso, 1992). This study of postrevolutionary melancholy was originally published in 1989, the year of the bicentenary of the French Revolution and also the fall of the Berlin Wall.

12. Derrida and Roudinesco, *For What Tomorrow*, 76.

13. Julie Fedor drew my attention to a fascinating detail: the first English translation by Helen MacFarlane (1850) rendered this line as "A frightful hobgoblin stalks through Europe." See, for example, "A Frightful Hobgoblin . . . ," DACH BLOG: The British Library's German, Austrian and Swiss Collections, February 25, 2010, http://britishlibrary.typepad.co.uk/dach/2010/02/a-frightful-hobgoblin.html.

14. Davis, *Haunted Subjects*, 13.

15. Derrida, *Specters of Marx*, 57.

16. Derrida and Roudinesco, *For What Tomorrow*, 81.

17. It is important in this respect that Derrida prefers to write "holocaust" with a small "h," alluding to the plurality of manmade catastrophes. See Eaglestone, *Holocaust and the Postmodern*, 292.

18. Derrida and Roudinesco, *For What Tomorrow*, 81.

19. Derrida, *Specters of Marx*, 121–122.

20. Ibid., 131.

21. Derrida and Roudinesco, *For What Tomorrow*, 80.

22. Jacques Derrida, "Heidegger's Silence," in *Martin Heidegger and National Socialism: Questions and Answers*, ed. Gunther Neske and Emil Kettering, trans. Joachim Neugroschel (New York: Paragon, 1990), 145–148. For discussion of this important text, see Dominick LaCapra, *Representing the Holocaust: History, Theory, Trauma* (Ithaca, N.Y.: Cornell University Press, 1994), 143–144; and Beril Lang, *Heidegger's Silence* (Ithaca, N.Y.: Cornell University Press, 1996), 29.

23. See Ernst Nolte, "Between Myth and Revisionism? The Third Reich in the Perspective of the 1980s," in *Aspects of the Third Reich*, ed. H. W. Koch (London: Macmillan, 1985): 17–38; LaCapra, *Representing the Holocaust*, chap. 5; Jorn Rusen, "The Logic of Historicization," *History and Memory* 9, nos. 1–2 (1997): 113–146; François Furet and Ernst Nolte, *Fascism and Communism*, trans. Katherine Golsan (Lincoln: University of Nebraska Press, 2001), 15.

24. Aleksandra Samarina's interview with Aleksandr Yakovlev, *Obshchaia gazeta*, October 18, 2001; Veniamin Iofe, "Reabilitatisiia kak istoricheskaia problema," in Iofe, *Granitsy smysla*, 7.

25. On rivalry and mimesis, see René Girard, *Violence and the Sacred*, trans. Patrick Gregory (Baltimore: Johns Hopkins University Press, 1977), and other his works. On codependencies of totalitarianisms, see Furet and Nolte, *Fascism and Communism*; Tzvetan Todorov, *Hope and Memory: Reflections on the Twentieth Century* (Princeton, N.J.: Princeton University Press, 2003) (Todorov presents Vasily Grossman as a precursor); Robert Gellately,

Lenin, Stalin, and Hitler (London: Vintage, 2008); and Timothy Snyder, *Bloodlands* (London: Bodley Head, 2010). See also Ian Kershaw and Moshe Lewin, eds., *Stalinism and Nazism: Dictatorships in Comparison* (Cambridge: Cambridge University Press, 1997); Henry Rousso and Richard Joseph Golsan, eds., *Stalinism and Nazism: History and Memory Compared* (Lincoln: University of Nebraska Press, 2004); and Geyer and Fitzpatrick, *Beyond Totalitarianism.*

26. Mikhail Geller, "Predislovie," in Varlam Shalamov, *Kolymskie rasskazy* (London: Overseas Publications Interchange, 1978), 8–9; see also his pioneering book: Mikhail Geller, *Kontsentratsionnyi mir i sovetskaia literatura* (London: Overseas Publications Interchange, 1974).

27. Alexander Mitscherlich and Margarete Mitscherlich, *The Inability to Mourn* (New York: Grove Press, 1975), 7, 14, 25.

28. Charles S. Maier, *The Unmasterable Past: History, Holocaust, and German National Identity* (Cambridge, Mass.: Harvard University Press, 1988); LaCapra, *Representing the Holocaust*; Andreas Huyssen, *Twilight Memories: Marking Time in a Culture of Amnesia* (New York: Routledge, 1995); Geoffrey H. Hartman, *The Longest Shadow: In the Aftermath of the Holocaust* (Bloomington: Indiana University Press, 1996); Robert R. Shandley, ed., *Unwilling Germans? The Goldhagen Debate* (Minneapolis: University of Minnesota Press, 1998); Aleida Assmann, *Erinnerungsraume: Formen und Wandlungen des kulturullen Gedachnisses* (Munich: Beck, 1999); James Young, *At Memory's Edge: After-Images of the Holocaust in Contemporary Art and Architecture* (New Haven, Conn.: Yale University Press, 2000); Oren Baruch Stier, *Committed to Memory: Cultural Mediations on the Holocaust* (Amherst: University of Massachusetts Press, 2003); and Daniel Levy and Natan Sznaider, *The Holocaust and Memory in the Global Age* (Philadelphia: Temple University Press, 2006).

29. For more details, see my essays "Post-Soviet Hauntology: Cultural Memory of the Soviet Terror," *Constellations* 16, no. 1 (2009): 182–200, and "The Kremlin's Double Monopoly," in *Russia Lost or Found?* (Helsinki: Ministry of Foreign Affairs, 2009), 186–213. See also an important analysis by Gasan Guseinov, who also approaches post-Soviet memory through the Mitscherlichs' lenses: Gasan Guseinov, "Iazyk i travma osvobozhdeniia," *Novoe literaturnoe obozrenie* 94 (2008): 130–147.

30. Rudolf Rummel, *Death by Government* (New York: Transaction Publishers, 1992).

31. Edmund Burke, *Reflections on the Revolution in France* (New York: Bobbs-Merrill, 1955), 110.

32. Benjamin, "Theses on the Philosophy of History," 254.

33. Derrida, *Specters of Marx*, xviii.

34. Irina Flige, personal communication, November 2002.

35. See, for example, Sarah E. Mendelson and Theodore P. Gerber, "Soviet Nostalgia: An Impediment to Russian Democratization," *Washington Quarterly* 29, no. 1 (2005): 83–96; Maria Ferretti, "Rasstroistvo pamiati: Rossiia i stalinizm," http://old.polit.ru/documents/517093.html; and Charles S. Maier, "Heißes und kaltes Gedachtnis: Uber die politische Halbwertszeit von Nazismus und Kommunismus," *Transit* 22 (Winter 2001–2002): 53–165. For a reevaluation of this position, see Tatiana Zhurzhenko, "The Geopolitics of Memory," *Eurozine*, May 10, 2007, www.eurozine.com/articles/2007–05–10-zhurzhenko-en.html.

36. Lawrence Langer, *Holocaust Testimonies: The Ruins of Memory* (New Haven, Conn.: Yale University Press, 1991).

37. *Osobennosti natsional'noi okhoty*, 1995, directed by Aleksandr Rogozhkin.

38. For theoretical discussion of the temporality of collective trauma, see Jenny Edkins, *Trauma and the Memory of Politics* (Cambridge: Cambridge University Press, 2003), chap. 2.

39. Katherine Verdery, *The Political Lives of Dead Bodies: Reburial and Postsocialist Change* (New York: Columbia University Press, 1999), 42–43.

40. A proliferation of ghosts and zombies in high and popular culture has been observed by scholars of postsocialist transformations in Poland, East Germany, Ukraine, and Russia. For a similar effect in South Africa after apartheid, see Jean Comaroff and John Comaroff, "Alien-Nation: Zombies, Immigrants, and Millennial Capitalism," *South Atlantic Quarterly* 104, no. 4 (2002): 779–805. While I am writing, the most recent example is a Cuban film, *Juan of the Dead*, described as "the blood-drenched tale of a slacker who decides to save the island from an invasion of cannibalistic zombies," though the film is also "scattered with allusions to traumatic moments in Cuba's recent history" (Victoria Burnett in the *New York Times*, December 10, 2011). See also *Haunted Futures*, edited by Debra Ferreday and Adi Kuntsman, a special issue of *Borderlands* 10, no. 2 (2011).

41. Santner, *On Creaturely Life*, 52; Etkind, "Post-Soviet Hauntology," 182–200.

42. *Nochnoi dozor* (2004) and *Dnevnoi dozor* (2005), script by Sergei Luk'ianenko, directed by Timur Bekmambetov.

43. These films have been the subject of several studies: Stephen M. Norris draws analogies between these films' plotlines and actual events in Russian politics in his "In the Gloom: The Political Lives of Undead Bodies in Timur Bekmambetov's *Night Watch*," *KinoKultura* 16 (2007), http://www.kinokultura.com/2007/16–norris.shtml; a glossy Russian volume demonstrates the "*kulturologia*" approach to these films and features essays by Boris Groys and Mikhail Ryklin, in *Dozor kak simptom*, ed. B. Kupriianov and M. Surkov (Moscow: Falanster 2006).

44. *Novaia Zemlia* (2008), script by Arif Aliev, directed by Aleksandr Mel'nik.

45. *Smert' Sovetskim Detiam* (2008), script by Denis Karyshev, directed by Vadim Shmelev.

46. *4* (2005), script by Vladimir Sorokin, directed by Ilia Khrzhanovsky.

47. Mikhail Idov, "The Movie Set That Ate Itself," *GQ* (November 2011), http://www.gq.com/entertainment/movies-and-tv/201111/movie-set-that-ate-itself-dau-ilya-khrzhanovsky?printable=true.

48. *Pokaianie* (1984), script by Nana Dzhanelidze, directed by Tengiz Abuladze.

49. Interestingly, the recent *Katyn* (2007) by Andrzej Waida, which shows the slaughter of thousands of Polish officers by their Russian "allies" in 1940, also refers to Antigone. A female character struggles to bury her brother who was murdered by the Russians; to earn money for the tombstone, she sells her hair to a Warsaw theater that needs wigs for its production of *Antigone*. See Etkind et al., *Remembering Katyn*.

50. *Zhivoi* (2006), script by Igor' Porublev, directed by Aleksandr Veledinsky.

51. Terry Castle, *The Female Thermometer: Eighteenth-Century Culture and the Invention of the Uncanny* (New York: Oxford University Press, 1995), 16.

52. Slavoj Žižek, *Looking Awry: An Introduction to Jacques Lacan through Popular Culture* (Cambridge, Mass.: MIT Press, 1991), 22; see also Carla Jodey Castricano, *Cryptomimesis: The Gothic and Jacques Derrida's Ghost Writing* (Montreal: McGill-Queen's University Press, 2001); and María del Pilar Blanco and Esther Peeren, eds., *Popular Ghosts: The Haunted Spaces of Everyday Culture* (New York: Continuum, 2010).

53. Hent de Vries and Lawrence Eugene Sullivan, eds., *Political Theologies: Public Religions in a Post-Secular World* (New York: Fordham University Press, 2006), 3.

54. Derrida, *Specters of Marx*, 221.

55. Ibid., xviii.

56. Tertz, *Golos iz khora*.

CHAPTER 11

1. Solzhenitsyn, *Gulag Archipelago*, ix–x. In English translation, the delicious creature is rendered as "salamander." Lost in translation, the aquatic aspect of Solzhenitsyn's monster alludes to the gulag archipelago, which in turn comes from the Solovetsky Archipelago. In Greek myths, Triton had a man's head, a fish's tail, and a conch shell to raise storms. As an oceanic beast, Triton is a distant relative of the Leviathan, the symbol of the state. See Carl Schmitt, *The Leviathan in the State Theory of Thomas Hobbes*, trans. George D. Schwab and Erna Hifstein (New York: Greenwood Press, 1996). A zoologist has identified the published source for

Solzhenitsyn's story of the triton; he believes that actually the convicts found and ate a frozen fish. Nikolai Formozov, "Metamorfoz odnoi metafory: Kommentarii zoologa k prologu 'Arkhipelaga Gulag,'" *Novyi mir* 10 (2011): 154–157.

2. Anna Akhmatova, "Northern Elegies," in *The Complete Poems of Anna Akhmatova*, trans. Judith Hemschemeyer (Somerville, Mass.: Zephyr Press, 1990), 2:351.

3. Anna Akhmatova, *Sobranie sochinenii v shesti tomakh*, vol. 2, book 2 (Moscow: Ėllis Lak, 1998); Akhmatova, "Northern Elegies," 351.

4. Akhmatova searched in vain for information about the site of her husband's grave. According to Veniamin Iofe, Gumilev was shot in Kovalevsky Forest near St. Petersburg. See Veniamin Iofe, "Pervaia krov': Petrograd, 1918–1921" (1997), *Nauchno-Informatsionnyi Tsentr "Memorial"* (St. Petersburg), http://www.memorial-nic.org/iofe/29.html.

5. Volkov, *Conversations with Joseph Brodsky*, 227–228. Czesław Miłosz wrote about this analysis of *Requiem* as "probably the deepest thing said about the creative process by anyone" (on the back cover of Volkov's *Conversations*). The theme of self-estrangement in mourning echoes *Hamlet*, "a play of contagious, almost universal self-estrangement." Greenblatt, *Hamlet in Purgatory*, 212.

6. Anna Akhmatova, "Poem without a Hero," in *Complete Poems*, 2:443.

7. In the European context, a number of scholars have speculated about the relations between the gothic novel and the terror of the French Revolution. See Ronald Paulson, "Gothic Fiction and the French Revolution," *English Literary History* 48, no. 3 (1981): 545–554; David Punter, *The Literature of Terror: A History of Gothic Fictions from 1765 to the Present Day* (London: Longman, 1980); and Markman Ellis, *The History of Gothic Fiction* (Edinburgh: Edinburgh University Press, 2000). For the classic study of Gothic motifs in nineteenth-century Russian literature, see Vadim Vatsuro, *Goticheskii roman v Rossii* (Moscow: NLO, 2002); see also N. D. Tamarchenko, ed., *Goticheskaia traditsia v russkoi literature* (Moscow: RGGU, 2008). Jimmie E. Cain, *Bram Stoker and Russophobia: Evidence of the British Fear of Russia in Dracula and the Lady of the Shroud* (Jefferson, N.C.: McFarland, 2006), lists numerous Russian allusions in central texts of the British Gothic. For Gothic metaphors in early Soviet literature, see Eric Naiman, *Sex in Public: The Incarnation of Soviet Ideology* (Princeton, N.J.: Princeton University Press, 1997); Muireann Maguire, "Soviet Gothic-Fantastic: A Study of Gothic and Supernatural Themes in Early Soviet Literature" (Ph.D. diss., University of Cambridge, 2008); and Muireann Maguire, *Stalin's Ghosts: Gothic Themes in Early Soviet Literature* (Berne: Peter Lang; forthcoming). For a Gothic reading of Putin's political culture, see Dina Khapaeva, *Goticheskoe obshchestvo: Morfologiia koshmara (*Moscow: NLO, 2007); for a similar take on the Russian prose of the period, see Olga Lebedushkina, "Nasha novaia gotika," *Druzhba narodov* 11 (2008): 188–199.

8. The name of this storyteller, Andrei Fedorovich Platonov, resembles the name of a Soviet writer whom Shalamov probably read or knew, Andrei Platonovich Platonov; his tale reads like an obituary of this author. Varlam Shalamov, *Kolymskie rasskazy* (London: Overseas Publications Interchange, 1978), 124.

9. In an interview with V. V. Bondarenko, Mamleev said that his father, Vitaly Ivanovich, had written a book, *Freudianism and Religion* ("Ya vezde— 'ne svoi chelovek'—interv'iu s Yuriem Mamleevym," *Lebed'*, 562, April 6, 2008, http://www.lebed.com/2008/art5285.htm). This could only be a reference to V. I. Maiskii, *Freidizm i religiia* (Moscow: Bezbozhnik, 1930).

10. Aleksandr Dugin, *Tampliery proletariata* (Moscow: Arktogeia, 1997).

11. Analytically, this difference is close to the distinction between "acting out" and "working through" trauma, as described by LaCapra, *Writing History, Writing Trauma*, 141. In this respect, cultural studies of horror films are inspiring: Paul Coates, *The Gorgon's Gaze: German Cinema, Expressionism, and the Image of Horror* (Cambridge: Cambridge University Press, 1991); Lowenstein, *Shocking Representation*.

12. Yefim Etkind, "'Chelovecheskaia komediia' Aleksandra Galicha," in *Psikhopoetika* (St. Petersburg: Iskusstvo, 2005), 697.

13. For a pioneering attempt to read Soviet folklore as the reflection of the socialist experience, see Marina Balina, Helena Goscilo, and Mark Lipovetsky, *Politicizing Magic: An Anthology of Russian and Soviet Fairy Tales* (Evanston, Ill.: Northwestern University Press, 2005).

14. Viktor Pelevin, "Zombifikatsiia," *Den' i noch'* (Krasnoiarsk) 4 (1994), republished in Viktor Pelevin, *Relics: Rannee i neizdannoe* (Moscow: EKSMO, 2005), 297–334.

15. Iofe, *Granitsy smysla*, 26.

16. Paul de Man, "Autobiography as De-Facement," in *The Rhetoric of Romanticism* (New York: Columbia University Press, 1984), 76.

17. A primitive variation on the same theme is Pavel Krusanov's *Ukus angela* (St. Petersburg: Amfora, 2000), which presents an alternative history of the victorious Russian Empire with a dictator of Russo-Chinese blood, a panoply of mages and miracles, a recognizable satire on "political technologists" of Putin's era, and a cannibalistic hermaphrodite to boot.

18. Viktor Pelevin, *Ampir "V"* (Moscow: EKSMO, 2006), 208; for reference to Count Dracula, see 352. Pelevin also refers to Franco Moretti, whose classical study of the affinity between money and vampires is Franco Moretti, "The Dialectic of Fear," *New Left Review* 1, no. 136 (1982): 67–85.

19. Paul Barber, *Vampires, Burial, and Death* (New Haven, Conn.: Yale University Press, 1988), 93. Basing his speculation on astrological teachings and Durer paintings, Walter Benjamin wrote that melancholy has a particular connection to dogs and stones. Benjamin, *Origin of German Tragic Drama*, 152, 154.

For a history of werewolves, see Giorgio Agamben, *The Open: Man and Animal*, trans. Kevin Attell (Stanford, Calif.: Stanford University Press, 2004).

20. Oleg Kulik was Vladimir Sorokin's coauthor on certain projects. For analysis of this post-Soviet artist-dog, see Mikhail Ryklin, "Pedigree Pal: Put' k angliiskomu dogu," in *Vremia diagnoza* (Moscow: Logos, 2003), 264–277.

21. Bykov's logic of torture differs from a more familiar understanding, which was articulated by Arthur Koestler in his *Darkness at Noon* (1940). In Koestler, torture convinces the true believer that the party really wants his confession as another sacrifice for its cause.

22. Bykov's works of the past decade include the historical novel *Orfografiia*, set in 1918; a satire called "How Putin Became the President of the USA: New Russian Fairytales"; a controversial biography of Boris Pasternak, which won two Russian literary prizes ("Great Book" and "National Best-Seller") in 2006; the grand-scale anti-utopia *ZhD*; and the fascinating series of off- and online performances of political poetry, *The Citizen Poet*, which led the reawakening of Russia's civil society in 2011.

23. This construction develops the better-known Russian speculation on "literary generations," which was authored by Viktor Shklovsky in his *O teorii prozy* (Moscow: Krug, 1925). Like this genealogical model, Bitov's and Bykov's characters dismiss immediate predecessors in favor of more distant forebears. In a similar construction, the Hungarian writer Peter Esterházy, in his novel *Corrected Edition*, tells the story of a son who finds evidence in the archive that his beloved father was a secret agent who denounced his friends and even his wife. See Peter Esterházy, *Javított kiadás: Melléklet a Harmonia cælestishez* (Budapest: Magveto, 2002); and the discussion of the Russian translation of this novel, edited by Ilia Kukulin in *Novoe literaturnoe obozrenie* 96 (2009), including A. Etkind, "Synov'ia katastrofy: Ot Esterházy obratno k Bitovu," 225–229. Esterházy's *Corrected Edition* is the sequel to the previous novel, which is available in English translation as *Celestial Harmonies* (New York: Harper, 2005).

24. Aleksandr Filippov, *Noveishaia istoriia Rossii, 1945–2006: Kniga dlia uchitelia* (Moscow: Prosveshchenie, 2007), 90. Despite the public outrage, the presidential administration supported the use of a modified version of Filippov's book in high schools.

25. Vladimir Sorokin, *Tridtsataia liubov' Mariny* (Moscow: AST, 1999), 122.

26. Derrida, *Specters of Marx*, 9.

27. This construction—managing an apocalypse by mutilating a target number of men and women—is probably taken from the central myth of the Skoptsy (castrates) sect. Mamleev's *Shatuny* (1988) features a character who was a Skopets; later, Russian sects have been important for Aleksandr Dugin's philosophical speculations. Vladimir Sharov's *Rehearsals (Repetitsii*, 1992) presents a wonderful fantasy of a sectarian community that extends from the seventeenth to the

late-twentieth century. Aleksei Ivanov's *Zoloto bunta* (2005) describes the fight between Old Believer communities over the treasure that the eighteenth-century rebel Pugachev allegedly left before his arrest. In Pavel Krusanov's *Ukus angela* (2000), a wandering Old Believer inspires the emerging dictator by citing Sigmund Freud and Johann Jakob Bachofen. For the role of sectarian themes in late nineteenth- and early twentieth-century Russian literature and thought, see Etkind, *Khlyst*. The reawakening of sectarian themes in post-Soviet literature deserves a special study.

28. Vladimir Sharov, "Istorii moego ottsa," *Znamia* 10 (2009).

29. Vladimir Sharov, interview to *Chastnyi korrespondent*, December 3, 2008.

30. Vladimir Sharov, "Ia ne chuvstvuiu sebia ni uchitelem, ni prorokom," *Druzhba narodov* 8 (2004): 114–122.

31. Sharov's hypothesis about Fedorov's influence on the Bolsheviks preceded historical writings on the subject. Post-Soviet literature often plays with the idea of reincarnation. Though this idea is perceived as characteristically Buddhist, it was also central for Russian mystical sects such as the Khlysty. See Caroline Humphrey, "Stalin and the Blue Elephant," in *Transparency and Conspiracy: Ethnographies of Suspicion in the New World Order*, ed. Harry G. West and Todd Sanders (Durham, N.C.: Duke University Press, 2003), 175–203, for reincarnation stories about Stalin, which are told by the Buddhist peoples of Russia.

32. Vladimir Sharov, "Eto ia prozhil zhizn'," *Druzhba narodov* 12 (2000).

33. Erika Haber, *The Myth of the Non-Russian: Iskander and Aitmatov's Magical Universe* (Lanham, Md.: Lexington Books, 2003); Vitaly Chernetsky, *Mapping Postcommunist Cultures: Russia and Ukraine in the Context of Globalization* (Montreal: McGill-Queen's University Press, 2007).

34. Wendy B. Faris, *Ordinary Enchantments: Magical Realism and the Remystification of Narrative* (Nashville, Tenn.: Vanderbilt University Press, 2004); see also Jean-Pierre Durix, *Mimesis, Genres, and Post-Colonial Discourse: Deconstructing Magic Realism* (London: Macmillan, 1998); and Maggie Ann Bowers, *Magic(al) Realism* (London: Routledge, 2004).

35. See Michael Taussig, *Shamanism, Colonialism, and the Wild Man: A Study in Terror and Healing* (Chicago: University of Chicago Press, 1987), chap. 8.

36. Salman Rushdie, *Midnight's Children* (London: Picador, 1982), 9.

37. See Peter Fritzsche, *Stranded in the Present: Modern Time and the Melancholy of History* (Cambridge, Mass.: Harvard University Press, 2004), 203.

38. Derrida, *Specters of Marx*, 24.

39. Grigorii Revzin, "O Tsaritsynskom dvortse i Iurii Luzhkove," http://www.gq.ru/exclusive/columnists/152/44235/.

40. Michael Wood, "In Reality," *Janus Head* 5, no. 2 (Fall 2002): 9–14.

41. For the recognition of influence of Latin American "magical realist" writers on Russian authors of the late-Soviet and post-Soviet periods, see Sergei

Chuprinin, "Eshche raz k voprosu o kartografii vymysla," *Znamia* 11 (2006): 171–184. The Russian mother of a founder of Latin American magical realism, Alejo Carpentier, and her alleged kinship to the poet Konstantin Balmont have been the subject of musings by Russian critics.

42. Freud, "Mourning and Melancholia," 253.

43. Freud, "Uncanny," in *The Uncanny*, 157–158.

44. After Filippov's textbook of Soviet history, which described Stalin as an "effective manager," Russian public debates use this figure of speech with invariable irony.

45. Among many debates about this novel and its author, the most informative is the discussion at Radio Liberty: "Pechal' i svet romana 'Okolonolia,'" *Radio Svoboda*, August 20, 2009, http://www.svobodanews.ru/content/transcript/1803941.html; and the review by Dmitrii Bykov, *Novaia gazeta*, August 19, 2009. For Surkov's own review of this novel, see Vladislav Surkov, "Korrumpirovannyi Shekspir," *Russkii pioner* 11 (2009), http://www.ruspioner.ru/otl.php?id_art=928; see also Peter Pomerantsev, "Putin's Rasputin," *London Review of Books* 33, no. 20 (October 2011): 3–6. Though it is possible that a ghostwriter wrote the novel, I can testify that both Kremlin insiders and the Moscow public firmly believe in Surkov's authorship.

46. Valerii Zor'kin, "Konstitutsiia protiv kriminala," *Rossiiskaia gazeta*, December 10, 2010, http://www.rg.ru/2010/12/10/zorkin.html. Zor'kin was the chairman of Russia's Constitutional Court from 1991 to 1993 and has served again from 2003.

47. A self-proclaimed sociologist, Kordonsky worked as the head of the Department of Experts of the Russian Presidential Administration in 2000–2004.

48. Simon Kordonskii, "Na polputi k sharashke," *polit.ru*, January 12, 2011, www.polit.ru/author/2011/01/12/modernization.html.

49. Gleb Pavlovsky, "Vatnaia situatsiia s zhivymi akulami," *Russkii zhurnal*, December 31, 2010, http://russ.ru/Mirovaya-povestka/Vatnaya-situaciya-s-zhivymi-akulami.

50. Oleg Kashin, "Dreif v storonu literatury," *Russkii zhurnal*, October 17, 2011, http://www.russ.ru/pole/Drejf-v-storonu-literatury.

CONCLUSION

1. See Hannah Arendt, *The Human Condition* (Chicago: University of Chicago Press, 1958). Lewis Hyde suggests that it is more appropriate to speak about "mourning labor" than the "work of mourning." Lewis Hyde, *The Gift: How the Creative Spirit Transforms the World* (Edinburgh: Canongate Books, 2007), 51–52.

2. Carl Schmitt, *The Concept of the Political*, trans. George Schwab (New Brunswick, N.J.: Rutgers University Press, 1976), 56.

3. Leon Trotsky, *The Revolution Betrayed: What Is the Soviet Union and Where Is It Going?* trans. Max Eastman (Mineola, N.Y.: Dover, 2004), 66, 86.
4. Freud, "Mourning and Melancholia," 11:245–268.
5. Il'ia Kalinin, "Boi za istoriiu: Proshloe kak ogranichennyi resurs," *Neprikosnovennyi zapas* 4, no. 78 (2011); http://magazines.russ.ru/nz/2011/4/ka29.html.
6. Ellen Barry, "Medvedev Called Russian Political System 'Exhausted,'" *Herald Tribune*, December 19, 2011, 3.

Index

Agamben, Giorgio, 28–29, 85–86, 97–98, 169–171, 184, 255n4, 257n15, 290n19
Akhmatova, Anna, 13, 36, 78–79, 99, 179–182, 189, 221–222, 259, 278, 282, 288n2–4
Aksenov, Vasily, 51
Alexeyeva, Liudmila, 37, 111, 259n35
allegory, 19, 47, 58, 81, 109, 171, 236, 244
Allilueva, Svetlana, 111, 135, 266n26, 271n4, 280n9
Althusser, Louis, 198–201, 283n5–11
Anikst, Aleksandr, 75–76, 266n27
anticipatory mourning, 3, 16, 35, 43, 149, 217
anti-Semitism, 79, 99, 115, 136
anti-utopias, 94, 117–118, 164, 188, 240
apocalyptic, 33, 96, 131, 146, 148, 198–199, 229, 231, 290n27
Arendt, Hannah, 27–28, 30–34, 38, 84–85, 118–119, 196, 200, 243, 256n11, 258n24, 268n6
Aristotle, 46, 74, 252n22, 261n9
Assmann, Aleida, XIII, 251, 259, 281, 285
atheism, 140, 192, 230
Auschwitz, 26, 34, 87, 101, 204

Bakhtin, Mikhail, 17, 55, 66–82, 94–98, 103, 128, 149, 160, 181, 263n26, 265n17–21, 266n24–5, 269n27, 277n28, 282n17
barracks, 5, 9, 22, 53, 60, 79, 102, 105, 123, 160, 183, 191–192
bare life, 28–30, 36, 57, 67, 86–89, 97–98, 107, 132, 140, 147, 159–162, 169–170, 188, 213

Batalov, Aleksei, 156–157, 278n51
Belinsky, Vissarion, 76–78
Belomor Canal, 8, 28, 61, 64, 67, 152, 172–174, 256n7
Benjamin, Walter, 13, 19, 21, 40, 74–75, 87–88, 93–94, 109, 130, 160, 165, 171, 207, 233, 251, 254, 266n25
Berggolts, Olga, 69–70, 265n16
Berman, Matvei, 8
Bitov, Andrei, 54–55, 105, 120, 227, 263n25–26, 290n23
Blok, Aleksandr, 13, 71, 126, 222, 265
boomerang effect, 31–34, 258n24–25
Bosch, Hieronymus, 73, 89, 209
Boym, Svetlana, XV, 250n9, 254n40, 257n16, 260n44
Brodsky, Joseph, 21, 54, 99–101, 107, 119, 179, 222, 254–245, 270n42, 280n8, 288n5
Brodsky, Yury, 7, 250, 264n8
Budaev, Andrei, 209
Burke, Edmund, 206–207, 218
Bykov, Dmitrii, XV, 226–229, 232, 234, 241, 249n5, 262n19, 273n47, 290n21

camp songs (blatnye pesni), 112–113, 279n9
carnival, 50, 66–75, 82, 94, 96, 103, 108, 117, 149–150, 181, 278n48,
Caucasus, 32–35, 54, 237–238
Césaire, Aimé, 37, 259n36
Chertkov, Leonid, 105–106, 270n47
Chudakova, Marietta, 41, 260n43, 264n12, 266n28

Chukovsky, Kornei, 78
Circassians, 32–33
Clorinda, 19–21, 169, 211, 218–221, 242, 254n34–6
Cold War, 38, 196–197, 226
Coleridge, Samuel, 15, 21
collapse of the gulag, 25, 34–38, 61, 119, 155
collapse of the USSR, 23, 35, 42, 98, 135, 147, 197, 201–203, 244, 248
collective body, 73, 93–94, 114
collectivization, 8, 33, 63, 70, 81, 250n5
colonization, internal vs. external, 32–34, 61–62, 81, 186, 252n22, 258n24, 264n11
Communism, 124, 131, 138, 164, 180, 197–202, 246
"companies" of the Thaw, 102, 107, *111*, 112–114, 116–117
Condee, Nancy, XV, 259n36–37, 282n14
Cosmic Academy, 64, 68
cosmopolitan memory, 23, 32, 38, 91, 134, 140, 194, 255n43
Counter-Reformation, 74, 89, 94
creaturely life, 29, 98, 107–108
Crosses (Kresty), a prison, 99–101, 181–182, 186, 189, 222, 282n20
crystallization of memory, 176–177, 183, 246

Daniel, Yuly, 99, 111–121, 128
Dante Alighieri, 72–73, 89, 123, 242, 265n23
Day of Memory of Victims of Political Repressions, 190
defamiliarization, 19, 21, 221, 245. *See also* estrangement
democide, 11, *206*, 251n12
Derrida, Jacques, 18, 141–142, 197–207, 218–289, 228, 234–235, 253n26, 283n3–11, 284n15–22
de-Stalinization, 34, 38, 41–42, 78, 194, 259n37
Diner, Dan, 39–40, 259n38
Dmitriev, Yury, 172–174, 177, 281n2
doctors in the gulag, 26, 86, 89–90, 113, 123, 263n28, 269n23, 280n7
Dodge, Norton, 38, 90–95, 103, 105, 108, 269n26–7
dogs, 46, 169, 208, 215, *226*, 249, 289n19, 290n20
Dostoevsky, Fyodor, 13, 16, 45, 72, 132, 139–140, 147, 150, 167
double mourning, 30, 134, 198
Druzhinin, Nikolai, 62–63, 264n3–4

Ehrenburg, Ilya, 38, 136–137, 146, 275n9
Eikhenbaum, Boris, 138, 276n16
enforced sociality, 68, 263n2
Epimenides, 36
estrangement, 17, 21, 48, 51, 103, 109, 288n5. *See also* defamiliarization
ethnography, 64–66, 78–82, 130
Etkind, Grigory, 44–45
Etkind, Mark, XIII, 38
Etkind, Yefim, XIII, 44–45, 83, 224, 260n2, 289n12
Etlis, Miron, 114

Fifty-Year Effect, 2–3
films, 2, 4, 13–14, 49–50, 97, 134–158, 159–171, 175, 208–217, 224, 226, 237, 244
Flakserman, Galina, 71
Formalist School, 21, 137, 276n13
Fraser, Nancy, 46, 261n8
Freud, Sigmund, 2, 14–22, 35–36, 52, 56, 73, 167, 196, 200, 218, 220–221, 223, 232, 236, 245, 252n21–24
Friedlander, Saul, 12, 251
Furet, François, 202

generations, 1–3, 14, 18, 23, 24, 29–30, 39–42, 63, 69, 96, 101, 107, 118, 129, 134, 151, 158, 177, 199, *203*, 207, 218, 227, 244, 252n20, 253n27, 254n29, 255n42, 276n13, 290n23
genocide, 11, 39, 251n12
German, Aleksei, 135, 159–171, 279n6, 280n9

ghosts, 7, 16–17, 37, 88, 122, 125–133, 138–142, 148, 199–207, 211–219, 233–236, 246, 286n40, 288n7
Ginzburg, Yevgenia, 51–52, 262n20
Girard, René, 169, 252n22, 284n25
Gnedich, Tatiana, 83–84
Gogol, Nikolai, 2, 45, 72, 76–78, 122–126, 130–133, 138–139, 167, 181, 222
Golomstock, Igor, 96, 113–114, 120
goners, 26, 28, 47–48, 57, 85–89, 95, 98, 123, 130–132, 161, 164, 170–171, 188, 256n8
Gorky, Maxim, 111, 131, 271n6
gothic realism, 17, 69, 73–75, 99, 288n7
Greenblatt, Stephen, XIII, 145, 261, 268n21, 277n27, 288n5
Grigoriev, Oleg, 108
Grossman, Vasily, 14, 31–39, 41, 52–54, 202, 258, 269n23, 284n25
grotesque, 56, 72–5, 129, 181, 266n26
Gulag, XI, 5, 8–10, 26–31, 34–35, 48, 58–59, 61, 63–64, 80–82, 87, 101–102, 119–121, 186, 190, 194
Gumilev, Lev, 79, 181, 267n36
Gumilev, Nikolai, 79, 222, 288n4

Habermas, Jürgen, 111, 179, 193, 202
Halbwachs, Maurice, 39–40
Hamlet, 9, 17, 46, 125, 134–159, 170, 199–200, 219, 224, 234, 237–238, 242
hardware vs. software vs. ghostware, 177–179, 183, 190, 193, 212, 246
hauntology, 199, 201, 217–219, 235
Hegel, Georg Wilhelm, 35–36, 46, 126, 198
Heidegger, Martin, 198, 201
Hirsch, Marianne, 14, 252 n20, 255 n42, 272 n11
Historians Affair, 61–63
historians as characters in Russian novels, 226–227
historians in the gulag, 60–82
Hobbes, Thomas, 89, 170, 188, 245
Hoffman, E. T. A., 17, 102, 122
Holocaust, 8–15, 23, 34–40, 48, 89, 101,
171, 178–193, 196–208, 250–252
homo sacer, 28–29, 88, 170, 184
horror doggerels, 107–108, 214, 271n51
humor, 2–3, 21, 23, 65, 68, 74, 81, 107, 109, 138, 149–150

intelligentsia, XIII, 7–8, 10, 37, 41, 53, 55, 63–64, 72, 76, 78, 81, 85, 102, 107–108, 112, 121, 130, 140, 144–145, 155–156, 158, 213, 217, 223, 227, 243–244
Iofe, Veniamin, XIII, 9–10, 172, 177, 184, 203–204, 207, 225, 250

Jaspers, Karl, 10, 250
Jews, 7, 32–33, 39, 79, 88, 100, 115, 136–140, 146, 168, 192, 204, 230
Judt, Tony, 11, 176–177, 251, 281, 283n11

Kabo, Vladimir, 81, 267n38
Kagan, Moisei, XIII
Kapler, Aleksei, 135–136, 138
Kashin, Oleg, 11, 241, 292
Kazakhstan, 49, 61, 66, 70, 73, 79, 102, 186, 212
Kazarnovsky, Yury 57, 263n28
Khlysty, 111, 131, 265n21, 271n6
Kholin, Igor, 103, 105
Khrushchev, Nikita, 4, 34–38, 78, 147, 150, 180–181, 186–188, 194, 197, 199, 203
Khrzhanovsky, Ilia, 214–215, 226
Klein, Lev, XIII, 79–81, 267n37
Kojève, Alexandre 46
Kolyma, 51, 76, 112–114, 132, 137, 188, 274n54
Kopelev, Lev, 60
Kordonsky, Simon, 240
Kotkin, Stephen XIV, 2, 281n2
Kozintsev, Grigory, 134–151, 154, 159, 274n1, 275n2–7
Kristeva, Yulia, 26, 256n8
Kropivnitsky, Lev, 102
Kropivnitsky, Yevgeny, 102, 106
"kulaks", 11, 39, 204

LaCapra, Dominick, XIV, 87, 251n13, 257n15, 278n39, 284n22, 289n11

laughter, 67–9, 73, 85, 181
Lermontov, Mikhail, 127, 130, 168, 222
Levi, Primo, 26, 48, 87, 178, 281n10
Lianozovo, 102–103, 105–107
Likhachev, Dmitry, XIII, 10, 63–70, 81–82, 127, 181, 264n7
Limonov, Eduard, 105
Liubavsky, Matvei, 61–62, 263n1
Lukichev, Aleksandr, 175
Lungin, Pavel, 162, 216

magical historicism, *233*–*236*, 238–239, 241, 244, 247
magical realism, 233–235, 291n34, 291n41
Mamleev, Yury, 223–224, 241, 289n9, 290n27
Mandelstam, Nadezhda, 12–14, 38, 47, 56–57, 102, 167, 261n12, 280n14
Mandelstam, Osip, 12–13, 25–28, 38, 47, 72, 78, 84–85, 123–124, 132, 255n9, 261n12, 265n23
Márquez, Gabriel García, 119, 235
Marxism, XIII, 35, 60, 71, 139–140, 197–201
Medvedev, Pavel, 71
melancholy, 9, 14, 18–19, 56–57, 68, 165, 171, 198–199, 211–215, 231, 236, 243–245, 248, 251–253
Meletinsky, Eleazar, 78, 267n36
melodrama, 141, 156, 158
memoirs, 14, 23, 35, 41, 44, 47–48, 51–52, 55–56, 60, 62, 68–69, 71, 78–86, 102, 113, 120, 135–136, 150, 180–181, 188, 192, 196, 241, 260n6, 261n16, 275n6, 275n9
Memorial Society, XIII, 9, 40, 114, 118, 184, 190–191, 194, 202, 207, 250, 281n2
memory events, *178–179*, 183, 189, 219, 244–246, 281n11
metonymies, 5, 17, 236
Mikhalkov, Nikita, 160, 209–210
Mikhoels, Solomon, 136, 146
mimetic mourning, 1–4, 13–14, 16, 21–22, 53, 69, 97–100, 106, 108–189, 119–120, 167–170, 224, 228, 237, 249, 252
misrecognition (anagnorisis), 44–59, 200, 212, 221, 261n9

Mitki, 99, 107–108, 270n51
Mitscherlich, Margaret and Alexander, 205–206
monsters, 17, 20–21, 73, 82, 89, 118, 124–132, 169–199, 186, 188, 201, 204, 211, 221–225, 236–239, 242, 246, 282n26, 287n1
monuments, 6, 22–23, 87, 99, 102, 114, 173–195, 211–212, 216–222, 228, 246, 250n7, 281n6, 282n14
multidirectional memory, 24, 255n43, 258n24
museums, 5–6, 22, 42, 87, 177, 183–184, 189–195, 205, 212, 260n46

Nabokov, Vladimir, 124, 163, 169, 235, 238
Necrorealists, 97–99, 106
Neizvestny, Ernst, 114, 186, 188
Nekrasov, Vsevolod, 106–107
"nepmen", 39, 44, 260n1
Nikon, Patriarch, 230
NKVD (People's Commissariat of Internal Affairs), 8, 172, 174, 185, 189, 229, 240
Nora, Pierre, 175–176
nostalgia, 10, 41, 207, 245, 260
novels, 14, 18, 23, 32–33, 45, 52, 54, 70, 111, 113, 114–125, 129, 163, 169, 202, 216, 223–239, 241, 276n13, 279n57

obelisks, 22–23, 173, 183, 186, 191
Oksman, Yulian, 25, 76–78, 137, 255n3, 263n26, 265n12, 266n28, 267n31–35
Okudzhava, Bulat, 48–51, 261n16, 262n19
Old Believers (Schismatics), 114, 130, 192, 229, 232, 290n27
Open Murder Day, 115–119
Orthodox Church, 5, 77, 88, 131, 162, 173, 185, 191–192, 209

Pankeev, Sergei, 18, 254n28, 283n1
Paperno, Irina, 85, 259n42, 281n2
Pasternak, Boris, 13, 126, 134, 144
Pavlovsky, Gleb, 240–241
Pelevin, Viktor, 129, 224–226, 229, 232–234, 239–240

phantoms, 19, 218, 254n28
pilgrims, 33, 54, *100*, 107, 119–120, 272n11
Pinsky, Leonid, 75–76, 137, 265n23, 272n25
postcatastrophic vs. post-traumatic, 3, 8, 14, 16, 19, 23, 41–42, 109, 171, 182, 211, 214–220, 223, 233, 236, 244–245
postmemory, 14, 42, 252 n20
post-Stalinism, 3, 37, 49, 74, 98, 116, 136–137, 141, 150, 157, 203, 271n9
Purgatory, 88–89, 268
Pushkin, Aleksandr, 13, 46, 49, 62, 76, 122–132, 179–180, 239

Rabin, Oskar, 102, 270n44
realization of metaphors, 121, *124*, 126–127, 142, 273n44
recognition, 11, 18, *46–47*, 57–58, 167, *219*, 261n7–9
redemptive narrative, 12, 87–88, 165, 171, 208, 251, 268n16
reenactment, 1, 16, 19, 34, 55, 98, 230, 244–245
rehabilitation, 10, 59, 66, 202, 253n25
repetition *vs.* remembering, 2, 15–21, 35, 43, 228, 234
repression(s), 8, 11, 35–*36*, *38*, 58, 175–179, 226
return of the repressed, 15–17, 25, 36–38, 48–59, 78, 100, 111, 120, 137, 165, 170, 217, 220, 225, 244–245
revenge, 3, *9*, 16, 78, 113, 116, 138, 142–149, 200, 214, 238
Riazanov, Eldar, 135, 150–155, 158, 278n 46–49
Rökk, Marika, 50, 262n18
Romanov, Boris, 66–7, 69–70, 264n12, 265n13
Rozanov, Vasily, 122, 125, 131, 133, 280n8
Russian *vs.* German memory, 10, 18, 22, 34, 39–41, 177, 183–184, 188, 192–193, 196–206, *246*

Sandarmokh, 172–173, 189, 192
Santner, Eric, 29, 98, 107, 257n17, 266n25, 279n4

Sapgir, Genrikh, 106, 270n49
Scarry, Elaine, 27–29, 256n12
Schmitt, Carl, 206, 244
sectarians, 82, 86, 111, 122–125, 130–131, 226, 229–232, 234, 239, 274n54, 290n27,
self-sacrificial mourning, 21, 47, 106, *119–120*, 171
serfdom, 33–34, 62–63, 77, 258n27
Shalamov, Varlam, 14, 41, 48, 86–90, 96, 98, 122, 128–129, 132, 204, 223, 237, 263, 268n14
Shakespeare, William, 2, 9, 15, 135–158, 200
Sharov, Vladimir, 119, 229–234
Shivarov, Nikolai, 26
Shostakovich, Dmitry, 14, 72, 84, 134–137, 144–145, 148, 153, 268, 275–276
Siberia, 26, 34, 62, 76, 79, 89, 99–100, 132, 186, 226–230
silences, 17, 117, 197–202, 284n22
Siniavsky, Andrei (Abram Tertz), 55–6, 78, 82, 96–133, 218–219, 265n23, 271n2, 273n44, 273n47
Skoptsy, 130–131, 290n27
smells, 53, 55, 87, 99, 146, 168
Smoktunovsky, Innokenty, 144–145, 151–155, 277n31
Solovetsky Special Purpose Camp, 5–9, 64–70, 82, 162, 172, 184–185, 190–192, 249–250, 263–264, 287
Solzhenitsyn, Aleksandr, 3, 5, 26, 38, 41, 60–61, 79, 86, 90, 119, 139, 143, 202, 220–221, 224, 230, 242, 255, 287n1
Sorokin, Vladimir, 99, 120, 215, 226, 228–229, 232–234, 238–239
sovereign, 28–29, 87–88, 98, 147, 159–162, *171*
Soviet Other, 65, 79, 82
Soviet terror, 8–13, 17–18, 26–32, 36–43, 58–59, 110, 115–117, 119, 204, 211, 243–245
Soviet subjectivity, *30*, 69–70, 257n18
Spiegelman, Art, 89
Stalin, Joseph, 11, 25, 30–38, 89, 116, 134–137, 159–164, 168, 199, 210–221, 231, 239. *See also* Stalinism, Post-Stalinism

Stalinism, 3, 5, 11–12, 28–37, 61–63, 80, 117–118, 125–128, 161–162, 166, 170, 197–204, 226–227, 244–245, 248, 257
Stalinist terror *vs.* the Nazi terror, 7–12, 22–29, 32–34, 39–40, 85–86, 101, 114, 170, 184, 196–208, 245–246, 285n28
Stalin Prize, 61, 63, 135, 280n7
Steinberg, Arkadii, 89–90, 102
Sukhanov, Nikolai, 71, 265n19
Surkov, Vladislav, 209, 236–238, 292n45
surrealism, 88, 93, 96, 100, 130–131, 269n25
survivors, 2, 14, 18, 27, 36, 48, 57, 81–82, 84–101, 107, 158
Sveshnikov, Boris, 72, 89–96, 102–104, 108–109, 113, 123, 125, 128, 269n24–27

Tancred, 19–21, 211, 218, 221, 254n35
Tarkovsky, Andrei, 135, 269n39, 275n4
Tarle, Yevgeny, 61–2
Tarusa, 102, 106
Tasso, Torquato, 19–21, 218, 254n54
Taussig, Michael, 16, 233, 252n21, 291n35
textual monuments, 180–182
Thaw, 4, 37–38, 41, 50–51, 54, 75, 98, 100, 102, 110–111, 116–117, 121, 128, 130, 134, 136–137, 144, 152, 156–158, 186, 203, 223, 259
thieves' argot, 64–66, 264n10
Tocqueville, Alexis, 40–41, 259n39
Todorov, Tzvetan 30
Tolstoy, Lev, 3, 63, 122, 130–131, 139, 146, 210, 238
torture camps vs. extermination camps, 3, *27*, 29, 256n12, 59
tortured life, *29*, 45, 57, 68, 70, 89, 96
totalitarianism, 29–30, 34, 114, 119, 164, 170, 196, 197–200, 203, 207
transformative torture, 9, 27–31, 44–45, 69, 89, 107, 226–228, 236, 256n12, 290n21
trauma, 2–4, 14–15, 18–21, 29, 42, 55, 66, 87, 107, 120, 232, 249, 252, 254, 264–265, 286n28
Trotsky, Lev, 93, 244–245, 293n1

Tumanov, Vadim, 112–113
Turovskaia, Maia, XV, 143–144, 277n28
Tynianov, Yury, 137–138, 276n13

Ukraine, 8, 32–4, 186, 286n40
uncanny, 11, 15–17, 36–37, 45, 56–59, 93–97, 167–169, 179, 180, 211–222, 234–236, 252n24
uncertainty of the loss, 10, 17–18, 47–48, 56–57, 169, 253n25

vampires, 125, 127–130, 149, *183*, 211, 213, 217, 222–223, 225–229, 232–234, 246
Victims' Balls (Bals des victims), 1–4, 13, 98, 119, 219
victims *vs.* perpetrators, 3, 7–11, 18, 20, 23–24, 33, 35–39, 42, 78, 86, 88–89, 106, 170–171, 174, 204, 217
violence, 4, 27, *30*, 31, 67, 80–81, 98, 116–120, 161, 206, 228, 237, 242, 258n20
Vologda, 87, 174–175, 190
Vysotsky, Vladimir, 50, 112–113, 119, 226, 271n9, 277n32

werewolves, 97, 114, *169*, 170, 225–226, 232, 234, 289n19
Wincott, Leonard, 83
Wood, Michael, 235, 291n40
world culture, 72, 76, 84–85, 89, 96, 99, 101, 103, 107
worldliness, *84–85*, 107, 217

X-shaped masterplot, 160–163, 170–171

Yakovlev, Aleksandr, 202
Yampolsky, Mikhail, 197–198, 282n14
Yenei, Yevgeny, 137, 144
Yevtushenko, Yevgeny, 113
Yufit, Yevgeny, 97–98
Yurchak, Alexei, XV, 30–31, 97–98, 258n21, 269n32

Zatochnik, Daniil, 67
Zorkin, Valery, 239–240

Cultural Memory | *in the Present*

Denis Guénoun, *About Europe: Philosophical Hypotheses*
Maria Boletsi, *Barbarism and Its Discontents*
Sigrid Weigel, *Walter Benjamin: Images, the Creaturely, and the Holy*
Roberto Esposito, *Living Thought: The Origins and Actuality of Italian Philosophy*
Henri Atlan, *The Sparks of Randomness, Volume 2: The Atheism of Scripture*
Rüdiger Campe, *The Game of Probability: Literature and Calculation from Pascal to Kleist*
Niklas Luhmann, *A Systems Theory of Religion*
Jean-Luc Marion, *In the Self's Place: The Approach of Saint Augustine*
Rodolphe Gasché, *Georges Bataille: Phenomenology and Phantasmatology*
Niklas Luhmann, *Theory of Society, Volume 1*
Alessia Ricciardi, *After* La Dolce Vita: *A Cultural Prehistory of Berlusconi's Italy*
Daniel Innerarity, *The Future and Its Enemies: In Defense of Political Hope*
Patricia Pisters, *The Neuro-Image: A Deleuzian Film-Philosophy of Digital Screen Culture*
François-David Sebbah, *Testing the Limit: Derrida, Henry, Levinas, and the Phenomenological Tradition*
Erik Peterson, *Theological Tractates*, edited by Michael J. Hollerich
Feisal G. Mohamed, *Milton and the Post-Secular Present: Ethics, Politics, Terrorism*
Pierre Hadot, *The Present Alone Is Our Happiness, Second Edition: Conversations with Jeannie Carlier and Arnold I. Davidson*
Yasco Horsman, *Theaters of Justice: Judging, Staging, and Working Through in Arendt, Brecht, and Delbo*
Jacques Derrida, *Parages*, edited by John P. Leavey
Henri Atlan, *The Sparks of Randomness, Volume 1: Spermatic Knowledge*
Rebecca Comay, *Mourning Sickness: Hegel and the French Revolution*

Djelal Kadir, *Memos from the Besieged City: Lifelines for Cultural Sustainability*

Stanley Cavell, *Little Did I Know: Excerpts from Memory*

Jeffrey Mehlman, *Adventures in the French Trade: Fragments Toward a Life*

Jacob Rogozinski, *The Ego and the Flesh: An Introduction to Egoanalysis*

Marcel Hénaff, *The Price of Truth: Gift, Money, and Philosophy*

Paul Patton, *Deleuzian Concepts: Philosophy, Colonialization, Politics*

Michael Fagenblat, *A Covenant of Creatures: Levinas's Philosophy of Judaism*

Stefanos Geroulanos, *An Atheism That Is Not Humanist Emerges in French Thought*

Andrew Herscher, *Violence Taking Place: The Architecture of the Kosovo Conflict*

Hans-Jörg Rheinberger, *On Historicizing Epistemology: An Essay*

Jacob Taubes, *From Cult to Culture*, edited by Charlotte Fonrobert and Amir Engel

Peter Hitchcock, *The Long Space: Transnationalism and Postcolonial Form*

Lambert Wiesing, *Artificial Presence: Philosophical Studies in Image Theory*

Jacob Taubes, *Occidental Eschatology*

Freddie Rokem, *Philosophers and Thespians: Thinking Performance*

Roberto Esposito, *Communitas: The Origin and Destiny of Community*

Vilashini Cooppan, *Worlds Within: National Narratives and Global Connections in Postcolonial Writing*

Josef Früchtl, *The Impertinent Self: A Heroic History of Modernity*

Frank Ankersmit, Ewa Domanska, and Hans Kellner, eds., *Re-Figuring Hayden White*

Michael Rothberg, *Multidirectional Memory: Remembering the Holocaust in the Age of Decolonization*

Jean-François Lyotard, *Enthusiasm: The Kantian Critique of History*

Ernst van Alphen, Mieke Bal, and Carel Smith, eds., *The Rhetoric of Sincerity*

Stéphane Mosès, *The Angel of History: Rosenzweig, Benjamin, Scholem*

Pierre Hadot, *The Present Alone Is Our Happiness: Conversations with Jeannie Carlier and Arnold I. Davidson*

Alexandre Lefebvre, *The Image of the Law: Deleuze, Bergson, Spinoza*

Samira Haj, *Reconfiguring Islamic Tradition: Reform, Rationality, and Modernity*

Diane Perpich, *The Ethics of Emmanuel Levinas*

Marcel Detienne, *Comparing the Incomparable*

François Delaporte, *Anatomy of the Passions*

René Girard, *Mimesis and Theory: Essays on Literature and Criticism, 1959–2005*

Richard Baxstrom, *Houses in Motion: The Experience of Place and the Problem of Belief in Urban Malaysia*

Jennifer L. Culbert, *Dead Certainty: The Death Penalty and the Problem of Judgment*

Samantha Frost, *Lessons from a Materialist Thinker: Hobbesian Reflections on Ethics and Politics*

Regina Mara Schwartz, *Sacramental Poetics at the Dawn of Secularism: When God Left the World*

Gil Anidjar, *Semites: Race, Religion, Literature*

Ranjana Khanna, *Algeria Cuts: Women and Representation, 1830 to the Present*

Esther Peeren, *Intersubjectivities and Popular Culture: Bakhtin and Beyond*

Eyal Peretz, *Becoming Visionary: Brian De Palma's Cinematic Education of the Senses*

Diana Sorensen, *A Turbulent Decade Remembered: Scenes from the Latin American Sixties*

Hubert Damisch, *A Childhood Memory by Piero della Francesca*

José van Dijck, *Mediated Memories in the Digital Age*

Dana Hollander, *Exemplarity and Chosenness: Rosenzweig and Derrida on the Nation of Philosophy*

Asja Szafraniec, *Beckett, Derrida, and the Event of Literature*

Sara Guyer, *Romanticism After Auschwitz*

Alison Ross, *The Aesthetic Paths of Philosophy: Presentation in Kant, Heidegger, Lacoue-Labarthe, and Nancy*

Gerhard Richter, *Thought-Images: Frankfurt School Writers' Reflections from Damaged Life*

Bella Brodzki, *Can These Bones Live? Translation, Survival, and Cultural Memory*

Rodolphe Gasché, *The Honor of Thinking: Critique, Theory, Philosophy*

Brigitte Peucker, *The Material Image: Art and the Real in Film*

Natalie Melas, *All the Difference in the World: Postcoloniality and the Ends of Comparison*

Jonathan Culler, *The Literary in Theory*

Michael G. Levine, *The Belated Witness: Literature, Testimony, and the Question of Holocaust Survival*

Jennifer A. Jordan, *Structures of Memory: Understanding German Change in Berlin and Beyond*

Christoph Menke, *Reflections of Equality*

Marlène Zarader, *The Unthought Debt: Heidegger and the Hebraic Heritage*

Jan Assmann, *Religion and Cultural Memory: Ten Studies*

David Scott and Charles Hirschkind, *Powers of the Secular Modern: Talal Asad and His Interlocutors*

Gyanendra Pandey, *Routine Violence: Nations, Fragments, Histories*

James Siegel, *Naming the Witch*

J. M. Bernstein, *Against Voluptuous Bodies: Late Modernism and the Meaning of Painting*

Theodore W. Jennings Jr., *Reading Derrida / Thinking Paul: On Justice*

Richard Rorty and Eduardo Mendieta, *Take Care of Freedom and Truth Will Take Care of Itself: Interviews with Richard Rorty*

Jacques Derrida, *Paper Machine*

Renaud Barbaras, *Desire and Distance: Introduction to a Phenomenology of Perception*

Jill Bennett, *Empathic Vision: Affect, Trauma, and Contemporary Art*

Ban Wang, *Illuminations from the Past: Trauma, Memory, and History in Modern China*

James Phillips, *Heidegger's* Volk: *Between National Socialism and Poetry*

Frank Ankersmit, *Sublime Historical Experience*

István Rév, *Retroactive Justice: Prehistory of Post-Communism*

Paola Marrati, *Genesis and Trace: Derrida Reading Husserl and Heidegger*

Krzysztof Ziarek, *The Force of Art*

Marie-José Mondzain, *Image, Icon, Economy: The Byzantine Origins of the Contemporary Imaginary*

Cecilia Sjöholm, *The Antigone Complex: Ethics and the Invention of Feminine Desire*

Jacques Derrida and Elisabeth Roudinesco, *For What Tomorrow . . . : A Dialogue*

Elisabeth Weber, *Questioning Judaism: Interviews by Elisabeth Weber*

Jacques Derrida and Catherine Malabou, *Counterpath: Traveling with Jacques Derrida*

Martin Seel, *Aesthetics of Appearing*

Nanette Salomon, *Shifting Priorities: Gender and Genre in Seventeenth-Century Dutch Painting*

Jacob Taubes, *The Political Theology of Paul*

Jean-Luc Marion, *The Crossing of the Visible*

Eric Michaud, *The Cult of Art in Nazi Germany*

Anne Freadman, *The Machinery of Talk: Charles Peirce and the Sign Hypothesis*

Stanley Cavell, *Emerson's Transcendental Etudes*

Stuart McLean, *The Event and Its Terrors: Ireland, Famine, Modernity*

Beate Rössler, ed., *Privacies: Philosophical Evaluations*

Bernard Faure, *Double Exposure: Cutting Across Buddhist and Western Discourses*

Alessia Ricciardi, *The Ends of Mourning: Psychoanalysis, Literature, Film*

Alain Badiou, *Saint Paul: The Foundation of Universalism*

Gil Anidjar, *The Jew, the Arab: A History of the Enemy*

Jonathan Culler and Kevin Lamb, eds., *Just Being Difficult? Academic Writing in the Public Arena*

Jean-Luc Nancy, *A Finite Thinking*, edited by Simon Sparks

Theodor W. Adorno, *Can One Live after Auschwitz? A Philosophical Reader*, edited by Rolf Tiedemann

Patricia Pisters, *The Matrix of Visual Culture: Working with Deleuze in Film Theory*

Andreas Huyssen, *Present Pasts: Urban Palimpsests and the Politics of Memory*

Talal Asad, *Formations of the Secular: Christianity, Islam, Modernity*

Dorothea von Mücke, *The Rise of the Fantastic Tale*

Marc Redfield, *The Politics of Aesthetics: Nationalism, Gender, Romanticism*

Emmanuel Levinas, *On Escape*

Dan Zahavi, *Husserl's Phenomenology*

Rodolphe Gasché, *The Idea of Form: Rethinking Kant's Aesthetics*

Michael Naas, *Taking on the Tradition: Jacques Derrida and the Legacies of Deconstruction*

Herlinde Pauer-Studer, ed., *Constructions of Practical Reason: Interviews on Moral and Political Philosophy*

Jean-Luc Marion, *Being Given That: Toward a Phenomenology of Givenness*

Theodor W. Adorno and Max Horkheimer, *Dialectic of Enlightenment*

Ian Balfour, *The Rhetoric of Romantic Prophecy*

Martin Stokhof, *World and Life as One: Ethics and Ontology in Wittgenstein's Early Thought*

Gianni Vattimo, *Nietzsche: An Introduction*

Jacques Derrida, *Negotiations: Interventions and Interviews, 1971–1998*, edited by Elizabeth Rottenberg

Brett Levinson, *The Ends of Literature: The Latin American "Boom" in the Neoliberal Marketplace*

Timothy J. Reiss, *Against Autonomy: Cultural Instruments, Mutualities, and the Fictive Imagination*

Hent de Vries and Samuel Weber, eds., *Religion and Media*

Niklas Luhmann, *Theories of Distinction: Re-Describing the Descriptions of Modernity*, edited and introduced by William Rasch

Johannes Fabian, *Anthropology with an Attitude: Critical Essays*

Michel Henry, *I Am the Truth: Toward a Philosophy of Christianity*

Gil Anidjar, *"Our Place in Al-Andalus": Kabbalah, Philosophy, Literature in Arab-Jewish Letters*

Hélène Cixous and Jacques Derrida, *Veils*

F. R. Ankersmit, *Historical Representation*

F. R. Ankersmit, *Political Representation*

Elissa Marder, *Dead Time: Temporal Disorders in the Wake of Modernity (Baudelaire and Flaubert)*

Reinhart Koselleck, *The Practice of Conceptual History: Timing History, Spacing Concepts*

Niklas Luhmann, *The Reality of the Mass Media*

Hubert Damisch, *A Theory of /Cloud/: Toward a History of Painting*

Jean-Luc Nancy, *The Speculative Remark: (One of Hegel's bon mots)*

Jean-François Lyotard, *Soundproof Room: Malraux's Anti-Aesthetics*

Jan Patočka, *Plato and Europe*

Hubert Damisch, *Skyline: The Narcissistic City*

Isabel Hoving, *In Praise of New Travelers: Reading Caribbean Migrant Women Writers*

Richard Rand, ed., *Futures: Of Jacques Derrida*

William Rasch, *Niklas Luhmann's Modernity: The Paradoxes of Differentiation*

Jacques Derrida and Anne Dufourmantelle, *Of Hospitality*

Jean-François Lyotard, *The Confession of Augustine*

Kaja Silverman, *World Spectators*

Samuel Weber, *Institution and Interpretation: Expanded Edition*

Jeffrey S. Librett, *The Rhetoric of Cultural Dialogue: Jews and Germans in the Epoch of Emancipation*

Ulrich Baer, *Remnants of Song: Trauma and the Experience of Modernity in Charles Baudelaire and Paul Celan*

Samuel C. Wheeler III, *Deconstruction as Analytic Philosophy*

David S. Ferris, *Silent Urns: Romanticism, Hellenism, Modernity*

Rodolphe Gasché, *Of Minimal Things: Studies on the Notion of Relation*

Sarah Winter, *Freud and the Institution of Psychoanalytic Knowledge*

Samuel Weber, *The Legend of Freud: Expanded Edition*

Aris Fioretos, ed., *The Solid Letter: Readings of Friedrich Hölderlin*

J. Hillis Miller / Manuel Asensi, *Black Holes / J. Hillis Miller; or, Boustrophedonic Reading*

Miryam Sas, *Fault Lines: Cultural Memory and Japanese Surrealism*

Peter Schwenger, *Fantasm and Fiction: On Textual Envisioning*

Didier Maleuvre, *Museum Memories: History, Technology, Art*

Jacques Derrida, *Monolingualism of the Other; or, The Prosthesis of Origin*

Andrew Baruch Wachtel, *Making a Nation, Breaking a Nation: Literature and Cultural Politics in Yugoslavia*

Niklas Luhmann, *Love as Passion: The Codification of Intimacy*

Mieke Bal, ed., *The Practice of Cultural Analysis: Exposing Interdisciplinary Interpretation*

Jacques Derrida and Gianni Vattimo, eds., *Religion*